JOHN WILLIS'

SCREEN WORLD

1981

Volume 32

CROWN PUBLISHERS, INC.

ONE PARK AVENUE

NEW YORK, NEW YORK 10016

TO

FRED ASTAIRE

who has danced his way into an irreplaceable niche in the hearts of millions around the world.

MARY TYLER MOORE, DONALD SUTHERLAND, TIMOTHY HUTTON
in "Ordinary People" © Paramount Pictures
1980 ACADEMY AWARD FOR BEST FILM

CONTENTS

EDITOR: JOHN WILLIS

Assistant Editor: Stanley Reeves

Staff: Joe Baltake, Marco Boyajian, Alberto Cabrera, Mark Cohen, Frances Crampon, Mark
Gladstone, Maltier Hagan, Miles Kreuger, William Schelble, Van Williams

Acknowledgments: This volume would not be possible without the cooperation of Harry Abranson, Deni Allaire, Tom Allen, Armondo Arrendondo, Fern Arenstein, Dianne Ball, Orley Berger, Mike Berman, Ronald Bowers, Kerry Boyle, Joseph Brenner, Susan Brockman, Barry Cahn, Curtis Campagna, Fabiano Canosa, Ed Cassidy, Maxi Cohen, Dian Collins, Jane Covner, J. C. Crampon, Lynne Dahlgren, Alberta D'Angelo, June Davenport, Nicholas Demetroules, Ira Deutchman, Robert Dorfman, Cilista Eberle, Vince Emery, Steve Fagan, Claudia Fallon, Suzanne Fedak, Bruce Feldman, Ray Fisher, Pam Fivack, Dore Freeman, Marvin Friedlander, Renee Furst, Charles Gardner, Bernie Glaser, James Gluckenhaus, Joseph Green, Jerry Gross, Valerie Gunderson, Earl Hadleberg, Allison Hanau, Richard Hassanein, Meg Higgins, Victoria Hill, Al Hindon, Andy Holtzman, Marjorie Hymowitz, Mark Itzkowitz, Barbara Javiz, Steve Johnston, Elenore Kane, Jack Kerness, Sam Kitt, Don Krim, Peter Krutzer, Janine Leonard, Wynn Lowenthal, Marian Luntz, William Lustig, Howard Mahler, Leonard Maltin, Louis Marino, Terri Martin, Priscilla McDonald, Peter Meyer, Tim Meyers, Terrance Mitchell, Patrick Montgomery, Ron Mutz, Eileen Nad, Eric Naumann, Frank Pergallia, Maria Peters, Jim Pike, Ruth Pologee Levinson, Mark Puckett, Sylvana Radman, Yevonne Rainer, Mike Rappaport, Jerry Rapport, Katherine Reilly, Robert Richter, Bruce Ricker, Reid Roosevelt, Sue Salter, Les Schecter, Carole Schwartz, Tom Schwartz, Richard Schwarz, Barbara Schwei, Art Schweitzer, Eve Segal, Jacqueline Sigmund, John Skauras, Gail Skilia, Paula Sprang, Alicia Springer, John Springer, Laurence Steinfeld, Jesse Sutherland, John Sutherland, Patricia Story, Cynthia Swartz, Dan Talbot, Chris Teseo, Bill Thompson, Jerry Ticman, Frank Tobin, Bruce Trinz, Ellen Trost, Don Velde, John West, Bob Winestein, Christopher Wood, Stew Zakim, Mindy Zepp.

1. Burt Reynolds

2. Robert Redford

3. Clint Eastwood

4. Jane Fonda

5. Dustin Hoffman

6. John Travolta

7. Sally Field

8. Sissy Spacek

9. Barbra Streisand

10. Steve Martin

11. John Belushi

12. Walter Matthau

13. Cheech & Chong

14. Jill Clayburgh

15. Meryl Streep

16. Bette Midler

TOP 25 BOX OFFICE STARS OF 1980

  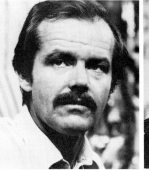 

17. George Burns   18. Brooke Shields   19. Jack Nicholson   20. Al Pacino

1980 RELEASES

January 1 through December 31, 1980

21. Dudley Moore   22. Chevy Chase   23. Woody Allen   24. Robert DeNiro

25. Goldie Hawn   Charles Bronson   Sophia Loren   Paul Newman

WINDOWS

(UNITED ARTISTS) Producer, Michael Lobell; Director, Gordon Willis; Screenplay, Barry Siegel; Associate Producer, John Nicolella; Editor, Barry Malkin; Music, Ennio Morricone; Designer, Melvin Bourne; Photography, Gordon Willis; Costumes, Clifford Capone; Art Director, Richard Fuhrman; In Technicolor; Rated R; 94 minutes; January release.

CAST

Emily Hollander	Talia Shire
Bob Luffrono	Joseph Cortese
Andrea Glassen	Elizabeth Ashley
Ida Marx	Kay Medford
Sam Marx	Michael Gorrin
Steven Hollander	Russell Horton
Dr. Marin	Michael Lipton
Obecny	Rick Petrucelli
Detective Swid	Ron Ryan
Policewoman	Linda Gillin
Nick	Tony Di Benedetto
Voice Over	Bryce Bond
Renting Agent	Ken Chapin
Ira	Marty Greene
Desk Officer	Bill Handy
Desk Sergeant	Robert Hodge
Detective	Kyle Scott Jackson
Doorman	Pat McNamara
Ben	Gerry Vichi

Left: Joseph Cortese, Rick Petrucelli
Top: Talia Shire, Elizabeth Ashley
© United Artists

8

Joseph Cortese, Talia Shire
Above: Key Medford

Elizabeth Ashley, Michael Lipton
Above: Talia Shire

FOR THE LOVE OF BENJI

(MULBERRY SQUARE) Written, Produced and Directed by
Joe Camp; Photography, Don Reddy; Music, Euel Box; Trainer,
Frank Inn; In color; Rated G; 85 minutes; January release.

CAST

Benji	Higgins
Mary	Patsy Garrett
Cindy Chapman	Cynthia Smith
Paul Chapman	Allen Fiuzat
Chandler Dietrich	Ed Nelson
Stelios	Art Vasil
Elizabeth	Bridget Armstrong
Ronald	Peter Bowles

Top: Benji Below Left: Patsy Garrett
Right: Benji © Mulberry Square

Ed Nelson, Benji

THE FOG

(AVCO EMBASSY) Director/Co-Author/Music, John Carpenter; Producer/Co-Author, Debra Hill; Executive Producer, Charles B. Bloch; Photography, Dean Cundey; Production Design/Co-Editor, Tommy Wallace; Co-Editor, Charles Bornstein; Assistant Producer, Pegi Brotman; Assistant Directors, Larry Franco, James Van Wyck; Costumes, Bill Whittens, Stephen Loomis; Art Director, Craig Stearns; An Entertainment Discoveries presentation; In Panavision and color; Rated R; 91 minutes; January release.

CAST

Stevie Wayne	Adrienne Barbeau
Father Malone	Hal Holbrook
Kathy Williams	Janet Leigh
Elizabeth Solley	Jamie Lee Curtis
Machen	John Houseman
Nick Castle	Tommy Atkins
Sandy Fadel	Nancy Loomis
Dan O'Bannon	Charles Cyphers
Al Williams	John Goff
Andy Wayne	Ty Mitchell
Tommy Wallace	George Buck Flower
Mayor	Jim Jacobus
Sheriff Simms	John Vick
Dick Baxter	Jim Canning
Mrs. Kobritz	Regina Waldon
Mel Sloan	Darrow Igus
Bartender	Bill Taylor
Hank Jones	Jim Haynie
Ashcroft	Fred Franklyn

Right: Adrienne Barbeau, Ty Mitchell
© AVCO Embassy

Janet Leigh, Hal Holbrook
Above: Jamie Lee Curtis, Nick Castle

Janet Leigh, Jamie Lee Curtis
Above: John Houseman

10

HERO AT LARGE

(UNITED ARTISTS/MGM) Producer, Stephen Friedman; Associate Producer, Roger M. Rothstein; Director, Martin Davidson; Screenplay, A. J. Carothers; Photography, David M. Walsh; Designer, Albert Brenner; Editors, Sidney Levin, David Garfield; Music, Patrick Williams; Assistant Directors, Jack Roe, John Kretchmer; Art Director, Norman Baron; Costumes, Sandra Davidson; In Metrocolor; Rated PG; 98 minutes; February release.

CAST

Steve Nichols	John Ritter
J. Marsh	Anne Archer
Walter Reeves	Bert Convy
Calvin Donnelly	Kevin McCarthy
Eddie	Harry Bellaver
Mrs. Havacheck	Anita Dangler
Gloria Preston	Jane Hallaren
Mayor	Leonard Harris
Milo	Rick Podell
Marty Fields	Allan Rich
Fireman	Kurt Andon
Heros at fire	Gerry Black, Gerald Castillo
Anthony Casselli	Tony Cacciotti
TV Moderator	William Bogert
Dr. Joyce Brothers	Herself
Firechief	Kenneth Tobey
TV Commentator	A. J. Carothers

and Natalie Cilona, Tony Crupi, Heidi Gold, Garry Goodrow, Michael Gorrin, Rod Haase, Henrietta Jacobson, Gary Klar, Michael Leon, Andrew Masset, Bryan O'Byrne, James O'Connell, Church Ortiz, William Robertson, Robin Sherwood, Marley Sims, Joseph Stern, Larry Attebery, Kevin Bacon, Vanda Barra, Neill Barry, Chris Borgen, David-James Carroll, Gary Combs, Rita Crafts, Carol Martin, Lionel Pina, Michael Prince, John Roland, Marilyn Salenger, Jack Somack, Rolland Smith, Willy Stern, Nancy Bleier, Robert Carricart, Frank Casey, Tracey Cohn, Kenneth Cory, Penny Crone, Alberto Ferrara, Lenny Geer, Tyler Horn, Peter Iacangelo

**Top: Kevin McCarthy, John Ritter,
Leonard Harris © MGM
Right Center: Willie Stern, John Ritter**

John Ritter, Anne Archer

COAL MINER'S DAUGHTER

(UNIVERSAL) Producer, Bernard Schwartz; Director, Michael Apted; Screenplay, Tom Rickman; Based on autobiography by Loretta Lynn with George Vecsey; Executive Producer, Bob Larson; Photography, Ralf D. Bode; Designer, John W. Corso; Editor, Arthur Schmidt; Associate Producer, Zelda Barron; Costumes, Joe I. Tomkins; Assistant Directors, Dan Kolsrud, Katy Emde; Set Designer, Lou Mann; In Technicolor; Rated PG; 125 minutes; February release.

CAST

Loretta	Sissy Spacek
Doolittle (Mooney) Lynn	Tommy Lee Jones
Ted Webb	Levon Helm
Clara Webb	Phyllis Boyens
Webb children	Bill Anderson, Jr., Foister Dickerson, Malla McCown, Pamela McCown, Kevin Salvilla
Junior Webb (at 16)	William Sanderson
Loretta and Mooney's children	Sissy Lucas, Pat Paterson, Brian Warf, Elizabeth Watson
Patsy Cline	Beverly D'Angelo
Bobby Day	Robert Elkins
Charlie Dick	Bob Hannah
Ernest Tubb	Himself
Patsy Lynn	Jennifer Beasley
Peggy Lynn	Jessica Easley
Storekeeper	Michael Baish
Girl at fairgrounds	Susan Kingsley
Doc Turner	David Gray
Hugh Cherry	Royce Clark
Radio Station Manager	Gary Parker
Speedy West	Billy Strange
Opry Stage Manager	Bruce Newman
Opry Announcer	Grant Turner

and Frank Mitchell, Merle Kilgore, Jackie Lynn Wright, Rhonda Rhoton, Vernon Oxford, Ron Hensley, Doug Bledsoe, Aubrey Wells, Russell Varner, Tommie O'Donnell, Lou Headley, Ruby Caudill, Charles Kahlenberg, Alice McGeachy, Ken Riley, Jim Webb

Left: Tommy Lee Jones Top: Levon Helm, Sissy Spacek © Universal Studios
1980 Academy Award to Sissy Spacek for Best Actress

(Left) Levon Helm, Phyllis Boyens, (second from right) Sissy Spacek

Sissy Spacek, and above and
top with Tommy Lee Jones

Sissy Spacek, also above, and top with Tommy Lee Jones

13

FOXES

(UNITED ARTISTS) Producers, David Puttnam, Gerald Ayres; Director, Adrian Lyne; Screenplay, Gerald Ayres; Associate Producers, Geoffrey Kirkland, Michael Seresin, Joel Blasberg, Gerry Hambling; Music, Giorgio Moroder; Photography, Leon Bijou; Art Director, Michael Levesque; Editor, Jim Coblentz; Assistant Directors, Stuart Gross, Carol Polakoff; In Technicolor; A Casablanca Record and Filmworks Production; Rated R; 106 minutes; February release.

CAST

Jeanie	Jodie Foster
Brad	Scott Baio
Mary	Sally Kellerman
Jay	Randy Quaid
Mrs. Axman	Lois Smith
Bryan	Adam Faith
Annie	Cherie Currie
Madge	Marilyn Kagan
Deirdre	Kandice Stroh
Loser	Jon Sloan
Sissie	Jill Barrie Bogart
Frank	Wayne Storm
Gladys	Mary Margaret Lewis
Greg	Grant Wilson
Bobby	Fredric Lehne
Scott	Robert Romanus
Counsellor	Roger Bowen
Detective	E. Lamont Johnson
Mrs. Steiner	Mary Ellen O'Neill

Buddy Foster, Ben Frank, Kay A. Tornberg, Scott Garrett, Laura Dern, Michael Taylor, Gino Baffa, Charles Shull, Tony Termini, Jeff Silverman, Mae Williams, R. Scott Thomson, Ron Lombard, Steve Jones, Jon Benson, Tom Pletts, Ken Novick

Right: Jodie Foster, Scott Baio
Top: Jodie Foster, Sally Kellerman
© United Artists

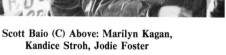

Scott Baio (C) Above: Marilyn Kagan,
Kandice Stroh, Jodie Foster

Kandice Stroh, Marilyn Kagan, Cherie Currie,
Jodie Foster, and above with Robert Romanus

14

SIMON

(ORION) Producer, Martin Bregman; Direction, Story and Screenplay, Marshall Brickman; Executive Producer, Louis A. Stroller; Music, Stanley Silverman; Design, Stuart Wurtzel; Photography, Adam Holender; Costumes, Santo Loquasto; Editor, Nina Feinberg; Assistant Directors, Michael Rauch, Bob Barth; Set, John Godfrey; In Technicolor; Rated R; 97 minutes; February release.

CAST

Simon	Alan Arkin
Cynthia	Madeline Kahn
Becker	Austin Pendleton
Lisa	Judy Graubart
Fichandler	William Finley
Barundi	Jayant
Van Dongen	Wallace Shawn
Hundertwasser	Max Wright
Korey	Fred Gwynne
Commune Leader	Adolph Green
Josh	Keith Szarabajka
Pam	Ann Risley
Military Aide at Map	Pierre Epstein
General's Aide	Roy Cooper
Army Doctor	Rex Robbins
Blades	David Warrilow
Voice of mother	Hetty Galen
Security Guard	David Gideon
Themselves	David Susskind, Dick Cavett
TV Newscaster	Remak Ramsay
TV Priest	Hansford Rowe
TV Philosopher	Yusef Bulos
TV Scientist	Jerry Mayer
TV Rabbi	Sol Frieder
TV Senator	William Griffis
TV Psychologist	Frank J. Lucas

Right: Alan Arkin, and above with Madeline Kahn
© Orion Pictures

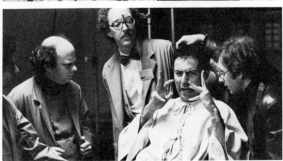

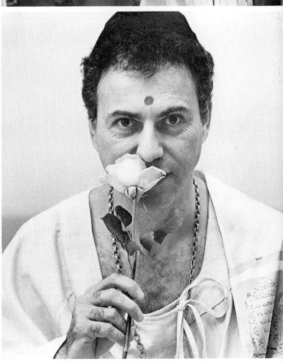

Jayant, Wallace Shawn, William Finley, Alan Arkin, Austin Pendleton Above: Arkin, Judy Graubart

Alan Arkin

AMERICAN GIGOLO

(PARAMOUNT) Producer, Jerry Bruckheimer; Executive Producer, Freddie Fields; Direction and Screenplay, Paul Schrader; Photography, John Bailey; Art Director, Ed Richardson; Editor, Richard Halsey; Music, Giorgio Moroder; Assistant Directors, Peter Bogart, Bill Beasley; Set Designer, Mark Fabus; In Metrocolor; Rated R; 117 minutes; February release.

CAST

Julian	Richard Gere
Michelle	Lauren Hutton
Sunday	Hector Elizondo
Anne	Nina Van Pallandt
Leon Jaimes	Bill Duke
Charles Stratton	Brian Davies
Lisa Williams	K Callan
Mr. Rheiman	Tom Stewart
Judy Rheiman	Patti Carr
Lt. Curtis	David Cryer
Mrs. Dobrum	Carole Cook
Mrs. Sloan	Carol Bruce
Mrs. Laudner	Frances Bergen
Hollywood actor	MacDonald Carey
Michelle's lawyer	William Dozier
Julian's lawyer	Peter Turgeon
Floyd Wicker	Robert Wightman
Mr. Williams	Richard Derr
Jill	Jessica Potter
Blind Boy	Gordon Haight
Salesman	Carlo Alonso
Jason	Michael Goyak

and Frank Pesce, Judith Ransdell, John Hammerton, Michele Drake, Linda Horn, Faye Michael Nuell, Eugene Jackson, Roma Alvarez, Dawn Adams, Bob Jardine, Harry Davis, Nanette Tarpey, Maggie Jean Smith, Pamela Fong, Randy Stokey, Harris Weingart, James Currie, Norman Stevans, Betty Canter, Laura Gile, Brent Dunsford, Barry Satterfield, Sam L. Nickens, William Valdez, Mary Helen Barro, John H. Lowe, Kopi Sotiropulos, Gordon W. Grant, Ron Cummins

Left: Nina Van Pallandt, Richard Gere
Above: Richard Gere, Lauren Hutton
© Paramount Pictures

Hector Elizondo, Richard Gere
Above: Frances Bergen, Gere

Richard Gere (C)

WISE BLOOD

NEW LINE CINEMA) Producers, Michael and Kathy Fitzgerald; Director, John Huston; Screenplay, Benedict Fitzgerald from the novel by Flannery O'Connor; Photography, Gerald Fisher; Editor, Roberto Silvi; Music, Alex North; Costumes and Sets, Sally Fitzgerald; In color; Not rated; 108 minutes; February release.

CAST

Hazel Motes	Brad Dourif
Hoover Shoates	Ned Beatty
Asa Hawks	Harry Dean Stanton
Enoch Emery	Daniel Shor
Sabbath Lilly:	Amy Wright
Landlady:	Mary Nell Santacroce
Grandfather	John Huston

**Top: Daniel Shor, Amy Wright,
Brad Dourif
© New Line Cinema**

Brad Dourif, Amy Wright

JUST TELL ME WHAT YOU WANT

(WARNER BROTHERS) Producers, Jay Presson Allen, Sidney Lumet; Director, Sidney Lumet; Executive Producer, Burtt Harris; Screenplay, Jay Presson Allen based on her novel; Music, Charles Strouse; Editor, John J. Fitzstephens; Designer, Tony Walton; Photography, Oswald Morris; Assistant Directors, Alan Hopkins, Robert E. Warren; Costumes, Tony Walton, Gloria Gresham; Art Director, John Jay Moore; In Technicolor; Rated R; 112 minutes; February release.

CAST

Bones Burton	Ali MacGraw
Max Herschel	Alan King
Stella Liberti	Myrna Loy
Seymour Berger	Keenan Wynn
Mike Berger	Tony Roberts
Steven Routledge	Peter Weller
Cathy	Sara Truslow
Baby	Judy Kaye
Connie Herschel	Dina Merrill
Dr. Coleson	Joseph Maher
Stan	John Walter Davis
New Baby	Annabel Lukins
Teddy	Jeffrey Anderson-Gunter
Lothar	Michael Gross
Julie Raskin	Joseph Leon
Dr. Jowdy	Raymond Thorne
Dr. Kierstein	Tom Batten
Hospital Nurse	Leslie Easterbrook
Mark Gosse	Paul E. Guskin
Bones' Lester	Stanley Greene
Party Major Domo	Lee H. Doyle
Dr. Benecek	Mike Howard

and Paddy Croft, Margie Swearingen, Lacey Neuhaus, Phil Leto, Tony Munafo, David Rasche, John Gabriel, Ruth Holden, Paul Farentino, Bill Masi, Ron Millkie

**Right: Peter Weller, Ali MacGraw
Top: Alan King, Ali MacGraw
© Warner Bros.**

Myrna Loy

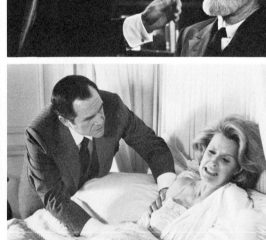

Alan King, Dina Merrill
Above: King, Keenan Wynn

18

CRUISING

(UNITED ARTISTS/LORIMAR) Producer, Jerry Weintraub; Direction and Screenplay, William Friedkin; Based on novel by Gerald Walker; Music, Jack Nitzsche; Photographer, James Contner; Designer, Bruce Weintraub; Art Director, Edward Pisoni; Costumes, Robert deMora; Editor, Bud Smith; Associate Producer, Burtt Harris; Assistant Directors, Alan Hopkins, Robert Warren; In Technicolor; Rated R; 106 minutes; February release.

CAST

Steve Burns	Al Pacino
Capt. Edelson	Paul Sorvino
Nancy	Karen Allen
Stuart Richards	Richard Cox
Ted Bailey	Don Scardino
Patrolman DiSimone	Joe Spinell
Skip Lee	Jay Acovone
Detective Lafransky	Randy Jurgensen
Dr. Rifkin	Barton Heyman
DaVinci	Gene Davis
Loren Lukas	Arnaldo Santana
Eric Rossman	Larry Atlas
Chief of Detectives	Allan Miller
Det. Blasio	Sonny Grosso
Det. Schreiber	Edward O'Neil
Det. Davis	Michael Aronin
Gregory	James Remar
Paul Gaines	William Russ
Patrolman Desher	Mike Starr
Martino	Steve Inwood
Joey	Keith Prentice
Jack Richards	Leland Starnes

and Robert Pope, Leo Burmester, Bruce Levine, Charles Dunlap, Powers Boothe, James Sutorius, Richard Jamieson, James Ray Weeks, David Winnie Hayes, Carmine Stipo, James Hyden, Todd Winters, Sylvia Gassell

Right: Don Scardino, Al Pacino
Top: Al Pacino, Karen Allen
© Lorimar Productions

Al Pacino, Richard Cox
Above: Al Pacino (C)

Paul Sorvino

SMOKEY AND THE BANDIT II

(UNIVERSAL) Producer, Hank Moonjean; Director, Hal Needham; Story, Michael Kane; Screenplay, Jerry Belson, Brock Yates; Based on Characters created by Hal Needham, Robert L. Levy; Photography, Michael Butler; Designer, Henry Bumstead; Editors, Donn Cambern, William Gordean; Music, Snuff Garrett; Art Director, Bernie Cutler; Associate Producer, Peter Burrell; Assistant Directors, David Hamburger, Frank Bueno, Bill Coker, Ronald G. Smith; Songs sung by Jerry Reed, Statler Brothers, Brenda Lee, Don Williams, Mel Tillis, Sons of the Pioneers, Tanya Tucker; In Technicolor; Rated PG; 101 minutes; March release.

CAST

Bandit	Burt Reynolds
Buford T. Justice, Reginald Van Justice, Gaylord Van Justice	Jackie Gleason
Cledus	Jerry Reed
Doc	Dom DeLuise
Carrie	Sally Field
Little Enos	Paul Williams
John Conn	David Huddleston
Junior	Mike Henry
Big Enos	Pat McCormick
Governor	John Anderson
Nice Lady	Brenda Lee
Statler Brothers	Phil Balsley, Lew DeWitt, Don Reid, Harold Reid
Fairground Owner	Mel Tillis
Themselves	Don Williams, Terry Bradshaw, "Mean Joe" Greene, Joe Klecko
Football Player	Jeffrey Bryan King
Ramona	Nancy Lenehan
P.T	John Megna

and Dudley Remus, Jerry Lester, Hal Carter, Rick Allen, Charles Yeager, Patrick Moody, John Robert Nicholson, Anthony T. Townes, Ritchey Brown, Nancy Lee Johnson, Gayle Davis, James L. Buchanan 2nd

Left: Jackie Gleason
Top: Burt Reynolds
© Universal Studios

Dom DeLuise, Burt Reynolds

Burt Reynolds, Sally Field
Above: Field, Jerry Reed
Top: Mike Henry, Jackie Gleason

Burt Reynolds, Sally Field
Top: Paul Williams, Pat McCormick

GILDA LIVE

(WARNER BROTHERS) Producer-Director, Lorne Michaels; Choreography, Patricia Birch; Design, Eugene and Franne Lee; Director, Mike Nichols; Written by Anne Beatts, Lorne Michaels, Marilyn Suzanne Miller, Don Novello, Michael O'Donoghue, Gilda Radner, Paul Shaffer, Rosie Shuster, Alan Zweibel; Associate Producer, Barbara Burns; In technicolor; Rated R; 95 minutes; March release.

CAST
Gilda Radner
Father Guido Sarducci
Paul Shaffer
Rouge

Left: Gilda Radner

© **Warner Bros.**

Gilda Radner, and above with Rouge

Gilda Radner Above: Father Guido Sarducci

22

LITTLE MISS MARKER

(UNIVERSAL) Producer, Jennings Lang; Direction and Screenplay, Walter Bernstein; Based on story by Damon Runyon; Executive Producer, Walter Matthau; Photography, Philip Lathrop; Designer, Edward C. Carfagno; Editor, Eve Newman; Music, Henry Mancini; Assistant Directors, Ronald J. Martinez, Judith Vogelsang; In color; Rated PG; 112 minutes; March release.

CAST

Sorrowful Jones	Walter Matthau
Amanda	Julie Andrews
Blackie	Tony Curtis
Regret	Bob Newhart
The Judge	Lee Grant
"The Kid"	Sara Stimson
Herbie	Brian Dennehy
Brannigan	Kenneth McMillan
Carter	Andrew Rubin
Benny	Joshua Shelley
Clerk	Randy Herman
Mrs. Clancy	Nedra Volz
Lola	Jacquelyn Hyde
Vittorio	Tom Pedi
Clerk	Jessica Rains
Teller	Henry Slate
Morris	Alvin Hammer
Sam	Don Bexley
Manager	Jack DeLeon
Clerk	John P. Finnegan

and Ralph Manza, Jack Mullaney, Mark Anger, Lennie Bremen, Maurice Marks, Colin Gilbert, Wynn Irwin, Joseph Knowland, Stanley Lawrence, Louis Basile, Ed Ness, H. B. Newton, Stanley E. Ritchie, William Ackridge, Alan Thomason, Charles A. Venegas, Sharri Zak, Robert E. Ball, Simmy Bow, Jorge B. Cruz

Top: Walter Matthau, Bob Newhart,
Sara Stimson Right: Sara Stimson,
Julie Andrews, Walter Matthau
Right Center: Tony Curtis, Walter
Matthau © Universal Studios

Julie Andrews, Sara Stimson,
Walter Matthau

A SMALL CIRCLE OF FRIENDS

(UNITED ARTISTS) Producer, Tim Zinnemann; Director, Rob Cohen; Screenplay, Ezra Sacks; Photography, Michael Butler; Designer, Joel Schiller; Editor, Randy Roberts; Music, Jim Steinman; Assistant Directors, Michael Haley, Lisa Hallas; Set Designers, Al Kemper, Nicolas Laborczy; Songs performed by Johnny Mathis, The Four Tops, The Rolling Stones, The Mamas and the Papas; In Technicolor; Rated R; 113 minutes; March release.

CAST

Leo DaVinci	Brad Davis
Jessica	Karen Allen
Nick Baxter	James Parker
Alice	Shelley Long
Haddox	John Friedrich
Greenblatt	Gary Springer
Harry	Craig Richard Nelson
Jimmy (The Cook)	Harry Caesar
Mrs. Baxter	Nan Martin
Crazy Kid	Dan Stern
Dorm Proctor	Jason Laskay
Karate Student	Jamie Squire
Girl in shower	Mary Margaret Amato
Crimson Editor	David Hollander
Crimson Editor #2	Frank Rich
Underground Woman	Pamela Cresant
Army Doctor	Nick Kairis
Art Professor	Severn Darden
Dean	Jonathan Moore
Karate Instructor	Nancy Penoyer
Sarah	Devorah Offner
Rizzo	John Peters

and Doug Llewelyn, Brett Smith, Jeannetta Arnette, Anita Sangiola, Michael Shaunessy, Doree Sitterly, Navabeh, Joe La Creta, William N. Chamberlain, Samson X. Greiff, Don Bennett, Amy Leitman, Annie McGuire, Peter Pollard, Lawrence Chevis Prince, William J. Sahlein, David Tomaras, Robert Underwood

Brad Davis, Karen Allen

Top: Brad Davis, Jameson Parker,
Karen Allen Left Center: Brad
Davis, Jameson Parker
© United Artists

Karen Allen, Jameson Parker
Above: Brad Davis, Parker Top:
Parker, Allen, Davis

Jameson Parker, Karen Allen,
Brad Davis Above: Davis,
John Friedrich

SERIAL

(PARAMOUNT) Producer, Sidney Beckerman; Director, Bill Persky; Screenplay, Rich Eustis, Michael Elias; Based on novel by Cyra McFadden; Photography, Rexford Metz; Editor, John W. Wheeler; Music, Lalo Schifrin; Lyrics, Norman Gimbel; Associate Producer, Mel Dellar; Art Director, Bill Sandell; Assistant Directors, Jerry Sobul, Herb Adelman; In MovieLab Color; Rated R; 92 minutes; March release.

CAST

Harvey	Martin Mull
Kate	Tuesday Weld
Joan	Jennifer McAlister
Bill	Sam Chew, Jr.
Martha	Sally Kellerman
Stokeley	Anthony Battaglia
Sam	Bill Macy
Angela	Nita Talbot
Carol	Pamela Bellwood
Vivian	Barbara Rhoades
Rachel	Ann Weldon
Leonard	Peter Bonerz
Wong	Jon Fong
Luckman/Skull	Christopher Lee
Stella	Patch MacKenzie
Marlene	Stacey Nelkin
Spike	Tom Smothers
Spenser	Clark Brandon
Paco	Paul Rossilli
Donald	Clyde Ventura

and Rosana Soto, Kevin O'Brien, Mark Taylor, Donna Ponterotto, Lee Wilkof, John Thompson, Kevyn Howard, Robin Sherwood, Bob Balhatchet, Victoria Huxtable, George American Horse, Peter Horton, Kenny Endoso, Jay Currin, Buddy Joe Hooker, Billy Sands, Sam Denoff, Melanie Workhoven, Mark Rasmussen, Bill Jelliffe, Scott Paulin, Anthony Fusco

Right: Sally Kellerman, Nita Talbot, Pamela Bellwood, Barbara Rhoades, Tuesday Weld
Top: Martin Mull, Weld, Jennifer McAllister, Tom Smothers © Paramount Pictures

Martin Mull, Tuesday Weld

Martin Mull, Patch Mackenzie
Above: Nita Talbot, Bill Macy

26

WHEN TIME RAN OUT

(WARNER BROTHERS) Producer, Irwin Allen; Director, James Goldstone; Screenplay, Carl Foreman, Stirling Silliphant; Based on novel "The Day the World Ended" by Gordon Thomas and Max Morgan Witts; Music, Lalo Schifrin; Designer, Philip M. Jefferies; Photography, Koennekamp; Associate Producers, Al Gail, George E. Swink; Assistant Directors, L. Andrew Stone, Robert P. Cohen, Emmitt-Leon O'Neil; Costumes, Paul Zastupnevich; Art Director, Russell C. Menzer; In Panavision and Technicolor; An International Cinema Corp. presentation; Rated PG; 121 minutes; March release.

CAST

Hank Anderson	Paul Newman
Kay Kirby	Jacqueline Bisset
Shelby Gilmore	William Holden
Brian	Edward Albert
Francis Fendly	Red Buttons
Iolani	Barbara Carrera
Rose Valdez	Valentina Cortesa
Nikki	Veronica Hamel
Tiny Baker	Alex Karras
Rene Valdez	Burgess Meredith
Tom Conti	Ernest Borgnine
Bob Spangler	James Franciscus
Webster	John Considine
Mona	Sheila Allen
Sam	Pat Morita
Kelly	Lonny Chapman
Webster's Assistant	Darrell Larson
Henderson	Sandy Kenyon
Wrangler	Marcus Mukai
Durant	Ted Gehring
Joe	Joe Papalimu

and Jaylin Maureen Acol, Reed Derwin Acol, Ava Readdy, Glynn Rubin, Takayo Doran, James Gavin, M. James Arnett, Marcia Nicholson, Barbara Costello, Bill Smillie, Steven Marlo, Esmond Chung, Jeffrey McDevitt, John Springer, Jr.

Right: William Holden, Jacqueline Bisset
Top: Bissett, Paul Newman
© Warner Bros.

Paul Newman, James Franciscus
Above: Ernest Borgnine, Red Buttons

Paul Newman, Jacqueline Bisset

27

THE BLACK MARBLE

(AVCO EMBASSY) Producer, Frank Capra, Jr.; Director, Harold Becker; Screenplay, Joseph Wambaugh; Photography, Owen Roizman; Design, Alred Sweeney; Editor, Maury Winetrobe; Music, Maurice Jarre; Costumes, Susan Becker; Assistant Directors, Tom Mack, Lou Race, Bill Elvin; In Panavision and DeLuxe Color; Rated PG; 113 minutes; March release.

CAST

Sgt. A. M. Valnikov	Robert Foxworth
Sgt. Natalie Zimmerman	Paula Prentiss
Fiddler	James Woods
Philo Sinner	Harry Dean Stanton
Madeline Whitfield	Barbara Babcock
Clarence Cromwell	John Hancock
Capt. Hipless Hooker	Raleigh Bond
Pattie Mae	Judy Landers
Itchy Mitch	Pat Corley
Dt. Bullets Bambarella	Paul Henry Itken
Alex Valnikov	Richard Dix
Russian Woman	Lidia Kristen
Marvis Skinner	Marilyn Chris
Harried woman	Doris Belack
Chester Biggs	Dallas Alinder
Receptionist	Elizabeth Farley
Millie's Houseboy	Michael Dudikoff
Limpwood	Lou Cuttell
Bessie Callahan	Anne Ramsey
Iosif	Ion Teodorescu
Capt. Jack Packerton	Michael Gainsborough

and Jorge Cervera, Jr., Tenaya, Art Kassul, Robin Raymond, Billy Beck, Adele Malis, Herta Ware, Jane Daly, Rev. F. Wilcock, Valery Klever, Natasha Plaksin, Christopher Lloyd

Left: Barbara Babcock Top: Paula Prentiss, Robert Foxworth
© AVCO Embassy

Robert Foxworth, Paula Prentiss, James Woods

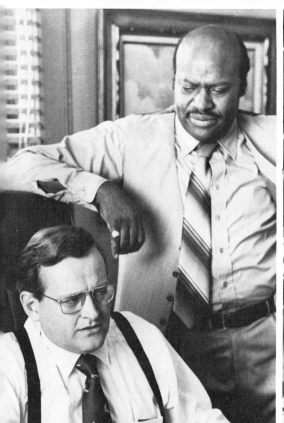

Paula Prentiss, Robert Foxworth
Top: (L) Raleigh Bond, John Hancock (R) Harry Dean Stanton, Judy Landers

HAPPY BIRTHDAY, GEMINI

(UNITED ARTISTS) Executive Producer, Alan King; Producer, Rupert Hitzig; Co-Producer, Bruce Calnan; Direction and Screenplay, Richard Benner; Based on play "Gemini" by Albert Innaurato; Photography, James B. Kelly; Editor, Stephan Fanfara; Music, Rich Look, Cathy Chamberlain; Designer, Ted Watkins; Costumes, D. Lynne MacKay; Assistant Director, Rob Malenfant; In color; Rated R; 107 minutes; April release.

CAST

Bunny Weinberger	Madeline Kahn
Lucille Pompi	Rita Moreno
Nick Geminiani	Robert Viharo
Francis Geminiani	Alan Rosenberg
Judith Hastings	Sarah Holcomb
Randy Hastings	David Marshall Grant
Herschel Weinberger	Timothy Jenkins
Sam Weinberger	David McIllwraith
Mary O'Donnel	Maura Swanson
Judge	Richert Easley
O'Donnel	John William Kennedy
Father McBride	Michael Donaghue
Dominique	Alberto de Rosa
Court Clerk	Michael Holton
Jerry	A. Frank Ruffo
Eddie	Dwayne McLean
Taxi Driver	Jeff Wincott

Left: Tim Jenkins, Madeline Kahn, Robert Viharo, Alberto deRosa, Rita Moreno, Sarah Holcomb Top: Viharo, Alan Rosenberg
© United Artists

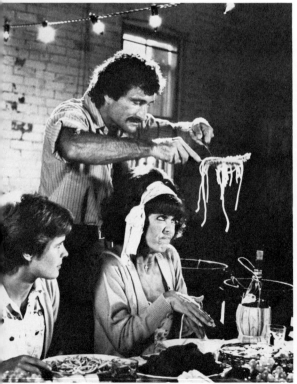

Sarah Holcomb, Robert Viharo
Rita Moreno

Madeline Kahn, Rita Moreno, Robert Viharo Above: David Marshall Grant, Sarah Holcomb

THE BALTIMORE BULLET

(AVCO EMBASSY) Executive Producers, William D. Jekel, Norman G. Rudman; Producer, John Brascia; Director, Robert Ellis Miller; Screenplay, John Brascia, Robert Vincent O'Neil; Associate Producer, Ted Goetz; Music, Johnny Mandel; Photography, James A. Crabe; Editor, Jerry Brady; Designer, Herman Blumenthal; Art Director, Adrian Gorton; Costumes, Patricia Ann Norris; Assistant Director, Dan Allingham; In color; Rated PG; 103 minutes; April release.

CAST

Nick Casey	James Coburn
The Deacon	Omar Sharif
Billie Joe Robbins	Bruce Boxleitner
Carolina Red	Ronee Blakley
Max	Jack O'Halloran
Snow White	Calvin Lockhart
Paulie	Michael Learner
Cosmo	Paul Barselou
Sportscasters	Jeff Temkin, Willie Mosconi
Sugar	Cissie Cameron
Robin	Shep Sanders
Baron	Jon Ian Jacobs
Skinny	Ed Bakey
Ricco	Robert Hughes
Gunner	Rocknee Tarkington
Al	Shay Duffin
Ernie	Thomas Castranova
Purvis	Eric Laneuville
Frankie	William M. Vint

and Lou Butera, Irving Crane, Richie Florence, Allen Hopkins, Peter Margo, Ray Martin, Jim Mataya, Steve Mizerak, Jim Rempe, Michael Sigel

Top: James Coburn, Omar Sharif, Ronee
Blakley, Bruce Boxleitner Below: Sharif,
Rocknee Tarkington Right: Coburn, Cissie
Cameron Top: Boxleitner, Coburn
© AVCO Embassy

James Coburn, Ronee Blakley, Bruce
Boxleitner Above: Omar Sharif, Coburn

SITTING DUCKS

(UNITED FILM DISTRIBUTION CO.) Producer, Meira Attia Dor; Direction and Screenplay, Henry Jaglom; Photography, Paul Glickman; Music, Richard Romanus; An International Rainbow Picture in color; Rated R; 90 minutes; April release.

CAST

Simon	Michael Emil
Sidney	Zack Norman
Jenny	Patrice Townsend
Leona	Irene Forrest
Moose	Richard Romanus
Jenny's friend	Henry Jaglom

Top: (and below) Michael Emil, Zack Norman
Right: Irene Forrest, Emil Below:
Norman, Richard Romanus

Patrice Townsend, Irene Forrest
Left: Michael Emil, Patrice Townsend

FFOLKES

(**UNIVERSAL**) Producer, Elliott Kastner; Director, Andrew V. McLaglen; Screenplay, Jack Davies from his novel "Esther, Ruth and Jennifer"; Executive Producer, Moses Rothman; Associate Producer, Denis Holt; Music, Michael J. Lewis; Photography, Tony Imi; Editor, Alan Strachan; Art Director, Bert Davey; Designer, Maurice Carter; Assistant Directors, Brian Cook, Terry Needham, Michael Stevenson; In color; Rated PG; 99 minutes; April release.

CAST

ffolkes	Roger Moore
Admiral Brinsden	James Mason
Kramer	Anthony Perkins
Shulman	Michael Parks
King	David Hedison
Olafsen	Jack Watson
Fletcher	George Baker
Tipping	Jeremy Clyde
Herring	David Wood
Prime Minister	Faith Brook
Sanna	Lea Brodie
Ackerman	Anthony Pullen Shaw
Webb	Philip O'Brien
Dawnay	John Westbrook
Sarah	Jennifer Hilary
Phillips	John Lee
Helicopter Pilot	Brook Williams
Harris	Tim Bentinck
Saburo	Saburo Kimura
Eiji	Eiji Kusuhara
Eriksen	David Landbury

and Alastair Llewellyn, Sean Arnold, Eric Mason, Thane Bettany, George Leach, Richard Graydon, Mathias Kilroy, Angela Thorne, Martin Matthews, Lindsay Campbell, Jonathan Nutt, Robert Swan, William Abney

Right: Eiji Kusuhara, Alastair Llewellyn, Lea Brodie, Saburo Kimura, Sean Arnold Top: David Hedison, James Mason, Philip O'Brien, Roger Moore © Universal Studios

Michael Parks, Anthony Perkins

Roger Moore, Lea Brodie Above: Anthony Pullen Shaw, Alastair Llewellyn, Anthony Perkins

FAME

(CINEMA INTERNATIONAL) Producers, Alan Marshall, David DeSilva; Director, Alan Parker; Screenplay, Christopher Gore; Music, Michael Gore; Lyrics, Dean Pitchford; Photography, Michael Seresin; Designer, Geoffrey Kirkland; Editor, Gerry Hambling; Choreography, Louis Falco; Assistant Directors, Robert F. Colesberry, Raymond L. Greenfield; Costumes, Kristi Zea; Art Director, Ed Wittstein; In Metrocolor and Dolby Stereo; Presented by MGM; Rated PG; 134 minutes; April release.

CAST

Angelo	Eddie Barth
Coco	Irene Cara
Bruno	Lee Curreri
Lisa	Laura Dean
Hilary	Antonia Franceschi
Michael	Boyd Gaines
Shorofsky	Albert Hague
Mrs. Finsecker	Tresa Hughes
Francois Lafete	Steve Inwood
Montgomery	Paul McCrane
Mrs. Sherwood	Anne Meara
Miss Berg	Joanna Merlin
Ralph	Barry Miller
Farrell	Jim Moody
Leroy	Gene Anthony Ray
Doris	Maureen Teefy
Lydia	Debbie Allen

and Richard Belzer, Frank Bongiorno, Bill Britten, Eric Brockington, Nicholas Bunin, Cindy Canuelas, Nora Controne, Mbewe Escobar, Gennady Filimonov, Victor Fischbarg, Penny Frank, Willie Henry, Jr., Steven Hollander, Sang Kim, Darrell Kirkman, Judith L'Heureux, Ted Lambert, Nancy Lee, Sara Malament, James Manis, Carol Massenburg, Issac Mizrahi, Raquel Mondin, Alba Oms, Frank Oteri, Traci Parnell, Sal Piro, Leslie Quickley, Ray Ramirez, Loris Sallahian, Ilse Sass, Dawn Steinberg, Jonathan Strasser, Yvette Torres, Frank X. Vitolo, Stefanie Zimmerman

Left: Barry Miller
© Cinema International

1980 Academy Awards for Best Original Song and Best Original Score

Irene Cara, Lee Curreri

Gene Ray (also top left)

Paul McCrane Above: Anne Meara,
Gene Ray Top: Paul McCrane,
Maureen Teefy

Irene Cara Above: Lee Curreri
Top: Antonia Franceschi

TOUCHED BY LOVE

(COLUMBIA/RASTAR) Producer, Michael Viner; Executive Producer, Peter E. Strauss; Director, Gus Trikonis; Screenplay, Hesper Anderson; Based on "To Elvis with Love" by Lena Canada; Photography, Richard H. Kline; Editor, Fred Chulack; Music, John Barry; Assistant Directors, Bert Gold, Joe Thornton; Art Director, Claudio Guzman; Costumes, Moss Mabry; Sets, Ray Molyneaux; In Metrocolor; Rated PG; 95 minutes; April release.

CAST

Lena Canada	Deborah Raffin
Karen	Diane Lane
Dr. Bell	Michael Learned
Tony	John Amos
Amy	Christina Raines
Margaret	Mary Wickes
Don Fielder	Clu Gulager
Monica	Twyla Volkins

and children and teachers from the Dr. Gordon Townsend School of Calgary, Canada.

Left: Diane Lane, Deborah Raffin
© Columbia Pictures

Michael Learned
Above: Clu Gulager

John Amos
Above: Christina Raines

THE WATCHER IN THE WOODS

(WALT DISNEY/BUENA VISTA) Producer, Ron Miller; Co-Producer, Tom Leetch; Director, John Hough; Screenplay, Brian Clemens, Harry Spalding, Rosemary Anne Sisson; From novel by Florence Engel Randall; Associate Producer, Hugh Attwool; Photography, Alan Hume; Music, Stanley Meyers; Designer, Elliot scott; Art Director, Alan Cassie; Editor, Geoffrey Foot; Costumes, Emma Porteous; Assistant Director, Richard Hoult; In Technicolor and Dolby Stereo; Rated G; 108 minutes; April release.

CAST

Mrs. Aylwood .... Bette Davis
Helen Curtis .... Carroll Baker
Paul Curtis .... David McCallum
Jan Curtis ....Lynn-Holly Johnson
Ellie Curtis ....Kyle Richards
John Keller .... Ian Bannen
Tom Colley ....Richard Pasco
Mary Fleming .... Frances Cuka
Mile Fleming...................................... Benedict Taylor
Mrs. Thayer .... Eleanor Summerfield
Young Mrs. Aylwood........................ Georgina Hale
Karen Aylwood................................Katherine Levy

**Top: David McCallum, Lynn-Holly Johnson
Kyle Richards, Carroll Baker
Right Center: Johnson, Bette Davis, Richards
© Walt Disney Productions**

Bette Davis, Kyle Richards

HEART BEAT

(ORION) Executive Producers, Edward R. Pressman, William Tepper; Producers, Alan Greisman, Michael Shamberg; Direction and Screenplay, John Byrum; Music, Jack Nitzsche; Photography, Laszlo Kovacs; Associate Producer, David R. Axelrod; Editor, Eric Jenkins; Costumes, Patricia Norris; Designer, Jack Fisk; Assistant Directors, Bill Scott, Dennis Capps; Set Designer, Peter Samish; In Panavision and Technicolor; Rated R; 109 minutes; April! release.

CAST

Neal Cassady	Nick Nolte
Carolyn Cassady	Sissy Spacek
Jack Kerouac	John Heard
Ira	Ray Sharkey
Stevie	Anne Dusenberry
Mrs. Kerouac	Margaret Fairchild
Dick	Tony Bill
Waitress	Mary Margaret Amato
Ogden	Kent Williams
Ogden's Secretary	Susan Niven
Receptionists	Marcia Nasatir, Mickey Kelly
Mexican Junkie	Luis Contreras
Blonde in car	Sharon Lee
Bob Bendix	Stephen Davies
Betty Bendix	Jenny O'Hara
Dispatcher	Don Brodie
Seaman	Tom Runyon
Cathy	Juliana Tutak
Claudia	Candy Brown
Steve Allen	Himself

and John Larroquette, John Hostetter, Billy Cross, Terry Winkless, Ray Vitte, Gary Baxley, Lloyd "Sunshine" Parker, Garth Eliassen

**Right: Nick Nolte, Sissy Spacek,
John Heard © Orion Pictures**

Sissy Spacek, Nick Nolte

**John Heard, Sissy Spacek, Nick Nolte
Above: John Heard, Sissy Spacek**

THE LONG RIDERS

(UNITED ARTISTS) Producer, Tim Zinnemann; Director, Walter Hill; Executive Producers, James Keach, Stacy Keach; Screenplay, Bill Bryden, Steven Phillip Smith, Stacy Keach, James Keach; Photography, Ric Waite; Designer, Jack T. Collis; Editor, David Holden; Music, Ry Cooder; Costumes, Bobbie Mannix; Art Director, Peter Romero; Editor, Freeman Davies; Assistant Directors, Peter Gries, Mary Lou MacLaury; Set, Bo Welch; Choreographer, Katina Sawidis; In Technicolor; Rated R; 100 minutes; May release.

CAST

Cole Younger	David Carradine
Jim Younger	Keith Carradine
Bob Younger	Robert Carradine
Jesse James	James Keach
Frank James	Stacy Keach
Ed Miller	Dennis Quaid
Clell Miller	Randy Quaid
John Younger	Kevin Brophy
George Arthur	Harry Carey, Jr.
Charlie Ford	Christopher Guest
Bob Ford	Nicholas Guest
Annie Ralston	Shelby Leverington
Mr. Reddick	Felice Orlandi
Belle Starr	Pamela Reed
Sam Starr	James Remar
Mrs. Samuel	Fran Ryan
Zee	Savannah Smith
Beth	Amy Stryker
Mr. Rixley	James Whitmore, Jr.
Mortician	John Bottoms

and West Buchanan, Edward Bunker, Martina Deignan, Allan Graf, Chris Mulkey, Thomas R. Myers, Marlise Pieratt, Glenn Robards, Tim Rossovich, Lin Shaye, Gary Watkins, Peter Jason, Steve Chambers, Duke Stroud, William Traylor, J. Don Ferguson, Hugh McGraw, Prentiss E. Rowe, Stuart Mossman, Michael Lackey, Mitch Greenhill, Bill Bryson, Tom Sauber, Jimmy Medearis, Edgar McLeod, Luis Contreras, Kalen Keach, R. B. Thrift

Top: (front) R. B. Thrift, Fran Ryan, James Keach, Savannah Smith, Amy Stryker, (back) David and Robert Carradine, Stacy Keach, Randy Quaid, Keith Carradine © United Artists

Pamela Reed Above: Christopher Guest, Nicholas Guest

39

TOM HORN

(WARNER BROTHERS) Executive Producer, Fred Weintraub; Director, William Wiard; Music, Ernest Gold; Screenplay, Thomas McGuane, Bud Shrake; Based on a true story; Art Director, Ron Hobbs; Photography, John Alonzo; Assistant Directors, Cliff Coleman, Ed Milkovich; Associate Producers, Michael Rachmil, Sandra Weintraub; In Panavision and Technicolor; Rated R; 98 minutes; May release.

CAST

Tom Horn	Steve McQueen
Glendolene Kimmel	Linda Evans
John Coble	Richard Farnsworth
Joe Belle	Billy Green Bush
Sam Creedmore	Slim Pickens
Assistant Prosecutor	Peter Canon
Stable Hand	Elisha Cook
Mendenhour	Roy Jenson
Arlo Chance	James Kline
Walter Stoll	Geoffrey Lewis
Burke	Harry Northup
Gentleman Jim Corbett	Steve Oliver
Ora Haley	Bill Thurman
Judge	Bert Williams
Corbett's Bodyguard	Bobby Bass
Brown's Hole Rustler	Mickey Jones
Cattle Baron	B. J. Ward
John Cleveland	Richard Kennedy
MacGregor	Larry Strawbridge

Top: Linda Evans, Steve McQueen
© Warner Bros.

Steve McQueen

BON VOYAGE, CHARLIE BROWN

(PARAMOUNT) Producers, Lee Mendelson, Bill Melendez; Director, Bill Melendez; Written and Created by Charles M. Schulz; Music, Ed Bogas, Judy Munsen; Co-Director, Phil Roman; Designed by Evert Brown, Bernard Gruver, Dean Spille, Lance Nolley; Editors, Chuck McCann, Roger Donley; In MovieLab Color; Rated G; 75 minutes; May release. Voices of Daniel Anderson, Casey Carlson, Patricia Patts, Arrin Skelley, Annalisa Bortolin, Scott Beach, Debbie Muller, Laura Planting, Bill Melendez, Roseline Rubens, Pascale DeBarolet

Right: Violet, Snoopy, Pig Pen, Sally, Schroeder, Charlie Brown, Peppermint Patty, Linus, Marcie, Lucy © Paramount Pictures

THE EMPIRE STRIKES BACK

(20th CENTURY-FOX) Producer, Gary Kurtz; Director, Irvin Kershner; Screenplay, Leigh Brackett, Lawrence Kasdan; Story-Executive Producer, George Lucas; Designer, Norman Reynolds; Photography, Peter Suschitzky; Editor, Paul Hirsch; Associate Producers, Robert Watts, James Bloom; Music, John Williams; Art Directors, Leslie Dilley, Harry Lange, Alan Tomkins; Set, Michael Ford; Costumes, John Mollo; Assistant Directors, David Tomblin, Steve Lanning, Roy Button: In Panavision, DeLuxe Color and Dolby Stereo; Rated PG; 124 minutes; May release.

CAST

Luke Skywalker	Mark Hamill
Han Solo	Harrison Ford
Princess Leia	Carrie Fisher
Lando Calrissian	Billy Dee Williams
C-3PO	Anthony Daniels
Darth Vader	David Prowse
Chewbacca	Peter Mayhew
R2-DR	Kenny Baker
Yoda	Frank Oz
Ben (Obi-Wan) Kenobi	Alec Guinness
Boba Fett	Jeremy Bulloch
Lando's Aide	John Hollis
Chief Ugnaught	Jack Purvis
Snow Creature	Des Webb
Performing Assistant for Yoda	Kathryn Mullen
Voice of Emperor	Clive Revill

Imperial Forces:
Kenneth Colley (Adm. Piett), Julian Glover (Gen. Veers), Michael Sheard (Adm. Ozzel), Michael Culver (Capt. Needa), John Dicks, Milton Johns, Mark Jones, Oliver Maguire, Robin Scoby (Officers)

Rebel Forces:
Bruce Boa (Gen. Rieekan), Christopher Malcolm (Zev), Dennis Lawson (Wedge), Richard Oldfield (Hobbie), John Morton (Dak), Ian Liston (Janson), John Ratzenberger (Maj. Derlin), Jack McKenzie (Deck Lt.), Jerry Harte (Head Controller), Norman Chancer, Norwich Duff, Ray Hassett, Brigitte Kahn, Burnell Tucker (Officers)

Left: Billy Dee Williams, Carrie Fisher, Peter Mayhew, Harrison Ford

© 20th Century-Fox

1980 Academy Award for Best Sound

Anthony Daniels (C-3PO), Kenny Baker (R2D2)

Peter Mayhew (Chewbacca)

Mark Hamill Above: Carrie Fisher,
Harrison Ford Top: David Prowse
(Darth Vader), Billy Dee Williams,
Jeremy Bulloch

Mark Hamill, David Prowse (also above)

THE SHINING

(WARNER BROTHERS) Producer-Director, Stanley Kubrick; Screenplay, Stanley Kubrick, Diane Johnson; Based on novel by Stephen King; Executive Producer, Jan Harlan; Photography, John Alcott; Designer, Roy Walker; Editor, Ray Lovejoy; Music, Bela Bartok; Assistant Director, Brian Cook; Costumes, Milena Canonero; Art Director, Les Tomkins; Produced in association with The Producer Circle Co; In color; Rated R; 146 minutes; May release.

CAST

Jack Torrance	Jack Nicholson
Wendy Torrance	Shelley Duvall
Danny	Danny Lloyd
Halloran	Scatman Crothers
Ullman	Barry Nelson
Grady	Philip Stone
Lloyd	Joe Turkel
Doctor	Anne Jackson
Durkin	Tony Burton
Young Woman in bathtub	Lia Beldam
Old Woman in bathtub	Billie Gibson
Watson	Barry Dennen
Forest Rangers	David Baxt, Manning Redwood
Grady Girls	Lisa Burns, Louise Burns
Nurse	Robin Pappas
Secretary	Alison Coleridge
Policeman	Burnell Tucker
Stewardess	Jana Sheldon
Receptionist	Kate Phelps
Injured Guest	Norman Gay

Left: Shelley Duvall, Danny Lloyd
Top: Barry Dennen, Barry Nelson,
Jack Nicholson © Warner Bros.

Scatman Crothers
Above: Jack Nicholson

Jack Nicholson, Shelley Duvall
Above: Nicholson, Joe Turkel

CARNY

(UNITED ARTISTS) Producer, Robbie Robertson; Director, Robert Kaylor; Executive Producer, Jonathan Taplin; Screenplay, Thomas Baum; Story, Phoebe Kaylor; Robert Kaylor, Robbie Robertson; Music, Alex North; Editor, Stuart Pappe; A Lorimar presentation; In color; Rated R: 107 minutes; June release.

CAST

Frankie	Gary Busey
Donna	Jodie Foster
Patch	Robbie Robertson
Gerta	Meg Foster
Heavy	Ken McMillan
Nails	Theodore Wilson
Skeet	John Lehne
Sugaree	Tina Andrews
Delno	Bert Remsen
Willie Mae	Alan Braunstein
Dill	Bill McKinney
On-Your-Mark	Elisha Cook

Top: Gary Busey, Meg Foster, Jodie Foster Below: Jodie Foster, Gary Busey Top Right: Elisha Cook, Jr. Below: Ken McMillan, Tina Andrews © United Artists

Gary Busey, Jodie Foster Robbie Robertson

45

THE BLUE LAGOON

(COLUMBIA) Producer-Director, Randal Kleiser; Co-Producer, Richard Franklin; Screenplay, Douglas Day Stewart; Based on novel by Henry Devere Stacpoole; Music, Basil Poledouris, Photography, Nestor Almendros; Editor, Robert Gordon; Art Director, Jon Dowding; Costumes, Jean-Pierre Dorleac; Assistant Director, Mark Piper; In Metrocolor; Rated R; 104 minutes; June release.

CAST

Emmeline	Brooke Shields
Richard	Christopher Atkins
Paddy Button	Leo McKern
Arthur LeStrange	William Daniels
Young Emmeline	Elva Josephson
Young Richard	Glenn Kohan
Captain	Alan Hopgood
Officer	Gus Mercurio
Lookout	Jeffrey Means
Little Paddy	Bradley Pryce
Infant Paddy	Chad Timmermans
Sailors	Gert Jacoby, Alex Hamilton, Richard Evanson

Above: Glenn Kohan, Elva Josephson and
Top with Leo McKern
© Columbia Pictures

Brooke Shields, Christopher Atkins
Above: Leo McKern

46

Brooke Shields, Christopher Atkins
(also at top)

Christopher Atkins, Brooke Shields

URBAN COWBOY

(PARAMOUNT) Executive Producer, C. O. Erickson; Producers, Robert Evans, Irving Azoff; Director, James Bridges; Screenplay, James Bridges, Aaron Latham; Story, Aaron Latham; Photography, Ray Villalobos; Designer, Stephen Grimes; Editor, Dave Rawlins; Score Adapter, Ralph Burns; Art Director, Stewart Campbell; Set, George R. Nelson; Choreographer, Patsy Swayze; Assistant Directors, Kim Kuramada, Albert Shapiro; In Panavision and Movielab Color; Rated PG; 135 minutes; June release.

CAST

Bud	John Travolta
Sissy	Debra Winger
Wes	Scott Glenn
Pam	Madolyn Smith
Uncle Bob	Barry Corbin
Aunt Corene	Brooke Alderson
Marshall	Cooper Huckabee
Steve Strange	James Gammon
Bud's Mom	Betty Murphy
Bud's Dad	Ed Geldart
Bud's Sister	Leah Geldart
Bud's Brothers	Keith Clemons, Howard Norman
Bud's Cousins	Sheryl Briedel, Sean Lawler
Gator	Gator Conley
Killer	David Ogle
Sissy's Mom	Bettye Fitzpatrick
Sissy's Dad	Jim Gough
Bubba	Christopher Saylors

and Mickey Gilley, Johnny Lee, Bonnie Raitt, Charlie Daniels Band, Minnie Elerick, Bret Williams, Tamara Matusian, Becky Conway, Sherwood Cryer, Jerry Hall, Cyndy Hall, Lucky Mosley, Zetta Raney, Ellen March, Gina Alexander, Steve Chambers, Anne Travolta, Anson Downs, W. P. Wright III, Steve Strange, Norman Tucker, Debie Tucker, Jessie LaRive, Connie Hanson, Glenn Holtzman, Daniel Heintschel, Jr., Ben F. Brannon III, Robert Herridge, Robert Bush, James N. Harrell, Julie Bailey, Gene McLaughlin

Left: John Travolta
© Paramount Pictures

Madolyn Smith, John Travolta

Debra Winger

Madolyn Smith Above: Scott Glenn,
Debra Winger Top: Brooke Alderson, John
Travolta, Debra Winger, Barry Corbin

John Travolta, and above with Debra
Winger, Madolyn Smith Top: Scott Glenn

THE LAST FLIGHT OF NOAH'S ARK

(BUENA VISTA) Producer, Ron Miller; Director, Charles Jarrott; Screenplay, Steven W. Carabatsos, Sandy Glass; George Arthur Bloom; Story, Ernest K. Gann; Co-Producer, Jan Williams; Photography, Charles F. Wheeler; Music, Maurice Jarre; Lyrics, Hal David; Art Director, John B. Mansbridge; Designer, Preston Ames; Editor, Gordon D. Brenner; Set, Norman Rockett; Assistant Directors, Richard Learman, Louis S. Muscate, Christopher D. Miller; In Technicolor; A Walt Disney Production; Rated G; 97 minutes; June release.

CAST

Noah Dugan	Elliott Gould
Bernadette Lafleur	Genevieve Bujold
Bobby	Ricky Schroder
Julie	Tammy Lauren
Stoney	Vincent Gardenia
Cleveland	John Fujioka
Hiro	Yuki Shimoda
Coslough	John P. Ryan
Benchley	Dana Elcar
Charlotte Braithwaite	Ruth Manning
Leipzig Manager	Arthur Adams
Slabotsky	Austin Willis
Irate Pilot	Pete Renaday
Chaplain	Bob Whiting

Left: (clockwise) Elliott Gould, Ricky Schroder, Genevieve Bujold, Tammy Lauren © Walt Disney Productions

Elliott Gould, Genevieve Bujold

Ricky Shroder, Tammy Lauren

THE BLUES BROTHERS

(UNIVERSAL) Producer, Robert K. Weiss; Director, John Landis; Executive Producer, Bernie Brillstein; Screenplay, Dan Aykroyd, John Landis; Photography, Stephen M. Katz; Designer, John J. Lloyd; Editor, George Folsey, Jr.; Costumes, Deborah Nadoolman; Choreographer, Carlton Johnson; Music, Ira Newborn; Associate Producers, George Folsey, Jr., David Sosna; Art Director, Henry Larrecq; Assistant Directors, David Sosna, Jerram Swartz, Leonard R. Garner, Jr., Randy Carter, Richard Espinoza, John Syrjamaki; In Technicolor; Rated R; 130 minutes; June release.

CAST

Joliet Jake	John Belushi
Corrections Officer	Frank Oz
Elwood	Dan Aykroyd
Sister Mary Stigmata	Kathleen Freeman
Curtis	Cab Calloway
Choirmaster	Alonzo Atkins
Rev. Cleophus James	James Brown
Choir Soloist	Chaka Khan
Prison Guards	Tom Erhart, Gerald Walling, S. J. Levine, Walter Levine
Mystery Woman	Carrie Fisher
Father	Ben Piazza
Head Nazi	Henry Gibson
Cafe Owner	Aretha Franklin
Ray	Ray Charles
Chic Lady	Twiggy

Top (C) Dan Aykroyd, John Belushi
and the Blues Brothers Band Below with
Ray Charles, Right: James Brown
Top: Aretha Franklin

Dan Aykroyd, John Belushi
Above: Twiggy, Aykroyd

51

THE ISLAND

(UNIVERSAL) Producers, Richard D. Zanuck, David Brown; Director, Michael Ritchie; Screenplay, Peter Benchley from his novel; Photography, Henri Decae; Designer, Dale Hennesy; Editor, Richard A. Harris; Music, Ennio Morricone; Costumes, Ann Roth; Set, Robert deVestel; Assistant Directors, Michel Cheyko, Chris Carreras, Peter Waller; In Technicolor, Panavision and Dolby Stereo; Rated R; 114 minutes; June release.

CAST

Maynard	Michael Caine
Nau	David Warner
Beth	Angela Punch McGregor
Windsor	Frank Middlemass
Rollo	Don Henderson
Dr. Brazil	Dudley Sutton
Hizzoner	Colin Jeavons
Wescott	Zakes Mokae
Stark	Brad Sullivan
Justin	Jeffrey Frank
Doctors	John O'Leary, Bruce McLaughlin, Jimmy Casino
Mrs. Burgess	Suzanne Astor
Kate	Susan Bredhoff
Jack the Bat	Reg Evans
Mr. Burgess	Cary Hoffman
Baxter	William Schilling
Hiller	Stewart Steinberg
Charter Boat Captain	Bob Westmoreland

Top: Michael Caine Below: David
Warner, Jeffrey Frank
© Universal Studios

Frank Middlemas
Top: Michael Caine

CAN'T STOP THE MUSIC

(ASSOCIATED FILM DISTRIBUTION) Producers, Allan Carr, Jacques Morali, Henri Belolo; Director, Nancy Walker; Screenplay, Bronte Woodward, Allan Carr; Music, Jacques Morali; Musical Staging-Choreography, Arlene Phillips; Associate Producer, Neil A. Machlis; Photography, Bill Butler; Costumes, Jane Greenwood, Theoni V. Aldredge; Art Director, Harold Michelson; Editor, John F. Burnett; Assistant Directors, Bill Beasley, Paul Moen; Special Effects, Michael Sullivan; Sets, Richard McKenzie, Eric Orbum; In Panavision, Metrocolor and Dolby Stereo; Rated PG; 118 minutes; June release.

CAST

Village People:
Policeman	Ray Simpson
Construction Worker	David Hodo
Indian	Felipe Rose
Cowboy	Randy Jones
Leatherman	Glenn Hughes
G. I.	Alex Briley
Samantha Simpson	Valerie Perrine
Ron White	Bruce Jenner
Jack Morell	Steve Guttenberg
Steve Waits	Paul Sand
Sydne Channing	Tammy Grimes
Helen Morell	June Havoc
Norma White	Barbara Rush
Alicia Edwards	Altovise Davis
Lulu Brecht	Marilyn Sokol
Richard Montgomery	Russell Nype
Benny Murray	Jack Weston
Claudia Walters	Leigh Taylor-Young
Record Store Manager	Dick Patterson
Bread Woman	Bobo Lewis
Stick-up Lady	Paula Trueman
Law Office Receptionist	Portia Nelson

Right: Steve Guttenberg, June Havoc, Paul Sand Top: Guttenberg, Valerie Perrine, Bruce Jenner © AFD

Russell Nype, Barbara Rush, Bruce Jenner Above: Valerie Perrine, Jenner, Ray Simpson, Altovise Davis

The Ritchie Family Above: Valerie Perrine and The Village People

BRUBAKER

(20th CENTURY-FOX) Producer, Ron Silverman; Director, Stuart Rosenberg; Screenplay, W. D. Richter; Story, W. D. Richter, Arthur Ross; Executive Producer, Ted Mann; Associate Producer, Gordon Webb; Photography, Bruno Nuytten; Art Director, J. Michael Riva; Editor, Robert Brown; Music, Lalo Schifrin; Assistant Directors, Jon C. Andersen, Scott Easton; Suggested by book by Thomas O. Murton and Joy Hyams; In DeLuxe color;' Rated R; 132 minutes; June release.

CAST

Brubaker	Robert Redford
Dickie Coombes	Yaphet Kotto
Lillian	Jane Alexander
Deach	Murray Hamilton
Larry Lee Bullen	David Keith
Walter	Morgan Freeman
Purcell	Matt Clark
Huey Rauch	Tim McIntire
Abraham	Richard Ward
Zaranska	Jon Van Ness
Rory Poke	Albert Salmi
Carol	Linda Haynes
Carldwell	Everett McGill
Wendel	Val Avery
Willets	Ronald C. Frazier
Duane Spivey	David D. Harris
Birdwell	Joe Spinell
Pinky	James Keane
Glenn Elwood	Konrad Sheehan
Dr. Gregory	Roy Poole
Leon Edwards	Nathan George
Warden Renfro	Lee Richardson
Senator Hite	John McMartin
Dr. Campbell	Harry Groener
Ackroyd	John R. Glover

and Alex A. Brown, John Chappell, Brent Jennings, William Newman, Noble Willingham, Wilford Brimley, Jane Cecil, Ebbe Roe Smith, Young Hwa Han, Vic Polizos, Jack O'Leary, James Dukas, J. C. Quinn, Jerry Mayer

Left: Robert Redford
© **20th Century-Fox**

Yaphet Kotto, Robert Redford

Robert Redford

Jane Alexander, Robert Redford Top: (L) Brent Jennings, Yaphet Kotto, Robert Redford, Kent Broadhurst Below: Robert Redford, Morgan Freeman Right: David Keith, Jon Van Ness, Robert Redford Top: Redford, Kotto

AIRPLANE!

(PARAMOUNT) Producer, Jon Davison; Executive Producers, Direction and Screenplay, Jim Abrahams, David Zucker, Jerry Zucker; Photography, Joseph Biroc; Designer, Ward Preston; Editor, Patrick Kennedy; Music, Elmer Bernstein; Set, Anne D. McCulley; Costumes, Rosanna Norton; Associate Producer, Hunt Lowry; Special Effects, Bruce Logan; Assistant Directors, Arne Schmidt, Ken Collins; Choreographer, Tom Mahoney; In Metrocolor; Rated PG; 88 minutes; June release.

CAST

Murdock .... Kareem Abdul-Jabbar
McCroskey .... Lloyd Bridges
Captain Oveur .... Peter Graves
Elaine.. Julie Hagerty
Ted Striker .... Robert Hays
Dr. Rumack .... Leslie Nielsen
Randy .... Lorna Patterson
Kramer .... Robert Stack
Johnny.. Stephen Stucker
Jive Lady...................................... Barbara Billingsley
Mrs. Davis.. Joyce Bulifant
Japanese General .... James Hong
Nun .... Maureen McGovern
Lt. Hurwitz .... Ethel Merman
Air Controller Neubauer .... Kenneth Tobey
Windshield Wiper Man .... Jimmie Walker
Man in taxi .... Howard Jarvis

Left: Robert Hays
© **Paramount Pictures**

Kareem Abdul-Jabbar, Frank Ashmore, Rossie Harris, Peter Graves

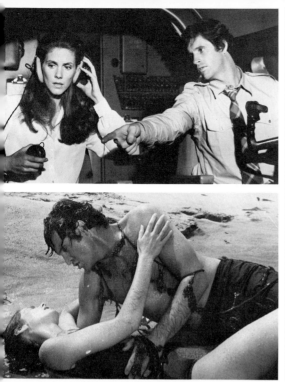

Kenneth Tobey, Lloyd Bridges, Robert Stack, Lee Terri Top Left: Julie Hagerty,
Robert Hays (also below and right)

BRONCO BILLY

(WARNER BROTHERS) Executive Producer, Robert Daley; Director, Clint Eastwood; Producers, Neal Dobrofsky, Dennis Hackin; Screenplay, Dennis Hackin; Associate Producer, Fritz Manes; Photography, David Worth; Editors, Ferris Webster, Joel Cox; Art Director, Gene Lourie; Assistant Directors, Stanley J. Zabka, Tom Joyner, Richard Graves, Fritz Mannes; Set, Ernie Bishop; In DeLuxe Color; Rated PG; 119 minutes; June release.

CAST

Bronco Billy	Clint Eastwood
Antoinette Lily	Sondra Locke
John Arlington	Geoffrey Lewis
Doc Lynch	Scatman Crothers
Lefty LeBow	Bill McKinney
Leonard James	Sam Bottoms
Chief Big Eagle	Dan Vadis
Lorraine Running Water	Sierra Pecheur
Sheriff Dix	Walter Barnes
Dr. Canterbury	Woodrow Parfrey
Irene Lily	Beverlee McKinsey
Lt. Wiecker	Douglas McGrath
Station Mechanic	Hank Worden
Edgar Lipton	William Prince
Mother Superior	Pam Abbass
Eloise	Edye Byrde
King	Michael Reinbold
Mitzi Fritts	Tessa Richarde
Doris Duke	Tanya Russell
Sister Maria	Valerie Shanks

and Douglas Copsey, John Wesley Elliott, Jr., Chuch Hicks, Bobby Hoy, Jefferson Jewell, Don Mummert, Lloyd Nelson, George Orrison, Sharon Sherlock, James Simmerhan, Roger Dale Simmons, Jenny Sternling, Chuck Waters, Jerry Willis

Left: Clint Eastwood
© **Warner Bros.**

Clint Eastwood, Sondra Locke

Clint Eastwood Top Left: Scatman Crothers Right: Sondra Locke

THE OUTSIDER

(PARAMOUNT) Executive Producer, Philippe Modave; Direction and Screenplay, Tony Luraschi; Based on novel "The Heritage of Michael Flaherty" by Colin Leinster; Photography, Ricardo Aronovich; Designer, Franco Fumagalli; Costumes, Judy Dolan; Assistant Directors, Giorgio Gentili, Bernard Farrel, Barry Blackmore, Robert Dwyer Joyce; Editor, Catherine Kelber; In color; Rated R; 128 minutes; June release.

CAST

Michael Flaherty	Craig Wasson
Siobhan	Patricia Quinn
Seamus Flaherty	Sterling Hayden
Farmer	Niall Toibin
Mrs. Cochran	Elizabeth Begley
John Russell	T. P. McKenna
Tony Coyle	Frank Grimes
Finbar Donovan	Bosco Hogan
Emmet Donovan	Niall O'Brien
Pat	Joe Dowling
Flynn	John Murphy
Ted	Conal Kearney
Tweeny	J. G. Devlin
Mrs. Flaherty	Avril Gentles
Mr. Flaherty	John Seitz
Hanlan	Aiden Grennell
Kevin McCann	Desmond Cave
Colonel O'Darell	Des Nealon
McDermot	Joseph McPartland
Thompson	Joy Lynch
Stanley	Allan Cuthbertson

Right: Craig Wasson
© Paramount Pictures

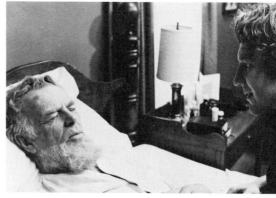

Craig Wasson (C)

Patricia Quinn, Craig Wasson
Above: Sterling Hayden, Craig Wasson

THE BIG RED ONE

(UNITED ARTISTS) Producer, Gene Corman; Direction and Screenplay, Samuel Fuller; Music, Dana Kaproff; Photography, Adam Greenberg; Editor, Morton Tubor; Assistant Directors, Arne L. Schmidt, Todd Corman; In Metrocolor and Dolby Stereo; A Lorimar Production; Rated PG; 113 minutes; July release.

CAST

Sergeant	Lee Marvin
Griff	Mark Hamill
Zab	Robert Carradine
Vinci	Bobby DiCicco
Johnson	Kelly Ward
Schroeder	Siegfried Rauch
Walloon	Stephane Audran
Rensonnet	Serge Marquand
General/Captain	Charles Macaulay
Broban	Alain Doutey
Vichy Colonel	Maurice Marsac
Dog Face POW	Colin Gilbert
Shep	Joseph Clark
Lemchek	Ken Campbell
Switolski	Doug Werner
Kaiser	Perry Lang
Smitty	Howard Delman
Madame Marbaise	Marthe Villalonga
Woman in Sicilian village	Giovanna Galetti
The Hun	Gregori Buimistre
German male nurse	Shimon Barr
Sicilian boy	Matteo Zoffoli
German Field Marshall	Avrahan Ronai
Pregnant Frenchwoman	Galit Rotman

Top: Mark Hamill, Robert Carradine, Bobby DiCicco, Kelly Ward Right: Lee Marvin © United Artists

Robert Carradine, Bobby DiCicco, Kelly Ward, Perry Lang

61

MY BODYGUARD

(20th CENTURY-FOX) Producer, Don Devlin; Director, Tony Bill; Screenplay, Alan Ormsby; Executive Producer, Melvin Simon; Associate Producer, Phillip Goldfarb; Music, Dave Grusin; Photography, Michael D. Margulies; Designer, Jackson DeGovia; Editor, Stu Linder; Assistant Directors, Michael Daves, Richard Prince; Set, Jeannine Oppewall; In C.F.I. Color and DeLuxe Prints; 96 minutes; July release.

CAST

Clifford	Chris Makepeace
Linderman	Adam Baldwin
Moody	Matt Dillon
Carson	Paul Quandt
Shelley	Joan Cusack
Hightower	Dean R. Miller
Koontz	Tim Reyna
Dubrow	Richard Bradley
Leilani	Denise Baske
Mike	Hank Salas
Freddy	Vicky Nelson
Gramma	Ruth Gordon
Mr. Peache	Martin Mull
Dobbs	John Houseman
Griffith	Craig Richard Nelson
Miss Jump	Kathryn Grody
Principal Rath	Richard Cusack
Librarian	Dorothy Scott
Basketball Coach	Angelo Buscaglia
Stewardess	Kitt York
Mrs. Linderman	Marge Kotusky

and Tom Reilly, Paul Charvonneau, Laura Salenger, Bert Hoddinott, Jonathan Turk, Cindy Russ, Laurie McEathron, Lori Mandell, Dean Devlin, Tim Kazurinsky, Bill Koza, Vivian Smolen, Bruce Jarchow, Andrea Dillon, Leonard Mack, George Wendt, Jerome Myers, Freddy Moss, Joseph Cohn, Patrick Billingsley, Barbara Hoddinott, Eddie Gomez

Top: Matt Dillon, Left: Chris Makepeace,
Adam Baldwin, Paul Quant Left Center:
Chris Makepeace, Paul Quant, Joan Cusak
© 20th Century-Fox

Martin Mull, Chris Makepeace,
Ruth Gordon

DRESSED TO KILL

(FILMWAYS) Producer, George Litto; Direction and Screenplay, Brian DePalma; Associate Producer, Fred Caruso; Photography, Ralf Bode; Designer, Gary Weist; Costumes, Ann Roth, Gary Jones; Editor, Jerry Greenberg; Assistant Director, Mike Rauch; Set, Gary Brink; A Samuel Z. Arkoff presentation in Panavision and color; A Cinema 77 Film; Rated R; 105 minutes; July release.

CAST

Dr. Robert Elliott	Michael Caine
Kate Miller	Angie Dickinson
Liz Blake	Nancy Allen
Peter Miller	Keith Gordon
Detective Marino	Dennis Franz
Dr. Levy	David Margulies
Warren Lockman	Ken Baker
Cleveland Sam	Brandon Maggart
Bobbi	Susanna Clemm
Mike Miller	Fred Weber
Museum Cabbie	Sean O'Rinn
Chase Cabbie	Bill Randolph
Hood #1	Robert Lee Rush
Woman in coffee shop	Mary Davenport

Right: Michael Caine
© **Filmways**

Nancy Allen (C)

Nancy Allen

NO NUKES

(WARNER BROTHERS) Producers, Julian Schlossberg, Danny Goldberg; Direction, Julian Schlossberg, Danny Goldberg, Anthony Potenza; Photography, Haskell Wexler; In Dolby Stereo and color; Rated PG; 103 minutes; July release; Based on the 1979 concerts and rallys protesting the use of nuclear energy.

CAST

Jackson Browne, Crosby Stills and Nash, The Doobie Brothers, John Hall, Graham Nash, Bonnie Raitt, Gil Scott Heron, Carly Simon, Bruce Springsteen, James Taylor, Jesse Colin Young

Below: James Taylor, Carly Simon
Left: Bruce Springsteen
© Lynn Goldsmith

Jesse Colin Young,
Jackson Browne

David Crosby, Stephen Stills
Above: Michael McDonald

THE HUNTER

(PARAMOUNT) Producer, Mort Engelberg; Director, Buzz Kulik; Screenplay, Ted Leighton, Peter Hyams; Photography, Fred J. Koenekamp; Designer, Ron Hobbs; Editor, Robert Wolfe; Music, Michel Legrand; Based on book by Christopher Keane and the life of Ralph Thorson; Assistant Directors, Richard Learman, Robert Dahlin; Set, Jim Tocci; In Metrocolor; Rated PG; 117 minutes; July release.

CAST

Papa Thorson	Steve McQueen
Ritchie Blumenthal	Eli Wallach
Dotty	Kathryn Harrold
Tommy Price	LeVar Burton
Sheriff Strong	Ben Johnson
Spota	Richard Venture
Rocco Mason	Tracey Walter
Bernardo	Tom Rosales
Winston Blue	Theodore Wilson
Luke Branch	Ray Bickel
Matthew Branch	Bobby Bass

and Karl Schueneman, Margaret O'Hara, James Spinks, Frank Delfino, Zora Margolis, Murray Rubin, Poppy Lagos, Dea St. La Mount, Lillian Adams, Thor Nielsen, Stan Wojno, Jr., Jodi Moon, Kathy Cunningham, Kelly Learman, Michael D. Roberts, Kevin Hagen, Luis Avalos, Wynn Irwin, Frank Arno, Ric DiAngelo, Ralph Thorson, Matilda Calnan, F. William Parker, Nathaniel Taylor, Tony Burton, Morgan Roberts, Frederick Sistaine, Taurean Blackque

Top: Steve McQueen, Ben Johnson
Below: McQueen, Kathryn Harrold
Right: McQueen, LeVar Burton
Top: McQueen, Eli Wallach
© Paramount Pictures

Steve McQueen

HONEYSUCKLE ROSE

(WARNER BROTHERS) Executive Producer, Sydney Pollack; Producer, Gene Taft; Director, Jerry Schatzberg; Screenplay, Carol Sobieski, William D. Wittliff, John Binder; Based on story by Gosta Steven, Gustav Molander; Photography, Robby Muller; Designer, Joel Schiller; Editors, Aram Avakian, Norman Gay, Marc Laub, Evan Lottman; Costumes, Jo Ynocencio; Songs composed and performed by Willie Nelson; Assistant Directors, David McGiffert, Nick Marck; In Panavision, Technicolor, and Dolby Stereo; Rated PG; 119 minutes; August release.

CAST

Buck	Willie Nelson
Viv	Dyan Cannon
Lily	Amy Irving
Garland	Slim Pickens
Jamie	Joey Floyd
Sid	Charles Levin
Rosella	Priscilla Pointer
Cotton	Mickey Rooney, Jr.
Rooster	Pepe Serna
Brag	Lane Smith
Jeanne	Diana Scarwid
Emmylou	Emmylou Harris
Tex	Rex Ludwick
Kelly	Mickey Raphael
Bo	Bee Spears
Easter	Chris Ethridge
Paul	Paul English
Bonnie	Bobby Nelson
Jonas	Jody Payne
Poodie	Randy Locke
Snake	T. Snake

and Johnny Gimble, Kenneth Threadgill, Grady Martin, Hank Cochran, Jeannie Seely, Gene Rader, Frank Stewart, Lubelle Camp, A. L. Camp, Jackie Ezzell, Bernedette Whitehead, Harvey Christiansen

Right: Willie Nelson, Dyan Cannon, Amy Irving Top: Nelson, Cannon
© Warner Bros.

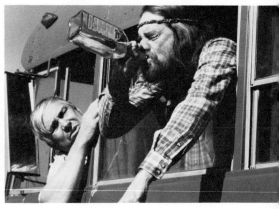

Willie Nelson

Slim Pickens, Willie Nelson
Above: Joey Floyd, Willie Nelson

THOSE LIPS, THOSE EYES

(UNITED ARTISTS) Producers, Steven-Charles Jaffe, Michael Pressman; Director, Michael Pressman; Screenplay, David Shaber; Executive Producer, Herb Jaffe; Associate Producer, Edward A. Teets; Music, Michael Small; Choreography, Dan Siretta; Editor, Millie Moore; Designer, Walter Scott Herndon; Photography, Bobby Byrne; Assistant Directors, Craig Huston, Toby Lovallo; Set, Blake Russell; In Technicolor; Rated R; 107 minutes; August release.

CAST

Harry Crystal	Frank Langella
Ramona	Glynnis O'Connor
Artie Shoemaker	Thomas Hulce
Mickey Bellinger	Kevin McCarthy
Mr. Shoemaker	Jerry Stiller
Dr. Julius Fuldauer	Herbert Berghof
Fibby Geyer	Joseph Maher
Sherman Spratt	George Morfogen
Cooky	Marshall Colt
D'Angeli	Anthony Mannino
Mrs. Shoemaker	Rose Arrick
Mr. Henry	William Robertson
Westervelt	Steve Levitt
Loomis	Mandy Stumpf
Hlavacek	Mark Keyloun
Stage Manager	Steve Nevil
Larry	Dan Siretta
Professor	Jordan Charney

and David Adams, Cheryl Armstrong, Providence Hollander, David O. Frazier, Don Kost, Chiara Peacock, J. Clayton Conroy, F. L. Schmidlapp, Frank Picard, Mel Pittenger, Susan Berlin, Heidi Albrecht, Nanci Glass, Jodi Moccia, Frank Hruby

Right: Thomas Hulce, Glynnis O'Connor
Top: Frank Langella (C)
© United Artists

Thomas Hulce, Jerry Stiller
Above: Frank Langella, George Morfogen

Frank Langella

THE FINAL COUNTDOWN

(UNITED ARTISTS) Producer, Peter Vincent Douglas; Executive Producer, Richard R. St. Johns; Director, Don Taylor; Screenplay, David Ambrose, Gerry Davis, Thomas Hunter, Peter Powell; Associate Producer, Lloyd Kaufman; Photography, Victor J. Kemper; Music, John Scott; Editor, Robert K. Lambert; Designer, Fernando Carrere; Assistant Directors, Pat Kehoe, Doug Wise, Ed Milkovich; Costumes, Ray Summers; In Panavision, Dolby Stereo and Technicolor; Rated PG; 104 minutes; August release.

CAST

Capt. Matthew Yelland	Kirk Douglas
Warren Lasky	Martin Sheen
Laurel Scott	Katharine Ross
Cdr. Richard Owens	James Farentino
Cdr. Dan Thurman	Ron O'Neal
Senator Chapman	Charles Durning
Black Cloud	Victor Mohica
Lt. Perry	James C. Lawrence
Simura	Soon-Teck Oh
Cdr. Damon	Joe Lowry
Kajima	Alvin Ing
Cpl. Kullman	Mark Thomas
Bellman	Harold Bergman
Navy Doctor	Dan Fitzgerald
Lt. Cdr. Kaufman	Lloyd Kaufman
Quartermaster	Peter Douglas
Admiral	Phil Philbin

and Ted Riehert, George Warren, Gary Morgan, Robert Goodman, Richard Liberty, Neil Ronco, William Couch, Jack McDermott, Masayuki Yamazuki, Orwin Harvey, Colby Smith, George H. Strohsahl, Jr., Ronald R. Stoops, Kenneth J. Jaskolski, Sergei M. Kowalchik, Jake Dennis, Jim Toone

Left: Kirk Douglas
© United Artists

Martin Sheen, James Farentino, Kirk Douglas

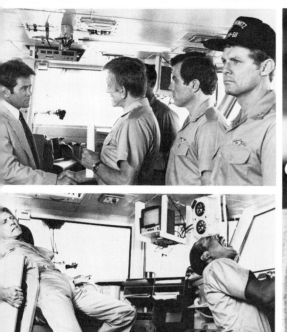

Katharine Ross, Charles Durning Top Left: Martin Sheen, Kirk Douglas Below: Douglas, Ron O'Neal Right: Ross, Soon-Teck Oh

THE FIENDISH PLOT OF DR. FU MANCHU

(ORION) Executive Producer, Hugh M. Hefner; Producers, Zev Braun, Leland Nolan; Director, Piers Haggard; Screenplay and story, Jim Moloney, Rudy Dochtermann; Based on characters in Sax Rohmer novels; Music, Marc Wilkinson; Associate Producer, Yannoulla Wakefield; Editor, Russell Lloyd; Costumes, John Bloomfield; Photography, Jean Tournier; Designer, Alex Trauner; Assistant Director, Paul Feyder; Choreographer, Barry Collins; In Technicolor; Rated PG; 106 minutes; August release.

CAST

Fu Manchu/Nayland Smith.................................. Peter Sellers
Alice Rage.. Helen Mirren
Sir Roger Avery .... David Tomlinson
Joe Capone .... Sid Caesar
Robert Townsend .... Simon Williams
Pete Williams .... Steve Franken
Ismail.. Stratford Johns
Perkins.. John LeMesurier
Sir Nules Thudd .... John Sharp
Dr. Wretch .... Clement Harari
Tong .... Lee Kwan-Young
and John Tan, Philip Tan, Serge Julien, Johns Rajohnson Pralith Jngam Oeurn, Lim Bun Song, Clive Dunn, Burt Kwouk, John Taylor, Katia Chenko, David Powers, Marc Wilkinson, Grace Coyle, Jacqueline Fogt, Iska Khan, George Hilsden, Rene Aranda

Top: Sid Caesar, Peter Sellers, Steve Franken, David Tomlinson, Simon Williams Below: Peter Sellers, Helen Mirren
© Orion Pictures

Peter Sellers
(also at top)

OH! HEAVENLY DOG

(**20th CENTURY-FOX**) Producer-Director, Joe Camp; Screenplay, Rod Browning, Joe Camp; Photography, Don Reddy; Associate Producer, Dan Witt; Music, Euel Box; Editor, Leon Seith; Designer, Garrett Lewis; Assistant Directors, Derek Cracknell, Raymond Becket; Art Director, George Richardson; In Panaflex, DeLuxe Color, Dolby Stereo; Rated PG; 103 minutes; August release.

CAST

Browning	Chevy Chase/Benji
Jackie	Jane Seymour
Malcolm Bart	Omar Sharif
Bernie	Robert Morley
Freddie	Alan Sues
Montanero	Donnelly Rhodes
Higgins	Stuart Germain
Alistair Becket	John Stride
Margaret	Barbara Leigh-Hunt
Lady Chalmers	Margaret Courtenay
Quimby Charles	Richard Vernon
Mr. Easton	Frank Williams
Pelican Man	Albin Pahernik
German Clerk	Susan Kellermann
Carlton	Lorenzo Music
Patricia Elliott	Marguerite Corriveau
Jeffrey Edgeware	Harry Hill

and Joe Camp, Stuart Germain, David Samain, Neil Affleck, Gerald Iles, Jennifer Foote, Dan Witt, Jerome Tiberghien, Norman Tavis, George E. Zeeman, Wendy Dawson, Jeannette Casenave, Gayle Garfinkle, Doris Malcolm, Mary Rathbone, Steve Michaels, Henry Hardy

Right: Chevy Chase, Jane Seymour, Benji
© **20th Century-Fox**

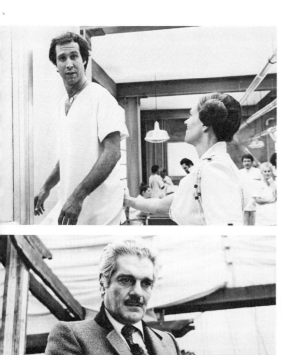

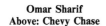

Omar Sharif
Above: Chevy Chase

Robert Morley

71

WILLIE AND PHIL

(20th CENTURY-FOX) Producers, Paul Mazursky, Tony Ray; Direction and Screenplay, Paul Mazursky; Photography, Sven Nykvist; Designer, Pato Guzman; Editor, Donn Cambern; Music, Claude Bolling; Costumes, Albert Wolsky; Associate Producer, Terry Donnelly; Assistant Directors, Terry Donnelly, Yudi Bennett; In Movielab Color; Rated R; 116 minutes; August release.

CAST

Willie	Michael Ontkean
Jeannette	Margot Kidder
Phil	Ray Sharkey
Mrs. Kaufman	Jan Miner
Mr. Kaufman	Tom Brennan
Mrs. D'Amico	Julie Bovasso
Mr. D'Amico	Louis Guss
Mrs. Sutherland	Kathleen Maguire
Patti	Kaki Hunter
Rena	Kristine DeBell
Wilson	Laurence Fishburne III
Official Clerk	Ed VanNuys
Jill	Jill Mazursky
Igor	Eivand Harum
Natalie Wood	Herself

and Alison Cass Shurpin, Christine Varnai, Walter N. Lowery, Jerry Hall, Helen Hanft, Sol Frieder, Donald Muhich, Anne E. Wile, Hubert J. Edwards, Allen C. Dawson, Alvin Alexis, Robert Townsend, Cynthia McPherson, Karen Montgomery, Tom Noonan, Ginny Ortix, Lionel Pina, Jr., Louis Cappeto, Karen Ford, Stephan Hart, Kitty Muldoon, Nikolas Irizarry, Madeline Moroff, R. M. Wexler, Mary-Pat Green

Left: Michael Ontkean, Margot Kidder, Ray Sharkey
© 20th Century-Fox

Margot Kidder, Michael Ontkean

Michael Ontkean, Margot Kidder, Ray Sharkey (also above)

MIDDLE AGE CRAZY

20th CENTURY-FOX) A Sid and Marty Krofft presentation; Producers, Robert Cooper, Ronald Cohen; Director, John Trent; Screenplay, Carl Kleinschmitt; Co-Producer, John M. Eckert; Music, Matthew McCauley; In color; Rated R; 95 minutes; August release.

CAST

Bobby Lee	Bruce Dern
Sue Ann	Ann-Margret
J. D.	Graham Jarvis
Tommy	Eric Christmas
Ruth	Helen Hughes
Greg	Geoffrey Bowes
Abe Titus	Michael Kane
Wanda Jean	Diane Dewey
Becky	Vivian Reis
Barbara Pickett	Patricia Hamilton
Janet	Anni Lantuch
Nancy	Deborah Wakeham
Linda	Gina Dick
Porsche Salesman	Thomas Baird
Valedictorian	Norma Dell'Agnesi
Condo Saleswoman	Shirley Solomon
Priest	Elias Zarou
Topless Dancer	Michele Chiponski
Limo Driver	Victor Sutton
Minister	Jack Mather
Nancy's Boyfriend	Jim Montgomery
Sportscaster's Voice	John Facenda

Top: Bruce Dern, Michael Kane, Graham
Jarvis Below: Geoffrey Bowes, Dern
Right: Dern, Deborah Wakeham Above:
Ann-Margret, Bruce Dern
© 20th Century-Fox

Ann-Margret, Bruce Dern

XANADU

(UNIVERSAL) Executive Producer, Lee Kramer; Producer, Lawrence Gordon; Director, Robert Greenwald; Screenplay, Richard Christian Danus, Michael Kane, Marc Reid Rubel; Photography, Vic Kemper; Editor, Dennis Virkler; Music, Barry DeVorzon, Jeff Lyne, John Farrar; In Dolby Stereo and color; Rated PG; 93 minutes; August release.

CAST

Kira	Olivia Newton-John
Danny McGuire	Gene Kelley
Sonny Malone	Michael Beck
Simpson	James Sloyan
Helen	Dimitra Arliss
Sandra	Katie Hanley
Richie	Fred McCarren
Jo	Ren Woods
Muses	Sandahl Bergman, Lynn Latham, Melinda Phelps, Cherise Bate, Juliette Marshall, Marilyn Tokunda, Yvette Van Voorhees, Teri Beckerman

Right: Gene Kelly
© **Universal Pictures**

Michael Beck, Gene Kelly, Olivia Newton-John Above: Newton-John, Beck

Gene Kelly, Olivia Newton-John Above: Kelly, Michael Beck

THE RETURN OF THE SECAUCUS SEVEN

(LIBRA) Producers, William Aydelott, Jeffrey Nelson; Directed, Written and Edited by John Sayles; Photography, Austin de Besche; Music, K. Mason Daring; A Salsipuedes Production in color; Not rated; 110 minutes; September release.

CAST

Jeff	Mark Arnott
Chip	Gordon Clapp
Frances	Maggie Cousineau
J. T.	Adam Lefevre
Mike	Bruce MacDonald
Irene	Jean Passanante
Katie	Maggie Renzi
Ron	David Strathairn
Maura	Karen Trott

Right: Karen Trott, Maggie Renzi
© Libra Films

Maggie Renzi, Bruce MacDonald, Jean Passanante Above: Maggie Cousineau-Arndt, David Strathairn

Jean Passanante, Maggie Renzi Above: Adam LeFevre, Karen Trott

MELVIN AND HOWARD

(UNIVERSAL) Producers, Art Linson, Don Phillips; Director, Jonathan Demme; Screenplay, Bo Goldman; Photography, Tak Fujimoto; Designer, Toby Rafelson; Editor, Craig McKay; Music, Bruce Langhorne; Associate Producer, Terry Nelson; Art Director, Richard Sawyer; Assistant Directors, Don Heitzer, Carol Jean Smetana, Wally Wallace; In Technicolor; Rated R; 95 minutes; September release.

CAST

Howard Hughes	Jason Robards
Melvin Dummar	Paul LeMat
Darcy Dummar	Elizabeth Cheshire
Lynda Dummar	Mary Steenburgen
Clark Taylor	Chip Taylor
Bus Depot Counterman	Melvin E. Dummar
Little Red	Michael J. Pollard
Lucy	Denise Galik
Mrs. Sisk	Gloria Grahame
Bonnie Dummar	Pamela Reed
Judge Keith Hayes	Dabney Coleman
Attorney Maxwell	Joseph Ragno
Attorney Freese	John Glover

and Gene Borkan, Lesley Margret Burton, Wendy Lee Couch, Marguerite Baierski, Janice King, Deborah Ann Klein, Theodora Thomas, Elise Hudson, Robert Ridgely, Susan Peretz, Robert Wentz, Hal Marshall, Naida Reynolds, Herbie Faye, Charles Napier, Jack Kehoe, Sonny Davis, Brendan Kelly, Danny Tucker, Shirley Washington, Cheryl Smith, John Thundercloud, Charlene Holt, Melissa Williams, Antony Alda, Rick Lenz, Gary Goetzman Kathleen Sullivan

Left: Mary Steenburgen, Paul LeMat
© Universal Studios

1980 Academy Awards for Best Supporting Actress (Mary Steenburgen) and Original Screenplay

Mary Steenburgen

Jason Robards

Mary Steenburgen, Matthew Hiers, Elizabeth Cheshire, Paul LeMat Top Left: Mary Steenburgen and below with Robert Ridgely Right: Paul LeMat and top with Jason Robards

DIVINE MADNESS

(WARNER BROTHERS) Producer-Director, Michael Ritchie; Executive Producer, Howard Jeffrey; Written by Jerry Blatt, Bette Midler, Bruce Vilanch; Music arranged and supervised by Tony Berg and Randy Kerber; Photography, William A. Fraker; Designer, Albert Brenner; Costumes, Robert DeMora; Editor, Glenn Farr; Choreography, Toni Basil; Assistant Directors, Jack Roe, John Kretchmer; In Panavision, Dolby Stereo and Technicolor; Rated R; 94 minutes; September release.

CAST

The Divine Miss M.	Bette Midler
The Harlettes	Jocyln Brown, Ula Hedwig, Diva Gray
Head Usher	Irving Sudrow
Band Vocals	Tony Berg, Jon Bonine, Joey Carbone, Randy Kerber

**Top: Bette Midler and below
with The Harlettes
© The Ladd Co.**

**Bette Midler (also top)
and above with The Harlettes**

CHEAPER TO KEEP HER

(AMERICAN CINEMA) Executive Producer, Jerry Frankel; Producer, Lenny Isenberg; Co-Producer, Corrine Mann; Director, Ken Annakin; Screenplay, Timothy Harris, Herschel Weingrod; Music, Dick Halligan; Lyrics, Carol Connors; Photography, Roland "Ozzie" Smith; Editor, Edward Warschilka; Assistant Directors, Rafael Elortegui, Kenneth Collins, Earl Mann; In color; Rated R; 92 minutes; September release.

CAST

Bill Dekker	Mac Davis
K. D. Locke	Tovah Feldshuh
Tony Turino	Art Metrano
Dr. Alfred Sunshine	Ian McShane
Theresa	Priscilla Lopez
Ida Bracken	Rose Marie
Stanley Bracken	Jack Gilford
Landlord	J. Pat O'Malley
Laura	Gwen Humble
Nora	Shannon Wilcox
Abe	Chuck Hicks
Leon	Bruce Flanders
Chuck	Joe Regalbuto
Brownmiller	Rod McCary
Peter	Steve Gagnon
Charlie	Fred Stuthman
Virginia	Jane Strudwick
Mugger	Wallace Shaun

Right: Tovah Feldshuh
© **Regal Productions**

Tovah Feldshuh, Mac Davis
Above: Art Metrano, Davis

Jack Gilford, Rose Marie
Above: Mac Davis, Priscilla Lopez　79

RESURRECTION

(UNIVERSAL) Producers, Renee Missel, Howard Rosenman; Director, Daniel Petrie; Screenplay, Lewis John Carlino; Photography, Mario Tosi; Designer, Paul Sylbert; Editor, Rita Roland; Music, Maurice Jarre; Art Director, Edwin O'Donovan; Assistant Directors, Craig Huston, Jerram Swartz; In Technicolor; Rated PG; 103 minutes; September release.

CAST

Edna	Ellen Burstyn
Cal	Sam Shepard
Esco	Richard Farnsworth
John Harper	Roberts Blossom
George	Clifford David
Margaret	Pamela Payton-Wright
Joe	Jeffrey DeMunn
Grandma Pearl	Eva LeGallienne
Kathy	Lois Smith
Ruth	Madeleine Thornton-Sherwood
Earl Carpenter	Richard Hamilton
Suzy Kroll	Carlin Glynn
Don	Lane Smith
Ellie	Penelope Allen
Hank Peterson	Ebbe Roe Smith
Dr. Herron	John Tillinger
Dr. Ellen Baxter	Trazana Beverley
Buck	Ralph Roberts
Dr. Hankins	George Sperdakos
Dr. Fisher	Bernard Behrens

and James Blendick, Vernon Weddle, David Calkins, Harvey Christiansen, Therese East, Lou Fant, Jessie Lee Fulton, David Haney, Claudette Harrell, James N. Harrell, Jennifer McAllister, Don Michaelson, A. G. Mills, Edith Mills, Tom Taylor, Sylvia Walden, Carol Williard, Tracy Wilson

Left: Eva LeGallienne, Ellen Burstyn
© Universal Studios

Sam Shepard, Ellen Burstyn

James Harrell, Lois Smith, Ellen Burstyn, David Haney Above: Burstyn, Jeffrey DeMunn

Ellen Burstyn and above with Richard
Farnsworth, top with Sam Shepard

Madeline Thornton-Sherwood,
Ellen Burstyn

BORDERLINE

(AFD) Producer, James Nelson; Director, Jerrold Freedman; Music, Gil Melle; Photography, Tak Fujimoto; Art Director, Michael Levesque; Editor, John F. Link II; Screenplay, Steve Kline, Jerrold Freedman; Assistant Directors, Charles A. Myers, Mary Ellen Canniff; In Panavision and Eastmancolor; Rated PG; 106 minutes; September release.

CAST

Jeb Maynard	Charles Bronson
Jimmy Fante	Bruno Kirby
Carl Richards	Bert Remsen
Henry Lydell	Michael Lerner
Malcolm Wallace	Kenneth McMillan
Hotchkiss	Ed Harris
Elena Morales	Karmin Murcelo
Arturo	Enrique Castillo
Scooter Jackson	A. Wilford Brimley
Willie Lambert	Norman Alden
Mirandez	James Victor
Benito Morales	Panchito Gomez
Charlie Monroe	John Ashton
Andy Davis	Lawrence Casey
Ski	Charles Cyphers
Mrs. Stine	Katherine Pass

and John Roselius, Murray MacLeod, Jerry DeWilde, Virgil Frye, Luis Contreras, Eduardo Ricard, John O'Banion, Rodger LaRue, Tanya Russell, Virginia Bingham, Anthony Munoz, Ray Ochoa, Ab Taylor, Tammy Wilson

Left: Charles Bronson

Bert Remsen, Ed Harris

Ed Harris Above: Charles Bronson (L)

HOPSCOTCH

(AVCO EMBASSY) Producers, Edie and Ely Landau; Director, Ronald Neame; Executive Producer, Otto Plaschkes; Associate Producers, Jonathan Bernstein, Brian Garfield; Music, Ian Fraser; Editor, Carl Kress; Photography, Arthur Ibbetson; Designer, William Creber; Screenplay, Brian Garfield, Bryan Forbes; Assistant Directors, Patrick Clayton, William Hassell; In Panavision and Movielab Color; Rated R; 104 minutes; September release.

CAST

Miles Kendig	Walter Matthau
Isobel von Schmidt	Glenda Jackson
Cutter	Sam Waterston
Myerson	Ned Beatty
Mikhail Yaskov	Herbert Lom
Ross	David Matthau
Westlake	George Baker
Ludlum	Ivor Roberts
Carla	Lucy Saroyan
Maddox	Severn Darden
Saint Breheret	George Pravda
Realtor	Jacquelyn Hyde
Alfie	Mike Gwilym
Chartermain	Allan Cuthbertson
Tobin	Terry Beaver
Clausen	Ray Charleson
Mrs. Myerson	Ann Haney

and Shan Wilson, Christopher Driscoll, Michael Cronin, Roy Sampson, Randy Patrick, Joe Dorsey, Candice Howard, Susan McShayne, Yolanda King, Anthony Carrick, Osman Ragheb, Roland Frohlich, Jeremy Young, Sally Nesbitt, Susan Engel, Joanna McCallum

Top: Sam Waterston, Ned Beatty
Below: Herbert Lom, Walter Matthau
Right: Glenda Jackson, Matthau
© AVCO Embassy

Glenda Jackson, Walter Matthau
(also above)

83

Gena Rowlands, Juan Adames

GLORIA

(COLUMBIA) Executive Producer, Sam Shaw; Producer-Director-Screenplay, John Cassavetes; Photography, Fred Schuler; Editor, Jack McSweeney; Associate Producer, Stephen Kesten; Designer, Rene D'Auriac; Costumes, Peggy Farrell; Assistant Directors, Mike Haley, Tom Fritz; In color; Rated R; 123 minutes; September release.

CAST

Gloria Swenson	Gena Rowlands
Philip Dawn	Juan Adames
Jack Dawn	Buck Henry
Jeri Dawn	Julie Carmen
Margarita Vargas	Lupe Guarnica
Joan Dawn	Jessica Castillo
1st Man/Gangster	Tony Knesich
Kid 1/Back of the bus	Ralph Dolman
Kid 2/Back of the bus	Israel Castro
Kid 3/back of the bus	Carlos Castro
Old Lady	Philomena Spagnolo
2nd Man/Gangster	Tom Noonan
Kid in elevator	Gregory Gleghorne
1st Policeman	Kyle-Scott Jackson
2nd Policeman	Gary Klarr
Escape Cab Driver	Ramon Rodriguez
Heavyset Man	George Yudzevich
3rd Man/Gangster	Ronnie Maccone
Cab Driver #2	Asa Quawee

Top: Julie Carmen
Left: Gena Rowlands
© Columbia Pictures

Juan Adames, Gena Rowlands (also top left)

STARDUST MEMORIES

(UNITED ARTISTS) Producer, Robert Greenhut; Direction and Screenplay, Woody Allen; Photography, Gordon Willis; Editor, Susan E. Morse; In black and white; Rated PG. 91 minutes; September release.

CAST

Sandy Bates	Woody Allen
Dorrie	Charlotte Rampling
Daisy	Jessica Harper
Isobel	Marie-Christine Barrault
Tony	Tony Roberts
Actor	Daniel Stern
Shelley	Amy Wright
Vivian Orkin	Helen Hanft
Jack Abel	John Rothman
Sandy's Sister	Anne DeSalvo
Sandy's Mother	Joan Neuman
Sandy's Father	Ken Chapin
Sandy's Analyst	Leonardo Cimino
Old Man	Eli Mintz
Jerry Abraham	Bob Maroff

Left: Woody Allen
© United Artists

Woody Allen, Anne DeSalvo, Jaqui Safra
Above: Marie-Christine Barrault, Allen

Woody Allen, Marie-Christine Barrault
Above: Woody Allen, Jessica Harper

86

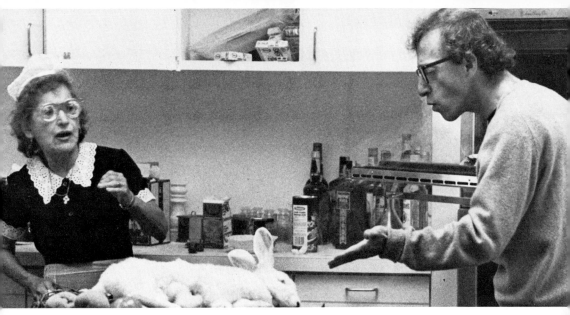

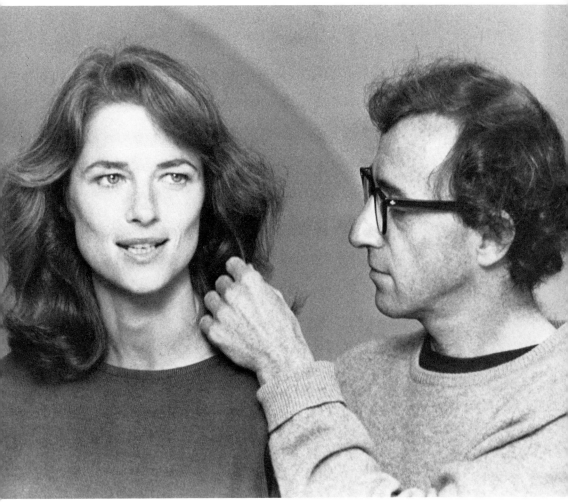

Charlotte Rampling, Woody Allen
Top: Dorothy Leon, Woody Allen

HE KNOWS YOU'RE ALONE

(MGM/UNITED ARTISTS) Producer, George Manasse; Director, Armand Mastroianni; Screenplay, Scott Parker; Executive Producers, Edgar Lansbury, Joseph Beruh; Co-Producers, Robert DiMilia, Nan Pearlman; Photography, Gerald Feil; Editor, George T. Norris; Music, Alexander and Mark Peskanov; Art Director, Susan Kaufman, Costa Mantis; In Metrocolor; Rated R; 94 minutes; September release.

CAST

Marvin	Don Scardino
Amy	Caitlin O'Heaney
Nancy	Elizabeth Kemp
Killer	Tom Rolfing
Gamble	Lewis Arlt
Joyce	Patsy Pease
Professor	James Rebhorn
Elliot	Tom Hanks
Diana	Dana Barron
Ralph the Tailor	Joseph Leon
Daley	Paul Gleason
Phil	James Carroll
Bernie	Brian Byers
Tommy	Curtis Hostetter
Ruthie	Robin Lamont
Marie	Robin Tilghman
Thompson	Peter Gumeny
Father McKenna	John Bottoms

and Debbie Novak, Russell Todd, Dorian Lopinto, Jamie Haskins, Barbara Quinn, Laurie Faso, Anthony Shaw, Ron Englehardt, Michael Fiorillo, Steve W. James

Right: Don Scardino
© MGM

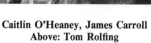
Caitlin O'Heaney, James Carroll
Above: Tom Rolfing

Lewis Arlt, Tom Rolfing
Above: Caitlin O'Heaney, Joseph Leon

ONE-TRICK PONY

(WARNER BROTHERS) Producer, Michael Tannern; Co-Producer, Michael Hausman; Director, Robert M. Young; Screenplay and Music, Paul Simon; Editors, Edward Beyer, Barry Malkin, David Ray; Designer, David Mitchell; Photography, Dick Bush; Associate Producer, Paul Martino; Assistant Directors, Michael Hausman, Joel Tuber; Costumes, Hilary Rosenfeld; Art Director, Woods MacIntosh; In Dolby Stereo and Technicolor; Rated R; 98 minutes; October release.

CAST

Jonah	Paul Simon
Marion	Blair Brown
Walter Fox	Rip Torn
Lonnie Fox	Joan Hackett
Cal Van Damp	Allen Goorwitz
Modeena Dandridge	Mare Winningham
Matty Levin	Michael Pearlman
Steve Kunelian	Lou Reed
Danny Duggin	Steve Gadd
Lee-Andrew Parker	Erid Gale
John DiBatista	Tony Levin
Clarence Franklin	Richard Tee
Bernie Wepner	Harry Shearer
Hare Krishna	Daniel Stern
Groupies	Lisa Carlson, Sameen Tarighati
Narrator at convention	Joe Smith
Lawyer	Noel L. Silverman
Lee Perry	Jordan Cael
Cal's Girlfriend	Susan Forristal
Moto Inn Clerk	Ann Karell
Chambermaid	Freda Scott

and The B 52's, The Lovin' Spoonful, Sam and Dave, Tiny Tim, Acappella Singers

Right: Paul Simon
© Warner Bros.

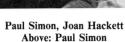

Paul Simon, Joan Hackett
Above: Paul Simon

Paul Simon, Blair Brown
Above: Simon, Michael Pearlman

89

THE STUNT MAN

(20th CENTURY-FOX) Producer-Director, Richard Rush; Screenplay, Lawrence B. Marcus; Adaptation, Richard Rush; From the novel by Paul Brodeur; Executive Producer, Melvin Simon; Photography, Mario Tosi; Associate Producer, Paul Lewis; Music, Dominic Frontiere; Lyrics, Norman Gimbel; Editors, Jack Hofstra, Caroline Ferriol; Art Director, James Schoppe; Assistant Directors, Frank Beetson, Paula Marcus; Costumes, Rosanna Norton; In color; Rated R; 129 minutes; October release.

CAST

Eli Cross	Peter O'Toole
Cameron	Steve Railsback
Nina Franklin	Barbara Hershey
Sam	Allen Goorwitz
Jake	Alex Rocco
Denise	Sharon Farrell
Raymond Bailey	Adam Roarke
Ace	Philip Bruns
Chuck Barton	Chuck Bail
Gabe/Eli's Cameraman	John Garwood
Henry/Eli's Camera Assistant	Jim Hess
Garage Guard	John B. Pearce
Burt	Michael Railsback
Father	George D. Wallace
Mother	Dee Carroll
Sister	Leslie Winograde
Lineman	Don Kennedy

Assistant Directors .... Whitey Hughes, Walter Robles and A. J. Bakunas, Gregg Berger, Ross Reynolds, Robert Caruso, Frank Avila, Stafford Morgan, John Alderman, James Avery, Leigh Webb, Frank Beetson, Jack Palinkas, Garrett McPherson, Nelson Tyler, Larry Dunn, Deanna Dae Coleman, Louie Gartner, Gordon Ross, Marion Wayne, William Joseph Arno

Left: Peter O'Toole
© **20th Century-Fox**

Steve Railsback, Chuck Bail

Barbara Hershey

Peter O'Toole, Steve Railsback (also above and top)

Jill Clayburgh, Michael Douglas

IT'S MY TURN

(COLUMBIA) Producer, Martin Elfand; Director, Claudia Weill; Screenplay, Eleanor Bergstein; Executive Producer, Jay Presson Allen; Photography, Bill Butler; Design, Jack DeGovia; Costumes, Ruth Myers; Editors, Byron Brandt, Marjorie Fowler, James Coblentz; Music, Patrick Williams; Title Song sung by Diana Ross; Associate Producer, Norman Gan; Assistant Directors, David McGiffert, Rafael Elortegui; Set, Geoff Hubbard; In color; Rated R; 91 minutes; October release.

CAST

Kate Gunzinger	Jill Clayburgh
Ben Lewin	Michael Douglas
Homer	Charles Grodin
Emma	Beverly Garland
Jacob	Steven Hill
Maryanne	Teresa Baxter
Rita	Joan Copeland
Hunter	John Gabriel
Gerome	Charles Kimbrough
Flicker	Roger Robinson
Maisie	Jennifer Salt
Cooperman	Daniel Stern
Gail	Dianne Wiest
Good Will Man	Robert Ackerman
Jerry Lanz Man	Ralph Mauro
Homer's son	Noah Hathaway
Homer's daughter	Marlyn Gates
Rabbi	Raymond Singer
Professors	Ronald C. Frazier, Edwin J. McDonough, Toshi Toda

Top: Michael Douglas, Jill Clayburgh
(also below) Left: Charles Grodin,
Jill Clayburgh
© Columbia Pictures

SAM MARLOW, PRIVATE EYE

(20th CENTURY-FOX) formerly "The Man with Bogart's Face"; Produced and Written by Andrew J. Fenady; Based on his novel; Director, Robert Day; Executive Producer, Melvin Simon; Photography, Richard C. Glouner; Designer, Robert Kinoshita; Associate Producer, Eddie Saeta; Editor, Houseley Stevenson; Music, George Dunning; Lyrics, A. J. Fenady; Assistant Directors, David McGiffert, Rafael Elortegui; Set, Richard McKenzie; In CFI Color; Rated PG; 111 minutes; October release.

CAST

Sam Marlow	Robert Sacchi
Hakim	Franco Nero
Gena	Michelle Phillips
Elsa	Olivia Hussey
Duchess	Misty Rowe
Commodore	Victor Buono
Mr. Zebra	Herbert Lom
Cynthia	Sybil Danning
Lt. Bumbera	Dick Bakalyan
Sgt. Hacksaw	Gregg Palmer
Wolf Zinderneuf	Jay Robinson
Petey Cane	George Raft
Theresa Anastas	Yvonne DeCarlo
Mike Mazurki	Himself
Chevalier	Henry Wilcoxon
Wing	Victor Sen Yung
Jock	Joe Theismann
Mother	A'Leshia Brevard
Nicky	Buck Kartalian
Spoony	Peter Mamakos
Horst Borsht	Martin Kosleck

and Philip Baker Hall, Mike Masters, Larry Pennell, Kathleen Bracken, Ed McCready, Alan Foster, Rozelle Gayle, Bill Catching, Everett Creach, Wally Rose, Ralph Carpenter, Jerry Somers, James Bacon, Frank Barron, Marilyn Beck, Robert Osborne, Will Tusher, Dick Whittington.

Right: Michelle Phillips, Robert Sacchi
© 20th Century-Fox

Robert Sacchi, Michelle Phillips, Victor Buono, Franco Nero, Jay Robinson Above: Dick Bakalyan, Olivia Hussey, Gregg Palmer, Sacchi

Robert Sacchi, Misty Rowe Above: Sybil Danning, Franco Nero, Sacchi, Michelle Phillips

PRIVATE BENJAMIN

(WARNER BROTHERS) Executive Producer, Goldie Hawn; Produced and Written by Nancy Meyers, Charles Shyer, Harvey Miller; Director, Howard Zieff; Photography, David M. Walsh; Designer, Robert Boyle; Editor, Sheldon Kahn; Music, Bill Conti; Assistant Directors, Jerry Sobul, Ross Brown; Costumes, Betsy Cox; Art Director, Jeff Howard; In Technicolor; Rated R; 110 minutes; October release.

CAST

Judy Benjamin	Goldie Hawn
Capt. Doreen Lewis	Eileen Brennan
Henri Tremont	Armand Assante
Col. Clay Thornbush	Robert Webber
Teddy Benjamin	Sam Wanamaker
Harriet Benjamin	Barbara Barrie
Pvt. Mary Lou Glass	Mary Kay Place
Sgt. Jim Ballard	Harry Dean Stanton
Yale Goodman	Albert Brooks
Rabbi	Alan Oppenheimer
Aunt Kissy	Gretchen Wyler
Helga	Sally Kirkland
Aunt Betty	Maxine Stuart

and Estelle Marlow, Everett Covin, Robert Hanley, Lee Wallace, James Dybas, Lillian Adams, Sandy Weintraub, Tim Haldeman, Kopi Sotiropulos, Stu Nahan, J. P. Bumstead, Hal Williams, Toni Kalem, Damita Jo Freeman, Alston Ahern, P. J. Soles, Craig T. Nelson, James R. Barnett, Ray Oliver, Robin Hoff, Ed Lewis, Carrol Davis Carson, Clayton Wright, Richard Herd, Denise Halma, Lilyan Chauvin, Elie Liardet

Left: Goldie Hawn
© **Warner Bros.**

Barbara Barrie, Sam Wanamaker, Goldie Hawn, Albert Brooks

Goldie Hawn, Armand Assante
Top: Goldie Hawn

THE FIRST DEADLY SIN

(FILMWAYS) Executive Producers, Frank Sinatra, Elliott Kastner; Producers, George Pappas, Mark Shanker; Director, Brian Hutton; Screenplay, Mann Rubin; Based on novel by Lawrence Sanders; Associate Producer, Fred C. Caruso; Photography, Jack Priestley; Art Director, Jack Priestley; Art Director, Woody Mackintosh; Costumes, Gary Jones; Editor, Eric Albertson; Assistant Director, Joe Napolitano; Music, Gordon Jenkins; An Artanis-Cinema VII Production in color; Rated R; 112 minutes; October release.

CAST

Edward Delaney	Frank Sinatra
Barbara Delaney	Faye Dunaway
Daniel Blank	David Dukes
Dr. Bernardi	George Coe
Monica Gilbert	Brenda Vaccaro
Christopher Langley	Martin Gabel
Doorman	Joe Spinell
Sgt. Fernandez	Jeffrey DeMunn
Capt. Broughton	Anthony Zerbe
Dr. Sanford Ferguson	James Whitmore
Delivery Man	Fred Fuster

Left: Frank Sinatra, Brenda Vaccaro
© Filmways

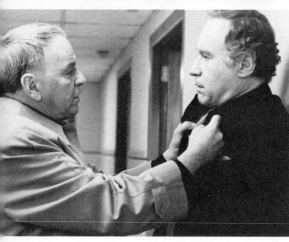

Frank Sinatra, George Coe
Above: James Whitmore, Sinatra

Frank Sinatra
Above: David Dukes

LOVING COUPLES

(20th CENTURY-FOX) Producer, Renee Valente; Executive Producer, David Susskind; Director, Jack Smight; Screenplay, Martin Donovan; Photography, Philip Lathrop; Music, Fred Karlin; Lyrics, Norman Gimbel; Art Director, Jan Scott; Editors, Greyfox, Frank Urioste; Associate Producer, Andrew Suskind; Costumes, Arnold Scaasi, Theoni V. Aldredge; Assistant Directors, Carl Olsen, Kathy Slakey, Mike Looney; Choreographer, Larry Vickers; In color; Rated PG; 97 minutes; October release.

CAST

Evelyn	Shirley MacLaine
Walter	James Coburn
Stephanie	Susan Sarandon
Gregg	Stephen Collins
Mrs. Liggett	Sally Kellerman
Walter's Nurse	Nan Martin
Dulcy	Shelly Batt
Elegant Doctor	Bernard Behrens
Nurse	Anne Bloom
Hotel Clerk	Fred Carney
Prudence	Helena Carroll
Sally	Marilyn Chris
Delmonico Clerk	Pat Corley
Ken	Michael Curry
Cop Partner	John Davis
Allan	John deLancie
Evelyn's Nurse	Edith Fields
Mrs. Herzog	Estelle Omens
Frank	Peter Hobbs
Salesgirl	Paula Jones
Drunk Doctor	Art Kassul
Nudist	Hap Lawrence

and Bob Levine, John Medici, David Murphy, June Sanders, Tony Travis, Sam Weisman

Top: Stephen Collins, Susan Sarandon,
James Coburn, Shirley MacLaine Right:
Stephen Collins, Sally Kellerman
Below: Collins, Sarandon
© 20th Century-Fox

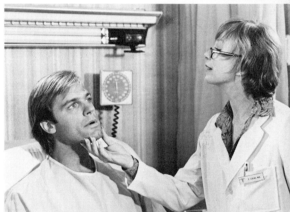

Stephen Collins, Shirley MacLaine
(also above)

George Burns

OH, GOD! BOOK II

(WARNER BROTHERS) Producer-Director, Gilbert Cates; Screenplay, Josh Greenfeld, Hal Goldman, Fred S. Fox, Seaman Jacobs, Melissa Miller; Story, Josh Greenfeld; Photography, Ralph Woolsey, Editor, Peter E. Berger; Music, Charles Fox; Design, Preston Ames; Set, Chris Westlund; Assistant Director, Tom Lofaro; In Technicolor; Rated PG; 94 minutes; October release.

CAST

God	George Burns
Paula	Suzanne Pleshette
Don	David Birney
Tracy	Louanne
Shingo	John Louie
Mr. Benson	Conrad Janis
Dr. Jerome Newell	Anthony Holland
Newscaster	Hugh Downs
Dr. Joyce Brothers	Herself
Dr. Barnes	Hans Conried
Judge Miller	Wilfrid Hyde-White

Marian Mercer, Bebe Drake Massey, Mari Gorman, Vernon Weddle, Alma Beltran

Top: Louanne, Suzanne Pleshette,
David Birney
© Warner Bros.

THE IDOLMAKER

(UNITED ARTISTS) Producers, Gene Kirkwood, Howard W. Koch, Jr.; Director, Taylor Hackford; Screenplay, Edward DiLorenzo; Photography, Adam Holender; Art Director, David L. Snyder; Editor, Neil Travis; Music and Lyrics, Jeff Barry; Choreography, Deney Terrio; Costumes, Rita Riggs; Associate Producers, R. J. Louis, David Nichols; Assistant Directors, Clifford C. Coleman, Hope Goodwin; Editors, Arthur Schmidt, Steve Potter; Set, Brandy Alexander; In Dolby Stereo and Technicolor; Rated PG; 119 minutes; November release.

CAST

Vincent Vacarri	Ray Sharkey
Brenda Roberts	Tovah Feldshuh
Caesare	Peter Gallagher
Tommy Dee	Paul Land
Gino Pilato	Joe Pantoliano
Ellen Fields	Maureen McCormick
Paul Vacarri	John Aprea
Uncle Tony	Richard Bright
Mrs. Vacarri	Olympia Dukakis
Mr. Vacarri	Steven Apostlee Peck
Luchetti	Leonard Gaines
Jerry Martin	Deney Terrio
Jesse	Charles Guardino
Ed Sharp	Michael Mislove
Walt Bennett	Kenneth O'Brien
Carlo	Michael Perotta
Delano	Jeffrey Tanner
Scapio	Howard Gordon

and Sweet Inspirations, London Fog

Right: Peter Gallagher, Ray Sharkey
© United Artists

Ray Sharkey, Tovah Feldshuh
Above: Sharkey, Paul Land

Ray Sharkey
Above: Paul Land

RAGING BULL

(UNITED ARTISTS) Producers, Irwin Winkler, Robert Chartoff; Director, Martin Scorsese; Associate Producer, Peter Savage; Screenplay, Paul Schrader, Mardik Martin; Based on book "Raging Bull" by Jake LaMotta with Joseph Carter, Peter Savage; Photography, Michael Chapman; Associate Producer, Hal W. Polaire; Editor, Thelma Schoonmaker; Designer, Gene Rudolf; Art Directors, Alan Manser, Kirk Axtell; Assistant Directors, Allan Wertheim, Jerry Grandey; In Dolby Stereo, black and white and color; Rated R; 129 minutes; November release.

CAST

Jake LaMotta	Robert DeNiro
Vickie LaMotta	Cathy Moriarty
Joey	Joe Pesci
Salvy	Frank Vincent
Tommy Como	Nicholas Colasanto
Lenore	Theresa Saldana
Patsy	Frank Adonis
Mario	Mario Gallo
Toppy/Handler	Frank Topham
Irma	Lori Anne Flax
Guido	Joseph Bono
Dr. Pinto	James V. Christy
Comedian	Bernie Allen
Reporter	Bill Mazer
Eddie Eagan	Bill Hanrahan
Emma (Miss 48's)	Rita Bennett
Sparring Partner	Mike Miles
Jimmy Reeves	Floyd Anderson
Sugar Ray Robinson	Johnny Barnes
Tony Janiro	Kevin Mahon
Billy Fox	Ed Gregory
Marcel Cerdan	Louis Raftis
Laurent Dauthuille	Johnny Turner
Barbizon Stagehand	Martin Scorsese

Left: Robert DeNiro
1980 Academy Awards for Best Actor
(DeNiro) and *Best Editing*
© United Artists

Robert DeNiro, Cathy Moriarty

Robert DeNiro, Joe Pesci

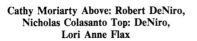

**Cathy Moriarty Above: Robert DeNiro,
Nicholas Colasanto Top: DeNiro,
Lori Anne Flax**

Robert DeNiro, and top with Martin
Denkin, Kevin Mahon (on mat)

101

THE FORMULA

(MGM/UNITED ARTISTS) Produced and Written by Steve Shagan; Based on his novel of the same title; Director, John G. Avildsen; Photography, James Crabe; Designer, Herman A. Blumenthal; Art Directors, Hans-Jurgen Keibach; Editor, David Bretherton; Music, Bill Conti; Assistant Directors, Dwight Williams, Candace Allen; Costumes, Bill Thomas; Set, Lee Poll; Associate Producer, Ken Swor; Choreographer, Bill Millie; In Metrocolor; Rated R; 118 minutes; December release.

CAST

Barney Caine	George C. Scott
Adam Steiffel	Marlon Brando
Lisa	Marthe Keller
Dr. Esau	John Gielgud
Clements	G. D. Spradlin
Kay Neeley	Beatrice Straight
Kladen/Tedesco	Richard Lynch
Hans Lehman	John Van Dreelen
Major Neeley	Robin Clarke
Tony	Ike Eisenmann
Geologist	Marshall Thompson
Assassin	Dieter Schidor
Schellenberg	Werner Kreindl
Gestapo Captain	Jan Niklas
Franz Tauber	Wolfgang Preiss
Sgt. Yosuta	Calvin Jung
Nolan	Alan North
Obermann	David Byrd
Siebold	Ferdy Mayne
Chauffeur	Gerry Murphy
Mendosa	Francisco Prado

Left: Marthe Keller, George C. Scott
© **United artists**

George C. Scott, Marlon Brando

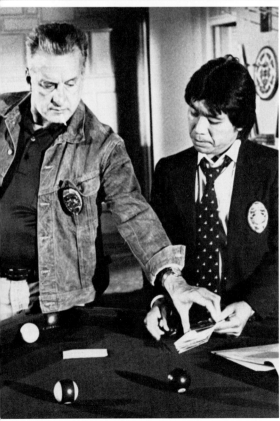

George C. Scott, Calvin Jung
Top: Scott, Marlon Brando

George C. Scott

POPEYE

(PARAMOUNT) Producer, Robert Evans; Director, Robert Altman; Screenplay, Jules Feiffer; Based on comic strip characters created by E. C. Segar; Executive Producer, C. O. Erickson; Music and Lyrics, Harry Nilsson; Photography, Giuseppe Rotunno; Designer, Wolf Kroeger; Editor, Tony Lombardo; Costumes, Scott Bushnell; Choreographers, Sharon Kinney, Hovey Burgess, Lou Wills; Associate Producer, Scott Bushnell; Assistant Directors, Bob Dahlin, Victor Tourjansky; In Technovision; Rated PG; 111 minutes; December release.

CAST

Popeye	Robin Williams
Olive Oyl	Shelley Duvall
Commodore	Ray Walston
Bluto	Paul Smith
Wimpy	Paul Dooley
Geezil	Richard Libertini
Nana Oyl	Roberta Maxwell
Taxman	Donald Moffat
Cole Oyl	MacIntyre Dixon
Castor Oyl	Donovan Scott
Rough House	Allan Nichols
Swee' Pea	Wesley Ivan Hurt
Ham Gravy	Bill Irwin
Bill Barnacle, town drunk	Robert Fortier
Harry Hotcash, gambler	David McCharen
Cherry, his moll	Sharon Kinney
Oxblood Oxheart, the fighter	Peter Bray
Mrs. Oxheart	Linda Hunt
LaVerne	Susan Kingsley
Mayor Stonefeller	Paul Zegler
Mrs. Stonefeller	Pamela Burrell
Preacher	Ray Cooper

and Geoff Hoyle, Wayne Robson, Larry Pisoni, Carlo Pellegrini, Michael Christensen, Noel Parenti, Karen McCormick, John Bristol, Julie Janney, Patty Katz, Diane Shaffer, Nathalie Blossom, Dennis Franz, Carlos Brown, Ned Dowd, Hovey Burgess, Roberto Messina

Left: Paul Dooley, Shelley Duvall, Robin Williams Top: Robin Williams
© **Paramount Pictures**

Ray Walston, Robin Williams

Robin Williams, Wesley Ivan Hurt

Paul Dooley, Wesley Ivan Hurt, Shelley Duvall, Robin Williams
Top: (L) Hurt, Paul Smith, Ray Walston, Below: Peter Bray, Robin Williams
(R) Paul Dooley Top: Robin Williams, Shelley Duvall

TELL ME A RIDDLE

(FILMWAYS) Executive Producer, Michael Rosenberg; Producers, Mindy Affrime, Rachel Lyon, Susan O'Connell; Director, Lee Grant; Screenplay, Joyce Eliason, Alev Lytle; Based on novella by Tillie Olsen; Photography, Fred Murphy; Designer, Patrizia von Brandenstein; Editor, Suzanne Pettit; Assistant Director, Peter Schindler; Music, Sheldon Shkolnik; A Godmother production in color; Rated PG; 90 minutes; December release.

CAST

David	Melvyn Douglas
Eva	Lila Kedrova
Jeannie	Brooke Adams
Vivi	Dolores Dorn
Sammy	Bob Elross
Mathew	Jon Harris
Paul	Zalman King
Hannah	Winifred Mann
Phil	Peter Owens
Nancy	Deborah Sussel
Mrs. Mays	Lili Valenty
Young Eva	Nora Hefflin
Young David	Peter Coyote
Lisa	Nora Bendich

Top: Brooke Adams, Lila Kedrova
(L) Brooke Adams, Melvyn Douglas
© Filmways

Melvyn Douglas, Lila Kedrova

A CHANGE OF SEASONS

(20th CENTURY-FOX) Producer, Martin Ransohoff; Director, Richard Lang; Screenplay, Erich Segal, Ronni Kern, Fred Segal; Story, Erich Segal, Martin Ransohoff; Executive Producer, Richard R. St. Johns; Associate Producer, Cathleen Summers; Photography, Philip Lathrop; Designer, Bill Kenney; Editor, Don Zimmerman; Music, Henry Mancini; Assistant Directors, Donald Heitzer, James Weatherill; In color; Rated R; 102 minutes; December release.

CAST

Karen Evans	Shirley MacLaine
Adam Evans	Anthony Hopkins
Lindsey Rutledge	Bo Derek
Pete Lachapelle	Michael Brandon
Kasey Evans	Marybeth Hurt
Steven Rutledge	Ed Winter
Paul DiLisi	Paul Regina
Alice Bingham	K Callan
Sam Bingham	Rod Colbin
Lance	Steve Eastin
Fritz	Christopher Coffey
Maitre d'	Albert Carriere
Older Man	Billy Beck
Young Girls	Blake Harris, Karen Philipp
Man at table	Paul Bryar
Woman at table	Anita Jodelsohn
Bartender	Tim Haldeman
Disco DJ	Paul Young
Truck Driver	James Jeter
Bubba Green	Stan Wright
Bobby Mason	Percy Davis
Charlie	Steve Myers
Basketball Player	John O'Connor

Right: Anthony Hopkins, Bo Derek
© 20th Century-Fox

Bo Derek, Anthony Hopkins, Shirley MacLaine, Michael Brandon

ANY WHICH WAY YOU CAN

(WARNER BROTHERS) Executive Producer, Robert Daley; Producer, Fritz Manes; Director, Buddy Van Horn; Screenplay, Stanford Sherman; Based on characters created by Jeremy Joe Kronsberg; Photography, David Worth; Design, William J. Creber; Editors, Ferris Webster, Ron Spang; Assistant Director, Tom Joyner; Set, Ernie Bishop; In DeLuxe Color; Rated PG; 116 minutes; December release.

CAST

Philo Beddoe	Clint Eastwood
Lynne Halsey-Taylor	Sondra Locke
Orville	Geoffrey Lewis
Jack Wilson	William Smith
James Beekman	Harry Guardino
Ma	Ruth Gordon
Patrick Scarfe	Michael Cavanaugh
Fat Zack	Barry Corbin
Moody	Roy Jenson
Dallas	Bill McKinney
Elmo	William O'Connell
Cholla	John Quade
Tony Paoli, Sr.	Al Ruscio
Frank	Dan Vadis
Hattie	Camila Ashlend
Baggage Man	Dan Barrows
Moustache Officer	Michael Brockman
Candy	Julie Brown
Glen Campbell	Himself
Jackson Officer	Dick Christie
Buxon Bess	Rebecca Clemons
Loretta Quince	Anne Ramsey
Luther Quince	Logan Ramsey
Long John	Jim Stafford
Honey Bun	Lynn Hallowell

Left: Clint Eastwood and Clyde
© Warner Bros.

Clint Eastwood, Sondra Locke, Ruth Gordon, Geoffrey Lewis

Sondra Locke, Clint Eastwood, also at top with William Smith

ALTERED STATES

(WARNER BROTHERS) Executive Producer, Daniel Melnick; Producer, Howard Gottfried; Director, Ken Russell; Screenplay, Sidney Aaron from the novel by Paddy Chayefsky; Music, John Corigliano; Special Effects, Bran Ferren; Costumes, Ruth Myers; Associate Producer, Stuart Baird; Editor, Eric Jenkins; Designer, Richard McDonald; Photography, Jordan Cronenweth; Assistant Directors, Gary Daigler, Peter Schindler; In Technicolor and Dolby Stereo; Rated R; 102 minutes; December release.

CAST

Eddie Jessup	William Hurt
Emily Jessup	Blair Brown
Arthur Rosenberg	Bob Balaban
Mason Parrish	Charles Haid
Eccheverria	Thaao Penghlis
Primal Man	Miguel Godreau
Sylvia Rosenberg	Dori Brenner
Hobart	Peter Brandon
The Brujo	Charles White Eagle
Margaret Jessup	Drew Barrymore
Grace Jessup	Megan Jeffers
Hector Ortego	Jack Murdock
Obispo	Frank McCarthy
Schizophrenic Patient	Deborah Baltzell
Young Rosenberg	Evan Richards
Endocrinology Fellow	Hap Lawrence
Medical Technician	John Walter Davis
Parrish's Girl	Cynthia Burr
Eccheverria's Girl	Susan Bredhoff
X-Ray Technician	John Larroquette
Dr. Wissenschaft	George Gaynes

and Ora Rubinstein, Paul Larson, Eric Forst, Adriana Shaw, Martin Fiscoe, Olivia Michelle, M. James Arnett

Left: Blair Brown, William Hurt
© **Warner Bros.**

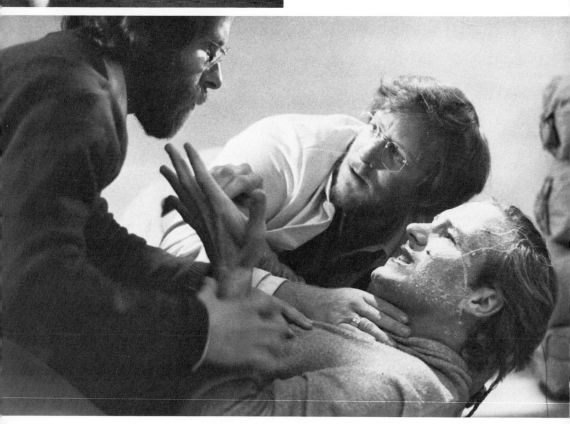

Bob Balaban, Charles Haid, William Hurt

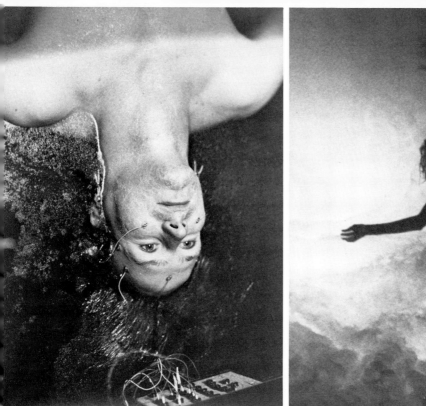

Blair Brown, William Hurt Top: (L) William Hurt (R) Blair Brown

NINE TO FIVE

(20th CENTURY-FOX) Producer, Bruce Gilbert; Director, Colin Higgins; Screenplay, Colin Higgins, Patricia Resnick; Story, Patricia Resnick; Photography, Reynaldo Villalobos; Music, Charles Fox; Title song written and sung by Dolly Parton; Designer, Dean Mitzner; Editor, Pembroke J. Herring; Assistant Directors, Gary Daigler, Chris Soldo; Art Director, Jack Gammon Taylor, Jr.; In DeLuxe Color; Rated PG; 110 minutes; December release.

CAST

Judy Bernly	Jane Fonda
Violet Newstead	Lily Tomlin
Doralee Rhodes	Dolly Parton
Franklin Hart, Jr.	Dabney Coleman
Tinsworthy	Sterling Hayden
Roz	Elizabeth Wilson
Hinkle	Henry Jones
Dick	Lawrence Pressman
Missy Hart	Marian Mercer
Barbara	Ren Woods
Betty	Norma Donaldson
Maria	Roxanna Bonilla-Giannini
Margaret	Peggy Pope
Meade	Richard Stahl
Eddie	Ray Vitte
Bob Enright	Edward Marshall
Chuck Strell	Alan Haufrect
Perkins	Earl Boen
Dwayne Rhodes	Jeffrey Douglas Thomas
Norman Lane	Tom Tarpey
Policeman	Terrence McNally
Buffy	Barbara Chase
Josh Newstead	David Price

and Michael Delnao, Gavin Mooney, Peter Hobbs, Esther Sutherland, Helene Heigh, Vicki Belmonte, Jerrold Ziman, Jessica Badovinac, Eric Mansker, Shirley Anthony, Michael Hehr, Gary Bisig, Raymond O'Keefe

Left: Jane Fonda, Dabney Coleman Top: Elizabeth Wilson, Fonda, Lily Tomlin
© 20th Century-Fox

Dabney Coleman, Dolly Parton

Lily Tomlin, Dolly Parton, Jane Fonda Above: Fonda, Tomlin

Jane Fonda, Lily Tomlin, Dolly Parton Top: (L) Dabney Coleman, Lily Tomlin Below:
Parton, Tomlin, Fonda (also right)

FIRST FAMILY

(WARNER BROTHERS) Producer, Daniel Melnick; Direction and Screenplay, Buck Henry; Photography, Fred J. Koenekamp; Editor, Stu Linder; Music, John Philip Sousa; In color; Rated R; 104 minutes; December release.

CAST

President Manfred Link	Bob Newhart
Gloria Link	Gilda Radner
Presidential Assistant Feebleman	Fred Willard
Press Secretary Bunthorne	Richard Benjamin
Vice President Shockley	Bob Dishy
Mrs. Link	Madeline Kahn
Ambassador Longo	Julius Harris
Ambassador Spender	Harvey Korman
Arab Delegate	Maurice Sherbanee
Alexander Grade	Austin Pendleton
Secretary of Defense Springfield	Dudley Knight
Secretary of State Reigie	Lou Felder
Father Sandstone	Buck Henry
President Mazai Kalundra	John Hancock
General Dumpston	Rip Torn

Top: Harvey Korman Below: Gilda Radner,
Austin Pendleton Left: Radner, Bob
Newhart, Madeline Kahn, and at top
© Warner Bros.

Madeline Kahn, Bob Newhart,
Gilda Radner

THE JAZZ SINGER

(ASSOCIATED FILM DISTRIBUTION) Producer, Jerry Leider; Director, Richard Fleischer; Screenplay, Herbert Baker; Adaptation, Stephen H. Foreman; Based on play by Samson Raphaelson; Song Score, Neil Diamond; Associate Producer, Joe Morwood; Photography, Isidore Mankofsky; Designer, Harry Horner; Costumes, Albert Wolsky; Editor, Frank J. Urioste; Art Director, Spencer Deverill; Assistant Directors, James Turley, Robert M. Webb; Set, Christopher Horner, Mark Poll; Choreographer, Don McKayle; In DeLuxe Color and Dolby Stereo; Rated PG; 115 minutes; December release.

CAST

Jess Robin	Neil Diamond
Cantor Rabinovitch	Laurence Olivier
Molly Bell	Lucie Arnaz
Rivka Rabinovitch	Catlin Adams
Bubba	Franklyn Ajaye
Keith Lennox	Paul Nicholas
Eddie Gibbs	Sully Boyar
Leo	Mike Bellin
Paul Rossini	James Booth
Teddy	Luther Waters
Mel	Oren Waters
Timmy	Rod Gist
Rabbi Birnbaum	Walter Janowitz
Aunt Tillie	Janet Brandt
M. C. Cinderella Club	John Witherspoon
Tommy	Dale Robinette
Peg	Judy Gibson
Police Sergeant	Hank Garrett
Barney Callahan	James Karen
Cowgirl	Jill Jaress
Irate Driver	Victor Paul

Right: Laurence Olivier, Neil Diamond
Top: Lucie Arnaz, Neil Diamond
© AFD

Neil Diamond, Franklyn Ajaye
Above: Catlin Adams, Diamond

Lucie Arnaz, Neil Diamond
Above: Neil Diamond

INSIDE MOVES

(ASSOCIATED FILM DISTRIBUTION) Producers, Mark M. Tanz, R. W. Goodwin; Director, Richard Donner; Screenplay, Valerie Curtin, Barry Levinson; Based on novel by Todd Walton; Photography, Laszlo Kovacs; Designer, Charles Rosen; Editor, Frank Morriss; Music, John Barry; Costumes, Ron Talsky; Assistant Directors, Michael F. Grillo, Paul Moen; Set, Boyd Willat; In Panavision and Technicolor; Rated PG; 113 minutes; December release.

CAST

Roary	John Savage
Jerry	David Morse
Louise	Diana Scarwid
Ann	Amy Wright
Lucius Porter	Tony Burton
Blue Lewis	Bill Henderson
Burt	Steve Kahan
Max	Jack O'Leary
Stinky	Bert Remsen
Wings	Harold Russell
Herrada	Pepe Serna
Alvin Martin	Harold Sylvester
Benny	Arnold Williams

And the Golden State Warriors

Left: John Savage
© **AFD**

Clockwise from Bill Henderson in wheelchair: Arnold Williams, Steve Kahan, David Morse, John Savage, Harold Russell, Bert Remsen, Jack O'Leary

Diana Scarwid, John Savage, and above
with Harold Sylvester Top: Bert Remsen,
Bill Henderson, Harold Russell

Amy Wright

THE COMPETITION

(COLUMBIA) Producer, William Sackheim; Direction and Screenplay, Joel Oliansky; Story, Joel Oliansky, William Sackheim; Executive Producer, Howard Pine; Photography, Richard H. Kline; Design, Dale Hennesy; Costumes, Ruth Myers; Music, Lalo Schifrin; Editor, David Blewitt; Assistant Directors, Jon C. Anderson, Paul Magwood; Set, Dianne Wager; In Dolby Stereo and Metrocolor; Rated PG; 129 minutes; December release.

CAST

Paul Dietrich	Richard Dreyfuss
Heidi Schoonover	Amy Irving
Greta Vandemann	Lee Remick
Erskine	Sam Wanamaker
Jerry DiSalvo	Joseph Cali
Michael Humphries	Ty Henderson
Tatiana Baronov	Vickie Kriegler
Mark Landau	Adam Stern
Mme. Gorshev	Bea Silvern
Mr. Dietrich	Philip Sterling
Mrs. Dietrich	Gloria Stroock
Mrs. DiSalvo	Delia Salvi
Mrs. Donellan	Priscilla Pointer
Brudnell	James B. Sikking
Mitzi	Elaine Welton Hill
Nichols	Ben Hammer
Karnow	Rhio H. Blair
Judge Heimling	Ross Evans
Rudko	Sterling Swanson
Vinnie DiSalvo	Jimmy Sturtevant
Denise DiSalvo	Kathy Talbot

Top: **Richard Dreyfuss, Amy Irving**
© Columbia Pictures

Lee Remick, Amy Irving

Richard Dreyfuss, Amy Irving (also at top)

STIR CRAZY

(COLUMBIA) Producer, Hannah Weinstein; Director, Sidney Poitier; Screenplay, Bruce Jay Friedman; Executive Producer, Melville Tucker; Associate Producer, Francoise deMenil; Photography, Fred Schuler; Music, Tom Scott; Editor, Harry Keller; Designer, Alfred Sweeney; Assistant Directors, Daniel J. McCauley, Joseph Moore, Don Wilkerson; Costumes, Patricia Edwards; Choreography, Scott Salmon; In color; Rated R; 114 minutes; December release.

CAST

Skip Donahue	Gene Wilder
Harry Monroe	Richard Pryor
Rory Schultebrand	Georg Stanford Brown
Meredith	Jobeth Williams
Jesus Ramirez	Miguelangel Suarez
Deputy Ward Wilson	Craig T. Nelson
Warden Walter Beatty	Barry Corbin
Blade	Charles Weldon
Warden Henry Sampson	Nicolas Coster
Len Garber	Joel Brooks
Jack Graham	Jonathan Banks
Grossberger	Erland Van Lidth De Jeude
Susan	Lee Purcell
Theresa Ramirez	Karmin Murcelo
Young Man in hospital	Franklyn Ajaye
Mrs. R. H. Broache	Estelle Omens
Big Mean	Cedrick Hardman
Ramon	Henry Kingi
Cook's Helper	Pamela Poitier
Korean Doctor	Alvin Ing
Ceasar Geronimo	Joseph Massengale
Alex	Herman Poppe
Chico	Luis Avalos
Sissie	Esther Sutherland

Left: Richard Pryor, Miguelangel Suarez, Georg Stanford Brown Top: Gene Wilder, Pryor
© Columbia Pictures

**Joseph Massengale, Gene Wilder
Above: Richard Pryor, Wilder**

Gene Wilder, Richard Pryor

SEEMS LIKE OLD TIMES

(COLUMBIA) Producer, Ray Stark; Director, Jay Sandrich; Screenplay, Neil Simon; Executive Producer, Roger M. Rothstein; Photography, David M. Walsh; Music, Marvin Hamlisch; Associate Producer, Margaret Booth; Editor, Michael A. Stevenson; Designed by Gene Callahan; Assistant Directors, Jack Aldworth, Venita Ozols; Costumes, Betsy Cox; Art Director, Pete Smith; In color; Rated PG; 102 minutes; December release.

CAST

Glenda	Goldie Hawn
Nick	Chevy Chase
Ira	Charles Grodin
Fred	Robert Guillaume
Judge	Harold Gould
Governor	George Grizzard
Aurora	Yvonne Wilder
Chester	T. K. Carter
Dex	Judd Omen
Bee Gee	Marc Alaimo
Thomas	Joseph Running Fox
Robert	Ray Tracey
Anne	Fay Hauser
Bank Teller	Carolyn Fromson
Jean	Sandy Lipton
Jack	Herb Armstrong
Rosita	Natividad Rios Kearsley
Conchita	Dolores Aguirre
Exra	Edmund Stoiber
Mrs. Ezra	Alice Sachs

Top: Goldie Hawn, Chevy Chase, Robert Guillaume Below: Harold Gould, Chase, Hawn, Charles Grodin Right: Hawn, Chase Top: Hawn, Grodin
© Columbia Pictures

Goldie Hawn, also above with T. K. Carter

Erich Von Stroheim, Denise Vernac
in "The Man You Loved to Hate"

THE MAN YOU LOVED TO HATE (Film Profiles) Producer-Director, Patrick Montgomery; Written and Researched by Richard Koszarski; Associate Producer, Gregg Burton; Editor, William Loeffler; Music, Herbert Deutsch; Narrator, Edward Binns; Produced in association with BBC, Killiam Shows, Fremantle International and Norddeutscher Rundfunk; In color, black and white; Not rated; 90 minutes; January release. A documentary on Erich Von Stroheim.

J-MEN FOREVER (International Harmony) A film by Proctor & Bergman of Firesign Theater; Music, Billy Preston, The Tubes, Badazz, Budgie, Head East, Richard Thiess; In color; Rated PG; 79 minutes; January release.

JOE AND MAXI (Cohen & Gold) Producer, Maxi Gold; Directors, Joel Gold, Maxi Cohen; Photography, Joel Gold; Editors, Pat Powell, Marion Kraft, Maxi Cohen; In color; Not rated; 80 minutes; January release. CAST: Joe Cohen (Father), Maxi Cohen (Daughter), Barry Cohen (Brother), Danny Cohen (Brother), Bea Metzman (Aunt), Dan Metzman (Uncle), Ronnie Kestenbaum (Barry's friend), Henrietta (Hank), Abrams (Joe's friend).

EVENTS (Alfred/Baker Films) Produced, Directed and Written by Fred Baker; In color; Rated R; 87 minutes; January release. CAST: Ryan Listman, Joy Wener, Frank Cavestani, Marsha Rossa

THE LEGEND OF COUGAR CANYON (First American Films) Producer-Director, James T. Flocker; Photography, David E. Jackson; Associate Producer, Peter Normandt; Music, William Loose; Animal Sequences, Monty Cox; Editorial Assistant, Lex Fletcher; In Eastman Color by Consolidated Film Industries; Rated G; 89 minutes; January release. CAST: Rex Allen (Storyteller), Holger Kasper (Walter), Steven Benally, Jr. (Steve), Johnny Guerro (Indian Guide) and members of the Navajo Nation

Anne Bancroft, Dom DeLuise, Estelle Reiner
in "Fatso" © 20th Century-Fox

JOURNEYS FROM BERLIN/1971 (Center for Public Cinema) Director-Editor, Yvonne Rainier; Photography, Michael Steinke; Carl Teitelbaum, Wolfgang Senn, Jon Else, Shinkichi Tajiri; In color, black and white; Not rated; 125 minutes; January release. CAST: Annette Michelson, Ilona Halberstadt, Gabor Vernon, Chad Wollen, Amy Taubin, Vito Acconci, Lena Hyun, Yvonne Rainier, Ruth Rainero, Leo Rainer, Cynthia Beatt, Antonio Skarmeta

DRACULA SUCKS (Kodiak Films) Executive Producer, David Emerich; Director, Philip Marshak; Screenplay, Darryl A. Marshak, David J. Kern; Photography, Hanania Baer; Set, Richard King; Associate Producers, David J. Kern, Nettie Pena; Editor, Nettie Pena; Music, Lional Thomas; Costumes, Barbara Ann Edelstein, Priscilla Morales; A Mr. Production Ltd. production in Panavision and Metrocolor; Rated R; 91 minutes; January release. CAST: Jamie Gillis (Dracula), Serena (Lucy), Annette Haven (Mina), John Leslie (Seward), Richard Bulik (Renfield), John Holmes (Stoker), Paul Thomas (Harker), Kay Parker (Sybil), Bill Margold (Henry), Detlef Van Berg (Helsing), Pat Manning (Irene), Mike Ranger (Bradley), Seka (Lawson), David Lee Bynum (Jarvis), Irene Best (Maid), George Lee (Cowboy), Kurt Sjoberg (Hitler), Renee Andre, Slavica (Handmaidens), Martin L. Dorf (Martin), Nancy Hoffman (Baby Jane), Ken Michaels, Mitch Morrill (Patients)

SMOKEY AND THE HOTWIRE GANG (NMD) Producer-Director-Editor, Anthony Cardoza; Story-Screenplay, T. Gary Cardoza; Music, Valerie Jeanne, Danny Bravin; Associate Producer, Bill Reardon; Photography, Gregory Sandor; Assistant Producer, Charles Samples; An Ace Pix Production in Movielab Color; Rated PG; 85 minutes; January release. CAST: James Keach (Joshua), Stanley Livingston (Russ), Tony Lorea (Filbert), Alvy Moore (Sheriff), Skip Young (Junior), Carla Ziegfield (Elena/Hotwire), George Barris (Billy), Ray Cantrell (Ron), Tanya George (Nancy), Albert Cole (Jack), Carol Connley (Diane), George Bryson (Dave), Randee Lynn Jensen (Cheryl), Timothy C. Burns (Rich), Anthony Sirico (Pete), Jerry Maren (Walt), Elizabeth Barrington (Pepper), Robert Gray (Razz), Mark Carlton (Tom), Anthony Cardoza (Wesley)

GIZMO! (New Line Cinema) Producer-Director, Howard Smith; Executive Producer, Francois de Menil; Editor, Terry Manning; Music, Dick Lavsky; Written by Kathleen Cox, Nicholas Hollander, Clark Whelton; In black and white and color; Rated G; 79 minutes; January release. Cast not submitted.

THE GODSEND (Cannon Group) Producer Director, Gabrielle Beaumont; Executive Producers, Menahem Golan, Yoram Globus; Screenplay, Olaf Pooley; Photography, Norman Warwick; Music, Roger Webb; Art Director, Tony Curtis; Based on novel by Bernard Taylor; In color; Rated R; 90 minutes; January release. CAST: Cyd Hayman (Kate Marlowe), Malcolm Stoddard (Alan Marlowe), Angela Pleasence (Stranger), Patrick Barr (Dr. Collins), Wilhelmina Green, Lee Gregory, Joanne Boorman

THE CARHOPS (NMD) Producer, Jim Buckley; Director, Peter Locke; Screenplay, Paul Ross, Michael Blank; Associate Producer, David Buckley; Music, Ronald Frangipane; Photography, Colin Campbell; Art Direction, Michael Sullivan, Peter Bramley; Editors, Rick Jackson, Wes Craven; Assistant Directors, Teri Schwartz, Dick Dixon; Editor, George Norris; In Eastman Color; Rated R; 88 minutes; January release. CAST: Kitty Carl (Kitty), Lisa Farringer (Cindy), Fay de Witt (Kitty's mother), Pamela Miller (Vicki), Marcie Barkin (Sherry), Jack DeLeon (MacGregor), Walter Wanderman (Albert), Asher Brauner (B.J.), David Debin (Tom), Don Baldwin (Pat), Paul Ross (Barry), Patricia Ann Parker (Nancy), Janus Blythe (Janet), Lee Moore (Charlie) and Anthony DeFonte, James Inch, Jack D. Miller, James Miles, Frederique, Jimmy Martinez, Peter Bramley, Janis Lynn, Michael Sullivan, Scott Patrick, B. G. Fisher, Vincent Barbi, Tiger Joe Marsh, Clover Mamone, Uschi Digard, Gene Darval

FATSO (20th CENTURY-FOX) Producer, Stuart Cornfield; Direction and Screenplay, Anne Bancroft; Photography, Brianne Murphy; Editor, Glenn Farr; Music, Joe Renzetti; Design, Peter Wooley; Set, Linda DeScenna; Costumes, Patricia Norris; Assistant Director, Mark Johnson; In Deluxe Color; Rated PG; 94 minutes; February release. CAST: Dom DeLuise (Dominick), Anne Bancroft (Antoinette), Ron Carey (Frankie), Candice Azzara (Lydia), Michael Lombard (Charlie), Sal Viscuso (Vito), Delia Salvi (Ida), Robert Costanzo (Johnny), Estelle Reiner (Mrs. Goodman), Richard Karron (Sonny)

Steve McQueen, Bibi Andersson
in "An Enemy of the People"
© Warner Bros.

Bob Dishy, Natalie Wood in "The Last Married
Couple . . ." © Universal Studios

MIDNIGHT MADNESS (Buena Vista) Producer, Ron Miller; Direction and Screenplay, David Wechter, Michael Nankin; Photography, Frank Phillips, Music, Julius Wechter; Editors, Norman R. Palmer, Jack Sekely; Art Directors, John B. Mansbridge, Richard Lawrence; In Technicolor; Rated PG; 110 minutes; January release. CAST: David Naughton (Adam), Debra Clinger (Laura), Eddie Deezen (Wesley), Brad Wilkin (Lavitas), Maggie Roswell (Donna), Stephen Furst (Harold), Irene Tedrow (Mrs. Grimhaus), Michael J. Fox (Scott), Joel P. Kenney (Flynch), Alan Solomon (Leon)

SPIRIT OF THE WIND (Raven Pictures) Director, Ralph Liddle; Screenplay, Ralph Liddle, John Logue; Photography, John Logue; Editor, Mark Goldblatt; Music, Buffy Sainte-Marie; In color; Not Rated; 98 minutes; January release. CAST: Pius Savage (George), Chief Dan George (Moses), Slim Pickens (Obie), George Clutesi (Father)

CARDIAC ARREST (Film Ventures International) Producer, Richard Helzberg; Direction and Screenplay, David Helzberg; Music, Andrew Kulberg; Associate Producer, Ned Kopp; In DeLuxe Color; Rated PG; 80 minutes; January release. CAST: Garry Goodrow, Mike Chan, Maxwell Gail, Susan O'Connell, Ray Reinhardt

HUMAN EXPERIMENTS (Essex) Producers, Summer Brown, Gregory Goodell; Director, Gregory Goodell; Executive Producer, Edwin Scott Brown; Screenplay, Richard Rothstein; Music, Marc Bucci; Photography, Joao Fernandes; In color; Rated R; 82 minutes; January release. CAST: Linda Haynes (Rachel), Geoffrey Lewis (Dr. Kline), Ellen Travolta, Aldo Ray, Jackie Coogan, Darlene Carviotto

DISCO GODFATHER (Transvue) A Generation International Pictures Presentation in color; Rated R; January release. CAST: Rudy Ray Moore, Jimmy Lynch, Jerry Jones, Lady Reed, Julius J. Carry III, Carol Speed

AN ENEMY OF THE PEOPLE (Warner Brothers) Producer-Director, George Schaefer; Executive Producer, Steve McQueen; Screenplay, Alexander Jacobs based on Arthur Miller's adaptation of Henrik Ibsen's play of the same title; Photography, Paul Lohmann; Editor, Sheldon Kahn; Music, Leonard Rosenman; Design, Eugene Lourie; Costumes, Noel Taylor; Assistant Director, Jack Aldworth; In Metrocolor; Rated G; 103 minutes; January release. CAST: Steve McQueen (Dr. Stockmann), Charles Durning (Peter Stockmann), Bibi Andersson (Catherine Stockmann), Eric Christmas (Morten Kiil), Michael Cristofer (Hovstad), Richard A. Dysart (Aslaksen), Michael Higgins (Billing), Richard Bradford (Capt. Forster), Ham Larsen (Morten Stockmann), John Levin (Ejlif Stockmann), Robin Pearson Rose (Petra Stockmann)

PACIFIC HIGH (Roy E. Disney) Producer, Roy E. Disney; Director, Michael Ahnemann; Photography, Stephen H. Burum; Editors, Thomas Stanford, Michael Ahnemann; Music, Robert F. Brunner; In Metro color; Rated R; 90 minutes; February release.

SURVIVAL RUN (Film Ventures International) Producer, Lance Hool; Director, Larry Spiegel; Executive Producers, Ruben Broido, Mel Bergman; Screenplay, Larry Spiegel, G. M. Cahill; Based on story by Cahill and Fredric Shore; Photography, Alex Phillips, Jr.; Music, Gary William Friedman; Editor, Chris Greenbury; In color; Rated R; 90 minutes; February release. CAST: Peter Graves, Ray Milland, Vincent Van Patten, Pedro Armendariz, Jr., Alan Conrad, Anthony Charnota, Gonzalo Vega, Cosie Costa, Randi Meryl, Marianne Sauvage, Robby Weaver, Danny Ades, Susan Pratt O'Hanlon

THE LAST MARRIED COUPLE IN AMERICA (Universal) Producers, Edward S. Feldman, John Herman Shaner; Director, Gilbert Cates; Screenplay, John Herman Shaner; Executive Producers, Gilbert Cates, Joseph Cates; Photography, Ralph Woolsey; Designer, Gene Callahan; Editor, Peter E. Berger; Costumes, Edith Head; Vicki Sanchez; Music, Charles Fox; Art Director, Peter Smith; Assistant Directors, Thomas Lofaro, Steve Lofaro; "We Could Have It All" sung by Maureen McGovern; Choreographer, Scott Salmon; "Do You Think I'm Sexy" sung by Rod Stewart, "Got to Be Real" sung by Cheryl Lynn; In Technicolor; 103 minutes; Rated R; February release. CAST: George Segal (Jeff), Natalie Wood (Mari), Richard Benjamin (Marv), Arlene Golonka (Sally), Alan Arbus (Al), Marilyn Sokol (Alice), Oliver Clark (Max), Priscilla Barnes (Helena), Dom DeLuise (Walter), Valerie Harper (Barbara), Bob Dishy (Howard), Mark Lonow (Tom), Sondra Currie (Lainy), Robert Wahler (Rick), and Catherine Hickland, Charlene Ryan, Murphy Dunne, David Rode, David Comfort, Ricky Segall, Stewart Moss, Colby Chester, Delia Salvi, Bebe Drake-Hooks, Edgy Lee, Mieko Kobayshi, Yvonne Wilder, Billy Holms, George Pentecost, David Bennett, Shari Summers, Jenny O'Hara, William Bogert, Robert Perault, Brad Maule, Jan Jorden, Vernon Weddle, G. Lewis Cates, Jenny Neumann, Lynne Marie Stewart, Oz Tortora

George Segal, Natalie Wood
in "The Last Married Couple . . ."
© Universal Studios
123

"Hot T-Shirts"

Heath Lamberts, Suzanne Somers
in "Nothing Personal"
© American International

THE AMERICAN SUCCESS COMPANY (Columbia) Producers, Daniel H. Blatt, Edgar J. Scherick; Director, William Richert; Screenplay, William Richert, Larry Cohen; Story, Larry Cohen; Music, Maurice Jarre; Photography, Anthony Richmond; Associate Producer, Pia I. Arnold; Designer, Rolf Zehetbauer; Costumes, Robert DeMora, Helga Pinnow; Editor, Ralph E. Winters; Art Director, Werner Achmann; Assistant Directors, Dietmar Siegert, Marijan Vajda; Choreographer, Cecilia Gruessing; In color; Rated PG; 94 minutes; March release. CAST: Jeff Bridges (Harry), Belinda Bauer (Sara), Ned Beatty (Elliot), Steven Keats (Rick), Bianca Jagger (Corinne), John Glover (Ernst), Mascha Gonska (Greta), Michael Durrell (Herman), Eva-Maria Meineke, Gunter Meisner, David Brooks, Marie Mardischewski, Sebastian Baur, Peer Brensing, Judy Brown, Michael Burger, Andrew Burleigh, Claudia Butenuth, Peter Capell, Loyd Catlett, Peter Chelsom, Conrad Dechert, Eunice Dechert, Erland Erlandson, Stephen Frances, Josef Frohlich, Claudia Golling, Wolfgang Klein, Ann Kligge, Regina Mardeck, Michaela May, Shelagh McLeod, Elisabeth Neumann-Viertel, Osman Ragheb, William Richert, Ute Willing

THE TRIALS OF ALGER HISS (Corinth Films) Producer-Director, John Lowenthal; Photography, Steven L. Alexander, Adam Giffard, Vic Losick, Mark Obenhaus, Edward Gray, William G. Markle; Editor, Marion Kraft; A History on Film presentation; In color, black and white; Not rated; 164 minutes; March release. A documentary.

TAKE IT TO THE LIMIT (Variety International Pictures) Producer-Director, Peter Starr; Executive Producer, Leroy Lefkowitz; Written by Charles Michael Lorre, Peter Starr; Photography, Michael Chevalier, Jeremy Lepard, Mark Zavad; Editor, John Bryant; Animation, Jon Wokuluk; Original Songs, Foreigner, Jean Luc Ponty, Arlo Guthrie, John McEuen, Tangerine Dream, Starwood; In DeLuxe Color; Rated PG; 95 minutes; March release. CAST: Barry Sheene, Russ Collins, Steve Baker, Scott Autrey, Mike Hailwood, Kenny Roberts

FORBIDDEN ZONE (Carl Borack) Producer-Director, Richard Elfman; Executive Producer, Gene Cunningham; Screenplay, Richard Elfman, M. Bright, Martin W. Nicholson, Nick Jones; Photography, Gregory Sandor; Editor-Associate Producer-Assistant Director, Martin W. Nicholson; Music, Danny Elfman; Design, Marie-Pascale Elfman; Art Director, David M. Makler; Set Design, Ken Corrone; In black and white; 76 minutes; Not rated; March release. CAST: Herve Villechaize (King Fausto), Susan Tyrrell (Queen), Marie-Pascale Elfman (Frenchy), Viva (Ex-Queen)

THE FIFTH FLOOR (Film Ventures International) Producer-Director, Howard Avedis; Story, Howard Avedis, Marlene Schmidt; Screenplay, Meyer Dolinsky; Executive Producer, Marlene Schmidt; Presented by Hickmar Productions in color; Rated R; 90 minutes; March release. CAST: Bo Hopkins, Dianne Hull, Patti D'Arbanville, Sharon Farrell, Mel Ferrer, Julie Adams, John David Carson

HOT T-SHIRTS (Cannon Group) Producer-Director, Chuck Vincent; Executive Producer, Tom Berman; Photography, Larry Revene; Screenplay, Chuck Vincent, Bill Slobodian; In color; Rated R; 86 minutes; March release. CAST: Ray Holland, Stephanie Lawlor, Pauline Rose, Corinne Alphen

THE LAST WORD (Variety International) formerly "Danny Travis"; Producers, Richard C. Abramson, Michael C. Varhol; Director, Roy Boulting; Screenplay, Michael Varhol, Greg Smith, L. M. Kit Carson; Based on story by Horatius Haeberle; Photography, Jules Brenner; Editor, George Grenville; Music, Carol Lees; Designer, Jack Collis; Executive Producers, A. J. Leydton, John Berglas, Reiner Walch; In color; Not rated; 105 minutes; March release. CAST: Richard Harris (Danny), Karen Black (Paula), Martin Landau (Garrity), Dennis Christopher (Ben), Biff McGuire (Gov. Davis), Christopher Guest (Roger), Penelope Milford (Denise), Bonnie Bartlett, Jorge Cervera, Nathan Cook, Linda Dangcil, Alex Henteloff, Pat McNamara, Michael Pataki, Netasha Ryan, Charles Siebert, James Staley, Richard Venture

Jan-Michael Vincent
in "Defiance"
© American International

Penelope Milford, Richard Harris, Dennis
Christopher in "The Last Word"

Donald Sutherland, Suzanne Somers
in "Nothing Personal"
© American International

Dan Grimaldi in "Don't Go In
the House" © Film Ventures

NOTHING PERSONAL (American International/Filmways)
Executive Producers, Alan Hamel, Jay Bernstein, Norman Hirschfield; Producer, David M. Perlmutter; Co-Producer. David Main; Director, George Bloomfield; Screenplay, Robert Kaufman; Photography, Laszlo George, Arthur Ibbetson; Art Director, Mary Kerr; Editor, George Appleby; Assistant Director, R. Martin Walters; Costumes, Lynda Kemp; In Movielab Color; Rated PG; 97 minutes; March release. CAST: Donald Sutherland (Prof. Roger Keller), Suzanne Somers (Abigail), Lawrence Dane (Robert), Roscoe Lee Brown (Paxton), Dabney Coleman (Tom), Saul Rubinek (Peter), Catherine O'Hara (Janet Samson), Maury Chakin (Kanook), Kate Lynch (Audrey), Hugh Webster (Ralph), Sean McCann (Jake), Ben Gordon, Eugene Levy, Rummy Bishop, Richard Monette, Gabe Cohen, Bonnie Brooks, Robert Benson, Ken Lamaire, Sam Moses, Pat Collins, Jack Duffy, Tony Rasato, Robert Christie

DEFIANCE (American International) Executive Producer, Robert J. Wunsch; Producers, William S. Gilmore, Jr., Jerry Bruckheimer; Director, John Flynn; Screenplay-Associate Producer, Thomas Michael Donnelly; Story, Thomas Michael Donnelly, Mark Tulin; Photography, Ric Waite; Editor, David Finfer; Designer, Bill Malley; Original Songs and Score, Gerard McMahon; A Necta Film in Movielab Color; Rated PG; 103 minutes; March release. CAST: Jan Michael Vincent (Tommy), Theresa Saldana (Marsha), Art Carney (Abe), Rudy Ramos (Angel), Joe Campanella (Karenski), Fernando Lopez (Kid), Danny Aiello (Carmine), Santos Morales (Paolo), Don Blakely (Abbie), Frank Pesce (Herbie), Lee Fraser (Bandana), Randy Herman (Tito), Alberto Vasquez (Slagg), Church Ortiz (Luis), East Carlo (El Bravo), Lenny Montana (Whacko), James Fictor (Father Rivera)

DRACULA'S LAST RITES (Cannon) Producer, Kelly Van Horn; Director, Domonic Paris; Screenplay, Ben Donnelly, Domonic Paris; Music, Paul Jost; A New Empire Feature Production in TVC color; Rated R; 88 minutes; March release. CAST: Patricia Lee Hammond, Gerald Fielding, Victor Jorge, Michael Lally

DON'T GO IN THE HOUSE (Film Ventures International) Producer, Ellen Hammill; Director, Joseph Ellison; Photography, Oliver Wood; Editor, Jane Kurson; Music, Richard Einhorn; Story, Joseph R. Masefield; Screenplay, Joseph Ellison, Ellen Hammill, Joseph R. Masefield; Associate Producers, Matthew Mallinson, Dennis Stephenson; Assistant Director, Monica Lange; Art Direction, Sarah Wood; Costumes, Sharon Lynch; Set Design, Peter Zsiba; In DeLuxe Color; Rated R; 90 minutes; March release. CAST: Dan Grimaldi (Donny), Robert Osth (Bobby), Ruth Dardick (Mrs. Kohler), Charlie Bonet (Ben), Bill Ricci (Vito), Dennis M. Hunter, John Hedberg, Johanna Brushay, Darcy Shean, Mary Ann Chin, Jim Donnegan, Claudia Folts, Denise Woods, Pat Williams, Colin McInness, Ralph D. Bowman, Joey Peschl, Connie Oaks, David McComb, Jean Manning, Ken Kelsch, Tom Brumberger, Nikki Kollins, Kim Roberts, Louise Grimaldi, Gloria Szymkovicz, David Brody, O'Mara Leary, Gail Turner, Eileen Dunn, Christian Isodore

STUCKEY'S LAST STAND (Royal Oak Films) Produced, Directed and Written by Lawrence G. Goldfarb; Executive Producer, Erich Von Forbes; Photography, Arthur J. Fitzsimmons; Music, Carson Whitsett; Art Director, Julia Norris; Editors, Arthur J. Fitzsimmons, Ethan Edwards; Assistant Director, Peg Berry; In color; Rated PG; 92 minutes; April release. CAST: Whit Reichert (Whit), Ray Anzalone (Russ), Will Shaw (Will), Tom Murray (Pete), Richard Consentino (Duke), Marilyn Terschluse (Billie), Jeanne L. Austin (Marianne), John Zimmerman (Gordon), Dan Dierdorf (Father), Pat Ball (Mother)

LIAR'S DICE Producers, Butros Makdissy, Ed Eubanks; Director, Issam B. Makdissy; Screenplay, Terry Eubanks Makdissy; Photography, Douglas Murray; Editor, Issam B. Makdissy; Music, Coleman Burke, Gary Yamani; In color; Not rated; 95 minutes; April release. CAST: Robert Ede (Joe), Terry Eubanks-Makdissy (Anne), Frank Triest (Jack), D. G. Buckles (Pete), Norma Small (Dottie), Phran Gauci (Janice), Rafik Assad (Jamil), Shirley James (Sharon), Phil DeCarla (Tony), Jerry LaRue (Mel), Judd Strelo (Boy), Jeannette Mignola (New Waitress), John Lovell (Father)

"Dracula's Last Rights"
© Cannon

Jan-Michael Vincent, Theresa Saldana
in "Defiance" © American International

Tatum O'Neal, Kristy McNichol
in "Little Darlings"
© Paramount Pictures

Gary Busey, Annette O'Toole in "Foolin'
Around" © Columbia Pictures

LITTLE DARLINGS (Paramount) Producer, Stephen J. Friedman; Director, Ronald F. Maxwell; Screenplay, Kimi Peck, Dalene Young; Story, Kimi Peck; Photography, Fred Batka; Music, Charles Fox; Lyrics, Carole Bayer Sager; Editor, Pembroke J. Herring; Associate Producer, Kimi Peck; Design, William Hiney; Costumes, Joseph Aulisi; Assistant Directors, Michael Daves, Bob Doherty; In Panavision and Metrocolor; Rated R; 95 minutes; March release. CAST: Tatum O'Neal (Ferris), Kristy McNichol (Angel), Armand Assante (Gary), Matt Dillon (Randy), Maggie Blye (Ms. Bright), Nicolas Coster (Whitney), Krista Errickson (Cinder), Alexa Kenin (Dana), Abby Bluestone (Chubby), Cynthia Nixon (Sunshine), Simone Schachter (Carrots), Jenn Thompson (Penelope), Troas Hayes (Diane), Mary Betten (Miss Nichols), Marianne Gordon (Mrs. Whitney), Paige Connor, Edith Ivey, J. Don Ferguson, Laura Whyte, Suzanne Illavacek, Scott MacLellan, Martha Wollbrinck, Bill Gribble, Cathy Larson

SATURN 3 (Associated Film Distribution) Executive Producer, Martin Starger; Producer-Director, Stanley Donen; Screenplay, Martin Amis; Story, John Barry; Photography, Billy Williams; Music, Elmer Bernstein; Editor, Richard Marden; Associate Producer, Eric Rattray; Designer, Stuart Craig; Art Director, Norman Dorme; In color and Dolby Sound; Rated R; 95 minutes; Presented by Lord Grade in association with Elliott Kastner; March release. CAST: Farrah Fawcett (Alex), Kirk Douglas (Adam), Harvey Keitel (Benson/James), Douglas Lambert (Capt. James), Ed Bishop (Harding), Christopher Muncke (2nd Crewman)

THE OFFENDERS (B Movies) Directed, Written and Photographed by Scott B and Beth B; Music, Bob Mason, Adele Bertei, Lydia Lunch, John Lurie, Scott B, Beth B, Terry Burns, Ed Steinberg, Alley; In color; Not rated; 100 minutes; March release. CAST: Adele Bertei (Laura), Bill Rice (Dr. Moore), John Lurie (The Lizard), Johnny O'Kane, Robin Winters, Pat Place, Laura Kennedy, Judy Nylon, Marcia Resnick, Evan Lurie, Walter Lure, Anna Sui, Barvara Klar, Cynthia Womersley, Diego Cortez, Lydia Lunch, Kristian Hoffman, Bradley Field, Edit De Ak, Robert Smith, Terry Robinson, Clio Young, Harry Spitz, Gerard Hovagimyan, Kirsten Bates, Scott B. Kristof Kolhofer

FOOLIN' AROUND (Columbia) Producer, Arnold Kopelson; Director, Richard T. Heffron; Story, David Swift; Screenplay, Mike Kane, David Swift; Music, Charles Bernstein; Associate Producer, Deborah Castle; Lyrics, Jim Seals; Editor, Peter Zinner; Designer, Fernando Carrere; Photography, Philip Lathrop; Assistant Directors, Craig Huston, Peter Schindler; Costumes, Joe Tompkins; In DeLuxe Color; Rated PG; 111 minutes; March release. CAST: Gary Busey (Wes), Annette O'Toole (Susan), John Calvin (Whitley), Eddie Albert (Daggett), Cloris Leachman (Samantha), Tony Randall (Peddicord), Michael Talbott (Clay), Shirley Kane (Aunt Eunice), W. H. Macy (Bronski), Beth Rosacker (Rickie), Roy Jenson (Blue), Gene Lebell (Paul)

HIDE IN PLAIN SIGHT (United Artists/MGM) Producers, Robert Christiansen, Rick Rosenberg; Associate Producer, Fred T. Gallo; Director, James Caan; Screenplay, Spencer Eastman; Based on book by Leslie Waller; Photography, Paul Lohmann; Design, Pato Guzman; Editors, Fredric Steinkamp, William Steinkamp; Music, Leonard Rosenman; Assistant Directors, David McGiffert, Fred Blankfein, C. Tad Devlin; In Panavision and Metrocolor; Rated PG; 98 minutes; March release. CAST: James Caan (Thomas Hacklin, Jr.), Jill Eikenberry (Alisa), Robert Viharo (Scolese), Joe Grifasi (Matty), Barbra Rae (Ruthie), Kenneth McMillan (Sam), Josef Sommer (Jason), Danny Aiello (Sal), Thomas Hill (Bobby), Chuck Hicks (Frankie), Andrew Gordon Fenwick (Andy), Heather Bicknell (Junie), David Clennon (Richard), Peter Maloney (Lee), Ken Sylk (Frantuzzi), Leonardo Cimino (Venucci), Nick Corello (Fiacco), Tom Signorelli (Moriarty), Alice Drummond (Mrs. Novack), Beatrice Winde (Unemployment Clerk), Anne Helm, Robert Gerringer, Terrence Currier, Josephine Nichols, Walter Scott, James DeCloss, Danny Costa, Charles Hallahan, Eddy Donno, Gerald Aleck Cantor, Dan Zanghi, H. Jack Jaeger, Nancy Weber, Sidney Ehrenreich, Gary Pace, Carolyn Ferrini, Vinnie DeCarlo, Vincent Cavalleri, Lorena McDonald, John Kiouses, Mina Evans, Jeff Ring, Keith Watts, H. P. Evetts, Ken Bellet, Frederick Seaton, Anne McLeod, Tony Mancini, Ben Gerard, Madonna Young, Sam Ippolito, Joey Giambra, Irv Weinstein

Farrah Fawcett, Kirk Douglas in "Saturn 3"
© AFD

James Caan, Jill Eikenberry in "Hide in Plain
Sight" © MGM

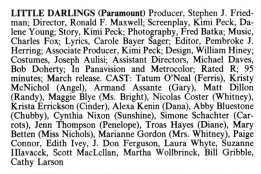

Doug McClure, Ann Turkel in "Humanoids"
© New World Pictures

"America Lost and Found"

HUMANOIDS FROM THE DEEP (New World) Producer, Martin B. Cohen; Director, Barbara Peeters; Story, Frank Arnold, Martin B. Cohen; Screenplay, Frederick James; Co-Producer, A. Hunt Lowry; Music, James Horner; Photography, Daniel Lacambre; Editor, Mark Goldblatt; Art Director, Michael Erler; Humanoids, Rob Bottin; In color; Rated R; 80 minutes; April release. CAST: Doug McClure (Jim), Ann Turkel (Susan), Vic Morrow (Hank), Cindy Weintraub (Carol), Anthony Penya (Johnny), Denise Galik (Linda), Lynn Theel (Peggy), Meegan King (Jerry), Breck Costin (Tommy), Hoke Howell (Deke), Don Maxwell (Dickie), David Strassman (Billy), Greg Travis, Linda Shayne, Lisa Glaser, Bruce Monette, Shawn Erler, Frank Arnold, Amy Barrett, Jo Williams, Henry T. Williams, Lyle Isom, Jonathan Lehan

WHERE THE BUFFALO ROAM (Universal) Producer-Director, Art Linson; Screenplay, John Kaye; Based on "The Twisted Legend of Dr. Hunter S. Thompson"; Music, Neil Young; Photography, Tak Fujimoto; Design, Richard Sawyer; Editor, Christopher Greenbury; Associate Producer, Mack Bing; Assistant Directors, Gene Law, Judith Vogelsang; In Technicolor; Rated R; 98 minutes; April release. CAST: Peter Boyle (Lazlo), Bill Murray (Hunter Thompson), Bruno Kirby (Marty), Rene Auberjonois (Harris), R. G. Armstrong (Judge), Danny Goldman (Porter), Rafael Campos (Rojas), Leonard Frey (Desk Clerk), Leonard Gaines (Super Fan), DeWayne Jessie (Man #1), Mark Metcalf (Dooley), Jon Matthews (Billy), Joseph Ragno (Willins), Quinn Redeker (Pilot), Lisa Taylor (Ruthie), Danny Tucker (Narcotics Agent), Susan Kellermann (Waitress), John Acevedo, Phillip L. Allan, Lee Allen, Juli Andelman, Janit Baldwin, Bruce Barbour, Marsha Bissler, Jack Caddin, David Castle, Linden Chiles, Suzanne Coltrin, Caesar Cordova, Michael Cornelison, Brian Cummings, Ron Cummins, Joshua Daniel, Sonny Davis, Richard M. Dixon; Susan Elliott, Suzanne Elliott, Les Engel, Reginald H. Farmer, Lou Felder, Randy Glass, Doris Hargrave, Jim Healy, Cork Hubbert, Doreen Jaros, Sunny Johnson, Garrie Kelly, Charles Konya, Marguerite Lamar, Jerry Maren, Miles McNamara, John Moio, Richard Seff

AMERICA LOST AND FOUND (Media Study) Producers and Directors, Tom Johnson, Lance Bird; Written by John Crowley; Editor, Kate Hirson; Assistant Producers, Matt Clarke, Rory Tetrault, Chrystie Munves; Music, Arthur Gorson; Narration spoken by Pat Hingle; Not rated; In black and white; 65 minutes; April release.

DON'T ANSWER THE PHONE! (Crown International) Producer-Director-Screenplay, Robert Hammer; Executive Producer, Michael Towers; Co-Producer-Writer, Michael Castle; Photography, James Carter; Music, Byron Allred; Editor, Joseph Fineman; A Scorpion Production; In Metrocolor; Rated R; 94 minutes; April release. CAST: James Westmoreland (Chris), Flo Gerrish (Dr. Gale), Ben Frank (Hatcher), Nicholas Worth (Kirk), Stan Haze (Adkins), Gary Allen (Feldon), Pamela Bryant (Sue), Ted Chapman (Bald Man), Denise Galick (Lisa), Dale Kalberg, Deborah Leah Land, Tom Lasswell, Ellen Karston, Mike Levine, Chuck Mitchell, Victor Mohica, Susanna Severeid, Paula Warner, Chris Wallace

ON THE NICKEL (Rose's Park Productions) Produced, Directed and Written by Ralph Waite; Associate Producer–Production Manager, William Bushnell; Photography, Ric Waite; Editor, Wendy Greene Bricmont; Music, Fredric Myrow; Title Song written and sung by Tom Waits; Assistant Directors, Ralph Ferrin, James M. Freitag; In color; Rated R; 96 minutes; April release. CAST: Donald Moffat (Sam), Ralph Waite (C. G.), Hal Williams (Paul), Penelope Allen (Rose), Jack Kehoe (Bad Mood), Danny Ades (God Bless), Paul Weaver (Hill), Ina Gould (Estelle), Jack O'Leary (Big William), Cano Graham (Sliver), James Gammon (Peanut John), Arthur Space (Soapy Post), Bert Conway (Bert), Jamie Sanchez (Joe), Tom Mahoney (Bobby D), Edmund Villa (Henry), Lane Smith (Preacher), Ellen Geer (Louise), Gayle Vance (Beatrice), Mike Robelo, Nathan Adler, Pattick Tovatt, George Loros, LeRoy Wheeler, Arnold Johnson, Carmen Filpi, Pat Corley, Melvin F. Allen, Hirsch Adell, Herb Evans, John Ryan, Peter Alsop, Charles Comfort, Kerry Shear Waite, Lou Gilbert, Cecil Jordan, Allen Buck, Sosimo, Charles Parks, John Perryman, Frank Savino. Steve Tucker

Bill Murray, Peter Boyle in "Where the Buffalo Roam" © Universal Studios

Ralph Waite, Penelope Allen in "On the Nickel" © Rose Park

Roger Corman in "Triple Play"

Kirk Douglas, Keith Gordon
in "Home Movies" © United Artists

THE PSYCHOTRONIC MAN (International Harmony) Producer, Peter Spelson; Director, Jack M. Sell; Screenplay, Spelson and Sell; Photography, Jack M. Sell; Score, Tommy Irons; Art Director, Fred Becht; Editor, Bill Reese; In AstroColor; Rated PG; 90 minutes; April release. CAST: Peter Spelson (Rocky), Christopher Carbis (O'Brien), Curt Colbert (Jackson), Robin Newton (Kathy), Paul Marvel (Steinberg), Jeff Caliendo (Maloney), Lindsey Novak (Mrs. Foscoe), Irwin Lewin (Prof), Corney Morgan (Gorman), Bob McDonald (Old Man)

TRIPLE PLAY: "Roger Corman, Hollywood's Wild Angel" produced and directed by Christian Blackwood; Narrated by Richard Koszarski; Music, Rich Look, Cathy Chamberlain; In color; 58 minutes. CAST: David Carradine, Peter Fonda, Martin Scorsese, Roger Corman. "Memoirs of a Movie Palace" produced and directed by Christian Blackwood; Commentary written by Elliott Stein; Narrated by Eli Wallach; 45 minutes. "Yesterday's Witness" produced and directed by Christian Blackwood; Written by Raymond Fielding; In black and white and color; Narrated by Lowell Thomas; 52 minutes; April release. CAST: Ed Herlihy, Lowell Thomas, Harry Von Zell

GET ROLLIN' (Get Rollin' Group) Produced, Directed and Written by J. Terrance Mitchell; Photography, Joseph J. Friedman; Editors, Terrance Mitchell, Peggy Ann Stulberg; Euphrates/Plotnick/DuArt Production in color; Not rated; 85 minutes; April release. CAST: Pat "The Cat" Richardson, Vinzerrelli Brown, Inez Daniels

HOW TO SCORE WITH GIRLS (NMD) Produced, Directed and Written by Ogden Lowell; Music, Earl Rose, Robert N. Langworthy; An Alpenglow production in Technicolor; Rated R; 82 minutes; April release. CAST: Ron Osborne (Steve), Larry Jacobs (Harry), Richard Young (Frank), Sandra McKnight (Joanna), Arlana Blue (Joy), Janice Fuller (Granola), Michelle Matthau (Sue), Grace Davies (Jean), Barbara Derecktor (Robin), Mary Ward (Mike), Adolphus King III, Richard Currier, Bill Richardson, Darlene Miller, Anne Wanders, Teddy Raye, Maureen Madden, Trish Garlan, Alan Miles, Pelati Pons, Dallas Mayr, Shakari Cichon, Cary Eckardt, Robin Ratner, Raymond Cortnee, Chris Chafouleas

ON COMPANY BUSINESS (Isla Negra) Producers, Howard Dratch, Allan Francovich; Director, Allan Francovich; Photography, Kevin Keating; Editor, Veronica Selver; Not rated; 180 minutes; April release. A documentary on the Central Intelligence Agency with Philip Agee, Victor Marchetti, John Stockwell.

DEVILS THREE (Aquarius) Producer-Director, Bobby A. Suarez; Screenplay, J. Zucherro, D. Adair; Executive Producer, Louis George; Music, Gene Kauer, Douglas Lackey; An Arista Films presentation in color; Rated R; May release. CAST: Marrie Lee, Johnny Wilson, Dick Adair, Cynthia Rodrigo, Ted Deelman, Danny Rojo

HOME MOVIES (United Artists Classics) Producers, Brian DePalma, Jack Temchin, Gil Adler; Director, Brian DePalma; Screenplay, Robert Harders, Gloria Norris, Kim Ambler, Dana Edelman, Stephen LeMay, Charles Loventhal; Story, Brian DePalma; Photography, James L. Carter; Editor, Corky Ohara; Art Director, Tom Surgal; Music, Pino Donaggio; In color; Rated PG; 90 minutes; May release. CAST: Kirk Douglas (Dr. Tuttle), Nancy Allen (Kristina), Keith Gordon (Denis), Gerrit Graham (James), Vincent Gardenia (Dr. Byrd), Mary Davenport (Mrs. Byrd)

KILL OR BE KILLED (Film Ventures International) Producer, Ben Volk; Director, Ivan Hall; Karate Sequences, Norman Robinson; Screenplay, C. F. Beyers-Boshoff; Photography, Mane Eotha; Editor, Brian Varaday; In color; Rated PG; 90 minutes; May release. CAST: James Ryan, Charlotte Michelle, Norman Combes, Daniel Du Plessis

THE HAPPY HOOKER (Cannon Group) Producer, Menahem Golan, Yoram Globus; Director, Alan Roberts; Photography, Stephen Gray; Music, Tom Perry, Don Bagley; Art Director, George Costello; Editor, Nicholas Wentworth; Associate Producer, Ronnie Hadar; Screenplay, Devin Goldenberg; In Color; Rated R; 88 minutes; May release. CAST: Martine Beswicke (Xaviera), Chris Lemmon (Robby), Adam West (Lionel), Richard Deacon (Joseph), Phil Silvers (Warkoff), Edie Adams (Rita)

Vinzerrelli Brown in "Get Rollin"

Martine Beswicke, Adam West in "The Happy Hooker Goes Hollywood" © Cannon

Walter Brooke, Don Adams, Patrick Gorman in "The Nude Bomb" © Universal Studios

Murray Langston, Chuck Barris in "The Gong Show Movie" © Universal Studios

THE NUDE BOMB (Universal) Producer, Jennings Lang; Director, Clive Donner; Screenplay, Arne Sultan, Bill Dana, Leonard B. Stern; Based on characters created by Mel Brooks and Buck Henry; Photography, Harry L. Wolf; Designer, William Tuntke; Editors, Walter Hannemann, Phil Tucker; Music, Lalo Schifrin; Assistant Directors, Don Zepfel, Chuck Sanford; Costumes, Burton Miller; In color; Rated PG; 94 minutes; May release. CAST: Don Adams (Maxwell), Sylvia Kristel (Agent 34), Rhonda Fleming (Edith), Dana Elcar (Chief), Pamela Hensley (Agent 36), Andrea Howard (Agent 22), Norman Lloyd (Carruthers), Bill Dana (Seigle), Gary Imhoff (Jerry), Sarah Rush (Pam), Vittorio Gassman (Nino), Walter Brooke (Ambassador), Thomas Hill (President), Ceil Cabot (Landlady), Joey Forman (Agent 13), Patrick Gorman (French Delegate), Earl Maynard (Jamaican Delegate), Alex Rodine (Russian Delegate), Richard Sanders (German Delegate), Vito Scotti (Italian Delegate), Byron Webster (English Delegate), Horst Ehrhardt (Polish Delegate), James Gavin, Gary Young

DIE LAUGHING (Orion) Executive Producer, Jon Peters; Producers, Mark Canton, Robby Benson; Director, Jeff Werner; Story, Scott Parker; Screenplay, Jerry Segal, Robby Benson, Scott Parker; Music, Robby Benson, Jerry Segal; Editor, Neil Travis; Designer, James H. Spencer; Photography, David Myers; Associate Producer, Don MacDonald; Assistant Directors, David Whorf, Steve Lofaro; In Technicolor; Rated PG; 108 minutes; May release. CAST: Robby Benson (Pinsky), Linda Grovenor (Amy), Charles Durning (Arnold), Elsa Lanchester (Sophie), Bud Cort (Mueller), Rita Taggart (Thelma), Mary Zagon (Friend), Larry Hankin (Bock), Sammuel Krachmalnick (Zhukov), Michael David Lee (Einstein), Peter Coyote (Davis), Charles Fleisher (Charlie), Charles Harwood, Melanie Henderson, Carel Struycken, Chuck Dorsett, Morgan Upton, Christopher E. Pray, John Bracci, James Cranna, Joe Bellan, John Tim Burrus, Maurice Argent, Rhoda Gemignani, Nick Outin

THE GONG SHOW MOVIE (Universal) Producer, Budd Granoff; Director, Chuck Barris; Screenplay, Chuck Barris, Robert Downey; Photography, Richard C. Glouner; Art Director, Robert K. Kinoshita; Editor, James Mitchell; Music, Milton DeLugg; Co-Producer, Byron Roberts; Associate Producer, Linda Howard; Assistant Directors, William H. White, Jonathan Zimmerman; Editors, Sam Vitale, Jacqueline Cambas; In color; Rated R; 89 minutes; May release. CAST: Robin Altman, Chuck Barris, Brian O'Mullin, Jack Bernardi, Satisfaction, William Tregoe, Harvey Alpert, Herman Alpert, Mabel King, Lillie Shelton, James B. Douglas, Harvey Lembeck, Ed Marinaro, Murray Langston, Melvin Presar, Steve Garvey, Jamie Farr, Pat Cranshaw, Cathleen Cordell, Jim Winburn, Bella Bruck, Starr Hester, David Sheiner, Pat McCormick, Patty Andrews, Jaye P. Morgan, Gary Mule Deer, Rip Taylor, Rosy Grier, Norman Blankenship, Darvy Traylor, Ronald Carr

THE HOLLYWOOD KNIGHTS (Columbia) Executive Producer, William Tennant; Producer, Richard Lederer; Direction and Screenplay, Floyd Mutrux; Story, Floyd Mutrux, Richard Lederer, William Tennant; Photography, William A. Fraker; Art Director, Lee Fischer; Editor, Stan Allen; Assistant Directors, Luigi Alfano, Chris Soldo; In Metrocolor; Rated R; 95 minutes; May release. CAST: Fran Drescher (Sally), Leigh French (Jacqueline), Randy Gornel (Wheatly), Gary Graham (Jimmy), Sandy Helberg (Officer), James Jeter (Smitty), Stuart Pankin (Dudley), P. R. Paul (Simpson), Michelle Pfeiffer (Suzie), Richard Schaal (Nevans), Gailard Sartain (Rimbeau), Robert Wuhl (Turk), Tony Danza (Duke)

UNDERGROUND U.S.A. (New Cinema) Produced-Directed and Written by Eric Mitchell; Photography, Tom DiCillo; Editor, J. P. Roland-Levy; Music, James White and the Blacks, Lounge Lizards, Walter Stedding; Co-Producer, Erdner Rauschalle; Assistant Director, Becky Johnston; In color; Not rated; 85 minutes; May release. CAST: Patti Astor (Vickie), Eric Mitchell (Hustler), Rene Ricard (Kenneth), Tom Wright (Frank), Jackie Curtis (Roommate), Cookie Mueller, Taylor Mead, Duncan Smith, Steve Mass, Terry Toye, John Lurie

Elsa Lanchester, Robby Benson in "Die Laughing" © Orion Pictures

Michelle Pfeiffer, Tony Danza in "Hollywood Knights" © Columbia Pictures

129

Adrienne King, Harry Crosby in "Friday
the 13th" © Paramount Pictures

Count Basie in "The Last of the
Blue Devils"

FRIDAY THE 13th (Paramount) Producer-Director, Sean S. Cunningham; Screenplay, Victor Miller; Associate Producer, Stephen Miner; Music, Harry Manfredini; Photography, Barry Abrams; Editor, Bill Freda; Art Director, Virginia Field; Assistant Directors, Cindy Veazey, Stephen Ross; In Panavision and color; Rated R; 95 minutes; May release. CAST: Betsy Palmer (Mrs. Voorhees), Adrienne King (Alice), Harry Crosby (Bill), Laurie Bartram (Brenda), Mark Nelson (Ned), Jeannine Taylor (Marcie), Robbi Morgan (Annie), Kevin Bacon (Jack), Peter Brouwer (Steve), Rex Everhart (Truck Driver), Ronn Carroll (Sgt. Tierney), Ron Millkie (Dorf), Walt Gorney (Crazy Ralph), Willie Adams (Barry), Debra S. Hayes (Claudette), Dorothy Kobs (Trudy), Sally Anne Golden (Sandy), Mary Rocco (Operator), Ken L. Parker (Doctor), Ari Lehman (Jason)

BEYOND EVIL (IFI/Scope III) Producers, David Baughn, Herb Freed; Executive Producer, Roven Akiba; Director, Herb Freed; Screenplay, Herb Freed, Paul Ross; Based on story by David Baughn; Photography, Ken Plotin; Editor, Rick Westover; In color; Rated R; 94 minutes; May release. CAST: John Saxon (Larry), Lynda Day George (Barbara), Michael Dante (Del), Mario Milano (Albanos), Janice Lynde (Alma), David Opatoshu (Dr. Solomon), Anne Marisse (Leia), Zitto Kazaan (Esteban)

THE HEARSE (Crown International) Executive Producer, Newton P. Jacobs; Producer, Mark Tenser; Director, George Bowers; Photography, Mori Kawa; Screenplay, William Bleich; Based on idea by Mark Tenser; Music, Webster Lewis; Editor, George Berndt; Art Director, Keith Michl; Assistant Directors, John Curran, Pete Robinson; In Metrocolor; Rated PG; 100 minutes; June release. CAST: Trish Van Devere (Jane), Joseph Cotten (Walter), David Gautreaux (Tom), Donald Hotton (Rev. Winston), Med Flory (Sheriff), Donald Petrie (Luke), Christopher McDonald (Peter), Perry Lang (Paul), Fredric Franklyn (Gordon), Olive Dunbar (Mrs. Gordon), Al Hansen (Bo), Dominic Barto (Driver), Nicholas Shields (Dr. Greenwalt), Chuck Mitchell (Counterman), Allison Balson (Alice), Jimmy Gatherum (Boy), Victoria Eubank (Lois), Tanya Bowers (Schoolgirl)

THE LAST OF THE BLUE DEVILS (Bruce Ricker) Producer-Director, Bruce Ricker; Executive Producer, Mitchell Donian; Editor, Thomasin Henkel; Written by John Arnoldy, Bruce Ricker; Co-Producer, Susan Strausberg; Associate Producers, Victoria Tarlow, John Arnoldly, Nick Napolitano, Timothy M. Taylor; Photography, Arne Johnson, Eric Menn, Bob Gardner; In color; Not rated; 91 minutes; June release. With Count Basie and His Orchestra, Big Joe Turner, Jay McShann, Buddy Anderson, Ernie Williams, Eddie Durham, Speedy Huggins, Budd Johnson, Baby Lovett, Charles McPherson, Paul Quinichette, Gene Ramey, Herman Walder, Jimmy Forrest, Crook Goodwin, Curtis Foster, Paul Gunther, Jo Jones, Sonny Kenner, Jesse Price, Buster Smith, Richard Smith, Claude Williams, Milton Morris, Charlie Parker, Lester Young

COVERT ACTION (21st Century) Director, Romolo Guerrieri; In color, Rated R; 80 minutes; June release. CAST: David Janssen, Corinne Clery, Maurizio Merli, Arthur Kennedy, Philippe Leroy

NIGHT OF THE JUGGLER (Columbia) Producer, Jay Weston; Director, Robert Butler; Screenplay, Bill Norton, Sr., Rick Natkin; From novel by William P. McGivern; Photography, Victor J. Kemper; Executive Producer, Arnold Kopelson; Associate Producer, Stephen F. Kesten; Editor, Argyle Nelson; Music, Artie Kane; Design, Stuart Wurtzel; Assistant Directors, Mike Haley, Ron Walsh, Mel Howard; Costumes, Peggy Farrell; Set, John Godfrey; In Technicolor; Rated R; 101 minutes; June release. CAST: James Brolin (Sean), Cliff Gorman (Gus), Richard Castellano (Tonelli), Linda G. Miller (Barbara), Barton Heyman (Preacher), Sully Boyar (Larry), Julie Carmen (Marie), Abby Bluestone (Kathy), Dan Hedaya (Barnes), Mandy Patinkin (Cabbie), Marco St. John (H.R. Clayton III), Frank Adu (Wino), Nancy Andrews (Mrs. Logan), Rick Anthony (M.C.), Tony Azito (Cashier), Tally Brown (Peep Show Owner), Blair Burrows, Joseph Carberry, Rosanna Carter, Rony Clanton, Mila Conway, Tito Goya, Delphi Harrington, Murray Horwitz, Frank Irizzary, Dorothy Lyman, Ruth Maynard, Ellen Parker, Samm-Art Williams, Arthur French, Richard Gant, James Moriarty

Trish Van Devere, David Gautreaux
in "The Hearse" © Crown International

Julie Carmen, James Brolin in "Night of the Juggler"
© Columbia Pictures

Stacey Nelkin, Hutch Parker in "Up the Academy" © Warner Bros.

Art Carney, Meat Loaf, Rhonda Bates in "Roadie" © United Artists

UP THE ACADEMY (Warner Brothers) Producers, Marvin Worth, Danton Rissner; Director, Robert Downey; Executive Producer, Bernie Brillstein; Screenplay, Tom Patchett, Jay Tarses; Photography, Harry Stradling; Designer, Peter Wooley; Editor, Bud Molin; Assistant Directors, James J. Quinn, Kalai Strode; Set, Mary Swanson; In Panavision, Technicolor, Dolby Stereo; Rated R; 96 minutes; June release; Presented by Mad Magazine. CAST: Wendell Brown (Ike), Tom Citera (Hash), J. Hutchison (Oliver), Ralph Macchio (Chooch), Harry Teinowitz (Ververgaert), Tom Poston (Sisson), Ian Wolfe (Commandant), Antonio Fargas (Coach), Stacy Nelkin (Candy), Barbara Bach (Bliss), Leonard Frey (Keck), Luke Andreas (Vitto), Candy Ann Brown, King Coleman, Rosalie Citera, Yvonne Francis, James G. Robertson, Rosemary Eliot, Louis Zorich, Robert Lynn Mock, Tyrees Allen, Eric Hanson, Ken White, Patrick McKenna, Robert Scopa

WHOLLY MOSES! (Columbia) Producer, Freddie Fields; Director, Gary Weis; Executive Producer, David Begelman; Screenplay, Guy Thomas; Music, Patrick Williams; Editor, Sidney Levin; Costumes, Buy Verhille; Design, Dale Hennesy; Photography, Frank Stanley; Assistant Directors, L. Andrew Stone, Herbert S. Adelman; Set, Diane Wager; Choreographer, Jaime Rogers; In Panavision and Metrocolor; Rated PG; 109 minutes; June release. CAST: Dudley Moore (Harvey/Herschel), Laraine Newman (Zoe/Zerelda), James Coco (Hyssop), Paul Sand (Angel of the Lord), Jack Gilford (Tailor), Dom DeLuise (Shadrach), John Houseman (Archangel), Madeline Kahn (Sorceress), David L. Lander (Beggar), Richard Pryor (Pharaoh), John Ritter (Devil), Richard B. Shull (Jethro), Tanya Boyd (Princess), Ruth Manning (Landlady), Walker Edmiston (Voice of God), Andrea Martin (Zipporah), Stan Ross (Mohammed), William Watson, Sam Weisman, Jeffrey Jacquet, Howard Mann, Charles Thomas Murphy, Hap Lawrence, David Murphy, Tom Baker, Sandy Ward, Lee Wilkof, Maryedith Burrell, Rod McCary, Brion James, Lois Robbins, Shelley Johnson, Michael Champion, Lauren Frost, Ion Teodorescu, Nick Mele

ROADIE (United Artists) Producer, Carolyn Pfeiffer; Director, Alan Rudolph; Screenplay, Big Boy Medlin, Michael Ventura; Executive Producer, Zalman King; Associate Producer, John E. Pommer; Photography, David Myers; Designer, Paul Peters; Music, Craig Hundley; Assistant Directors, Ed Ledding, Bruce Solow; In Dolby Stereo and Technicolor; Rated PG; 106 minutes; June release. CAST: Meat Loaf (Travis), Kaki Hunter (Lola), Art Carney (Corpus), Gailard Sartain (B. B.), Don Cornelius (Mohammed), Rhonda Bates (Alice), Joe Spano (Ace), Richard Marion (George), Sonny Davis, Ginger Varney, Cindy Wills, Allan Graf, Merle Kilgore, Ramblin' Jack Elliott, Roy Orbison, Hank Williams, Jr., Hector Britt, Larry Lindsey, Hamilton Camp, Deborah Harry, Ray Benson, Alice Cooper, Larry Marshall, Alvin Crow

HOW TO BEAT THE HIGH COST OF LIVING (Filmways) Executive Producer, Samuel Z. Arkoff; Producers, Jerome M. Zeitman, Robert Kaufman; Director, Robert Scheerer; Screenplay, Robert Kaufman; Story Leonora Thuna; Associate Producer, Robin Krause; Photography, Jim Crabe; Assistant Director, Irby Smith; Designer, Larry Paull; Editor, Bill Butler; Music, Patrick Williams; A Cinema 77 Film in color; Rated PG; 110 minutes; June release. CAST: Susan Saint James (Jane), Jane Curtin (Elaine), Jessica Lange (Louise), Richard Benjamin (Albert), Fred Willard (Robert), Eddie Albert (Max), Dabney Coleman (Heintzel), Art Metrano (Attendant), Ronnie Schell (Bill), Garrett Morris (Power and Light Man), Cathryn Damon (Natalie), Sybil Dannind (Charlotte), Al Checco (Tim), Carmen Zapata (Mama), Dru Wagner (Harriet)

GALAXINA (Crown International) Producer, Marylin J. Tenser; Executive Producer, Newton P. Jacobs; Direction and Screenplay, William Sachs; Photography, Dean Cundy; Designer, Tom Turlley; Editor, Larry Bock; In Panavision and color; Rated R; 95 minutes; June release. CAST: Stephen Macht (Thor), Dorothy R. Stratten (Galaxina), James David Hinton (Buzz), Avery Schreiber (Capt. Butt), Ronald Knight (Ordric), Lionel Smith (Maurice), Tad Horino (Sam), Herb Kaplowitz (Kitty), Nancy McCauley (Elexia), Fred D. Scott (Commander), George E. Mather (Horn Man)

Laraine Newman, Dudley Moore in "Wholly Moses!" © Columbia

James David Hinton, Dorothy Stratten, Stephen Macht in "Galaxina" © Crown International **131**

Bill Murray, Chevy Chase in "Caddyshack"
© Orion Pictures

Treat Williams, Lisa Eichhorn in "Why Would
I Lie?" © United Artists

CADDYSHACK (Orion) Executive Producer, Jon Peters; Producer, Douglas Kenney; Director, Harold Ramis; Screenplay, Brian Doyle-Murray, Harold Ramis, Douglas Kenney; Photography, Stevan Larner; Designer, Stan Jolley; Songs, Kenny Loggins; Music, Johnny Mandel; Editor, William Carruth; Associate Producer, Don MacDonald; Assistant Directors, David Whorf, Charles Persons; Editor, Robert Barrere; Art Director, George Szeptycki; In Technicolor; Rated R; 99 minutes; July release. CAST: Chevy Chase (Ty), Rodney Dangerfield (Al), Ted Knight (Judge), Michael O'Keefe (Danny), Bill Murray (Carl), Sarah Holcomb (Maggie), Scott Colomby (Tony), Cindy Morgan (Lacey), Dan Resin (Dr. Beeper), Henry Wilcoxon (Bishop), Elaine Aiken (Mrs. Noonan), Albert Salmi (Noonan), Ann Ryerson (Grace), Brian Doyle Murray (Lou), Hamilton Mitchell (Motormouth), Peter Berkrot (Angie), John F. Barmon, Jr. (Spaulding), Lois Kibbee (Mrs. Smalls), Brian McConnachie (Scott), Scott Powell, Ann Crilley, Cordis Heard, Scott Sudden, Jackie Davis, Thomas Carlin, Minerva Scelza, Chuck Rodent

RAISE THE TITANIC! (Associated Film Distribution) Executive Producer, Martin Starger; Producer, William Frye; Director, Jerry Jameson; Screenplay, Adam Kennedy; Adaptation, Eric Hughes; Based on novel by Clive Cussler; Photography, Matthew F. Leonetti; Music, John Barry; Design, John F. De Cuir; Editors, J. Terry Williams, Robert F. Shugrue; Assistant Directors, Jim Westman, Scott Easton, Paul Chavez; Art Director, John F. DeCuir, Jr.; Presented by Lord Grad; In Technivision, DeLuxe Color, and Dolby Stereo; Rated PG; 122 minutes; July release. CAST: Jason Robards (Adm. Sandecker), Richard Jordan (Dirk Pitt), David Selby (Dr. Seagram), Anne Archer (Dana), Alec Guinness (Bigalow), J. D. Cannon (Capt. Burke), Bo Brundin (Capt. Prevlov), M. Emmet Walsh (MCPO Giordino), Robert Broyles (Willis), Norman Bartold (Kemper), Elya Baskin (Marganin), Dirk Blocker (Merker), Paul Carr (Nicholson), Michael C. Gwynne, Harvey Lewis, Charles Macaulay, Stewart Moss, Michael Pataki, Marvin Silbersher, Mark L. Taylor, Maurice Kowalewski, Nancy Nevinson, Trent Dolan, Paul Tuerpe, Sander Vanocur, Ken Place, Michael Ensign, Craig Shreeve, Brendan Burns, Jonathan Moore, George Whiteman, Hilly Hicks, Mike Kulcsar, David Hammond, Mark Hammer, Ron Evans

THE LITTLE DRAGONS (Aurora) Producers, Hannah Hempstead, Curtis Hanson; Executive Producers, Tony Bill, Robert Bremson; Director, Curtis Hanson; Screenplay, Harvey Applebaum, Louis G. Atlee, Rudolph Borchert, Alan Ormsby; Photography, Stephen Katz; Music, Ken Lauber; Art Director, Spencer Quinn; Assistant Director, Rick Whiting; An Eastwind production in color; Rated PG; 90 minutes; July release. CAST: Charles Lane (J. J.), Ann Sothern (Angel), Chris Petersen (Zack), Pat Petersen (Woody), Sally Boyden (Carol), Rick Lenz (Dick), Sharon Weber (Ruth), Joe Spinell (Yancey), John Chandler (Carl), Clifford A. Pellow (Sheriff), Tony Bill (Niles), Stephen Young (Lunsford), Pat Johnson, Master Bong Soon Han, Donnie Williams, Brad Gorman

CATHY'S CURSE (21st Century) Producers, N. Mathieu, Nicole Boisvert, Eddy Matalon; Director, Eddy Matalon; In Eastmancolor; Rated R; 88 minutes; July release. CAST: Alan Scarfe, Beverley Murray, Randi Allen

WHY WOULD I LIE? (United Artists) Executive Producers, Rich Irvine, James L. Stewart; Producer, Pancho Kohner; Director, Larry Peerce; Screenplay, Peter Stone; Based on novel "The Fabricator" by Hollis Hodges; Music, Charles Fox; Photography, Gerald Hirschfeld; Art Director, James Schoppe; Editor, John C. Howard; Associate Producers, Shelly Abend, Stuart Wallach; Assistant Directors, Steve Barnett, Chase Newhart; Costumes, Al Lehman; An MGM presentation in Metrocolor; Rated PG; 105 minutes; July release. CAST: Treat Williams (Cletus), Lisa Eichhorn (Kay), Gabriel Swann (Jeorge), Susan Heldfond (Amy), Anne Byrne (Faith), Valerie Curtin (Mrs. Bok), Jocelyn Brando (Mrs. Crumpe), Nicolas Coster (Walter), Severn Darden (Dr. Barbour), Sonny Davis (Paul), Jane Burkett (Natalie), Kay Cummings (Edith), Mia Bendixsen (Thelma), Ilene Kristen (Waitress), Harriet Gibson, Cynthia Hoppenfeld, Mitzi Hoag, Natalie Core, Shirley Slater, Elizabeth Kerr, Michael Shane, Eric Haims, Marcia Nicholson, Sheila Kandlbinder, Gino Ardito, Martin Cassidy, Susan Elliot, Lonnie Lloyd, Mary Kay Pupo, Jan D'Arcy, Marian Gants, Joe Gillis, Ron Graves

Richard Jordan, David Selby, Jason Robards
in "Raise the Titanic!" © AFD

Earl Owensby, Ginger Alden in "Living
Legend" © Maverick Pictures

Charles M. Smith, Elyssa Davalos, Cloris Leachman, Joaquin Garay, Stephan Burns in "Herbie Goes Bananas" © Walt Disney

Richard Marin, Thomas Chong in "Cheech and Chong's Next Movie" © Universal Studios

LIVING LEGEND (Maverick) Producer, Earl Owensby; Director, Worth Keeter; Screenplay, Tom McIntyre; Photography, Darrell Cathcart; Editor, Richard Aldridge; In CFI Color; Rated PG; 92 minutes; July release. CAST: Earl Owensby (Eli), William T. Hicks (Jim), Ginger Alden (Jeannie), Jerry Rushing (Chad), Greg Carswell (Teddy), Toby Wallace (Dean), Kristina Reynolds (Susan)

HERBIE GOES BANANAS (Buena Vista) Producer, Ron Miller, Director, Vincent McEveety; Screenplay, Don Tait; Based on characters created by Gordon Buford; Co-Producers, Kevin Corcoran, Don Tait; Photography, Frank Phillips; Music, Frank DeVol; Art Directors, John B. Mansbridge, Rodger Maus; Editor, Gordon D. Brenner; Assistant Director, Win Phelps; In Technicolor; Rated G; 100 minutes; July release. CAST: Cloris Leachman (Aunt Louise), Charles Martin Smith (D.J.), John Vernon (Prindle), Stephan W. Burns (Pete), Elyssa Davalos (Melissa), Joaquin Garay III (Paco), Harvey Korman (Capt. Blythe), Richard Jaeckel (Shepard), Alex Rocco (Quinn), Fritz Feld (Steward), Vito Scotti (Armando), Jose Gonzalez Gonzalez, Rubin Moreno, Tina Menard, Jorge Moreno, Allan Hunt, Tom Scott, Hector Morales, Iris Adrian, Ceil Cabot, Patricia Van Patten, Jack Perkins, Henry Slate

THE MOUNTAIN MEN (Columbia) Executive Producer, Richard R. St. Johns; Producers, Martin Shafer, Andrew Scheinman; Director, Richard Lang; Screenplay, Fraser Clarke Heston; Photography, Michael Hugo; Designer, Bill Kenney; Music Michel Legrand; Editor, Eva Ruggiero; Associate Producer, Cathleen Summers; Assistant Directors, Steven H. Perry, Paul Moen; In Panavision and Metrocolor; Rated R; 102 minutes; July release. CAST: Charlton Heston (Bill Tyler), Brian Keith (Henry), Victoria Racimo (Running Moon), Stephen Macht (Heavy Eagle), John Glover (Nathan), Seymour Cassel (LaBont), David Ackroyd (Medicine Wolf), Cal Bellini (Cross Otter), Bill Lucking (Jim), Ken Ruta (Fontenelle), Victor Jory (Iron Belly), Danny Zapien, Tim Haldeman, Buckley Norris, Daniel Knapp, Michael Greene, Stewart East, Terry Leonard, Steve D. Chambers, Bennie Dobbins, Suzanna Trujillo, Melissa Sylvia, James Ecoffey

CHEECH AND CHONG'S NEXT MOVIE (Universal) Producer, Howard Brown; Associate Producer, Peter MacGregor-Scott; Director, Thomas Chong; Screenplay, Thomas Chong, Cheech Marin; Photography, King Baggot; Designer, Fred Harpman; Editor, Scott Conrad; Costumes, Joe I. Tompkins; Music, Mark Davis; Performed by Killer; Assistant Directors, Newton Arnold, Tom Doherty; Editor, Tom Avildsen; Animation, Paul Power; In Technicolor; Rated R; 99 minutes; July release. CAST: Richard Marin (Cheech), Thomas Chong (Chong), Evelyn Guerrero (Donna), Betty Kennedy (Candy), Sy Kramer (Neatnik), Rikki Marin (Gloria), Peter Bromilow, Paul "Mousie" Garner, Jonathan T. Moore, Lupe M. Ontiveros, Ed Peck, Marguerite Ray, John Steadman, Jake Steinfeld, Robert Ackerman, Lita Aubry, Jonnie Barnett, Shelby Chong, Carolyn Conwell, Don Davis, Margarita Garcia, Mark H. Gilman, Kim S. Hopkins, Robert Linder, Susan Mechsner, Frank Picard, Ben Powers, Michael Winslow, Malcolm Drummond, Natividad Vacio, Tony Viscarra, Marcus Wyatt, Alvin Childress, DeForest Covan, Nan Mason

IN GOD WE TRUST (Universal) Producers, Howard West, George Shapiro; Executive Producer, Norman T. Herman; Associate Producer, Lauretta Feldman; Director, Marty Feldman; Screenplay, Marty Feldman, Chris Allen; Photography, Charles Correll; Designer, Lawrence G. Paull; Editor, David Blewitt; Costumes, Ruth Myers; Music, John Morris; "Good for God" written and sung by Harry Nilsson; Assistant Directors, Stephen Barnett, Chase Newhart, David Valdes; Choreographer, Dee Dee Wood; In Technicolor; Rated PG; 97 minutes; July release. CAST: Marty Feldman (Brother Ambrose), Peter Boyle (Dr. Melmoth), Louise Lasser (Mary), Richard Pryor (God), Andy Kaufman (Thunderbird), Severn Darden (Priest), Wilfrid Hyde-White (Abbot), Eddie Parkes, Stephanie Ross, Richard A. Roth, Barbara Ann Walters, John J. Koshel, Peter Koshel, Lynda Chase-Chankin, Brayton "Bob" Yerkes, David Bond, Norman Bartold, Len Lawson, Peter Nyberg, Paul Baxley, Larri Thomas, David Burton, Kaisen Chu, Chuck Hicks, Rose Michtom, Sue Angelyn Strain, Terry L. Finch, David Francis Banks

Charlton Heston, Victoria Racimo in "The Mountain Men" © Columbia Pictures

Marty Feldman, Louise Lasser in "In God We Trust" © Universal Studios

Darren McGavin in "Hangar 18"
© Sunn Classic Pictures

Leslie Nielsen, Jamie Lee Curtis, Michael Tough
in "Prom Night" © AVCO Embassy

HANGAR 18 (Sunn Classic) Producer, Charles E. Sellier, Jr.; Director, James L. Conway; Screenplay, Steven Thornley; Story, Tom Chapman, James L. Conway; Based on novel by Robert Weverka, Charles E. Sellier, Jr.; Music, John Cacavas; Photography, Paul Hipp; Designer, Paul Staheli; Editor, Michael Spence; Assistant Directors, Henning Schellerup, Leon Dudevoir; Associate Producer, Bill Cornford; Costumes, Julie Staheli; Art Director. Chip Radaelli; Assistant Producer, Carole Fontana; In color; Rated PG; 97 minutes; July release. CAST: Darren McGavin (Forbes), Robert Vaughn (Gordon), Gary Collins (Steve), James Hampton (Lew), Philip Abbott (Frank), Pamela Bellwood (Sarah), Tom Hallick (Phil), Steven Keats (Paul), William Schallert (Mills), Cliff Osmond (Sheriff), Andrew Bloch (Neal), Stuart Pankin (Sam), Betty Ann Carr (Flo), H. M. Wynant, Bill Zuckert, Jesse Bennett, Robert Bristol, Ed E. Carroll, J. R. Clark, Craig Clyde, John William Galt, Anne Galvan, Ken Hapner, Michael Irving, Bruce Katzman, Peter Liakakis, Debra MacFarlane, Chet Norris, H. E. D. Redford, Max Robinson, Ocie Robinson, Michael Ruud

BATTLE BEYOND THE STARS (New World) Executive Producer, Roger Corman; Producer, Ed Carlin; Director, Jimmy T. Murakami; Screenplay, John Sayles; Story, John Sayles, Anne Dyer; Photography, Daniel Lacambre; Editors, Allan Holtzman, Bob Kizer; Music, James Horner; Associate Producer, Mary Ann Fisher; Assistant Directors, Jim Sbartellati, Frank Martinez, Don Opper; Art Directors, Jim Cameron, Charles Breen; Costumes, Durinda Rice Wood; Special Effects, C. Comisky, Ken Jones; In color; Rated PG; 104 minutes; July release. CAST: Richard Thomas (Shad), Robert Vaughn (Gelt), John Saxon (Sador), Darlanne Fluegel (Nanelia), George Peppard (Cowboy), Sam Jaffe (Dr. Hephaestus), Jeff Corey (Zed), Sybil Danning (St. Exmin), Morgan Woodward (Cayman), Steve Davis (Quopeg), Earl Boen, John McGowans, Larry Meyers, Laura Cody, Lynne Carlin, Julia Duffy, Eric Morris, Marta Kristen, Doug Carleson, Ron Ross, Terrence McNally, Don Thompson, Daniel Carlin, Ansley Carlin, Whitney Rydbeck, Dallas Clarke, Dan Vincent, Rick Davidson, Ron Henschel, Brian Coventry, Kerry Frank

PROM NIGHT (AVCO Embassy) Producer, Peter Simpson; Associate Producer, Richard Simpson; Director, Paul Lynch; Screenplay, William Gray, from a story by Robert Guza, Jr.; Photography, Robert New; Music, Carl Zittrer, Paul Zaza; Editor, Brian Ravok; Assistant Directors, Steve Wright, Lee Knippelberg, Martha Hendricks; Art Director, Reuben Freed; In color; Rated R; 91 minutes; July release. CAST: Leslie Nielsen (Hammond), Jamie Lee Curtis (Kim), Casey Stevens (Nick), Eddie Benton (Wendy), Antoinette Bower (Mrs. Hammond), Michael Tough (Alex), Robert Silverman (Sykes), Pita Oliver (Vicki), David Mucci (Lou), Jeff Wincott (Drew), Marybeth Rubins (Kelly), George Touliatos (McBride), Melanie Morse MacQuarrie (Henri-Anne), David Gardner (Fairchild), Joy Thompson (Jude), Sheldon Rybowski, Rob Garrison, David Bolt, Beth Amos, Sonia Zimmer, Sylvia Martin, Liz Stalker-Mason, Pam Henry, Ardon Bess, Lee Wildgen, Brock Simpson, Debbie Greenfield, Tammy Bourne

HEALTH (20th Century-Fox) A Lion's Gate Films production; Director, Robert Altman; Screenplay, Frank Barhydt, Paul Dooley, Robert Altman; Photography, Edmond Koons; Editor, Dennis M. Hill; In color; Rated PG; 102 minutes; August release. CAST: Glenda Jackson, Carol Burnett, James Garner, Lauren Bacall, Dick Cavett, Paul Dooley, Henry Gibson

STEEL (World Northal) Producers, Peter S. Davis, William N. Panzer; Director, Steve Carver; Screenplay, Leigh Chapman; Story, Rob Ewing, Peter S. Davis, William N. Panzer; Music, Michel Colombier; Executive Producer, Lee Majors; Associate Producer, Neal Machlis; Photography, Roger Shearman; Editor, David Blewitt; Assistant Directors, Tom Connors, Richard Hashimoto; In Panavision and Movielab Color; Rated PG; 100 minutes; August release. CAST: Lee Majors (Mike), Jennifer O'Neill (Cass), Art Carney (Pignose), George Kennedy (Lew), Harris Yulin (Eddie), Redmond Cleason (Harry), Terry Kiser (Valentino), Richard Lynch (Dancer), Ben Marley (Kid), Roger Mosley (Lionel), Albert Salmi (Tank), Robert Tessier (Cherokee), Hunter Von Leer (Surfer), R. G. Armstrong (Kellin), Joseph DeNicola (Tom)

Robert Vaughn, Richard Thomas in "Battle Beyond
the Stars" © New World

Lee Majors, Jennifer O'Neill in "Steel"
© World Northal

Jose Ferrer, Kristine DeBell, Jackie Chan
in "The Big Brawl" © Warner Bros.

Stacy Keach (R) in "Twinkle, Twinkle,
Killer Kane" © UFD

THE BIG BRAWL (Warner Brothers) Executive Producer, Raymond Chow; Producers, Fred Weintraub, Terry Morse, Jr; Direction and Screenplay, Robert Clouse; Photography, Robert Jessup; Music, Lalo Schifrin; Editor George Grenville; Art Director, Joe Altadonna; Assistant Director, Craig Huston; A Golden Harvest presentation in Panavision and Technicolor; Rated R; 95 minutes; August release. CAST: Jackie Chan (Jerry), Jose Ferrer (Dominici), Kristine DeBell (Nancy), Mako (Herbert), Ron Max (Leggetti), David Sheiner (Morgan), Rosalind Chao (Mae), Lenny Montana, Pat Johnson, Mary Ellen O'Neill, H. B. Haggerty, Chao-Li Chi, Joycelyne Lew

LOOSE SHOES (Atlantic) Producer, Joel Chernoff; Director, Ira Miller; Screenplay, Varley Smith, Ian Paiser, Royce D. Applegate, Ira Miller; Executive Producers, Byron Lasky, Lee D. Weisel; Photography, John P. Beckett; Music, Murphy Dunne; Assistant Directors, Richie Shor, Beth Rodgers, Rick Braverman; Art Director, Mike McCloskey; Choreography, Ceil Gruessing; In CFI Color; Rated R; August release. CAST: Lewis Arquette (Warden), Danny Dayton (Bartender), Buddy Hackett (Himself), Ed Lauter (Sheriff), Jaye P. Morgan (Stop-it Nurse), Bill Murray (Lefty), Avery Schreiber (Theatre Manager), Susan Tyrrell (Boobies), narrated by Gary Goodrow, Pamela Hoffman, Gary Owens, Roger Peltz, Harry Shearer

THE KIDNAPPING OF THE PRESIDENT (Crown International) Presented by Sefel Pictures International; Executive Producer, Joseph Sefel; Co-Producers, George Mendeluk, John Ryan; Director, George Mendeluk; Screenplay, Richard Murphy; Based on book by Charles Templeton; Photography, Michael Molloy; In Panavision and color; Rated R; 113 minutes; August release. CAST: William Shatner (Jerry), Hal Holbrook (President Adam Scott), Van Johnson (VP Richards), Ava Gardner (Beth Richards), Miguel Fernandes (Assanti), Cindy Girling (Linda), Michael J. Reynolds (MacKenzie), Elizabeth Shepherd (Joan), Gary Reineke (Deitrich), Maury Chaykin (Harvey), Murray Westgate (Archie), Michael Kane (Herb), Jackie Burroughs, Aubert Pallascio, Virginia Podesser, Elias Zarov, Larry Duran, Patrick Brymar, Gershon Resnik, John Stocker, Chappelle Jaffe, John Romaine

TWINKLE, TWINKLE, "KILLER" KANE (UFD) Produced, Directed and Written by William Peter Blatty; Based on his novel; Photography, Gerry Fisher; Music, Barry DeVorzon; Executive Producer, William Paul; Associate Producer, Tom Shaw; Designers, Bill Malley, J. Dennis Washington; Editors, T. Battle Davis, Peter Lee-Thompson, Roberto Silvi; Assistant Director, Tom Shaw; In Panavision and color; Rated R; 102 minutes; August release. CAST: Stacy Keach (Col. Kane), Scott Wilson (Capt. Cutshaw), Jason Miller (Lt. Reno), Ed Flanders (Col. Fell), Neville Brand (Himself), George DiCenzo (Capt. Fairbanks), Moses Gunn (Maj. Nammack), Robert Loggia (Lt. Bennish), Joe Spinell (Spinell), Alejandro Rey (Lt. Gomez), Tom Atkins (Sgt. Krebs), Steve Sandor, Richard Lynch, Mark Gordon, Bill Lucking, Stephen Powers, David Healy, William Paul, Tom Shaw, Gordon K. Kee, Bruce Boa, Linda Blatty, Marilyn Raymon, Hobby Gilman, Bobby Bass, Billy Blatty

USED CARS (Columbia) Producer, Bob Gale; Director, Robert Zemeckis; Screenplay, Robert Zemeckis, Bob Gale; Executive Producers, Steven Spielberg, John Milius; Photography, Donald M. Morgan; Designer, Peter M. Jamison; Editor, Michael Kahn; Music, Patrick Williams; Lyrics, Norman Gimbel; Associate Producer, John G. Wilson; Assistant Directors, Richard Luke Rothschild, Joseph A. Ingraffia; In Metrocolor; Rated R; 111 minutes; August release. CAST: Kurt Russell (Rudy), Jack Warden (Roy & Luke Fuchs), Gerrit Graham (Jeff), Frank McRae (Jim), Deborah Harmon (Barbara), Joseph P. Flaherty (Sam), David L. Lander (Freddie), Michael McKean (Eddie), Michael Talbott (Mickey), Harry Northup (Carmine), Alfonso Arau (Manuel), Al Lewis, Woodrow Parfrey, Andrew Duncan, Dub Taylor, Claude Earl Jones, Dan Barrows, Cheryl Rixon, Marc McClure, Susan Donovan, Don Ruskin, Jan Sandwich, Tracy Lee Rowe, Kurtis Sanders, Clint Lilley, Patrick McMorrow, Joseph Barnaba, Diane Hill, Dick Miller, Rita Taggart, Dave Herrera, Walter Jackson, Gene Blakely

Hal Holbrook (L), Miguel Fernandes (R) in
"Kidnapping of the President"
© Crown International

Deborah Harmon, Kurt Russell in "Used Cars"
© Columbia Pictures

Chuck Norris, Karen Carlson in "Octagon"
© American Cinema

George Stover in "Fiend"
© Cinema Enterprises

THE OCTAGON (American Cinema) Producer, Joel Freeman; Director, Eric Karson; Screenplay, Leigh Chapman; Story, Paul Aaron, Leigh Chapman; Executive Producers, Michael Leone, Alan Belkin; In color; Rated R; 103 minutes; August release. CAST: Chuck Norris (Scott), Karen Carlson (Justine), Lee Van Cleef (McCarn), Art Hindle (A. J.), Carol Bagdasarian (Aura), Kim Lankford (Nancy), Tadashi Yamashita (Seikura), Kurt Grayson (Doggo), Yuki Shimoda (Katsumoto), Larry D. Mann (Tibor), John Fujioka (Isawa), Jack Carter (Sharkey)

MOTHER'S DAY (UFD) Producers; Michael Kravitz, Charles Kaufman; Director, Charles Kaufman; Screenplay, Charles Kaufman, Warren D. Leight; Photography, Joe Mangine; Associate Producers, Lloyd Kaufman, Michael Hertz; Music, Phil Gallo, Clem Vicari; In color; Not rated; 98 minutes; September release. CAST: Nancy Hemdrickson (Abbey), Deborah Luce (Jackie), Tiana Pierce (Trina), Holden McGuire (Ike), Billy Ray McQuade (Addley), Rose Ross (Mother), Kevin Loew (Ted), Karl Sandys (Brad), Ed Battle (Doorman), Stanley Knapp (Charlie), Marsella Davidson (Terry), Robert Carnegie (Tex), Scott Lucas (Storekeeper), Bobby Collins (Ernie)

THE TRAP DOOR (B Movies) Directed, Written and Photographed by Beth B and Scott B; Music, Bob Mason, Beth B, Scott B; In color; Not rated; 70 minutes; September release. CAST: John Ahearn (Jeremy), Colen Fotzgibbon (Movie Actress), Mary-Lou Fogarty (Ms. Hanimex), Robin Harvey (Secretary), Jenny Holzer (Ms. Fist), Gary Indiana (Judge), Dany Johnson (Girlfriend), Richard Prince (Dickie), Marcia Resnick (Bird Woman), Bill Rice (Duller Brush Man), Jack Smith (Dr. Shrinkelstein), Robin Winters (Movie Actor)

SHOCK WAVES (Joseph Brenner) Producer, Reuben Trane; Director, Ken Wiederhorn; Screenplay, John Harrison, Ken Wiederhorn; Music, Richard Einhorn; A Zopix Presentation in Eastmancolor; Rated PG; 90 minutes; September release. CAST: Peter Cushing, Brooke Adams, Jack Davidson, D. J. Sidney, John Carradine, Fred Buch, Luke Halprin, Don Stout

FIEND (Cinema Enterprises) Written, Directed, Edited by Don Dohler; Photography, Richard Geiwitz; Special Effects, David W. Renwick; Music, Paul Woznicki; Set, Mark Supensky; In color; Not rated; 93 minutes; September release. CAST: Don Leifert (Eric), Richard Nelson (Gary), Elaine White (Marsha), George Stover (Dennis), Greg Dohler (Scotty), Del Winans (Jimmy), Kim Dohler (Kristy), Pam Merenda (Jane), Anne Fritch (Katie), Steve Vertlieb (Announcer)

PHOBIA! (Paramount) Executive Producers, Larry Spiegel, Mel Bergman; Producer, Zale Magder; Director, John Huston; Story, Gary Sherman, Ronald Shusett; Screenplay, Lew Lehman, Jimmy Sangster, Peter Bellwood; Photography, Reginald H. Morris; Music, Andre Gagnon; Assistant Directors, David Robertson, Richard Flower; Art Director, David Jaquest; Editor, Stan Cole; In color; Rated R; 94 minutes; September release. CAST: Paul Michael Glaser (Dr. Peter Ross), John Colicos (Inspector Barnes), Susan Hogan (Jenny), Alexandra Stewart (Barbara), Robert O'Ree (Bubba), David Bolt (Henry), David Eisner (Johnny), Lisa Langlois (Laura), Kenneth Welsh (Sgt. Wheeler), Neil Vipond (Dr. Clegg), Patricia Collins (Dr. Toland), Marian Waldman (Mrs. Casey), Gwen Thomas (Dr. Clemens), Paddy Campanero, Gerry Salsberg, Peter Hicks, Joan Fowler, John Stoneham, Terry Martin, Ken Anderson, Janine Cole, Karen Pike, Wendy Jewel, Coleen Embry, Diane Lasko

WITHOUT WARNING (Filmways) Producer-Director, Greydon Clark; Executive Producers, Skip Steloff, Paul Kimatian; Associate Producers, Curtis Burch, Milton Spender; Screenplay, Lyn Freeman, Daniel Grodnik, Ben Nett, Steve Mathis; Music, Dan Wyman; Editor, Curtis Burch; Photography, Dean Cundey; Assistant Director, Caren Singer; Designer, Jack DeWolf; In Movielab Color; Rated R; 89 minutes; September release. CAST: Jack Palance (Taylor), Martin Landau (Fred), Tarah Nutter (Sandy), Christopher S. Nelson (Greg), Cameron Mitchell (Hunter), Neville Brand (Leo), Sue Ane Langdon (Aggie), Ralph Meeker (Dave), Larry Storch (Scoutmaster), Lynn Theel (Beth), David Caruso (Tom), Darby Hinton (Randy)

"Mother's Day"
© UFD

Paul Michael Glaser, Robert O'Ree
in "Phobia" © Paramount Pictures

136

Samantha Eggar, Christopher George in "The Exterminator" © AVCO Embassy

Robin Johnson, Trini Alvarado in "Times Square" © AFD

THE EXTERMINATOR (AVCO Embassy) Producer, Mark Buntzman; Direction and Screenplay, James Glickenhaus; Music, Joe Renzetti; Songs, The Tramps, Roger Bowling; Photography, Robert M. Baldwin; Editor, Corky O'Hara; Assistant Directors, Jane Hershcopf, Mark Slater; In Dolby Stereo and color; Rated R; 101 minutes; September release. CAST: Christopher George (Det. Dalton), Samantha Eggar (Dr. Stewart), Robert Ginty (John Eastland), Steve James (Michael), Tony Di Benedetto (Chicken Pimp), Dick Boccelli (Gino), Patrick Farrelly (C.I.A. Agent), Michele Harrell (Maria), David Lipman (State Senator), Cindy Wilks (Candy), Dennis Boutsikaris (Frankie)

FREEZE BOMB (Movietime Films) Producer, Harry Hope; Director, Al Adamson; Executive Directors, Dick Randall, Oscar Nichols; In Metrocolor; Rated R; 91 minutes; September release. CAST: George Lazenby, Jim Kelly, Harold Sakata, Aldo Ray, Terry Moore, Myron Bruce Lee

SCHIZOID (Cannon Group) Producers, Menahem Golan, Yoram Globus; Direction and Screenplay, David Paulsen; Photography, Norman Leigh; Music, Craig Hundley; Editors, Robert Fitzgerald, Dick Brummer; In color by TVC; Rated R; 91 minutes; September release. CAST: Klaus Kinski (Dr. Fales), Mariana Hill (Julie), Craig Wasson (Doug), Donna Wilkes (Alison), Richard Herd (Donahue), Joe Regalbuto (Jake), Christopher Lloyd (Gilbert), Flo Gerrish (Pat), Kiva Lawrence (Rosemary), Claude Duvernoy (Francoise), Cindy Dolan (Sally)

UNION CITY (Kinesis) Producer, Graham Belin; Associate Producer, Ron Mutz; Direction and Screenplay, Mark Reichert; Based on short story "The Corpse Next Door" by Cornell Woolrich; Photography, Edward Lachman; Art Director, George Stavrinos; Music, Chris Stein; In color; Rated PG; 87 minutes; September release. CAST: Dennis Lipscomb (Harlan), Deborah Harry (Lillian), Irina Maleeva (Contessa), Everett McGill (Longacre), Sam McMurray (Vagrant), Terina Lewis (Evelyn), Pat Benatar (Jeanette), Tony Azito (Alphonse), Paul Andor (Ludendorf), Taylor Mead (Man in taxi), Cynthia Crisp (Woman in taxi), Charles Rydell (Cabbie)

TIMES SQUARE (AFD) Executive Producers, Kevin McCormick, John Nicolella; Producers Robert Stigwood, Jacob Brackman; Director, Alan Moyle; Screenplay, Jacob Brackman; Story, Alan Moyle, Leanne Unger; Associate Producer, Bill Oakes; Photography, James A. Contner; Editor, Tom Priestley; Assistant Directors, Alan Hopkins, Robert Warren; In Technicolor, Dolby Stereo; Rated R; 111 minutes; September release. CAST: Tim Curry (Johnny), Trini Alvarado (Pamela), Robin Johnson (Nicky), Peter Coffield (David), Herbert Berghof (Dr. Huber), David Margulies (Dr. Zymansky), Anna Maria Horsford (Rosie), Michael Margotta (JoJo), J. C. Quinn (Simon), Miguel Pinero (Roberto), Ronald "Smoky" Stevens (Heavy), Tiger Haynes (Andy), Billy Mernit, Paul Sass, Artie Weinstein, Tim Choate, Elizabeth Pena, Kathy Lojac, Susan Merson, George Morfogen, Charles Blackwell, Bill Anagnos, Tammas J. Hamilton, Franklyn Scott, Jane Solar, Victoria Vanderkloot, Steve W. James, Jay Acovone, Alice Spivak, Calvin Ander, Peter Iacangelo, Michael Riney

THE AWAKENING (Orion) Producer, Robert Solo; Director, Mike Newell; Co-Producers, Andrew Scheinman, Martin Shafer; Screenplay, Allan Scott, Chris Bryant, Clive Exton; Based on novel "The Jewel of Seven Stars" by Bram Stoker; Photography, Jack Cardiff; Designer, Michael Stringer; Music, Claude Bolling; Associate Producer, Harry Benn; Editor, Terry Rawlings; Assistant Directors, Neill Vine-Miller, Peter Kohn, Hugh O'Donnell; Costumes, Phyllis Dalton; Art Director, Lionel Couch; In Dolby Stereo and Technicolor; Rated R; 102 minutes; October release. CAST: Charlton Heston (Matthew Corbeck) Susannah York (Jane), Jill Townsend (Anne), Stephanie Zimbalist (Margaret), Patrick Drury (Paul), Bruce Myers (Khalid), Nadim Sawalha (El Sadek), Ian McDiarmid (Richter), Ahmed Osman (Yussef), Miriam Margolyes (Kadira), Michael Mellinger (Hamid), Leonard Maguire (John), Ishia Bennison (Nurse), Madhav Sharma (Doctor), Chris Fairbanks (Porter), Michael Halphie, Roger Kemp (Doctors)

Klaus Kinski, Donna Wilkes in "Schizoid" © Cannon

Stephanie Zimbalist, Charlton Heson in "The Awakening" © Warner Bros.

137

**Dennis Christopher, Linda Kerridge
in "Fade to Black" © American Cinema**

**John Roselius, Robert Blake, Dyan Cannon
in "Coast to Coast" © Paramount**

FADE TO BLACK (American Cinema) Executive Producers, Irwin Yablans, Sylvio Tabet; Producers, George Braunstein, Ron Hamady; Direction and Screenplay, Vernon Zimmerman; Story, Irwin Yablans; Photography, Alex Phillips, Jr.; Assistant Directors, Ron Fury, Paul Chavez; Editor, Howard Kunin; In color; Rated R; 100 minutes; October release. CAST: Dennis Christopher (Eric), Linda Kerridge (Marilyn), Tim Thomerson (Dr. Moriarty), Morgan Paull (Gary), Hennen Chambers (Bart), Marya Small (Doreen), Eve Brent Ashe (Aunt Stella), Bob Drew (Rev. Shick), Gwynn Gilford (Anne), John Steadman (Sam), Mickey Rourke (Richie), Bruce Reed (Franco), Melinda Fee (TV Hostess), Jane K. Wiley (Go-fer), Al Tafoya (Newscaster), Peter Horton (Joey), James Luisi (Gallagher), Anita Converse (Deedee), Marcie Barkin (Stacy), Gilbert Lawrence Kahn (Counterman)

THE CREEPER (Coast) Producer, Lawrence Dane; Director, Peter Carter; Screenplay, Ian Sutherland; Presented by Howard Willette; Rated R; In color; October release. CAST: Hal Holbrook, Lawrence Dane, Robin Gammell, Ken James

COAST TO COAST (Paramount) Producers, Steve Tisch, Jon Avnet; Director, Joseph Sargent; Screenplay, Stanley Weiser; Music, Charles Bernstein; Editor, George Jay Nicholson; Executive Producer, Terry Carr; Photography, Mario Tosi; Art Director, Hilyard Brown; Associate Producer, Vince Cannon; Costumes, Sandra Davidson; Assistant Directors, Michael Daves, Robert Doherty; In Movielab Color; Rated PG; 95 minutes; October release. CAST: Dyan Cannon (Madie), Robert Blake (Charlie), Quinn Redeker (Benjamin), Michael Lerner (Dr. Froll), Maxine Stuart (Sam), Bill Lucking (Jules), Ellen Gerstein, Patricia Conklin (Nurses), David Moody (Chester), Rozelle Gayle (Orderly), Martin Beck (Albert), Karen Rushmore (Charlie's wife), Mae Williams (Waitress), George P. Wilbur (Billy Ray), Tom Pletts (Attendant), Henry Wills (Chef), Hap Lawrence (Mechanic), Tom J. Delaney, Darwin Joston (Drunken Truckers), Dick Durock (Greg), Grace Spence, Dorothy Frazier (Salesladies), Joe Finnegan, Jerry Gatlin, Leonard P. Geer, Cassandra Peterson, Karen Montgomery, Arsenio Trinidad, Vicki Frederick, John Roselius, Al Robertson, Clarke Gordon, Cynthia Gable

MOTEL HELL (United Artists) Produced and Written by Steven-Charles Jaffe, Robert Jaffe; Director, Kevin Connor; Executive Producer, Herb Jaffe; Photography, Thomas Del Ruth; Art Director, Joseph M. Altadonna; Editor, Bernard Gribble; Music, Lance Rubin; Associate Producer, Austen Jewell; Assistant Directors, Jack Barry, Richard Allen; Set, Jim Teegarden; In Dolby Stereo and Technicolor; A Camp Hill Production; Rated R; 92 minutes; October release. CAST: Rory Calhoun (Vincent), Paul Linke (Bruce), Nancy Parsons (Ida), Nina Axelrod (Terry), Wolfman Jack (Rev. Billy), Elaine Joyce (Edith), Dick Curtis (Guy), Monique St. Pierre (Debbie), Rosanne Katon (Suzi), E. Hampton Beagle (Bob), Everett Creach (Bo), Michael Melvin (Ivan), John Ratzenberger, Marc Silver, Victoria Hartman, Gwil Richards, Toni Gillman, Shaylin Hendrixson, Heather Hendrixson, Margot Hope, Barbara Goodson, Kim Fowler

JONI (World Wide) Producer, Frank R. Hacobson; Executive Producer, William F. Brown; Direction and Screenplay, James F. Collier; Based on book by Joni Eareckson; Photography, Frank Raymond; Editor, Duane Hartzell; Music, Ralph Carmichael; Art Direction, Bill Ross; Assistant Director, Stephen Lim; In Metrocolor; Rated G; 108 minutes; October release. CAST: Joni Eareckson (Joni), Bert Remsen (Eareckson), Katherine DeHetre (Jay), Cooper Huckabee (Dick), John Milford (Doctor), Michael Mancini (Don), Richard Lineback (Steve), Jay W. MacIntosh, Louise Hoven, Cloyce Morrow

**Dick Curtis, Rory Calhoun, Elaine Joyce
in "Motel Hell" © United Artists**

**"Teen Mothers"
© Cannon**

Oliver Reed, Virgil Frye in "Dr Heckyl
and Mr. Hype" © Cannon Films

"Gates of Heaven"
© New Yorker

DR. HECKYL AND MR. HYPE (Cannon Group) Producers,
Menahem Golan, Yoram Globus; Associate Producer Jill
Griffith; Direction and Screenplay, Charles B. Griffith; Music,
Richard Band; Photography, Robert Carras; Designer, Maxwell
Mendes; Art Director, Bob Ziembiki; Editor, Skip Schoolnik;
Assistant Directors, Peter Manoogian, Darryl Michelson; In
color; Rated R; 99 minutes; October release. CAST: Oliver Reed
(Dr. Heckyl/Mr. Hype), Sunny Johnson (Coral), Maia Danziger
(Miss Finegum), Virgil Frye (Il Topo), Mel Welles (Dr. Hinkle),
Kedric Wolfe (Dr. Hoo), Jackie Coogan (Sgt. Fleacollar), Co-
rinne Calvet (Pizelle), Sharon Compton (Mrs. Quivel), Denise
Hayes (Liza), Charles Howerton, Dick Miller, Jack Warford,
Lucretia Love, Ben Frommer, Mickey Fox, Catalaine Knell,
Jacque Lynn Colton, Lisa Zebro, Stan Ross, Joe Anthony Cox,
Duane Thomas, Michael Ciccone, Steve Ciccone, Candi Brough,
Randi Brough, Dan Sturkie, Yehuda Efroni, Herta Ware, Samuel
Livneh, Dana Feller, Katherine Kirkpatrick, Carin Berger, Cindy
Riegel, Merle Ann Taylor, Ed Randolph

TEEN MOTHERS (Cannon Group) formerly "Seed of Inno-
cence"; Producer, Yoram Globus; Director, Boaz Davidson;
Screenplay, Stuart Krieger; Assistant Directors, Tom Rolapp,
Ami Amir; Designer, Brent Swift; Art Director, Dan Linkmeyer;
Photography, Adam Greenberg; Editor, Jon Koslowsky; Music,
Shalom Chanach; In color; Rated R; 90 minutes; October release.
CAST: Timothy Wead (Danny), Mary Cannon (Alice), Vincent
Schiavelli (Leo), T. K. Carter (Captain), Azizi Johari (Denise),
Julianna McCarthy (Nadine), Sonja O. Menor (Teacher), Mary
Ellen O'Neill (Sister Mary), Monika Ramirez (Jane), John
Miranda (Dr. Walthour), Brad Gorman (Barney), Shirley Stoler
(Corky), Gloria Stroock (Sophie), Robert Alan Brown (Dale),
Bonnie Bartlett (Velma), Jane Drennan (Marie), Russ Marin
(Marv), Bart Burns (Ray), William J. Sanderson, Scott Edmund
Lane, Art Bradford, John Wheeler, Jeremy West, Tony Plana,
Lanny Duncan, Earl Montgomery, Barbara Lyle, Hillary Horan

PLAYGROUND IN THE SKY (Kino International) Producer,
Ted Webster; Director, Carl Boenish; Music, Michael Lloyd; Editor, Richard Meystre; In color; Rated G; 85 minutes; October
release. A documentary on parachute jumping and hang-gliding.

GATES OF HEAVEN (New Yorker) Produced, Directed, Edited by Errol Morris; Photography, Ned Burgess; In color; Not
rated; 85 minutes; October release. A documentary on cemeteries
for pets with Floyd McClure, Joe Allen, Martin Hall, Mike Ko-
ewler, Ed Quye, Lucille Billingsley, Zella Graham, Florence Rasmussen, Cal Harberts, Scottie Harberts, Phil Harberts, Dan
Harberts

AMERICAN RASPBERRY (Cannon) Executive Producer,
Robin French; Music, Ken Lauber; Screenplay, Stephen Feinberg, John Baskin, Roger Shulman, Bradley R. Swirnoff; Producer, Marc Trabulus; Director, Bradley R. Swirnoff; In color;
Rated R; 75 minutes; October release.

THE SWAP (Cannon Group) Producer, Christopher C. Dewey;
Director, John Shade; Additional scenes written and directed by
John C. Broderick; Photography, Alex Phillips, Jr.; In color;
Rated R; 84 minutes; October release. CAST: Robert DeNiro
(Sammy), Anthony Charnota (Vito), Jennifer Warren, Jerry
Mickey, Terrayne Crawford, Martin Kelley, Lisa Blount, Sybil
Danning, John Medici, James Brown, Sam Anderson, Tony
Brande, Matt Green, Alvin Hammer, Jack Slater

THE ATTIC (Atlantic) Producers, Raymond M. Dryden, Phillip
Randall; Director, George Edwards; Executive Producers, Rob-
ert H. Becker, Mel Edelstein; Screenplay, Tony Crechales,
George Edwards; Co-Producers, Max Greenburg, Martin Wivi-
ott; Associate Producer, Tony Crechales; Photography, Gary
Graver; Editor, Derek Parsons; Music, Hod David Schudson; Art
Director, Tom Rasmussen; Set, Tana Cunningham-Curtis; Assis-
tant Director, Susan Kay Ferris; CFI Color; Rated R; 97 minutes;
October release. CAST: Carrie Snodgress (Louise), Ray Milland
(Wendell), Ruth Cox (Emily), Angel (Dickey), Rosemary Mur-
phy (Mrs. Perkins), Francis Bay (Librarian), Marjorie Eaton
(Mrs. Fowler), Fern Barry (Mrs. Mooney), Michael Rhodes
(Sailor), Patrick Brennan (David), Mark Andrews (Gardener),
Dick Welsbacher (Bureau of Missing Persons), Phil Speary
(Travel Agent)

Robert DeNiro in "The Swap"
© Cannon

Ray Milland, Carrie Snodgress
in "The Attic" © Atlantic

Catherine Mary Stewart in "The Apple"
© Cannon Group

Tim Conway, Don Knotts in "The Private
Eyes" © New World

BLANK GENERATION (International Harmony) Producer, Roger Deutsch; Director, Ulli Lommel; Music, Elliot Goldenthal; Songs, Richard Hell; In color; Rated R; 90 minutes; October release. CAST: Carole Bouquet, Richard Hell, Andy Warhol

BLOODEATERS (Parker National) Produced, Directed and Written by Chuck McCrann; Photography, David Sperling; Editors, Chuck McCrann, David Sperling; Music, Ted Shapiro; Assistant Director, Jenny Lee; In color; Rated R; 84 minutes; October release. CAST: Charles Austin (Cole), Beverly Shapiro (Polly) Dennis Helfend (Hermit), Paul Haskin (Briggs), John Amplas (Phillips)

THE APPLE (Cannon Group) Producers, Menahem Golan, Yoram Globus; Direction and Screenplay, Menahem Golan; Music, Coby Recht; Lyrics, Iris Recht, George Clinton; Story, Coby and Iris Recht; Choreography, Nigel Lythgoe; Photography, David Gurfinkel; Costumes, Ingrid Zore; Editor, Alain Jakubowicz; Designer, Jurgen Kiebach; Assistant Directors, Martin Honer, Haim Idan, Dori Lubliner; In Dolby Stereo, Panavision and color; Rated PG; 94 minutes; November release. CAST: Catherine Mary Stuart (Bibi), George Gilmour (Alphie), Grace Kennedy (Pandi), Allan Love (Dandi), Joss Ackland (Topps), Vladek Sheybal (Boogalow), Ray Shell (Shake), Miriam Margolyes (Landlady), Leslie Meadows (Ashley), Derek Deadman (Bulldog), Gunter Notthoff (Fatdog), Michael Logan (James), Clem Davies (Clark), George S. Clinton (Joe), Coby Recht (Jean-Louis), Francesca Poston (Vampire), Iris Recht (Domini)

HEAVEN'S GATE (United Artists) Producer, Joann Carelli; Direction and Screenplay, Michael Cimino; Photography, Vilmos Zsigmond; Editors, Tom Rolf, William Reynolds. Lisa Fruchtman, Gerald Greenberg; Music, David Mansfield, Michael Cimino; In color; Rated R; 225 minutes; November release. CAST: Kris Kristofferson (Averill), Christopher Walken (Champion), John Hurt (Irvine), Sam Waterston (Canton), Brad Dourif (Mr. Eggleston), Isabelle Huppert (Ella), Joseph Cotten (Reverend Doctor), Jeff Bridges (John H. Bridges)

THE PRIVATE EYES (New World) Producers, Lang Elliott, Wanda Dell; Director, Lang Elliott; Screenplay, Tim Conway, John Myhers; Photography, Jacques Haitkin; Art Director, Vincent Peranio; Editor, Patrick M. Crawford; Music, Peter Matz; Costumes, Christine Goulding; Assistant Directors, Doub Wise, Jimmy Simons; Color by TVC; Rated PG; 92 minutes; November release. CAST: Tim Conway (Dr. Tart), Don Knotts (Insp. Winship), Trisha Noble (Phylis), Bernard Fox (Justin), Grace Zabriskie (Nanny), John Fujoika (Mr. Uwatsum), Stan Ross (Tibet), Irwin Keyes (Jock), Suzy Mandel (Hilda), Fred Stuthman (Lord Morley), Mary Nell Santacroce (Lady Morley), Robert V. Barron (Gas Station Attendant), Patrick Cranshaw (Roy)

THE DAY TIME ENDED (Compass International) Executive Producer, Charles Band; Producers, Wayne Schmidt, Steve Neill, Paul W. Gentry; Director, John "Bud" Cardos; Screenplay, Wayne Schmidt, J. Larry Carroll, David Schmoeller; Story, Steve Neill; Photography, John Murill; Editor, Ted Nicolaou; Music, Richard Band; Assistant Directors, Bob Shue, Kathy Slakey, Debra Michaelson; Art Director, Rusty Rosene; In Metrocolor and Panavision; Rated PG; 79 minutes; November release. CAST: Jim Davis (Grant), Chris Mitchum (Richard), Dorothy Malone (Ana), Marcy Lafferty (Beth), Natasha Ryan (Jenny), Scott Kolden (Steve)

THE BOOGEY MAN (Jerry Gross) Produced, Directed and Written by Ulli Lommel; Screenplay, Ulli Lommel, Suzanna Love, David Herschel; Executive Producer, Wolf Schmidt; Associate Producer, Terrell Tannen; Photography, David Sperling, Jochen Breitenstein; Art Director, Robert Morgan; Editor, Terrell Tannen; Music, Tim Krog; In color; Rated R; 86 minutes; November release. CAST: Suzanna Love (Lacey), Ron James (Jake), John Carradine (Dr. Warren), Nicholas Love (Willy), Raymond Boyden (Kevin), Felicite Morgan (Helen), Bill Rayburn (Uncle Ernest), Llewelyn Thomas (Father Reily), Jay Wright (Young Willy), Natasha Schiano (Young Lacey), Gillian Gordon (Mother), Howard Grant (Lover), Jane Pratt (Jane), Lucinda Ziesing (Susan), David Swim, Katie Casey, Ernest Meier, Stony Richards, Claudia Porcelli, Catherine Tambini

Jim Davis, Dorothy Malone (R) in "The Day
Time Ended" © Compass International

Jay Wright, Natasha Schiano in "The
Boogey Man" © Jerry Gross

"Space Movie"
© International Harmony

Joe Spinell, Caroline Munro in "Maniac"
© Magnum

THE SPACE MOVIE (International Harmony) Producers, Richard Branson, Simon Draper; Director, Tony Palmer; Music, Mike Oldfield with the Royal Philharmonic Orchestra; A Virgin Films production; Not rated; 82 minutes; November release. A documentary of compiled footage from the National Aeronautics and Space Administration and the National Archives.

AGEE Produced, Directed and Written by Ross Spears; Photography, Anthony Forma; Music, Kenton Coe; Associate Producer, Jude Cassidy; In black and white and color; Not rated; 96 minutes; November release. A documentary on the life of James Agee with Jimmy Carter, Father James Flye, Robert Saudek, Olivia Wood, Dwight Macdonald, Robert Fitzgerald, Elizabeth Tingle, Mae Burroughs, Alma Neuman, Mia Agee, John Huston, Earl McCarroll as voice af Agee, voice of Walker Evans.

ALLIGATOR (Group 1) Producer, Brandon Chase; Executive Producer, Robert S. Bremson; Director, Lewis Teague; Screenplay, John Sayles; Photography, Joseph Mangine; In DeLuxe Color; Rated R; 94 minutes; November release. CAST: Robert Forster (David), Robin Riker (Marisa), Michael Gazzo (Police Chief), Perry Lang (Kelly), Jack Carter (Mayor), Henry Silva (Col Brock), Bart Braverman (Reporter), Dean Jagger (Tycoon), Sidney Lassick, Sue Lyon, Angel Tompkins

FALLING IN LOVE AGAIN (International Picture Show) Executive Producer, Hank Paul; Producer-Director, Steven Paul; Co-Producer, Patrick Wright; Screenplay, Steven Paul, Ted Allan, Susannah York; Music, Michel Legrand; Associate Producers, Dan Murphy, Dorothy Koster-Paul; Photography, Michael Mileham, Dick Bush, Wolf Suschitzky; Editors, Bud Smith, Doug Jackson, Jacqueline Cambas; In color; Rated PG; 103 minutes; November release. CAST: Elliott Gould (Harry Lewis), Susannah York (Sue), Stuart Paul (Pompadour), Michelle Pfeiffer (Sue 1940), Kaye Ballard (Mrs. Lewis), Robert Hackman (Mrs. Lewis), Cathy Tolbert (Cheryl), Steven Paul (Stan), Todd Helper (Alan), Herb Rudley (Mr. Wellington), Marion McCargo (Mrs. Wellington), Bonnie Paul (Hilary)

NEW YEAR'S EVIL (Cannon) Executive Producer, Billy Fine; Producers, Menahem Golan, Yoram Globus; Associate Producer, Christopher Pearce; Director, Emmett Alston; Screenplay, Leonard Neubauer; Story, Leonard Neubauer, Emmett Alston; Music, Laurin Rinder, W. Michael Lewis; In color; Rated R; December release. CAST: Roz Kelly, Kip Niven, Chris Wallace, Grant Cramer, Louisa Moritz, Jed Mills

MANIAC (Films Around the World) Producers, Andrew Garroni, William Lustig; Executive Producers, Jose Spinell, Judd Hamilton; Associate Producer, John Packard; Director, William Lustig; Story, Joe Spinell; Screenplay, C. A. Rosenberg, Joe Spinell; Music, Jay Chattaway; Editor, Lorenzo Marinelli; Photography, Robert Lindsay; Songs performed by Gino Braniere, Don Armando's 2nd Avenue Rhumba Band; In TVC color and Dolby Stereo; Not rated; 87 minutes; December release. CAST: Joe Spinell (Frank), Caroline Munro (Anna), Gail Lawrence (Rita), Kelly Piper (Nurse), Rita Montone (Hooker), Tom Savini (Disco Boy), Hyla Marrow (Disco Girl), James Brewster (Beach Boy), Linda Lee Walter (Beach Girl), Tracie Evans, Sharon Mitchell, Carol Henry, Nelia Bacmeister, Louis Jawitz, Denise Spagnuolo, Billy Spagnuolo, Frank Pesce, Candice Clements, Diane Spagnuolo, Kim Hudson, Terry Gagnon, Joan Baldwin, Jeni Paz, Janelle Winston, Randy Jurgensen, Jimmy Aurichio

BELOW THE BELT (Atlantic) Executive Producer, Joseph Miller; Producers, Robert Fowler, Joseph Miller; Screenplay, Robert Fowler, Sherry Sonnett; Suggested by novel "To Smithereens": by Rosayln Drexler; Associate Producers, Bill Botts, Steven Marshall, Carol Seal; Photography, Alan Metzger, Misha Suslov; Music, Jerry Fielding; Lyrics, David Mackechnie; Songs sung by Billy Preston; In Technicolor; Rated R; 90 minutes; December release. CAST: Regina Baff (Rosa), John C. Becher (Bobby), Mildred Burke (Millie), James Gammon (Luke), Annie McGreevey (Lee), Billie Mahoney (Jean), Ric Mancini (Tio), Jane O'Brien (Terrible Tommy), Titi Paris (Hilda), Sierra Pecheur (Verne), Gregory Rozakis (Peddler), Frazer Smith (Terry), Shirley Stoler (Trish), Dolph Sweet (LeRoi), K. C. Townsend (Thalia), Paul Brennan (Stepfather), Ray Scott, Voices of the Firesign Theater

Susannah York, Elliot Gould in "Falling in Love Again" © International Picture Show

Regina Baff in "Below the Belt" © Atlantic Releasing

141

ACADEMY AWARDS OF 1980

(Presented Tuesday, March 31, 1981)

ORDINARY PEOPLE

(PARAMOUNT) Producer, Ronald L. Schwary; Director, Robert Redford; Screenplay, Alvin Sargent; Based on book by Judith Guest; Assistant Directors, Steven Perry, Michael Britton; Photography, John Bailey; Editor, Jeff Kanew; Art Directors, Phillip Bennett, Michael Riva; Costumes, Barnie Pollack; A Wildwood Enterprises production in color; Rated R; 124 minutes; September release.

CAST

Calvin	Donald Sutherland
Beth	Mary Tyler Moore
Conrad	Tim Hutton
Berger	Judd Hirsch
Karen	Dinah Manoff
Jeanine	Elizabeth McGovern
Swim Coach	Emmett Walsh
Lazenby	Fredrick Lehne
Stillman	Adam Baldwin
Bucky	Scott Doebler

Left: Judd Hirsch
© Paramount Pictures
1980 Academy Awards for Best Picture, Supporting Actor (Timothy Hutton), Director, Adapted Screenplay

Donald Sutherland, Mary Tyler Moore

1980 ACADEMY AWARD FOR BEST PICTURE

Judd Hirsch, Timothy Hutton Above: Donald Sutherland, Hutton Top: Mary Tyler Moore, Hutton

Timothy Hutton, Dinah Manoff
Above: Hutton, Elizabeth McGovern

Robert Redford directing Mary Tyler Moore
and Timothy Hutton at top
in "Ordinary People" © Paramount Pictures

ROBERT DeNIRO
in "Raging Bull" © United Artists
1980 ACADEMY AWARD FOR BEST ACTOR   145

SISSY SPACEK
in "Coal Miner's Daughter" © Universal Studios
1980 ACADEMY AWARD FOR BEST ACTRESS

TIMOTHY HUTTON
in "Ordinary People" © Paramount Pictures
1980 ACADEMY AWARD FOR BEST SUPPORTING ACTOR

147

MARY STEENBURGEN
in "Melvin and Howard" © Universal Studios
1980 ACADEMY AWARD FOR BEST SUPPORTING ACTRESS

FROM MAO TO MOZART:
Isaac Stern in China

(HARMONY FILM GROUP) Produced and Directed by Murray Lerner; Artistic Supervisor, Allan Miller; Film Editor, Thomas Haneke; Assistant Editor, Donald George Klocek; Executive Producer, Walter Scheuer; Photography, Nic Knowland, Nick Doob, David Bridges; A Hopewell Foundation production in color; Not rated; 84 minutes; December release. CAST: Isaac Stern, David Golub, Tan Shuzhen.

1980 Academy Award for Best Feature Documentary

Right: Isaac Stern and young Chinese musicians

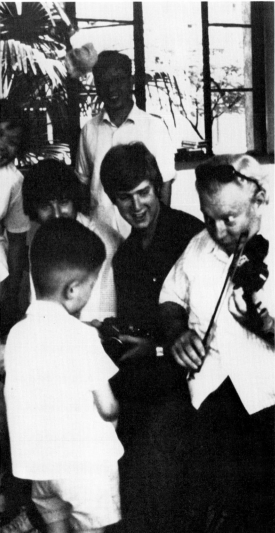

Isaac Stern (R)

Isaac Stern and young Chinese musicians

1980 ACADEMY AWARD FOR BEST DOCUMENTARY FEATURE

149

MOSCOW DOESN'T BELIEVE IN TEARS

(INTERNATIONAL FILM EXCHANGE) Director, Vladimir Menshov; Screenplay, Valentin Chiornykh; Photography, Igor Slabnevitch; A Mosfilm production in color; 150 minutes; December release.

CAST

Katerina	Vera Alentova
Liudmila	Irina Muravyova
Antonina	Raisa Ryazanova
Alexandra	Naralia Vavilova
Gosha	Alexei Batalov
Gurin	Alexander Fatiushin
Nikolai	Boris Smorchkov
Rashkov	Yury Vasiliev

1980 Academy Award for Best Foreign-Language Film

Left: Irina Muravyova, Vera Alentova

Irina Muravyova, Zora Fyodorova

1980 ACADEMY AWARD FOR BEST FOREIGN-LANGUAGE FILM

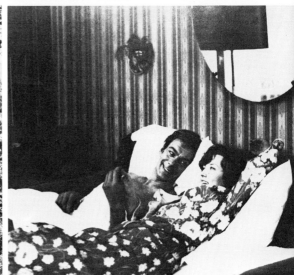

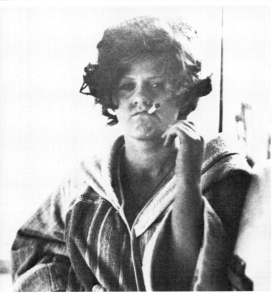

Irina Muravyova, and above with Vera Alentova
Top: Victor Uralsky, Valentina Ushakova

Natalia Vavilova Top: Alexei Batalov,
Vera Alentova

| Jose Ferrer | Janet Gaynor | Cliff Robertson | Gale Sondergaard | Maximilian Schell | Claire Trevor |

PREVIOUS ACADEMY AWARD WINNERS

(1) Best Picture, (2) Actor, (3) Actress, (4) Supporting Actor, (5) Supporting Actress, (6) Director,
(7) Special Award, (8) Best Foreign Language Film

1927–28: (1) "Wings," (2) Emil Jannings in "The Way of All Flesh," (3) Janet Gaynor in "Seventh Heaven," (6) Frank Borzage for "Seventh Heaven," (7) Charles Chaplin.

1928–29: (1) "Broadway Melody," (2) Warner Baxter in "Old Arizona," (3) Mary Pickford in "Coquette," (6) Frank Lloyd for "The Divine Lady."

1929–30: (1) "All Quiet on the Western Front," (2) George Arliss in "Disraeli," (3) Norma Shearer in "The Divorcee," (6) Lewis Milestone for "All Quiet on the Western Front."

1930–31: (1) "Cimarron," (2) Lionel Barrymore in "A Free Soul," (3) Marie Dressler in "Min and Bill," (6) Norman Taurog for "Skippy."

1931–32: (1) "Grand Hotel," (2) Fredric March in "Dr. Jekyll and Mr. Hyde" tied with Wallace Beery in "The Champ," (3) Helen Hayes in "The Sin of Madelon Claudet," (6) Frank Borzage for "Bad Girl."

1932–33: (1) "Cavalcade," (2) Charles Laughton in "The Private Life of Henry VIII," (3) Katharine Hepburn in "Morning Glory," (6) Frank Lloyd for "Cavalcade."

1934: (1) "It Happened One Night," (2) Clark Gable in "It Happened One Night," (3) Claudette Colbert in "It Happened One Night," (6) Frank Capra for "It Happened One Night," (7) Shirley Temple.

1935: (1) "Mutiny on the Bounty," (2) Victor McLaglen in "The Informer," (3) Bette Davis in "Dangerous," (6) John Ford for "The Informer," (7) D. W. Griffith.

1936: (1) "The Great Ziegfeld," (2) Paul Muni in "The Story of Louis Pasteur," (3) Luise Rainer in "The Great Ziegfeld," (4) Walter Brennan in "Come and Get It," (5) Gale Sondergaard in "Anthony Adverse," (6) Frank Capra for "Mr. Deeds Goes to Town."

1937: (1) "The Life of Emile Zola," (2) Spencer Tracy in "Captains Courageous," (3) Luise Rainer in "The Good Earth," (4) Joseph Schildkraut in "The Life of Emile Zola," (5) Alice Brady in "In Old Chicago," (6) Leo McCarey for "The Awful Truth," (7) Mack Sennett, Edgar Bergen.

1938: (1) "You Can't Take It with You," (2) Spencer Tracy in "Boys' Town," (3) Bette Davis in "Jezebel," (4) Walter Brennan in "Kentucky," (5) Fay Bainter in "Jezebel," (6) Frank Capra for "You Can't Take It with You," (7) Deanna Durbin, Mickey Rooney, Harry M. Warner, Walt Disney.

1939: (1) "Gone with the Wind," (2) Robert Donat in "Goodbye, Mr. Chips," (3) Vivien Leigh in "Gone with the Wind," (4) Thomas Mitchell in "Stagecoach," (5) Hattie McDaniel in "Gone with the Wind," (6) Victor Fleming for "Gone with the Wind," (7) Douglas Fairbanks, Judy Garland.

1940: (1) "Rebecca," (2) James Stewart in "The Philadelphia Story," (3) Ginger Rogers in "Kitty Foyle," (4) Walter Brennan in "The Westerner," (5) Jane Darwell in "The Grapes of Wrath," (6) John Ford for "The Grapes of Wrath," (7) Bob Hope.

1941: (1) "How Green Was My Valley," (2) Gary Cooper in "Sergeant York," (3) Joan Fontaine in "Suspicion," (4) Donald Crisp in "How Green Was My Valley," (5) Mary Astor in "The Great Lie," (6) John Ford for "How Green Was My Valley," (7) Leopold Stokowski, Walt Disney.

1942: (1) "Mrs. Miniver," (2) James Cagney in "Yankee Doodle Dandy," (3) Greer Garson in "Mrs. Miniver," (4) Van Heflin in "Johnny Eager," (5) Teresa Wright in "Mrs. Miniver," (6) William Wyler for "Mrs. Miniver," (7) Charles Boyer, Noel Coward.

1943: (1) "Casablanca," (2) Paul Lukas in "Watch on the Rhine," (3) Jennifer Jones in "The Song of Bernadette," (4) Charles Coburn in "The More the Merrier," (5) Katina Paxinou in "For Whom the Bell Tolls," (6) Michael Curtiz for "Casablanca."

1944: (1) "Going My Way," (2) Bing Crosby in "Going My Way," (3) Ingrid Bergman in "Gaslight," (4) Barry Fitzgerald in "Going My Way," (5) Ethel Barrymore in "None but the Lonely Heart," (6) Leo McCarey for "Going My Way," (7) Margaret O'Brien, Bob Hope.

1945: (1) "The Lost Weekend," (2) Ray Milland in "The Lost Weekend," (3) Joan Crawford in "Mildred Pierce," (4) James Dunn in "A Tree Grows in Brooklyn," (5) Anne Revere in "National Velvet," (6) Billy Wilder for "The Lost Weekend," (7) Walter Wanger, Peggy Ann Garner.

1946: (1) "The Best Years of Our Lives," (2) Fredric March in "The Best Years of Our Lives," (3) Olivia de Havilland in "To Each His Own," (4) Harold Russell in "The Best Years of Our Lives," (5) Anne Baxter in "The Razor's Edge," (6) William Wyler for "The Best Years of Our Lives," (7) Laurence Olivier, Harold Russell, Ernst Lubitsch, Claude Jarman, Jr.

1947: (1) "Gentleman's Agreement," (2) Ronald Colman in "A Double Life," (3) Loretta Young in "The Farmer's Daughter," (4) Edmund Gwenn in "Miracle On 34th Street," (5) Celeste Holm in "Gentleman's Agreement," (6) Elia Kazan for "Gentleman's Agreement," (7) James Baskette, (8) "Shoe Shine."

1948: (1) "Hamlet," (2) Laurence Olivier in "Hamlet," (3) Jane Wyman in "Johnny Belinda," (4) Walter Huston in "The Treasure of the Sierra Madre," (5) Claire Trevor in "Key Largo," (6) John Huston for "The Treasure of the Sierra Madre," (7) Ivan Jandl, Sid Grauman, Adolph Zukor, Walter Wanger, (8) "Monsieur Vincent."

1949: (1) "All the King's Men," (2) Broderick Crawford in "All the King's Men," (3) Olivia de Havilland in "The Heiress." (4) Dean Jagger in "Twelve O'Clock High," (5) Mercedes McCambridge in "All the King's Men," (6) Joseph L. Mankiewicz for "A Letter to Three Wives," (7) Bobby Driscoll, Fred Astaire, Cecil B. DeMille, Jean Hersholt, (8) "The Bicycle Thief."

1950: "All about Eve," (2) Jose Ferrer in "Cyrano de Bergerac," (3) Judy Holliday in "Born Yesterday," (4) George Sanders in "All about Eve," (5) Josephine Hull in "Harvey," (6) Joseph L. Mankiewicz for "All about Eve," (7) George Murphy, Louis B. Mayer, (8) "The Walls of Malapaga."

1951: (1) "An American in Paris," (2) Humphrey Bogart in "The African Queen," (3) Vivien Leigh in "A Streetcar Named Desire," (4) Karl Malden in "A Streetcar Named Desire," (5) Kim Hunter in "A Streetcar Named Desire," (6) George Stevens for "A Place in the Sun," (7) Gene Kelly, (8) "Rashomon."

1952: (1) "The Greatest Show on Earth," (2) Gary Cooper in "High Noon," (3) Shirley Booth in "Come Back, Little Sheba," (4) Anthony Quinn in "Viva Zapata," (5) Gloria Grahame in "The Bad and the Beautiful," (6) John Ford for "The Quiet Man," (7) Joseph M. Schenck, Merian C. Cooper, Harold Lloyd, Bob Hope, George Alfred Mitchell, (8) "Forbidden Games."

1953: (1) "From Here to Eternity," (2) William Holden in "Stalag 17," (3) Audrey Hepburn in "Roman Holiday," (4) Frank Sinatra in "From Here to Eternity," (5) Donna Reed in "From Here to Eternity," (6) Fred Zinnemann for "From Here to Eternity," (7) Pete Smith, Joseph Breen.

1954: (1) "On the Waterfront," (2) Marlon Brando in "On the Waterfront," (3) Grace Kelly in "The Country Girl," (4) Edmond O'Brien in "The Barefoot Contessa," (5) Eva Marie Saint in "On the Waterfront," (6) Elia Kazan for "On the Waterfront," (7) Greta Garbo, Danny Kaye, Jon Whitely, Vincent Winter, (8) "Gate of Hell."

1955: (1) "Marty," (2) Ernest Borgnine in "Marty," (3) Anna Magnani in "The Rose Tattoo," (4) Jack Lemmon in "Mister Roberts," (5) Jo Van Fleet in "East of Eden," (6) Delbert Mann for "Marty," (8) "Samurai."

1956: (1) "Around the World in 80 Days," (2) Yul Brynner in "The King and I," (3) Ingrid Bergman in "Anastasia," (4) Anthony Quinn in "Lust for Life," (5) Dorothy Malone in "Written on the Wind," (6) George Stevens for "Giant," (7) Eddie Cantor, (8) "La Strada."

1957: (1) "The Bridge on the River Kwai," (2) Alec Guinness in "The Bridge on the River Kwai," (3) Joanne Woodward in "The Three Faces of Eve," (4) Red Buttons in "Sayonara," (5) Miyoshi Umeki in "Sayonara," (6) David Lean for "The Bridge on the River Kwai," (7) Charles Brackett, B. B. Kahane, Gilbert M. (Bronco Billy) Anderson, (8) "The Nights of Cabiria."

1958: (1) "Gigi," (2) David Niven in "Separate Tables," (3) Susan Hayward in "I Want to Live," (4) Burl Ives in "The Big Country," (5) Wendy Hiller in "Separate Tables," (6) Vincente Minnelli for "Gigi," (7) Maurice Chevalier, (8) "My Uncle."

1959: (1) "Ben-Hur," (2) Charlton Heston in "Ben-Hur," (3) Simone Signoret in "Room at the Top," (4) Hugh Griffith in "Ben-Hur," (5) Shelley Winters in "The Diary of Anne Frank," (6) William Wyler for "Ben-Hur," (7) Lee de Forest, Buster Keaton, (8) "Black Orpheus."

1960: (1) "The Apartment," (2) Burt Lancaster in "Elmer Gantry," (3) Elizabeth Taylor in "Butterfield 8," (4) Peter Ustinov in "Spartacus," (5) Shirley Jones in "Elmer Gantry," (6) Billy Wilder for "The Apartment," (7) Gary Cooper, Stan Laurel, Hayley Mills, (8) "The Virgin Spring."

1961: (1) "West Side Story," (2) Maximilian Schell in "Judgment at Nuremberg," (3) Sophia Loren in "Two Women," (4) George Chakiris in "West Side Story," (5) Rita Moreno in "West Side Story," (6) Robert Wise for "West Side Story," (7) Jerome Robbins, Fred L. Metzler, (8) "Through a Glass Darkly."

1962: (1) "Lawrence of Arabia," (2) Gregory Peck in "To Kill a Mockingbird," (3) Anne Bancroft in "The Miracle Worker," (4) Ed Begley in "Sweet Bird of Youth," (5) Patty Duke in "The Miracle Worker," (6) David Lean for "Lawrence of Arabia," (8) "Sundays and Cybele."

1963: (1) "Tom Jones," (2) Sidney Poitier in "Lilies of the Field," (3) Patricia Neal in "Hud," (4) Melvyn Douglas in "Hud," (5) Margaret Rutherford in "The V.I.P's," (6) Tony Richardson for "Tom Jones," (8) "8½."

1964: (1) "My Fair Lady," (2) Rex Harrison in "My Fair Lady," (3) Julie Andrews in "Mary Poppins," (4) Peter Ustinov in "Topkapi," (5) Lila Kedrova in "Zorba the Greek," (6) George Cukor for "My Fair Lady," (7) William Tuttle, (8) "Yesterday, Today and Tomorrow."

1965: (1) "The Sound of Music," (2) Lee Marvin in "Cat Ballou," (3) Julie Christie in "Darling," (4) Martin Balsam in "A Thousand Clowns," (5) Shelley Winters in "A Patch of Blue," (6) Robert Wise for "The Sound of Music," (7) Bob Hope, (8) "The Shop on Main Street."

1966: (1) "A Man for All Seasons," (2) Paul Scofield in "A Man for All Seasons," (3) Elizabeth Taylor in "Who's Afraid of Virginia Woolf?," (4) Walter Matthau in "The Fortune Cookie," (5) Sandy Dennis in "Who's Afraid of Virginia Woolf?," (6) Fred Zinnemann for "A Man for All Seasons," (8) "A Man and A Woman."

1967: (1) "In the Heat of the Night," (2) Rod Steiger in "In the Heat of the Night," (3) Katharine Hepburn in "Guess Who's Coming to Dinner," (4) George Kennedy in "Cool Hand Luke," (5) Estelle Parsons in "Bonnie and Clyde," (6) Mike Nichols for "The Graduate," (8) "Closely Watched Trains."

1968: (1) "Oliver!," (2) Cliff Robertson in "Charly," (3) Katharine Hepburn in "The Lion in Winter" tied with Barbra Streisand in "Funny Girl," (4) Jack Albertson in "The Subject Was Roses," (5) Ruth Gordon in "Rosemary's Baby," (6) Carol Reed for "Oliver!," (7) Onna White for "Oliver!" choreography, John Chambers for "Planet of the Apes" make-up, (8) "War and Peace."

1969: (1) "Midnight Cowboy," (2) John Wayne in "True Grit," (3) Maggie Smith in "The Prime of Miss Jean Brodie," (4) Gig Young in "They Shoot Horses, Don't They?," (5) Goldie Hawn in "Cactus Flower," (6) John Schlesinger for "Midnight Cowboy," (7) Cary Grant, (8) "Z."

1970: (1) "Patton," (2) George C. Scott in "Patton," (3) Glenda Jackson in "Women in Love," (4) John Mills in "Ryan's Daughter," (5) Helen Hayes in "Airport," (6) Franklin J. Schaffner for "Patton," (7) Lillian Gish, Orson Welles, (8) "Investigation of a Citizen above Suspicion."

1971: (1) "The French Connection," (2) Gene Hackman in "The French Connection," (3) Jane Fonda in "Klute," (4) Ben Johnson in "The Last Picture Show," (5) Cloris Leachman in "The Last Picture Show," (6) William Friedkin for "The French Connection," (7) Charles Chaplin, (8) "The Garden of the Finzi-Continis."

1972: (1) "The Godfather," (2) Marlon Brando in "The Godfather," (3) Liza Minnelli in "Cabaret," (4) Joel Grey in "Cabaret," (5) Eileen Heckart in "Butterflies Are Free," (6) Bob Fosse for "Cabaret," (7) Edward G. Robinson, (8) "The Discreet Charm of the Bourgeoisie."

1973: (1) "The Sting," (2) Jack Lemmon in "Save the Tiger," (3) Glenda Jackson in "A Touch of Class," (4) John Houseman in "The Paper Chase," (5) Tatum O'Neal in "Paper Moon," (6) George Roy Hill for "The Sting," (8) "Day for Night."

1974: (1) "The Godfather Part II," (2) Art Carney in "Harry and Tonto," (3) Ellen Burstyn in "Alice Doesn't Live Here Anymore," (4) Robert DeNiro in "The Godfather Part II," (5) Ingrid Bergman in "Murder on the Orient Express," (6) Francis Ford Coppola for "The Godfather Part II," (7) Howard Hawks, Jean Renoir, (8) "Amarcord."

1975: (1) "One Flew over the Cuckoo's Nest," (2) Jack Nicholson in "One Flew over the Cuckoo's Nest," (3) Louise Fletcher in "One Flew over the Cuckoo's Nest," (4) George Burns in "The Sunshine Boys," (5) Lee Grant in "Shampoo," (6) Milos Forman for "One Flew over the Cuckoo's Nest," (7) Mary Pickford, (8) "Dersu Uzala."

1976: (1) "Rocky," (2) Peter Finch in "Network," (3) Faye Dunaway in "Network," (4) Jason Robards in "All the President's Men," (5) Beatrice Straight in "Network," (6) John G. Avildsen for "Rocky," (8) "Black and White in Color."

1977: (1) "Annie Hall," (2) Richard Dreyfuss in "The Goodbye Girl," (3) Diane Keaton in "Annie Hall," (4) Jason Robards in "Julia," (5) Vanessa Redgrave in "Julia," (6) Woody Allen for "Annie Hall," (7) Margaret Booth (film editor), (8) "Madame Rosa."

1978: (1) "The Deer Hunter," (2) Jon Voight in "Coming Home," (3) Jane Fonda in "Coming Home," (4) Christopher Walken in "The Deer Hunter," (5) Maggie Smith in "California Suite," (6) Michael Cimino for "The Deer Hunter," (7) Laurence Olivier, King Vidor, (8) "Get Out Your Handkerchiefs."

1979: (1) "Kramer vs. Kramer," (2) Dustin Hoffman in "Kramer vs. Kramer," (3) Sally Field in "Norma Rae," (4) Melvyn Douglas in "Being There," (5) Meryl Streep in "Kramer vs. Kramer," (6) Robert Benton for "Kramer vs. Kramer," (7) Robert S. Benjamin, Hal Elias, Alec Guinness, (8) "The Tin Drum."

PROMISING NEW ACTORS 1980

BEVERLY D'ANGELO

WILLIAM HURT

TIMOTHY HUTTON

ROBYN DOUGLASS

KRISTY McNICHOL

DAVID MORSE

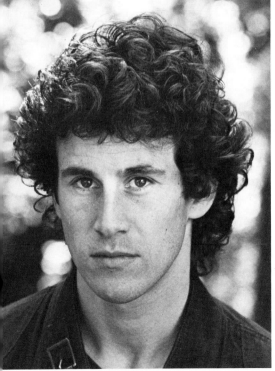

MICHAEL ONTKEAN

DINAH MANOFF

CATHY MORIARTY

STEVE RAILSBACK

RAY SHARKEY

DIANA SCARWID

FOREIGN FILMS

ANGI VERA

(NEW YORKER) Director, Pal Gabor; Screenplay, Pal Gabor from novel by Endre Veszi; Photography, Lajos Koltai; Art Director, Andras Gyorky; Music, Gyorgy Selmeczi; Editor, Eva Karmento; Costumes, Eva Zs. Varga; Assistant Director, Dezso Koza; In Hungarian with English subtitles; In color; Not rated; 96 minutes; January release.

CAST

Vera Angi	Veronika Papp
Anna Trajan	Erzsi Pasztor
Maria Muskat	Eva Szabo
Istvan Andre	Tamas Dunai
Comrade Sas	Laszlo Halasz
Josef Neubauer	Laszlo Horvath

Right: Veronika Papp
© New Yorker Films

Veronika Papp, Tamas Dunai

TO FORGET VENICE

(QUARTET FILMS) Story and Direction, Franco Brusati; Screenplay, Franco Brusati, Jaja Fiastri; Photography, Romano Albani; Music, Benedetto Ghiglia; Art Director, Luigi Scaccianoce; Costumes, Luca Sabatelli; Editor, Ruggero Mastroianni; A Rizzoli Film-Action Films Co-Production; A Robert A. McNeil presentation in color; Not rated; 110 minutes; January release.

CAST

Nicky	Erland Josephson
Anna	Mariangela Melato
Claudia	Eleonora Girogi
Picchio	David Pontremoli
Marta	Hella Petri
Rossino	Fred Personne

Left: Eleonora Giorgi, Mariangel Melato
© **Quartet Films**

**Erland Josephson, and above
with David Pontremoli**

**Eleonora Giorgi, Mariangela Melato
Above: David Pontremoli, Melato**

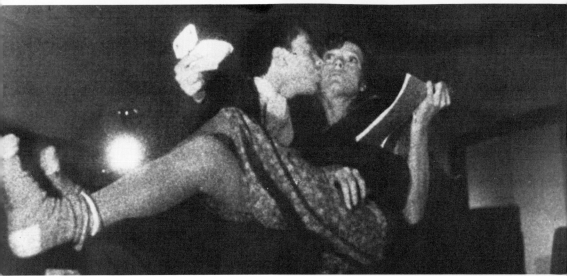

WHY SHOOT THE TEACHER

(QUARTET FILMS) Producer, Lawrence Hertzog; Director, Silvio Narizzano; Executive Producer, Fil Fraser; Screenplay, James DeFelice from the novel of the same name by Max Braithwaite; Photography, Marc Champion; Art Director, Karen Bromley; Music, Ricky Hyslop; Editors, Bruce Nyznik, Ian McBride, Peter Thillaye; In color; Not rated; 96 minutes; January release.

CAST

Max Brown	Bud Cort
Alice Field	Samantha Eggar
Lyle Bishop	Chris Wiggins
Harris Montgomery	Gary Reineke
Dave McDougall	John Friesen
Bert Field	Michael J. Reynolds
Jake Stevenson	Dale McGowan

Top: Samantha Eggar, Bud Cort
© Quartet Films

Bud Cort

MOZART—A CHILDHOOD CHRONICLE

Directed and Written by Klaus Kirschner; Producer, Bayerischer Rundfunk Artfilm Pitt Koch; In black and white; Not rated; 224 minutes; January release.

CAST

Mozart at 7	Pavlos Bekiaris
Mozart at 12	Diago Crovetti
Mozart at 20	Santiago Ziesmer
Mozart's Mother	Marianne Lowitz
His Sister Nannerl at 11	Ingeborg Schroeder
Nannerl at 17	Nina Palmers
Cousin Basle	Elisabeth Bronten
Alofsia Weber	Dietlind Hubner
Mozart's Father, Leopold	Karl-Maria Schley

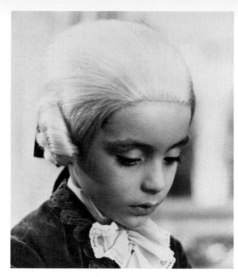

Pavlos Bekiaris
in "Mozart . . ."

THE APPLE GAME

(ARGENT ARTS/ENTERTAINMENT MARKETING) Producer, Antonin Vanek; Director, Vera Chytilova; Screenplay, Vera Chytilova, Kristina Vlachova; Photography, Frantisek Vlcek; Assistant Director, Petr Sveda; Art Director, Vladimir Labsky; Music, Miroslav Korinek; Editor, Alois Fisarek; In color; Rated R; 94 minutes; January release.

CAST

Anna	Dagmar Blahova
Dr. John	Jiri Menzel
Marta	Evelyna Steimarova-Ytirova
Pavel	Jiri Kodet

"The Apple Game'

COUP DE TETE
("Hothead")

(QUARTET FILMS) Director, Jean-Jacques Annaud; Executive Producer, Alain Poire; Screenplay, Francis Veber, Jean-Jacques Annaud for an original idea by Alain Godard; Dialogue, Francis Veber; Photography, Claude Agostini; Music, Pierre Bachelet; A Robert A. McNeil Presentation in color; Editor, Noelle Boisson; Art Director, Alain Maunoury; A Gaumont-S.F.P. Co-Production; Not rated; 87 minutes; January release.

CAST

Francois Perrin	Patrick Dewaere
Stephanie	France Dougnac
Team Owner	Jean Bouise
Team Manager	Michel Aumont

and Paul LePerson, Robert Dalban, Michel Fortin, Mario David, Dora Doll, Catherine Samie, Corinne Marchand, Maurice Barrier, Corothe Jemma

Patrick Dewaere (L)
in "Coup de Tete"

OUR HITLER

(OMNI ZOETROPE) Written and Directed by Hans-Jurgen Syberberg; Photography, Dietrich Lohmann; Assistant Directors, Gerhard von Halem, Michael Sedevy; Editor, Jutta Brandstaedter; Art Director, Hans Gailling; Costumes, Barbara Gailling, Brigitte Kuhlenthal; Puppets, Barbara Buchwald, Hans M. Stummer; Executive Producer, Bernd Eirchinger; A 7 hour film cycle in 4 parts: "The Grail," "A German Dream," "The End of Winter's Tale," "We Children of Hell"; Not rated; January release. CAST: Heinz Schubert, Peter Kern, Hellmut Lange, Rainer von Artenfels, Martin Sperr, Peter Moland, Johannes Buzalski, Alfred Edel, Amelie Syberberg, Harry Baer, Peter Luhr, Andre Heller

MY BRILLIANT CAREER

(ANALYSIS FILMS) Producer, Margaret Fink; Director, Gillian Armstrong; Photography, Don McAlpine; Designer, Luciana Arrighi; Screenplay, Eleanor Witcombe; Adapted from novel by Miles Franklin; Costumes, Anna Senior; In color; Not rated; 101 minutes; February release.

CAST

Sybylla Melvyn	Judy Davis
Harry Beecham	Sam Neill
Aunt Helen	Wendy Hughes
Frank Hawdon	Robert Grubb
Mr. McSwat	Max Cullen
Aunt Gussie	Pat Kennedy
Grandma Bossier	Aileen Brittain
Uncle Julius	Peter Whitford
Mr. McSwat	Carole Skinner
Father	Alan Hopgood
Mother	Julia Blake
Peter McSwat	Tony Hughes
Lizer McSwat	Tina Robinson
Jimmy McSwat	Aaron Corrin
Sarah McSwat	Sharon Crouch
Willie McSwat	Robert Austin
Tommy McSwat	Mark Spain
Mary Anne McSwat	Simone Buchanan
Rosie Jane McSwat	Haylely Anderson
Horace	David Franklin
Gertie	Marion Schad
Stanley	Aaron Wood
Mr. Harris	Max Meldrum
Biddy	Suzanne Roylance
Ethel	Zelda Smyth
Mrs. Butler	Bobby Ward
Blanche Derrick	Amanda Pratt

Left: Judy Davis
© **Analysis Films**

Judy Davis, Sam Neill

Robert Grubb, Judy Davis

THE IMMORTAL BACHELOR

(S. J. INTERNATIONAL) Producer, Elio Scardamaglia; Director, Marcello Fondato; Story and Screenplay, Marcello Fondato, Francesco Scardamaglia; Music, Guido DeAngelis; Art Director, Luciano Ricceri; Costumes, Luca Sabatelli; In color; Rated PG; 95 minutes; February release.

CAST

Gino Benacio	Giancarlo Giannini
Tina Candela	Monica Vitti
Andrea Sansoni	Vittorio Gassman
Gabriella Sansoni	Claudia Cardinale
Fulvio	Renato Pozzetto

Top: Vittorio Gassman, Claudia Cardinale

Monica Vitti, Giancarlo Giannini

THE HUMAN FACTOR

(MGM/UNITED ARTISTS) Producer-Director, Otto Preminger; Screenplay, Tom Stoppard; Based on novel by Graham Greene; Music, Richard Logan, Gary Logan; Executive Producer, Paul Crosfield; Associate Producer, Chris Dillinger; Production Supervisor/Associate Producer, Val Robins; Photography, Mike Molloy; Editor, Richard Trevor; Art Director, Ken Ryan; Costumes, Hope Bryce; In Technicolor; Rated R; 115 minutes; February release.

CAST

Colonel Daintry	Richard Attenborough
Cornelius Muller	Joop Doderer
Brigadier Tomlinson	John Gielgud
Davis	Derek Jacobi
Percival	Robert Morley
Castle's Mother	Ann Todd
Sir John Hargreaves	Richard Vernon
Castle	Nicol Williamson
Sarah	Iman
Porter	Keith Marsh
Dr. Barker	Anthony Woodruff
Sam	Gary Forbes
Lady Mary Hargreaves	Angela Thorne
Buffy	Tony Haygarth
Halliday	Paul Curran
Cynthia	Cyd Haygarth
Messenger	Ken Jones
Shop Assistant	Paul Seed
Stripper	Chantal Gray
Elizabeth	Fiona Fullerton
Sylvia	Adrienne Corri

and Walter Hinds, Philip Chege, Tony Vogel, Norbert Okare, Vicky Udall, Brian Epson, Mike Andrews, Leon Green, Martin Benson, Giles Watling, Marianne Stone, Edward Dentith, Robert Dorning, Patrick O'Connell, Sean Caffrey, Clifford Earl, Tom Chatto, Rawyn Blade, Glenna Forster-Jones, Sylvia Coleridge, Boris Isarov, Dennis Hawthorne, Frank Williams

Top: Gary Forbes, Nicol Williamson, Iman, Derek Jacobi Left Center: John Gielgud, Richard Attenborough

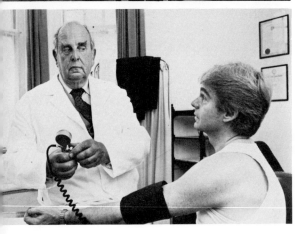

Robert Morley, Derek Jacobi

ZULU DAWN

(AMERICAN CINEMA) Executive Producer, Barrie Saint Clair; Producer, Nate Kohn; Co-Producer, James Faulkner; Associate Producer, Dieter Nobbe; Director, Douglas Hickox; Story and Screenplay, Cy Endfield, Anthony Storey; Music, Elmer Bernstein; Photography, Ousama Rawi; Editor, Malcolm Cooke; In Technicolor, Panavision and Dolby Stereo; Rated PG; 98 minutes; February release.

CAST

Col. Durnford	Burt Lancaster
Lord Chelmsford	Peter O'Toole
William Vereker	Simon Ward
Sir Bartle Frere	John Mills
Col. Hamilton-Brown	Nigel Davenport
Col. Crealock	Michael Jayston
Norris Newman	Ronald Lacey
Lt. Col. Pulleine	Denholm Elliott
Bishop Colenso	Freddie Jones
Lt. Coghill	Christopher Cazenove
Lt. Harford	Ronald Pickup
Major Russell	Donald Pickering
Fanny Colenso	Anna Calder-Marshall
Lt. Melvill	James Faulkner
Quartermaster Sergeant	Peter Vaughn
Capt. Shepstone	Graham Armitage
Sgt. Major Williams	Bob Hoskins
Pvt. Williams	Dai Bradley
Pvt. Storcy	Paul Copley

and Chris Chittell, Nicholas Clay, Patrick Mynhardt, Brian O'Shaughnessy, Simon Sabela, Midge Carter, Phil Daniels, Raymond Davies, Ken Gampu.

**Right: Seated: John Mills, Peter O'Toole
Standing: Burt Lancaster, Simon Ward**
© American Cinema

Denholm Elliott (R)

Peter O'Toole

CLAIR DE FEMME

(ATLANTIC) Producer, Georges Alain Vuille; Direction and Screenplay, Costa-Gavras; Based on a novel by Romain Gary; Photography, Ricardo Aranovich; Music, Jean Musy; Editor, Francoise Bonnot; Art Directors, Mario Chiari, Eric Simon; In color; Not rated; 103 minutes; March release.

CAST

Michel .... Yves Montand
Lydia .... Romy Schneider
Senor Galba.. Romolo Valli
Sonia .... Lila Kedrova
Georges .... Heinz Bennent

Left: Yves Montand, Romy Schneider
© Atlantic Films

Yves Montand, Romy Schneider

THE CHANGELING

(ASSOCIATED FILM DISTRIBUTION) Producers, Joel B. Michaels, Garth H. Drabinsky; Director, Peter Medak; Photography, John Coquillon; Designer, Trevor Williams; Music, Rick Wilkins; Story, Russell Hunter; Screenplay, William Gray, Diana Maddox; In Dolby Stereo and color; Rated R; 113 minutes; March release.

CAST

John Russell	George C. Scott
Claire Norman	Trish Van Devere
Senator Joe Carmichael	Melvyn Douglas
Captain DeWitt	John Colicos
Mrs. Russell	Jean Marsh
Dr. Pemberton	Barry Morse
Robert Lingstrom	Bernard Behrens
Eva Lingstrom	Roberta Maxwell
Tuttle	Chris Gampel
Mrs. Norman	Madeleine Thornton-Sherwood
Eugene Carmichael	James B. Douglas
Minnie Huxley	Ruth Springford
Leah Harmon	Helen Burns
Albert Harmon	Eric Christmas

**Top: Trish Van Devere, George C. Scott
Below: Scott, Melvyn Douglas (also top
right)
© AFD**

**Trish Van Devere, George C. Scott
(also above)**

NIJINSKY

(PARAMOUNT) Producers, Nora Kaye, Stanley O'Toole; Director, Herbert Ross; Screenplay, Hugh Wheeler; Executive Producer, Harry Saltzman; Photography, Douglas Slocombe; Editor, William Reynolds; Associate Producer, Howard Jeffrey; Music, John Lanchbery; Designer, Alan Barrett; Assistant Director, Ariel Levy; Art Directors, Tony Roman, George Richardson; A Hera Production in Dolby Stereo and Metrocolor; Rated R; 129 minutes; March release.

CAST

Sergei Diaghilev	Alan Bates
Vaslav Nijinsky	George De La Pena
Romola De Pulsky	Leslie Browne
Baron De Gunzburg	Alan Badel
Tamara Karsavina	Carla Fracci
Vassili	Colin Blakely
Igor Stravinsky	Ronald Pickup
Leon Bakst	Ronald Lacey
Sergei Grigoriev	Vernon Dobtcheff
Mikhail Fokine	Jeremy Irons
Gabriel Astruc	Frederick Jaeger
Maestro Cecchetti	Anton Dolin
Emilia Marcus	Janet Suzman
Adolph Bolm	Stephan Chase
Magda	Henrietta Baynes
Lady Ripon	Sian Phillips
Argentinian Ambassador	Charles Kay
Young Man on the beach	Tomas Milian, Jr.
Maria Piltz	Monica Mason
Lydia Nelidova	Valerie Aitken
Ludmilla Schollar	Genesia Rosato
Maria Stepanova	June Brown
Lisl	Blaise Mills
Marie Rambert	Kim Miller
Page	Dean McMillan
Baron Adolphe De Meyer	Mart Crowley
Signora Cerchetti	Olga Lowe
Gavrilov	Geoffrey Hughes
The Doll	Patricia Ruanne
Max Froman	Ben Van Cauwenbergh

Top: Alan Bates, Carla Fracci
Left: Bates, George de la Pena
© Paramount Pictures

George de la Pena, Leslie Browne
Above: Alan Badel, George de la Pena

EBOLI

(FRANKLIN MEDIA) Producers, Franco Cristaldi, Nicola Carraro; Director, Francesco Rosi; Screenplay, Rosi, Tonino Guerra, Raffaele La Capria from a novel by Carlo Levi; Photography, Pasqualino DeSantis; Art Director, Andrea Crisanti; Editor, Ruggero Mastroianni; Music, Piero Piccioni; Set, Andrea Cristanti; Costumes, Enrico Sabbatini; In color; Not rated; 150 minutes; March release.

CAST

Carlo Levi	Gian Maria Volonte
Don Luigi Magalone	Paolo Bonacelli
Baron Rotundo	Alain Cuny
Luisa Levi	Lea Massari
Giulia	Irene Papas
Don Traiella	Francois Simon

Right: Gian Maria Volonte, Irene Papas
© Franklin Media

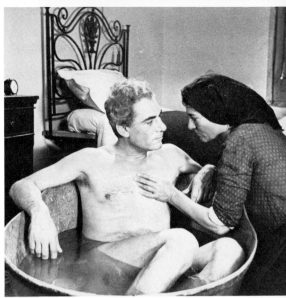

Gian Maria Volonte
Above: Irene Papas

Gian Maria Volonte

NIGHT GAMES

(AVCO EMBASSY) Executive Producer, Raymond Chow; Producers, Andre Morgan, Roger Lewis; Director, Roger Vadim; Story, Anton Diether, Barth Jules Sussman; Screenplay, Anton Diether, Clarke Reynolds; Editor, Peter Hunt; Music, John Barry; Photography, Dennis Lewiston; Designer, Robert Laing; Art Director, Frank Israel; Assistant Director, Denys Grenier DeFerr; In Technicolor; Rated R; 100 minutes; April release.

CAST

Valerie	Cindy Pickett
Julie	Joanna Cassidy
Jason	Barry Primus
Sion	Paul Jenkins
Timothy	Gene Davis
Alicia	Juliet Fabriga
Jun	Clem Parsons
Valerie at 13	Carla Reynolds
Blake	Rene Knecht
Sandra	Pamela Mellish
Rapist	Walter Fagerstrom
Medavoy	Clarke Reynolds
Jewelry Shop Salesgirl	Hermin Aslanian
Dress Shop Salesman	Mario Munder
Policemen	George Weber, Bob Mallett

Left: Barry Primus, Cindy Pickett
© AVCO Embassy

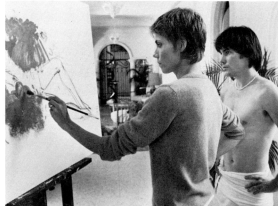

Cindy Pickett and above
with Joanna Cassidy

Joanna Cassidy, Paul Jenkins, Cindy Pickett
Above: Pickett, Gene Davis

KNIFE IN THE HEAD

(NEW YORKER) Director, Reinhard Hauff; Screenplay, Peter Schneider; Photography, Frank Bruhne; Editor, Peter Przygodda; Music, Irmin Schmidt; Art Director, Heidi Ludi; Costumes, Monika Altmann; Assistant Director, Peter Fratzscher; Executive Producer, Eberhard Junkersdorf; In German with English subtitles; In color; Not rated; 108 minutes; April release.

CAST

Bertolt Hoffmann	Bruna Ganz
Ann Hoffmann	Angela Winkler
Anleitner	Hans Christian Blech
Volker Kohler	Heinz Honig
Scholz	Hans Brenner
Schurig	Udo Samel
Dr. Groske	Eike Gallwitz
Nurse Angelika	Carla Egerer
Nurse Emmilie	Gabriele Dossi
Chefarzt	Hans Fuchs
Trau Institute Director	Gerd Burkhard
Patient	Karl Heinz Merz
Mrs. Schurig	Christa Lessoing
Architect	Roland Teubner
TV Journalist	Hans Noever
Police Inspectors	Heinz Hurlander, Karl Scheydt, Alois Mayer

Top: Angela Winkler, Heinz Honig, Bruno Ganz
Below: Hans Christian Blech, Ganz
(R) Angela Winkler, Heinz Honig
© New Yorker Films

Bruno Ganz

IN A YEAR OF THIRTEEN MOONS

(NEW YORKER) Executive Producer, Screenplay, Editing, Art Direction, Photography and Direction by Rainer Werner Fassbinder; In color; Not rated; 129 minutes; In German with English subtitles; June release.

CAST

Elvira Weishaupt	Volker Spengler
Zora	Ingrid Caven
Anton Saitz	Gottfried John
Irene, Elvira's ex-wife	Elisabeth Trissenaar
Marie-Ann, Elvira's daughter	Eva Mattes
J. Smolik	Gunter Kaufmann
Sister Gudrun	Lilo Pempeit
Sybille	Isolde Barth
Christoph Hacker	Karl Scheydt
Soul Friede	Walter Bockmayer
Bum	Bob Dorsey
Cleaning Woman	Ursula Lillig
H. H. Brei	Gunther Holzapfel
Oskar Pleitgen	Janoz Bermez
Poet	Gerhard Zwerenz

Top: Elisabeth Trissenaar, Volker Spengler,
Eva Mattes Below: Lilo Pempeit, Volker
Spengler, Ingrid Caven Left: Gottfried John,
Ingrid Caven Top: Volker Spengler (on ground)
© New Yorker Films

Volker Spengler, Karl Scheydt

ROUGH CUT

(PARAMOUNT) Producer, David Merrick; Director, Donald Siegel; Screenplay, Francis Burns; Based on novel "Touch the Lion's Paw" by Derek Lambert; Photography, Freddie Young; Designer, Ted Haworth; Editor, Doug Stewart; Music, Duke Ellington, Nelson Riddle; Assistant Directors, David Tringham, Andy Armstrong, Waldo Roeg; Costumes, Anthony Mendelson; In color; Rated PG; 112 minutes; June release

CAST

Jack Rhodes	Burt Reynolds
Gillian Bromley	Lesley-Anne Down
Chief Inspector Cyril Willis	David Niven
Nigel Lawton	Timothy West
Ernst Mueller	Patrick Magee
Ferguson	Al Matthews
Shelia	Susan Littler
Inspector Vanderveld	Joss Ackland
Mrs. Willis	Isobel Dean
DeGooyer	Wolf Kahler
Pilbrow	Andrew Ray
Ronnie Taylor	Julian Holloway
Maxwell Levy	Douglas Wilmer
Tobin	Geoffrey Russell
Captain Small	Ronald Hines
1st Officer Palmer	David Howey
Sir Samuel Sacks	Alan Webb

and Frank Mills, Roland Culver, Cassandra Harris, Sue Lloyd, Hugh Thomas, Paul McDowell, Stephen Reynolds, David Eccles, Stephen Moore, Peter Schofield, Jonathan Elsom, Ron Pember, Cyril Appleton, John Slavid, Brian Tipping, Carol Rydall

Right: Burt Reynolds, Lesley-Anne Down
(also at top)
© Paramount Pictures

David Niven, Lesley-Anne Down

Burt Reynolds, Lesley-Anne Down

PRACTICE MAKES PERFECT

(QUARTET FILMS) Producers, Georges Dancigers, Alexandre Mnouchkine; Director, Philippe de Broca; Screenplay, Philippe de Broca, Michel Audiard; Photography, Jean-Paul Schwartz; Editor, Henri Lanoe; Music, Bach, Beethoven, Schumann, Offenbach, Georges Delerue; In color; Not rated; 104 minutes; June release.

CAST

Edouard Choiseul	Jean Rochefort
Marie-France	Nicole Garcia
Lucienne	Annie Girardot
Suzanne Taylor	Danielle Darrieux
Murielle	Catherine Alric
Olga	Lila Kedrova
Charles-Edmond	Jean Dessailly
Pompom	Carole Lixon
Valentine	Catherine LePrince
LeGoff	Jacques Jouanneau

Left: Jean Rochefort (also top)
© Quartet Films

BAROCCO

(ROBERT A. McNEIL) Producers, Andre Genoves, Alain Sarde; Direction and Screenplay, Andre Techine; Photography, Bruno Nuytten; Music, Philippe Sarde; In Eastmancolor; Not rated; 102 minutes; July release.

CAST

Laure	Isabelle Adjani
Samson	Gerard Depardieu
Nelly	Marie-France Pisier
Walt	Jean Claude Brialy
Gauthier	Julien Guiomar
Antoinette	Helene Surgere
Jules	Claude Brasseur

Top: Gerard Depardieu, Isabelle Adjani
Below: Marie-France Pisier, Depardieu
Right: Depardieu, Adjani Top: Claude
Brasseur, Pisier
© Robert A. McNeil

Isabelle Adjani, Gerard Depardieu

STRANGE MASQUERADE

(PIKE FILMS) Director, Pal Sandor; Screenplay, Zsuzsa Toth; Photography, Elemer Ragalyi; Music, Zdenko Tamassy; Hungarian with English subtitles; In Eastmancolor; Not rated; 89 minutes; July release.

CAST

The Boy (Sarolta Galambos)	Endre Holman
Nurse Zsofi	Erzsebet Kutvolgyi
Head Masseuse	Ildiko Pecsi
Dr. Wallach	Sandor Szabo
Old Ladies	Margit Dayka, Irma Patkos, Maria Lazar
Miss Agota	Hedi Temessy
Itinerant Photographer	Dezso Garas
Italian Woman	Carla Romanelli

Right: Endre Holman
© Pike Films

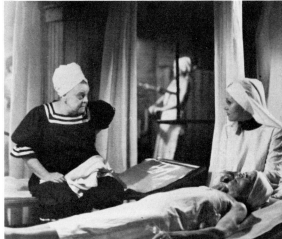

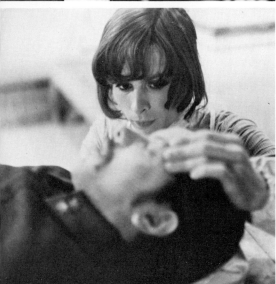

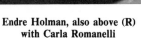

Endre Holman, also above (R) with Carla Romanelli

Endre Holman, Carla Romanelli

THE ADVENTURES OF PICASSO

(DOME PRODUCTIONS) Presented by Albert Schwartz, Renee Furst; Director, Tage Danielsson; Screenplay, Hans Alfredson, Tage Danielsson; Picasso's pictures painted by Per Ahlin; Not rated; 92 minutes; August release.

CAST

Picasso	Gosta Ekman
Picasso's Father	Hans Alfredson
Picasso's Mother	Margaretha Krook
Gertrude Stein	Bernard Cribbins
Alice B. Toklas	Wilfrid Brambell
Apollinaire	Per Socarsson
Rousseau	Lennart Nyman
Sirkkat	Lena Nyman
Ingrid Svensson Guggenheim	Birgitta Andersson

Right: Gosta Ekman, Lena Olin
© Dome Productions

Bernard Cribbons, Wilfrid Brambell
Above: Gosta Ekman

Lena Nyman

LOVERS AND LIARS

(LEVITT-PICKMAN) Producer, Alberto Grimaldi; Director, Mario Monicelli; Screenplay, Paul Zimmerman, Mario Monicelli; Photography, Tonino Belli Colli; Music, Ennio Morricone; Rated R; 96 minutes; August release.

CAST

Anita	Goldie Hawn
Guido	Giancarlo Giannini
Elisa	Claudine Auger
Cora	Aurore Clement
Laura	Laura Betti
Noemi	Andrea Ferreol

Top: Goldie Hawn, Giancarlo Giannini
(also below, left and top)

Giancarlo Giannini, Goldie Hawn

THE CHANT OF JIMMIE BLACKSMITH

(**NEW YORKER**) Producer, Fred Schepisi; Associate Producer, Roy Stevens; Direction and Screenplay, Fred Schepisi; From the novel by Thomas Keneally; Photography, Ian Baker; Designer, Wendy Dickson; Editor, Brian Kavanagh; Music, Bruce Smeaton; Assistant Directors, Ken Ambrose, Greg Allen; Costumes, Bruce Finlayson, Daro Gunzberg; In color and Panavision; Not rated; 108 minutes; September release.

CAST

Jimmie Blacksmith	Tommy Lewis
Mort	Freddy Reynolds
Gilda	Angela Punch
Constable Farrell	Ray Barrett
Tabidgi	Steve Dodds
Rev. Neville	Jack Thompson
Mrs. Neville	Julie Dawson
Healy	Tim Robertson
Mrs. Healy	Jane Harders
McCready	Peter Carroll
Mrs. McCready	Robyn Nevin
Mr. Newby	Don Crosby
Mrs. Newby	Ruth Cracknell
Miss Graf	Elizabeth Alexander
Peter Newby	Marshall Crosby
Young Newby	Matthew Crosby
Jane Newby	Rosie Lilley
Vera Newby	Katie Lilley
Dowie Stead	Peter Sumner
Dud Edmonds	Ray Meagher
Hyberry	Brian Anderson
Claude Lewis	Rob Steele
Cook	Thomas Keneally
Kelly	Bryan Brown

Right: Tommy Lewis, Freddy Reynolds
Top: Lewis, Jack Thompson, Julie Dawson
© New Yorker Films

Angela Punch, Tommy Lewis

Tommy Lewis, Don Crosby

BAD TIMING/A SENSUAL OBSESSION

(WORLD NORTHAL) Producer, Jeremy Thomas; Director, Nicolas Roeg; Screenplay, Yale Udoff; Associate Producer, Tim Van Rellim; Editor, Tony Lawson; Music, Richard Hartley; Photography, Anthony Richmond; A Sondra Gilman/Louise Westergaard presentation in Technovision and color; Not rated; 122 minutes; September release.

CAST

Dr. Alex Linden	Art Garfunkel
Milena Flaherty	Theresa Russell
Inspector Fredrich Netusil	Harvey Keitel
Stefan Vognic	Denholm Elliott
Foppish Man	Daniel Massey
Amy	Dana Gillespie

Left: Art Garfunkel
© World Northal

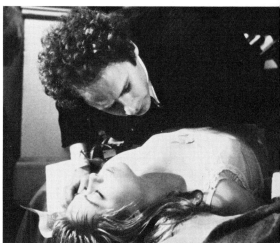

Theresa Russell, Art Garfunkel
(also above)

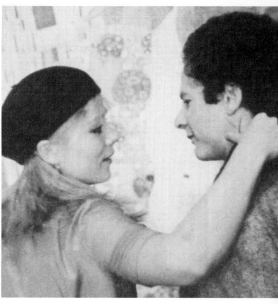

Theresa Russell, Art Garfunkel
(also above)

THE THIRD GENERATION

(NEW YORKER) Producer, Harry Zottl; Direction, Screenplay, Photography, Rainer Werner Fassbinder; Design and Setting, Raul Gimenez, Volker Spengler, Y Sa Lo; Music, Peer Raben; Editor, Juliane Lorenz; In German with English subtitles; In color; Not rated; 111 minutes; September release.

CAST

P. J. Lurz	Eddie Constantine
Police Chief Gerhard Gast	Hark Bohm
Gerhard's son Edgar	Udo Kier
Edgar's wife Susanne	Hanna Schygulla
August	Volker Spengler
Rudolf Mann	Harry Baer
Petra	Margit Carstensen
Hilde	Bulle Ogier
Paul	Raul Gimenez
Ilse Hoffmann	Y Sa Lo
Franz Walsch	Gunther Kaufmann
Bernhard von Stein	Vitus Zeplichal
Grandpa Gast	Claus Holm
Mother Gast	Lilo Pempeit

Top: Hanna Schygulla, Eddie Constantine
Below: Margit Carstensen, Gunther Kaufmann
Right: Vitus Zeplichal
© New Yorker Films

Eddie Constantine

Jose Wilker Left: Fabio Junior,
Betty Faria (also below)
© Carnaval Unifilm

BYE-BYE BRAZIL

(CARNAVAL/UNIFILM) Producer, Lucy Barreto; Direction and Screenplay, Carlos Diegues; Title Song, Roberto Menescal, Chico Buarque; Associate Producers, Walter Clark, Bruno Barreto, Carlos Henrique Braga, Luciola Villela; Presented by Luiz Carlos Barreto; In color; Not rated; 110 minutes, October release.

CAST

Lord Gypsy	Jose Wilker
Salome	Betty Faria
Cico	Fabio Junior
Dasdo	Zaira Zambelli
Swallow, the Muscle King	Principe Nabor
Ze da Luz	Jofre Soares
Agent	Marcos Vinicius
Assistant	Jose Maria Lima
Mayor	Emanoel Cavalcanti
Mayor's Assistant	Jose Marcio Passos
Indian Chief	Rinaldo Gines
Truck Driver	Carlos Kroeber
Smuggler	Oscar Reis
Peasant	Rodolfo Arena
Widow	Catalina Bonaki
Social Worker	Marieta Severo
Customer	Cleodon Gondin
Steward	Jose Carlos Lacerda

Jose Wilker

WORLDS APART

(SCANLON) Producers, Amos Kollek, Rafi Reibenbach; Director, Barbara Noble; Screenplay, Amos Kollek from his novel "Don't Ask Me If I Love"; Additional Dialogue, Mark Dickerman; Photography, David Gurfinkel; Editor, Alain Jakubowicz; Music, Nurit Hirsh; Art Director, Shlomo Zafrir; Assistant Director, Zion Haen; In Panavision and color; Not rated; 94 minutes; October release.

CAST

Assaf	Amos Kollek
Lee	Shelby Leverington
Ram	Joseph Cortese
Father	Joseph Yadin
Mustafa	Shraga Harpaz
Rotman	Joseph Pollak
Mother	Lia Konig
Mickey	Gidi Gov
Muhammed	Avi Luzia
Ruthi	Lea Orshar
Nomi	Esti Zebko

Right: Amos Kollek
© **Scanlon**

Amos Kollek, Shelby Leverington
(also above)

Shelby Leverington, Amos Kollek

KAGEMUSHA
(The Shadow Warrior)

(20th Century Fox) Executive Producers, Akira Kurosawa, Tomoyuki Tanaka; Assistant Producer, Teruyo Nogami; Director, Akira Kurosawa; Screenplay, Akira Kurosawa, Masato Ide; Photography, Takao Saito, Shoji Ueda; Art Director, Yoshiro Muraki; Music, Shinichiro Ikebe; Presented by George Lucas and Francis Ford Coppola; In Panavision and Eastmancolor; Rated PG; 160 minutes; October release.

CAST

Shingen Takeda, Lord of Kai	Tatsuya Nakadai
Kagemusha, Shingen's double	Tatsuya Nakadai
Nobukado Takeda, Shingen's younger brother	Tatsuya Nakadai
Katsuyori, Shingen's son	Kenichi Hagiwara
Sohachiro Tsuchiya, bodyguard	Jinpachi Nezu
Masakage Yamagata, Fire General	Shuji Otaki
Nobunaga Oda	Daisuke Ryu
Ieyasu Tokugawa	Masayuki Yui
Otsuyanokata, Shingen's mistress	Kaori Momoi
Oyunokata, Shingen's mistress	Nitsuko Baisho
Takemaru Takeda, Shingen's heir	Kota Yui
Takeda Clan Generals	Hideo Murota, Koji Shimizu, Sen Yamamoto, Takayuki Shiho, Noboru Shimizu, Shuhei Sugimori
Takemaru's Nurse	Kumeko Otowa
Ranmaru Mori, Nobunaga's Page	Yasuhito Yamanaka
Nagahide Niwa, Nobunaga's Aide	Tetsuo Yamashita
Shingen's Bodyguards	Kai Ato, Yutaka Shimaka
Shingen's Pages	Eiichi Kanakubo, Yugo Miyazaki
Spy disguised as priest	Takashi Ebata
Spy disguised as salt merchant	Yoshimitsu Yamaguchi

Left: Tatsuya Nakadai
© 20th Century-Fox

Tatsuya Nakadai

Kenichi Hagiwara (Center)
Top: Tatsuya Nakadai

Teresa Wright, Christopher Reeve

SOMEWHERE IN TIME

(UNIVERSAL) Producer, Stephen Deutsch; Director, Jeannot Szwarc; Screenplay, Richard Matheson from his novel "Bid Time Return"; Photography, Isidore Mankofsky; Designer, Seymour Klate; Editor, Jeff Gourson; Music, John Barry; Associate Producer, Steven Bickel; Costumes, Jean-Pierre Dorleac; Assistant Directors, Buet Bluestein, Lorraine Senna; Set, Chris Burian-Mohr; In Technicolor; Rated PG; 103 minutes; October release.

CAST

Richard Collier	Christopher Reeve
Elise McKenna	Jane Seymour
W. F. Robinson	Christopher Plummer
Laura Roberts	Teresa Wright
Arthur	Bill Erwin
Dr. Gerald Finney	George Voskovec
Older Elise	Susan French
Arthur's Father	John Alvin
Genevieve	Eddra Gale
Richard's Date	Audrey Bennett
Critics	W. H. Macy, Laurence Coven
Penelope	Susan Bugg
Beverly	Christy Michaels
Students	Ali Matheson, George Wendt
Hippie	Steve Boomer
Professor	Patrick Billingsley
Agent	Ted Liss
Desk Clerk	Francis X. Keefe
Maitre D'	Taylor Williams
Librarian	Noreen Walker
Coin Shop Operator	Evans Ghiselli
Hotel Manager	David Hull
Doctor	Paul M. Cook

and Barbara Giovannini, Don Franklin, Victoria Michaels, William P. O'Hagen, Maud Strand, Bo Clausen, James P. Dunnigan, Sean Hayden, Hal Frank, Hayden Jones, Val Bettin

Top: Christopher Plummer, Jane Seymour
Below: Christopher Reeve, Plummer
Left: Jane Seymour, Christopher Reeve
(also at top)
© Universal Studios

EVERY MAN FOR HIMSELF

(ZOETROPE/NEW YORKER) Producers, Alain Sarde, Jean-Luc Godard; Associate Producer, Marin Karmitz; Director, Jean-Luc Godard; Screenplay, Jean-Claude Carriere, Anne Marie Mieville; Art Director, Romain Goupil; Photography, William Lubchansky, Renato Berta; Music, Gabriel Yared; Editors, Anne Marie Mieville, Jean-Luc Godard; In color; Not rated; 87 minutes; October release.

CAST

Isabelle Riviere	Isabelle Huppert
Paul Godard	Jacques Dutronc
Denise Rimbaud	Nathalie Baye
Second Costumer	Roland Amstutz
Isabelle's Sister	Anna Baldaccini
First Costumer	Fred Personne
Woman	Nicole Jacquet
Elevator Attendant	Dore DeRosa
Opera Singer	Monique Barscha
Paul's Daughter	Cecile Tanner
Second Guy	Roger Jendly
Piaget	Michel Cassagne
Paul's Ex-wife	Paule Muret
Farm Girl	Catherine Freiburghaus
First Guy	Bernard Cazassus
Character	Eric Desfosses
Woman	Nicole Wicht
Stranger	Claude Champion
Motorcyclist	Gerard Battaz
Italian Fiance	Angelo Napoli
Coach	Marie-Luce Felber

Right: Jacques Dutronc
© **Zoetrope/New Yorker**

Isabelle Huppert

Nathalie Baye

THE ELEPHANT MAN

(PARAMOUNT) Producer, Jonathan Sanger; Director, David Lynch; Screenplay, Christopher DeVore, Eric Bergren, David Lynch; Based on "The Elephant Man and Other Reminiscences" by Sir Frederick Treves, and in part on "The Elephant Man: A Study in Human Dignity" by Ashley Montagu; Music, John Morris; Editor, Anne V. Coates; Design, Stuart Craig; Photography, Freddie Francis; Costumes, Patricia Norris; Art Director, Bob Cartwright; Assistant Directors, Anthony Waye, Gerry Cavigan; In Panavision, Dolby Stereo, black and white; Rated PG; 125 minutes; October release.

CAST

Frederick Treves	Anthony Hopkins
John Merrick	John Hurt
Mrs. Kendal	Anne Bancroft
Carr Gomm	John Gielgud
Mothershead	Wendy Hiller
Bytes	Freddie Jones
Night Porter	Michael Elphick
Mrs. Treves	Hannah Gordon
Princess Alex	Helen Ryan
Fox	John Standing
Bytes' Boy	Dexter Fletcher
Nora	Lesley Dunlop
Merrick's Mother	Phoebe Nicholls
Fairground Bobby	Pat Gorman

and Claire Davenport (Fat Lady), Orla Pederson (Skeleton Man), Patsy Smart (Distraught Woman), Frederick Treves (Alderman), Stromboli (Fire Eater), Richard Hunter (Hodges), James Cormack (Pierce), Robert Bush (Messenger), Roy Evans (Cabbie), Joan Rhodes (Cook), Nula Conwell (Nurse), Tony London (Porter), Alfie Curtis (Milkman), Bernadette Milnes, Brenda Kempner (Fighting Women), Carole Harrison (Tart), Hugh Manning, Dennis Burgess, Fanny Carby, Morgan Sheppard, Kathleen Byron, Gerald Case, David Ryall, Deirdre Costello, Pauline Quirke, Kenny Baker, Chris Greener, Marcus Powell, Gilda Cohen, Lisa Scoble, Teri Scoble, Eiji Kusuhara, Robert Day, Patricia Hodge, Tommy Wright, Peter Davidson, John Rapley

Left: Anthony Hopkins Top: Hopkins, Freddie Jones, Dexter Fletcher
© Paramount Pictures

Wendy Hiller

Anne Bancroft

John Hurt Top: (L) Anthony Hopkins, John Hurt Below: Hopkins, Helen Ryan, John Gielgud (R) Anthony Hopkins, and at top with John Gielgud

LOULOU

(NEW YORKER) Executive Producers, Klaus Hellwig, Yves Gasser, Yves Peyrot; Director, Maurice Pialat; Screenplay, Arlette Langmann, Maurice Pialat; Story, Arlette Langmann; Photography, Pierre William Glenn, Jacques Loiseleux; Editors, Yann Dedet, Sophie Coussein; Assistant Directors, Patrick Grandperret, Dominique Bonnaud, Pierre Wallon; Set, Max Berto; French with English subtitles; In color; Not rated; 110 minutes; October release.

CAST

Nelly, 24 years old	Isabelle Huppert
Loulou (Louis), 28 years old	Gerard Depardieu
Andre, 36 years old, Nelly's husband	Guy Marchand
Michel, Nelly's brother	Humbert Balsan
Remy	Bernard Troncyzyk
Pierrot	Christian Boucher
Dominique	Frederique Cerbonnet
Loulou's Mother	Jacqueline Dufranne
Jean-Louis	Willy Safar
Cathy	Agnes Rosier
Marite	Patricia Coulet
Man with knife	Jean-Claude Meilland
Thomas	Patrick Playez
Lulu	Gerald Garnier
Marie-Jo	Catherine de Guirchitch
Rene	Jean Van Herzeele
Philippe	Patrick Poivey
Bernard	Xavier Saint Macary

Top: (R) Isabelle Huppert, Gerard Depardieu
© **New Yorker Films**

Gerard Depardieu, Isabelle Huppert

190

FROM THE LIFE OF THE MARIONETTES

(**ASSOCIATED FILM DISTRIBUTION**) Directed and Written by Ingmar Bergman; In German with English subtitles; Photography, Sven Nykvist; Editors, Petra Von Oelffen; Music, Rolf Wilhelm; Executive Producers, Lord Grade, Martin Atarger; An ITC Entertainment release; In black and white and color; Rated R; 104 minutes; November release.

CAST

Peter Egerman	Robert Atzorn
Katarina	Christine Buchegger
Mogens Jensen	Martin Benrath
Ka	Rita Russel
Cordella Egerman	Lola Muethel
Tim	Walter Schmidinger
Arthur Brenner	Heinz Bennent
Nurse	Ruth Olafs
Interrogator	Karl Heinz Pelser
Secretary	Gaby Dohrr
Doorman	Toni Berger

Right: Christine Buchegger

©AFD

Robert Atzorn, Christine Buchegger

THE HOUND OF THE BASKERVILLES

(HEMDALE INTERNATIONAL/ATLANTIC) Producer, John Goldstone; Director, Paul Morrissey; Executive Producers, Michael White, Andrew Braunsberg; Screenplay, Peter Cook, Dudley Moore, Paul Morrissey; Based on novel by Sir Arthur Conan Doyle; Photography, Dick Bush; Music, Dudley Moore; Editors, Richard Marden, Glenn Hyde; Designer, Roy Smith; Costumes, Charles Knode; Associate Producer, Tim Hampton; In color; Not rated 84 minutes; November release.

CAST

Sherlock Holmes	Peter Cook
Dr. Watson	Dudley Moore
Stapleton	Denholm Elliott
Beryl Stapleton	Joan Greenwood
Dr. Mortimer	Terry-Thomas
Barrymore	Max Eall
Mrs. Barrymore	Irene Handl
Sir Henry Baskerville	Kenneth Williams
Frankland	Hugh Griffith
Mrs. Holmes/Mr. Spiggot	Dudley Moore
Mary	Dana Gillespie
Seldon	Roy Kinnear
Glynis	Prunella Scales
Massage Parlor Receptionist	Penelope Keith
Baskerville Police Force	Spike Milligan

Left: Dudley Moore, Peter Cook
© Atlantic Releasing Corp.

Hugh Griffith (R)

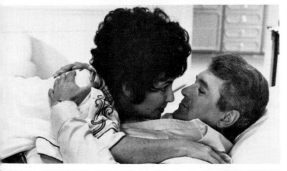

THE MIRROR CRACK'D

(ASSOCIATED FILM DISTRIBUTION) Producers, John Brabourne, Richard Goodwin; Director, Guy Hamilton; Screenplay, Jonathan Hales, Barry Sandler; Music, John Cameron; Photography, Christopher Challis; Designer, Michael Stringer; Costumes, Phyllis Dalton; Editor, Richard Marden; Based on novel by Agatha Christie; Assistant Director, Derek Cracknell; Art Director, John Roberts; In Technicolor; Rated PG; 105 minutes; December release.

CAST

Miss Marple	Angela Lansbury
Cherry	Wendy Morgan
Mrs. Bantry	Margaret Courtenay
Bates the Butler	Charles Gray
Heather Babcock	Maureen Bennett
Miss Giles	Carolyn Pickles
The Major	Eric Dodson
Vicar	Charles Lloyd-Pack
Dr. Haydock	Richard Pearson
Mayor	Thick Wilson
Mayoress	Pat Nye
Scoutmaster	Peter Woodthorpe
Ella Zielinsky	Geraldine Chaplin
Marty N. Fenn	Tony Curtis
Inspector Craddock	Edward Fox
Jason Rudd	Rock Hudson
Lola Brewster	Kim Novak
Marina Rudd	Elizabeth Taylor
Margot Bence	Marella Oppenheim
Sir Derek Ridgeley	Anthony Steel
Lady Amanda Ridgeley	Dinah Sheridan
Kate Ridgeley	Oriana Grieve
Charles Foxwell	Kenneth Fortescue
Lady Foxcroft	Hildegard Neil
Peter Montrose	Allan Cuthbertson
DaSilva	George Silver
Barnsby	John Bennett
Inspector Gates	Nigel Stock

Top: Elizabeth Taylor, Rock Hudson
Below: Geraldine Chaplin, Edward Fox
Right: Angela Lansbury, Edward Fox
© AFD

Kim Novak, Rock Hudson, Elizabeth
Taylor Above: Geraldine Chaplin,
Rock Hudson

THE PURPLE TAXI

(QUARTET) Director, Yves Boisset; Music, Philippe Sarde; Performed by The Chieftans; Presented by Giselle Rebillon, Catherine Winter; In color; Rated R; 107 minutes; December release.

CAST
Sharon	Charlotte Rampling
Dr. Scully	Fred Astaire
Taubelman	Peter Ustinov
Jerry	Edward Albert
Philip	Philippe Noiret
Anne Taubelman	Agostina Belli

Right: Philippe Noiret, Fred Astaire
© Quartet Films

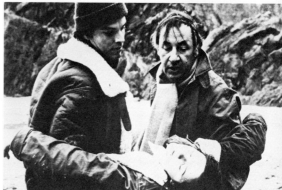

Peter Ustinov, Agostina Belli, Fred Astaire, Charlotte Rampling, Philippe Noiret
Center: (L) Edward Albert, Peter Ustinov, Philippe Noiret (R) Albert, Noiret

FLASH GORDON

(UNIVERSAL) Producer, Dino DeLaurentiis; Director, Mike Hodges; Screenplay, Lorenzo Semple, Jr.; Adaptation, Michael Allin; Based on characters created by Alex Raymond; Music, Queen, Howard Blake; Editor, Malcolm Cooke; Photography, Gil Taylor; Executive Producer, Bernard Williams; Production, Costumes, Sets designed by Danilo Donati; Art Director, John Graysmark; Special Effects, George Gibbs; Art Director, Norman Dorme; Assistant Director, Brian Cook; In Todd-AO, Technicolor and Dolby Stereo; Rated PG; 110 minutes; December release.

CAST

Flash Gordon	Sam J. Jones
Dale Arden	Melody Anderson
Dr. Hans Zarkov	Topol
Emperor Ming	Max von Sydow
Princess Aura	Ornella Muti
Prince Barin	Timothy Dalton
Prince Vultan	Brian Blessed
Klytus	Peter Wyngarde
Kala	Mariangela Melato
Arborian Priest	John Osborne
Fico	Richard O'Brien
Luro	John Hallam
Zogi, the High Priest	Philip Stone
Serving Girl	Suzanne Danielle
Munson	William Hootkins
Hedonia	Bobbie Brown
Biro	Ted Carroll
Vultan's Daughter	Adrienne Kronenberg
Mongon Doctor	Stanley Lebor
Airline Pilots	John Morton, Burnell Tucker

Top: Timothy Dalton, Sam Jones Below: Jones
Right: Jones Top: Topol
© Universal Studios

Max von Sydow, Ornella Muti

195

TRIBUTE

(20th CENTURY-FOX) Producers, Joel B. Michaels, Garth H. Drabinsky; Director, Bob Clark; Screenplay, Bernard Slade from his play of the same title; Photography, Reginald H. Morris; Editor, Richard Halsey; Music, Kenn Wannberg, Barry Manilow, Jack Lemmon, Alan Jay Lerner; In color; Rated PG; December release.

CAST

Scottie Templeton	Jack Lemmon
Jud Templeton	Robby Benson
Maggie Stratton	Lee Remick
Gladys Petrelli	Colleen Dewhurst
Lou Daniels	John Marley
Sally Haines	Kim Cattrall
Hilary	Gale Garnett
Evelyn	Teri Keane
Poker Players	Rummy Bishop, John Dee, Bob Windsor

Left: Robby Benson, Jack Lemmon
© **20th Century-Fox**

Lee Remick, Jack Lemmon
Above: Lemmon, Robby Benson

Robby Benson, Kim Cattrall
Above: Benson, Lee Remick

Kim Cattrall, Jack Lemmon, Robby Benson
Above: Benson, Lemmon, Lee Remick

Jack Lemmon, and top with Colleen Dewhurst
Above: Robby Benson, Kim Cattrall

MON ONCLE D'AMERIQUE

(NEW WORLD) Executive Producer, Michel Faure; Producer, Philippe Dussart; Director, Alain Resnais; Screenplay, Jean Gruault; Photography, Sacha Vierny; Set Design, Jacques Saulnier; Music, Arie Dzierlatka; Editor, Albert Jurgenson; Assistant Directors, Florence Malraux, Jean Leon; In color; Rated PG; 123 minutes; December release.

CAST

Rene Ragueneau	Gerard Depardieu
Janine Garnier	Nicole Garcia
Jean Le Gall	Roger-Pierre
Therese Ragueneau	Marie Dubois
Arlette Le Gall	Nelly Borgeaud
Zambeaux	Pierre Arditi
Veerstrate	Gerard Darrieu
Michel Aubert	Philippe Laudenbach

Right: Gerard Depardieu, Nicole Garcia
© **New World Pictures**

Nicole Garcia, Roger-Pierre
Above: Nelly Borgeaud, Garcia

Gerard Depardieu Above: Nicole
Garcia, Roger-Pierre

BREAKER MORANT

(NEW WORLD/QUARTET) Producer, Matt Carroll; Director, Bruce Beresford; Screenplay, Bruce Beresford, Jonathan Hardy, David Stevens; Based on play by Kenneth Ross; Photography, Don McAlpine; A South Australian Film Corp. presentation; In color; Not rated; 107 minutes; December release.

CAST

Lt. Harry Morant	Edward Woodward
Maj. J. F. Thomas	Jack Thompson
Capt. Alfred Taylor	John Waters
Lt. Peter Handcock	Bryan Brown
Lt. Col. Denny	Charles Tingwell
Dr. Johnson	Frank Wilson
Capt. Simon Hunt	Terence Donovan
Col. Ian Hamilton	Vincent Vall
Lt. George Witton	Lewis Fitz-Gerald
Maj. Charles Bolton	Rod Mullinar

Right: Edward Woodward, Bryan Brown
© New World/Quartet Films

Edward Woodward, and above with Bryan
Brown, Lewis Fitz-Gerald

Edward Woodward, Jack Thompson, and above
with Bryan Brown, Lewis Fitz-Gerald

TESS

(COLUMBIA) Producer, Claude Berri; Co-Producer, Timothy Burrill; Associate Producer, Jean-Pierre Rassam; Executive Producer, Pierre Grunstein; Director, Roman Polanski; Screenplay, Gerard Brach, Roman Polanski, John Brownjohn; Based on novel "Tess of the D'Urbervilles" by Thomas Hardy; Music, Philippe Sarde; Designer, Pierre Guffroy; Costumes, Anthony Powell; Photography, Geoffrey Unsorth, Ghislain Cloquet; Editors, Alastair McIntyre, Tom Priestley; Art Director, Jack Stephens; Choreographer, Sue Lefton; Assistant Director, Thierry Chabert; A Franco-British Co-Production; In Panavision, Eastmancolor, Dolby Stereo; Rated PG; 170 minutes; December release.

CAST

John Durbeyfield	John Collin
Parson Tringham	Tony Church
Tess	Nastassia Kinski
Angel Clare	Peter Firth
Felix Clare	John Bett
Cuthbert Clare	Tom Chadbon
Mrs. Durbeyfield	Rosemary Martin
Alec d'Urberville	Leigh Lawson
Mrs. d'Urberville	Sylvia Coleridge
Vicar of Marlott	Richard Pearson
Marian	Carolyn Pickles
Izz	Suzanna Hamilton
Retty	Caroline Embling
Mercy Chant	Arielle Dombasle
Rev. Mr. Clare	David Markham
Mrs. Clare	Pascale de Boysson
Girls in meadow	Brigid Erin Bates, Jeanne Biras
Religious Fanatic	Peter Benson
Mrs. Crick	Josine Comellas
Housekeeper	Patsy Smart
Constable	Graham Weston

Top: Carolyn Pickles, Caroline Embling,
Suzanna Hamilton, Nastassia Kinski
© Columbia Pictures

Nastassia Kinski

1980 Academy Awards for Best Cinematography, Costume Design, Art Direction

Leigh Lawson, Nastassia Kinski
Top: Peter Firth, Nastassia Kinski

Setsuko Hara, Ken Uehara in "Sounds
from the Mountains" © Corinth

Stuart Whitman, Gene Barry in "Guyana . . ."
© Universal Studios

SOUNDS FROM THE MOUNTAINS (Corinth Films) Director, Mikio Naruse; Screenplay, Yoko Mizuki from novel by Yasunari Kawabata; Photography, Masao Tamai; Art Director, Satoru Chuko; Music, Ichiro Saito; In color; 95 minutes; Not rated; January release. CAST: So Yamamura (Old Man), Teruko Nagaoka (His wife), Ken Uehara (His son), Setsuko Hara (Son's wife), Chieko Nakakita (Old Man's daughter)

THE SUPER-JOCKS (Joseph Brenner) Produced and Written by Emil Nofal; Directors, Emil Nofal, Ray Sargeant; In color; Rated R; 100 minutes; January release. CAST: Joe Stewardson (Will), Ken Leach (Tony), John Higgins (Barry), Richard Loring (Paul), Jenny Meyer (Sandra), Madeleine Usher, Diane Ridler, Tony Jay

THE HATCHET MURDERS (Directors-Mahler Films) formerly "Deep Red"; A Lea J. Marks/Radcliffe Associates Ltd. film in color; Rated R; 100 minutes; January release. CAST: David Hemmings, Daria Nicolodi

NO TIME FOR BREAKFAST (Daniel Bourla) Producer, Yves Gasser; Director, Jean-Louis Bertucelli; Screenplay, Andre G. Brunelin, M. Bertucelli based on book "Un Cri" by Noelle Loriot; In color; Not rated; 100 minutes; January release. CAST: Annie Girardot, Jeane-Pierre Cassel, Isabelle Huppert, Francois Perrier, William Coryn, Suzanne Flon, Anouc Fergac, Michael Subor, Josephine Chaplin, Andre Falcon, Jacqueline Doyen, Margolion, Jacques Richard

M3: THE GEMINI STRAIN (Group 1) Produced and Written by Ed Hunt, Barry Pearson; Director, Ed Hunt; Music, Ric Robertson; A Harmony Ridge production in DeLuxe Color; Rated PG; 88 minutes; January release. CAST: Daniel Pilon (Bill), Kate Reid (Jessica), Celine Lomez (Teacher), Michael J. Reynolds

SACRIFICE (Joseph Brenner) Producers, Giorgio C. Rossi, Ovidio G. Assonitis; Director, Umberto Lenzi; In Technicolor and Techniscope; Rated R; 90 minutes; January release. CAST: Ivan Rassimov, Me Me Lay

GUYANA, CULT OF THE DAMNED (Universal) Producer-Director, Rene Cardona, Jr.; Story and Screenplay, Carlos Valdemar, Rene Cardona, Jr.; Associate Producer, Alfonso Lopez Negrete; Co-Produced with Izaro Films Spain, Conacine Mexico, Care Productions Panama; Music, Nelson Riddle, Bob Summers, George S. Price; Photography, Leopoldo Villasenor; Editor, Earl Watson; Assistant Director, Robert Schlosser; In C.F.I. Color; Rated R; 90 minutes; January release. CAST: Stuart Whitman (Rev. Johnson), Gene Barry (O'Brien), John Ireland (Cole), Joseph Cotten (Gable), Bradford Dillman (Dr. Shaw), Jennifer Ashley (Anna), Yvonne DeCarlo (Susan), Nadiuska (Leslie), Tony Young (Ron), Erika Carlsson (Marilyn), Robert Doqui (Oliver), Hugo Stiglitz (Cliff), Carlos East (Mike)

PRIMAL FEAR (Nu-Image Film) Producers, Anne Claire Poirier, Jacques Gagne: Director, Anne Claire Poirier; Screenplay, Anne Claire Poirier, Marthe Blackburn; Executive Producer, Laurence Pare; Photography, Michel Brault; Editor, Andre Corriveau; Music, Maurice Blackburn; In color; Not rated; 96 minutes; January release. CAST: Julie Vincent (Suzanne), Germain Houde (Rapist), Paul Savoie (Phillippe), Monique Miller (Director), Micheline Lanctot (Editor), Pierre Gobeil (Police), Andre Page (Gynecologist), Michele Mercure (Phillippe's sister), Luce Guilbeault (Patient), Christiane Raymond (Disciple), Louise Portal (Actress), Murielle Dutil (Wife), Julie Morand (Secretary), Leo Munger (Victim), voice of Jean-Pierre Masson

WHO HAS SEEN THE WIND (Cinema World) Executive Producer, Pierre Lamy; Director, Allan King; Screenplay, Patricia Watson from the novel by W. O. Mitchell; Photography, Richard Leiterman; Art Director, Anne Pritchard; Editor, Arla Saare; Music, Eldon Rathburn; Assistant Director, Patricia Watson; In color; Not rated; 100 minutes; January release. CAST: Brian Painchaud (Brian), Douglas Junor (Young Ben), Gordon Pinsent (Gerald), Chapelle Jaffe (Maggie), Jose Ferrer (Ben), Charmian King (Mrs. Abercrombie), David Gardner (Rev. Powelly), Patricia Hamilton (Miss McDonald), Helen Shaver (Ruth), Tom Hauff (Digby), Gerard Parkes (Sean), Nan Stewart (Mrs. MacMurray)

Ivan Rassimov, Me Me Lay
in "Sacrifice" © Joseph Brenner

Daria Nicolodi, David Hemmings
in "Hatchet Murders"

Julie Vincent, Germaine Houde in "Primal
Fear" © Nu-Image Films

Richard Loring, Ken Leach, Joe Stewardson
in "Super-Jocks" © Joseph Brenner

SUPERSONIC MAN (Topar) Director, Juan Piquer; Screenplay, Sebastian Moi, Juan Piquer; Photography, Juan Marine; Editor, Pedro del Rey; Music, Gino Peguri, Juan Luis Izaguirre, Carlos Attias; Sets, Emilio Ruiz, Francisco Prosper; In Eastmancolor, Supercolor and Dinavision; Not rated; 85 minutes; January release. CAST: Michael Coby, Cameron Mitchell, Richard Yesteran, Diana Polakov, Jose Maria Caffarel, Frank Brana, Javier de Campos, Tito Garcia, Quique Camoiras, Louis Barboo, Angel Ter

BEYOND EROTICA (Joseph Brenner) Director, Jose Maria Forque; Screenplay, Hermogenes Sainz, Jose Maria Forque; In color; Rated R; 90 minutes; January release. CAST: David Hemmings (Juan), Alida Valli (Louise), Andrea Rau (Lola),

THE NEW ADVENTURES OF SHOW WHITE (NMD) Written and Directed by Rolf Thiel; English version supervised by Perry Oxenhorn; Written by Tom Baum; Director, Helen Gary; Music, Joe Beck, Regis Mull; In DeLuxe Color and Widescreen; Rated R; 76 minutes; January release. CAST: Marie Liljedahl (Snow White), Eva V. Rueber-Staier (Cinderella), Ingrid Van Bergen (Wicked Queen), Gaby Fuchs (Sleeping Beauty), Kitty Gschopf, Evelin Dutree (Wicked Sisters), Walter Giller (Hans), Peter Hohberger (Heinz), Hugo Lindinger (Farmer), Isolde Stiegler (Old One)

THE WRONG MOVE (Bauer International) Producer, Peter Genee; Director, Wim Wenders; Screenplay, Peter Handke; In German with subtitles; Photography, Robbie Miller; In black and white and color; Not rated; 103 minutes; January release. CAST: Rudiger Vogler (Wilhelm), Hanna Schygulla (Therese), Hans Christian Blach (Laertes), Peter Kern (Landau), Natassia Kinski (Mignon)

THE DRUGSTORE (Cinema Perspectives) an excerpt from "How Yukong Moved the Mountains" by Joris Ivens and Marceline Loridan; Running time, 81 minutes; January release. A documentary on the running of a big-city pharmacy in China.

DEATH ON CREDIT (Joseph Green) Producers, V. Petrashevich, Fred I. Jasons; Director, Victor Petrashevich; Music, Chuck Mymit; Editor, Debbie Brownstein; Photography, Petrashevich; Screenplay, Inese L. Apelis; In Eastmancolor; Rated R; 81 minutes; January release. CAST: Linda Boyce (Linda), Kent Bateman (Ken), Caesar Cordova (Caesar), Joseph Lewis (Chauffeur), Lucky Kargo, Billy Jackson, Patrick Wright, Nikko Karant, Luke Walter

DOUBLE IDENTITY (Joseph Green) Director, Franz Peter Wirth; Screenplay, Oliver Storz, Karl Heinz Willcheri, Wilfried Schroder; Photography, Gernot Roll; Art Director, Gotz Weidner, Helmut Gassner; Editor, Hannes Nikel; Music, Horst Jankowski; Costumes, Monika Bauert; Producer, Oliver Storz; In Eastmancolor; Rated PG; 100 minutes; January release. CAST: Jean Claude Bouillon (Mike), Hansjorg Felmy (Muller), Marina Malfatti (Sonja), Gabriella Farinon (Laureen), Martin E. Brooks (Camden), Konrad Georg (Semmerling), Alfons Hockmann (Schubert), Charlotte Kerr (Maude), Franz Mosthav (Micnic)

THE CREATURES FROM BEYOND THE GRAVE (Howard Mahler) Producers, Max J. Rosenberg, Milton Subotsky; Associate Producer, John Dark; Screenplay, Robin Clarke, Raymond Christodoulou; Director, Kevin Connor; An Amicus production in Technicolor; Rated PG; 100 minutes; January release. CAST: Ian Bannen, Ian Carmichael, Peter Cushing, Diana Dors, Margaret Leighton, Donald Pleasence, Nyree Dawn Porter, David Warner, Ian Ogilvy, Lesley-Anne Down

MOLIERE (New Yorker) Written and Directed by Ariane Mnouchkine; Photography, Bernard Zitzerman; Editor, Francoise Javet, Georges Klotz; Art Director, Guy-Claude Francois; Music, Rene Clemencie; In Eastmancolor; Not rated; 225 minutes; January release. CAST: Phillippe Caubere (Moliere), Marie-France Audollent (Forest), Jonathan Sutton (LaGrange), Frederic Ladonne (Moliere as child), Odile Cointepas (Mother), Armand Delcampe (Father), Jean Daste (Cesse), Francoise Jamet (Genevieve), Jean-Claude Penchenat (Louis XIV)

David Hemmings, Andrea Rau in "Beyond
Erotica" © Joseph Brenner

Ian Bannen in "The Creatures from
Beyond the Grave" © Howard Mahler

**Ingrid Thulin, Erland Josephson
in "One & One" © New Line Cinema**

**Franco Nero, Lisa Gastoni
in "Submission" © Joseph Brenner**

KING OF KUNG FU (Cinematic) Producer, Robert Jeffrey; Director, Joseph Velasco; Associate Producer, Serafim Karalexis; Action Director, Ron Van Clief; In color; Rated R; February release. CAST: Yang Tse, Robert Colts, Ben Clayton, Peter Tai, Lee Hai San, Lan Fun, Rod Cooper, John Taylor, Jr.

THE CASE AGAINST FERRO (Specialty) Director, Alain Corneau; Screenplay, Corneau, Daniel Boulanger; Photography, Etienne Becker; Editor, Marie-Joseph Yoyotte; Music, Georges Delerue; In Eastman Color; Not rated; 125 minutes; February release. CAST: Yves Montand (Ferro), Simone Signoret (Therese), Francois Perier (Ganay), Stefania Sandrelli (Sylvia), Mathieu Carriere (Menard)

ONE AND ONE (New Line) Story, Screenplay and Direction by Erland Josephson; Executive Producer, Katinka Farago; In Eastmancolor; Not rated; 90 minutes; February release. CAST: Erland Josephson, Ingrid Thulin

BLOOD FEUD (AFD) Written and Directed by Lina Wertmuller; Photography, Tonino Delli Colli; Editor, Franco Fraticelli; Music, Dangio, Nando DeLuca; In Eastmancolor; Rated R; 112 minutes; February release. CAST: Sophia Loren (Titina Paterno), Marcello Mastroianni (Spallone), Giancarlo Giannini (Nick), Turi Ferro (Baron)

CALIGULA (Penthouse Films) Producers, Bob Guccione, Franco Rossellini; Adapted by Gore Vidal; Art Director, Danilo Donati; Photography, Silvano Ippoliti, Tinto Brass; Editors, Nino Baragli, Bob Guccione, Franco Rossellini; Music, Paul Clemente, Khatchaturian, Prokofiev; Assistant Director, Piernico Solinas; Choreographers, Tito DeDuc, Pino Pennesi; In color; Not rated 156 minutes; February release. CAST: Malcolm McDowell (Caligula), Teresa Ann Savoy (Drusilla), Guido Mannari (Macro), John Gielgud (Nerva), Peter O'Toole (Tiberius), Giancarlo Badessi (Claudius), Bruno Brive (Gemellus), Adriana Asti (Ennia), Leopoldo Trieste (Charicles), Paolo Bonacelli (Chaerea), John Steiner (Longinus), Mirella Dangelo (Livia), Helen Mirren (Caesonia), Richard Parets (Mnester), Paula Mitchell (Subura Singer), Osiride Pevarello (Giant), Donato Placido (Proculus), Anneka DiLorenzo (Messalina), Lori Wagner (Agrippina)

SIMONE DE BEAUVOIR (Center for Public Cinema) A documentary by Josee Dayan and Malka Ribowska; French with subtitles; Not rated 110 minutes; February release.

THE MIDDLEMAN (Bauer International) Executive Producer, Subir Guha; Direction, Music and Screenplay, Satyajit Ray; In Bengali with subtitles; Photography, Soumendu Ray; Editor, Dulal Dutta; Not rated; 125 minutes; February release. CAST: Pradip Mukherlee (Samnath), Staya Baneriee (Father), Dipankar Dey (Brother), Lily Chekravorty (His Wife), Utpal Dut (Bishu), Rabi Ghost (Mitter), Subeshna Das Sharma (Juana), Aparna Ser (Somnath's fiancee)

SUBMISSION (Joseph Brenner) Producer, Silvio Clementelli; Director, Salvatore Samperi; Screenplay, Ottavio Jemma, Salvatore Samperi; Photography, Vittorio Storaro; Music, Riz Ortolani; Art Director, Ezio Altieri; Editor, Sergio Montanari; Costumes, Gitt Magrini; In Technicolor; Rated R; 107 minutes; February release. CAST: Lisa Gastoni (Eliane), Franco Nero (Armand), Raymond Pellegrin (Henri), Andrea Ferreol (Juliette), Claudia Marsani (Justine)

GOLIATHON (World Northal) Producer, Runme Shaw; Director, Homer Gaugh; Special Effects, Andrew Rayan; A Shaw Brothers presentation in color; Rated PG; 83 minutes; March release. CAST: Lee Hassen, Evelyne Kraft

DAYS OF FURY (Picturemedia Ltd.) Executive Producer, Doro Vlado Hreljanovic; Producers, Doro Vlado Hreljanovic, Fred Warshofsky; Associate Producer, Donald Stillman, Jr.; Direction and Screenplay, Fred Warshofsky; A Markwood Productions Ltd. picture; In color; Rated PG; 97 minutes; March release. CAST: Vincent Price as host and narrator.

BLAISE PASCAL (Entertainment Marketing) Producer-Director, Roberto Rossellini; Screenplay, Marcella Mariani, Luciano Scaffa, Roberto Rossellini; Photography, Mario Fioretti; In Italian with English subtitles; In color; Not rated; 135 minutes; March release. CAST: Pierre Arditi as Blaise Pascal

**Leopoldo Trieste, Malcolm McDowell
in "Caligula" © Penthouse Films**

**Evelyne Kraft in "Goliathon"
© World Northal**

Herbert Lom, Elliott Gould, Cybill Shepherd
in "The Lady Vanishes" © Group 1

Bruno Ganz, Edith Clever in "The Left-
Handed Woman" © New Yorker Films

BRUCE LEE: HIS LAST DAYS, HIS LAST NIGHTS (World Northal) Director, Lo Mar; A Shaw Brothers presentation in color; Rated R; March release. CAST: Li Hsiu Hsien, Betty Ting Pei

THE LADY VANISHES (Group 1) Producer, Tom Sachs; Executive Producers, Michael Garreras, Arlene Sellers, Alex Winitsky; Director, Anthony Page; Screenplay, George Axelrod based on novel by Ethel Lina White; Photography, Douglas Slocombe; Editor, Russell Lloyd; Music, Richard Hartley; Design, Wilfred Shingleton; Art Director, Bill Alexander; Costumes, Emma Porteus; Assistant Directors, Michael Dryhurst, Michael Mertineit; A Hammer Film in color; Rated PG; 99 minutes; March release. CAST: Elliott Gould (Condon), Cybill Shepherd (Amanda), Angela Lansbury (Miss Froy), Herbert Lom (Dr. Hartz), Arthur Lowe (Charters), Ian Carmichael (Caldicott), Gerald Harper (Todhunter), Jean Anderson (Baroness), Jenny Runacre (Mrs. Todhunter), Vladek Sheybal (Trainmaster), Madlena Nedeva (Nun), Madge Ryan, Rosalind Knight, Jonathan Hackett, Barbara Markham, Hillevi, Garry McDermott, Jacki Harding

EMPIRE OF PASSION (Barbary Coast) Direction and Screenplay, Nagisa Oshima; Based on book by Itoko Nakamura; Photography, Yoshio Miyajima; Editor, Keiichu Uraoka; Art Director, Jusho Toda; Music, Toru Takemitsu; In Eastmancolor; Not rated; 108 minutes; March release. CAST: Kazuko Yoshiyuki (Seki), Tatsuya Fuji (Toyoji), Takahiro Tamura (Gisaburo), Takuzo Kawatani (Hotta), Akiko Koyama (Boss), Taiji Tonoyama (Toichiro)

THE WORLD IS FULL OF MARRIED MEN (New Line Cinema) Executive Producer, Adrienne Fancey; Producers, Malcolm Fancey, Oscar S. Lerman; Screenplay, Jackie Collins from her novel of same title; Director, Robert Young; Title Song performed by Bonnie Tyler, Mick Jackson; In color; Rated R; 109 minutes; March release. CAST: Anthony Franciosa, Carroll Baker, Gareth Hunt, Georgina Hale, Anthony Steel, Sherrie Lee Cronin, Paul Nicholas, Jean Gilpin, John Nolan, Hot Gossip

THE LEFT-HANDED WOMAN (New Yorker) Direction and Screenplay, Peter Handke; Photography, Robby Muller; Editor, Peter Pryzgodda; Executive Producer, Renee Gundelach; Associate Producer, Joachim von Mengershausen; Assistant Directors, F. C. Maye, Peter Jungk; Costumes, Domenica Kaesdorf; In German with English subtitles; A Road Movies Filmproduktion in color; Not rated; 119 minutes; March release. CAST: Edith Clever (The Woman), Markus Muhleisen (Stefan), Bruno Ganz (Bruno), Michel Lonsdale (Waiter), Angela Winkler (Franziska), Bernhard Wicki (Publisher), Nicolas Novikoff (Driver), Bernhard Minetti (Father), Rudiger Vogler (Actor)

THE BATTLE OF CHILE PART 3 (Unifilm) Director, Patricio Guzman; Editor, Pedro Chaskel; Photography, Jorge Muller; Assistant Director, Jose Pino; In Spanish with subtitles; In black and white; Not rated; 82 minutes; April release. Part of the documentary trilogy.

THE COED MURDERS (NMD) Producer, Primex Italiana; Director, Massimo Dallamano; Music, Stelvio Cipriani; Presented by Nicholas Demetroules; In Movielab Color; Rated R; 96 minutes; April release. CAST: Giovanna Ralli, Claudio Cassinelli, Mario Adorf, Franco Fabrizi, Farley Granger

FIST OF FURY PART 2 (21st Century) Producer-Director, Jimmy Shaw; Martial Arts Director, Tommy Lee; In color; Rated R; 92 minutes; April release. CAST: Bruce Li, Lo Lieh, Ti Fung, Lee Quinn, Yasuyoshi Shikamura, Jimmy Nam

DEATH SHIP (Avco Embassy) Executive Producer, Sandy Howard; Producers, Derek Gibson, Harold Greenberg; Director, Alvin Rakoff; Screenplay, John Robins; Associate Producer, Adrian Hughes; Photography, Rene Verzier; Assistant Directors, Charles Braive, Pedro Gandol; Art Directors, Chris Burke, Michel Proulx; Editor, Mike Campbell; In color; Rated R; 91 minutes; April release. CAST: George Kennedy (Ashland), Richard Crenna (Trevor), Nick Mancuso (Nick), Sally Ann Howes (Margaret), Kate Reid (Sylvia), Victoria Burgoyne (Lori), Jennifer McKinney (Robin), Danny Highham (Ben), Saul Rubinek (Jackie)

Carroll Baker, Anthony Franciosa in "The
World Is Full of Married Men" © New Line

Kate Reid, George Kennedy, Richard Crenna
in "Death Ship" © AVCO Embassy

Karen Dotrice, Robert Powell in "39 Steps" © International Picture Show

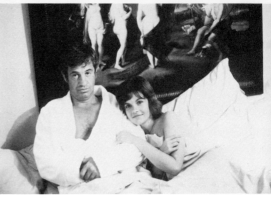

Jean-Paul Belmondo, Genevieve Bujold in "The Incorrigible" © EDP

SOUPCON (Roy Durham/Jeffie Pike) Producers, Roy Durham, Jeffie Pike; Direction and Screenplay, Jean-Charles Tacchella; Music, Gerard Anfosso; Photography, Georges Lendi; In color; Not rated; 91 minutes; April release. CAST: Jean Carmet (Francois Dupuis), Marie Dubois (Brigitte Dupuis), Rachel Jenevein (Nathalie), Jose Luccioni (Roger), Gael Gautier (Macho), Gilles Laurent (Gilbert), Christine Deschaumes (Josyane), Mathieu Verlier (Their Son), Marie-Veronique Maurin (Sophie), Alain Doutey (Gerard), Clement Michu, Jean-Philippe Ancelle, Marianne Valentin, Georges Montal, Anne-Marie Bacquie, Jacqueline Ricard, Jacqueline Fontaine, Francoise Caillaud, Joseph Quere

THE THIRTY-NINE STEPS (International Picture Show) Executive Producer, James Kenelm-Clarke; Producer, Greg Smith; Director, Don Sharp; Screenplay, Michael Robson; Based on novel by John Buchan; Associate Producer, Frank Bevis; Photography, John Coquillion; Designer, Harry Pottle; Music, Ed Welch; Editor, Eric Boyd-Perkins; Assistant Director, Barry Langley; A Rank Film in color; Rated PG; 102 minutes; April release. CAST: Robert Powell (Hannay), David Warner (Appleton), Eric Porter (Lomas), Karen Dotrice (Alex), John Mills (Scudder), George Baker (Bullivant), Ronald Pickup (Bayliss), Donald Pickering (Marshall), Timothy West (Porton), Miles Anderson (David), Andrew Keir (Rohan), Robert Flemyng (Magistrate), William Squire (Harkness), Paul McDowell (McLean), David Collings (Tillots), John Normington (Fletcher), John Welsh (Belthane), Edward DeSouza (Woodville), Tony Steedman (Admiral), John Grieve (Forbes), Andrew Downie (Stewart), Donald Bisset (Renfrew), Derek Anders (Donald), Oliver Maquire (Martins), Joan Henley (Lady Nettleship), Prentis Hancock (Perryman), Leo Dolan (Milkman), Artro Morris (Scott), James Garbutt (Miller), Robert Gillespie (Crombie), Raymond Young (Guide), Paul Jerricho (P. C. Scott), Michael Bilton (Vicar)

MANNEQUIN (Joseph Brenner) Producer, Alain Vallier; Director, Claude Pessis; In Eastmancolor; Rated R; 81 minutes; April release. CAST: Nadine Perles (Natalie), Elton Frame (Pierre), Alain Schwartz, Karen Mayer

INCORRIGIBLE (EDP Films) Producers, Alexandre Mnouchkine, Georges Dancigers; Director, Philippe DeBroca; Screenplay, Michel Audiard; Music, Georges Delerue; In color; Not rated; 93 minutes; April release. CAST: Jean-Paul Belmondo, Genevieve Bujold, Julien Cuiomar, Charles Gerard, Capucine, Danie Ceccaldi

EAGLE'S WING (International Picture Show) Executive Producer, Peter Shaw; Producer, Ben Arbeid; Director, Anthony Harvey; Screenplay, John Briley; Based on story by Michael Syson; Photography, Billy Williams; Editor, Lesley Walker; Music, Marc Wilkinson; Designer, Herbert Westbrook; Costumes, Tim Hutchinson; Assistant Directors, Jake Wright, Manuel Munoz; In color; Rated PG; 104 minutes; May release. CAST: Martin Sheen (Pike), Sam Waterston (White Bull), Harvey Keitel (Henry), Stephane Audran (Widow), Caroline Langrishe (Judith), John Castle (Priest), Jorge Luke (Red Sky), Jose Carlos Ruiz (Lame Wolf), Manuel Ojeda (Miguel), Jorge Russek (Gonzalo), Pedro Damieari (Jose), Farnesio DeBernal (Monk), Cecilia Camacho (Girl), Claudio Brook (Sanchez), Julio Lucena (Luis), Enrique Lucero (Shaman)

SNAKE FIST VS. THE DRAGON (21st Century) Producer, Alex Gouw; Action Choreography, Wilson Tong; In Eastmancolor; Rated R; 85 minutes; May release. CAST: Johnny Chang, Wilson Tong, Charlie Chan, Hau Tsau Seng, Pom Pom Shi, Wong Chun Leung

RUNNIN' AFTER LOVE (Bauer International) Producer-Director, Carlos Hugo Christensen; Screenplay, Mr. Christensen, Pericles Leal; In Portugese with subtitles; Photography, Antonio Goncalves; Editor, Ozen Sermet; Music, New York City Four; Not rated; 90 minutes; May release. CAST: Bibi Vogel (Marlene), Wagner Montes (Beto), Osmar de Mattos (Nando), Jayme Barcellos (Delgado), Fernando de Almeida (Ramiro), Sonia de Morale (Vitoria), Roberto Faissal (Ruf), Domicio Costa (Tony), Darcy de Souza (Jurema), Marcos Andre (Serjao), Ricardo Barros (Giba), Ricardo Faissal (Paulinho), Tatiana Leal (Girl on phone), Affonso Brage (Detective)

Nadine Perles, Elton Frame in "Mannequin" © Joseph Brenner

Martin Sheen in "Eagle's Wing" © International Picture Show

Ginette Garcin, Nelly Kaplan, Daniel
Ceccaldi in "Charles and Lucie"

Hugh Griffith, Josephine Chaplin in
"Canterbury Tales" © United Artists

CHARLES AND LUCIE (Nu-Image Film) Producer, Claude
Makovski; Director, Nelly Kaplan; Screenplay, Nelly Kaplan,
Jean Chapot, Claude Makovski; Executive Producer, Jean Chapot; Photography, Gilbert Sandoz; Editors, Nelly Kaplan, Jean
Chapot; Music, Pierre Perret; Assistant Directors, Andre Delacroix, Jean-Claude Robert; In French with English subtitles; In
color; 97 minutes; May release. CAST: Daniel Ceccaldi (Charles),
Ginette Garcin (Lucie), Nelly Kaplan (Nostradama), Claude
Makovski (Curator), Jean-Marie Proslier (Leon), Georges Claisse
(Nerac), Guy Grosso, Henri Tisot, Feodor Atkine, Pierre Repp,
Jacques Maury, Renne Duncan, Samson Fainsilber

THE CANTERBURY TALES (United Artists) Producer, Alberto Grimaldi; Direction and Screenplay, Pier Paolo Pasolini;
Based on Geoffrey Chaucer's "Canterbury Tales:' Photography,
Tonino Delli Colli; Art Director, Dante Ferzetti; Costumes,
Danilo Donati; Editor, Nino Baragli; Assistant Directors, Sergio
Citti, Umberto Angelucci, Peter Shepherd; In Technicolor; 109
minutes; May release. CAST: Pier Paolo Pasolini (Chaucer),
Hugh Griffith (Sir January), Laura Betti (Wife of Bath), Ninetto
Davoli (Peterkin), Franco Citti (Devil), Josephine Chaplin (May),
Alan Webb (Old Man), Jenny Runacre (Alison), John Francis
Lane (Friar), Tom Baker (Jenkin), Oscar Fochetti (Damian),
Robin Asquith (Ruffo), Derek Deadman (Pardoner), George Bethell Datch (Host), Guiseppe Arrigo (Pluto), Elizabetta Genovese
(Prosperine), Daniel Buckler (Summoner), Dan Thomas (Nicholas), Michael Balfour (Carpenter), Peter Cain (Absolom), Eamann Howell (John), Patrick Duffett (Alan), Albert King
(Miller)

PASTORAL HIDE AND SEEK (Unifilm) Producers, Eiko
Kujo, Hiroko Govaers; Direction and Screenplay, Shuji
Terayama; Photography, Tatsuo Suzuki; Music, J. A. Seazer; Art
Director, Kiyoshi Awazu; Designer, Kazuichi Hanawa; Editor,
Sachiko Yamaji; In color; Not rated; 102 minutes; June release.
CAST: Kantaro Suga (Author), Hiroyuki Takano (Boy), Chigusa
Tayakama (Mother), Keiko Niitaka (Unwed Mother), Masumi
Harukawa, Masaharu Saito, Kaoru Yachigusa, Yoshio Harada,
Izumi Hara, Isao Kimura, Salvador Tali, Mister Pon, Yoko Ran,
Kin Omae, Masako Ono, Kan Mikami, Kiyoshi Awazu

EFFECTS (International Harmony) Producers, John Harrison,
Pasquale Buba; Direction and Screenplay, Dusty Nelson; Photography, Carl Augenstein; An Image Works Production presented
by Stuart S. Shapiro; In color; Rated R; 87 minutes; June release.
CAST: Joseph Pilato, Susan Chapek, John Harrison, Bernard
McKenna, Debra Gordon, Tom Savini

SUMMER SHOWERS (Unifilm) Executive Producer, Luiz Fernando Goulart; Direction and Screenplay, Carlos Diegues; Photography, Jose Medeiros; Editor, Mair Tavares; In color; Not
rated; 86 minutes; June release. CAST: Jofre Soares (Afonso),
Mirian Pires (Isaura), Cristian Ache (Lurdinha), Daniel Filho
(Geraldinho), Emanuel Cavalcanti, Gracinda Freire, Jorge Coutinho, Luiz Antonio, Lurdes Mayer, Marieta Severo, Carlos Gregorio, Paulo Cesar Pereio, Procopio Mariano, Rodolfo Arena,
Sady Cabral

MAD MAX (American International/Filmways) Producer, Byron Kennedy; Director, George Miller; Screenplay, James
McCausland; Direction, George Miller; Art Director, Jon Dowding; Photography, David Eggby; Editor, Tony Paterson; Costumes, Clare
Griffin; Music, Brian May; Associate Producer, Bill Miller; Assistant Director, Ian Goddard; A Samuel Z. Arkoff presentation in
Movielab Color; Rated R; 93 minutes; June release. CAST: Mel
Gibson (Max), Joanne Samuel (Jessie), Hugh Keays-Byrne (Toecutter), Steve Bisley (Goose), Tim Burns (Johnny), Roger Ward
(Fifi Macaffee)

HOG WILD (AVCO Embassy) Producer, Claude Heroux; Director, Les Rose; Screenplay, Andrew Peter Marin; Photography,
Rene Verzier; Art Director, Carol Spier; Editor, Dominique Boisvert; Costumes, Delphine White; Executive Producers, Pierre David, Victor Solnicki, Stephen Miller; In color; Rated PG; 97
minutes; June release. CAST: Michael Biehn (Tim), Patti D'Arbanville (Angie), Tony Rosato (Bull), Angelo Rizacos (Bean),
Martin Doyle (Shadow), Matt Craven (Chrome), Matt Birman-Feldman (Lead), Claude Philippe (Indian), Thomas C. Kovacs
(Veel), Jacoba Knaapan (Tina), Michael Zelniker (Pete), Karen
Stephen (Brenda)

"Pastoral Hide and Seek"
© Unifilm

Michael Biehn, Patti D'Arbanville
in "Hog Wild" © AVCO Embassy

"Floating Cloud"
© Corinth Films

"The Children"
© World Northal

FLOATING CLOUD (Corinth) An Akira Kurosawa film in black and white; 123 minutes; June release. CAST: Hideko Takamine, Masayuki Mori, Daisuke Kato

CRY ONION (Joseph Green) Producer, Zev Braun; Director, Enzo G. Castellari; Executive Producer, Ronald A. Tash; Story and Screenplay, Liciano Vincenzoni, Serio Donati; Art Director, Alberto Boccianti; Costumes, Enrico Job; Photography, Alegandro Ullba; Music, Gianfranco Plenizio; In Eastmancolor; Rated PG; 92 minutes; June release. CAST: Franco Nero, Martin Balsam, Sterling Hayden, Emma Cohen, Leo Anchoriz, Romano Ruppo, Neno Zamperla, Massimo Vanni, Helmut Brash, Duillio Cruciani, Fernado Castro, Wal Davis, Dan Van Husen, Dick Butkus

A HARD WAY TO DIE (Transmedia) Producer, Pal Ming; An Eterna Film production in color; Rated R; June release. CAST: Billy Chong, Carl Scott, Louis Neglia

DINNER FOR ADELE (New Yorker/Dimension) Director, Oldrich Lipsky; Screenplay, Jiri Brdecka; Photography, Jaroslav Kucera; Music, Lubos Fiser; In Eastmancolor; Not rated; 102 minutes; June release. CAST: Michal Docolomansky (Nick), Rudolf Hrusinsky (Josef), Milos Kopecky (Kratzman), Ladislav Pesek (Bocek), Nada Konvalinkova (Kvetusa), Martin Ruzek (Inspector), Vaclav Lohnisky (Servant), Olga Schoberova (Irma), Kveta Fialova (Countess)

ROCKERS (New Yorker) Producer, Patrick Hulsey; Direction and Screenplay, Theodoros Bafaloukos; Photography, Peter Sova; Editor, Susan Steinberg; Associate Producer, Avrom Robin; Associate Producer-Manager, David Streit; Art Director, Lilly Kilvert; Costumes, Eugenie Bafaloukos; Assistant Director, Walter Rearick; In color; Not rated; 99 minutes; June release. CAST: Leroy Horsemouth Wallace, Richard Dirty Harry Hall, Marjorie Sunshine Norman, Jacob Miller, Gregory Jah Tooth Isaacs, Peter Honeyball, Monica Madgie Craig, Winston Burning Spear Rodney, Ashley Higher Harris, L. Jack Ruby Lindo, Frank Riddus Dowding, Robert Robbie Shakespeare, Peter Tosh, Bynn Wailer

THE CHILDREN (World Northal) Producer, Carlton J. Albright; Director, Max Kalmanowicz; Screenplay, Carlton J. Albright, Edward Terry; In Panavision and color; Rated R; 89 minutes; June release. CAST: Martin Shakar, Gil Rogers, Gale Garnett

DAISY CHAIN (Joseph Green) Producer, Joe Juliano; Director, Ralph Olsen, Ralph Thiel; Screenplay, Ed Marcus, Joe Juliano; Music, Erwin Hall, Joe Juliano, Sam Spence; Photography, Rene Guissart, Ralph Worth; Costumes, Charlotte Fleming; Editor, Max Saldinger; Associate Producer, Carl Spice; Assistant Director, Peter Semp; In Eastmancolor; Rated PG; 86 minutes; June release. CAST: Catherine Deneuve, Anita Ekberg, Curt Jurgens, Gert Froebe, Steve Eckart, Nadja Tiller, Ivan Desny, Peter Alexander, Gunther Philips

PORTRAIT OF TERESA (Unifilm) Director, Pastor Vega; Story and Screenplay, Pastor Vega, Ambrosio Fornet; Photography, Livio Delgado; Editor, Mirita Lores; Music, Carlos Farinas; In color; Not rated; 103 minutes; June release. CAST: Daisy Granados (Theresa), Adolfo Llaurado (Ramon), Raul Pomares (Tomas), Alina Sanchez (Teresa's friend)

MICHAEL KOHLHAAS (Columbia) Producer, Jerry Bick; Director, Volker Schlondorff; Screenplay, Edward Bond, Clement Biddle-Wood, Volker Schlondorff; Based on novella by Heinrich von Kleist; Photography, Willy Kurant; Editor, Claus von Boro; In German with subtitles; Not rated; 95 minutes; June release. CAST: David Warner (Michael), Anna Karina (Elisabeth), Reila Basic (Nagel), Anita Pallenberg (Katrina), Inigo Jackson (Junker), Michael Gothard (John), Anton Diffring (Elector), Anthony May (Peter), Tim Ray (Tony), Iwan Palluch (Stern), Kurt Meisel (Chancellor), Vaclav Lohninsky (Herse), Emanuel Schmied (Steward), Thomas Holtzman (Martin Luther)

THE PATRIOT GAME (Icarus/Cinema Perspectives) Director, Arthur MacCaig; Photography, Arthur MacCaig, Theo Robichet; Editors, MacCaig, Dominique Greussay; Commentary voice, Winnie Marshall; In black and white; Not rated; 93 minutes; June release. A documentary on events in Northern Ireland.

Leroy "Horsemouth" Wallace
in "Rockers" © New Yorker

Adolfo Llaurado, Daisy Granados
in "Portrait of Teresa" © Unifilm

"No Regrets for Our Youth"
© Corinth Films

Tisa Farrow, Ian McCulloch
in "Zombie" © Jerry Gross

NO REGRETS FOR OUR YOUTH (Corinth) A film by Akira Kurosawa in black and white; Not rated; 111 minutes; June release. CAST: Setsuko Hara, Denjiro Okochi, Susumu Fujita, Haruko Sugimura

THE HUNTER (WILL GET YOU!) (Joseph Green) Producer, Alain Belmondo; Direction and Screenplay, Philippe Labro; Photography, Jean Penzer; Music, Michel Columbier; Editor, Jean Revel; In Eastmancolor; Rated PG; 107 minutes; June release. CAST: Jean-Paul Belmondo (The Hunter), Bruno Cremer (The Hawk), Patrick Fierry (Costa Valdez), Jean Negroni (Spitzer), Jean-Pierre Jorris (Salicetti), Victor Garrivier (Doumecq)

THE MURDERER OF PEDRALBES Executive Producer, Pepon Coromina; Direction, Gonzalo Herralde; Photography, Juame Peracaula; Editor, Teresa Alcocer; Spanish with subtitles. Not rated; 86 minutes; June release. CAST: Jose Luis Cerveto (Murderer), Fernando Chamorra (Prison Doctor), Matrimonio Pastor (Cerveto), Antonio Garcia (Childhood friend), Rafael Gavilan (Chief Administrator), Jose Marti Gomez (Newspaperman), Francisco Mas (Chauffeur), Juan Merelo (Defense Lawyer),

THE BROTHERS KARAMAZOV (Columbia) Direction and Screenplay, Ivan Pyriev; Based on novel by Fyodor Dostoyevsky; Photography, Sergev Vronsky; Music, Isaac Schwartz; In Russian with subtitles; Not rated; 125 minutes; June release. CAST: Mikhail Oulinov (Dmitry), Lionella Pyrieva (Grushenka), Kirili Lavrov (Ivan), Andre Miagkiv (Alyosha), Marc Proudkine (Fyodor Pavolvich)

ARABIAN NIGHTS (United Artists) Direction and Screenplay, Pier Paolo Pasolini; Photography, Giuseppe Ruzzolini; Editors, Enzo Ocone, Nino Baragil, Tatiana Casini; Music, Ennio Morricone; Producer, Alberto Grimaldi; In color; 130 minutes; July release. CAST: Ninetto Devoli, Franco Meril, Ines Pellegrini, Luigina Rocchi, Francesco Paolo Governale, Zeudi Biasolo, Elisabetta Vito Genovesi, Abadit Ghidel, Salvatore Verdetti, Cristian Allgny, Luigi Antonio Gurra

ZOMBIE (Jerry Gross) Producers, Ugo Tucci, Fabrizio de Angelis; Director, Lucio Fulci; Screenplay, Elisa Briganti; Photography, Sergio Salveti; Editor, Vincenzo Tomassi; Music, Fabio Frizzi, Giorgio Tucci; In Technicolor; Not rated; 91 minutes; July release. CAST: Tisa Farrow (Anne), Ian McCulloch (Peter), Richard Johnson (Dr. Menard), Al Cliver (Brian), Arnetta Gay (Susan), Olga Karlatos (Mrs. Menard), Stefania D'Amario (Nurse)

LES PETITES FUGUES (New Yorker) "Little Escapes"; Executive Producer, Robert Boner; Assistant Producer, Christine Pascal; Director, Yves Yersin; Screenplay, Ives Yersin, Claude Muret; Photography, Robert Alazraki; Editors, Yves Yersin, Marianne Monnier; Music, Leon Francioli. Guillermo Villegas, Jean-Francois Farjon; Art Director, Jean-Claude Maret; Assistant Director, Jean-Daniel Bloesch; Costumes, Marianne Monnier, Vercellotti Freres; In French with English subtitles; In color; Not rated; 137 minutes; July release. CAST: Michel Robin (Pipe), Fabienne Barraud (Joseiane), Dore DeRosa (Luigi), Fred Personne (Father), Mista Prechac (Mother), Laurent Sandoz (Son), Nicole Vautier (Marianne), Leo Maillard (Stephane), Pierre Bovet, Roland Amstutz, Joseph Leiser, Gerald Battiaz, Martine Simon, Pierre Malkini, Therese Storck, Bernd van Doornick, Yvette Theraulaz

LUDWIG (American Zoetrope) Producers, TMS Film, Hans-Jurgen Syberberg; Direction and Screenplay, Hans-Jurgen Syberberg; Photography, Dietrich Lohmann; Editor, Peter Przygodda; In German with subtitles; Not rated 140 minutes; July release. CAST: Harry Baer (Ludwig), Balthasar (Ludwig as a child), Peter Kern (Lakal Mayr), Peter Moland (Lutz), Gunter Kaufmann (Hoinstein), Waldemar Brem (Prof. von Gudden), Gert Haucke (Baron Freyschiag), Eynon Hanfstangl (Durckheim), Oscar von Schab (Ludwig I), Siggi Graue (Prince Otto), Rudi Schelbengraber (Luitpoid), Gerhard Marz (Wagner I), Anette Tirier (Wagner II), Ingrid Caven (Lola Montez), Hanna Kohler (Sissi), Ursula Stratz (Norne), Liesl Haller (Anna Vogl), Johannes Buzalski (Emmanuel Geibel/Hitler)

Jean-Paul Belmondo, Patrick Fierry
in "The Hunter (Will Get You!)"

Dore DeRosa, Michel Robin, Fabienne Barraud
in "Les Petites Fugues" © New Yorker

Thomas Milian in "Almost Human"
© Joseph Brenner

ALMOST HUMAN (Joseph Brenner) Producer, Luciano Martino; Director, Umberto Lenzi; In Eastmancolor; Rated R; 90 minutes; July release. CAST: Tomas Milian, Laura Belli, Henry Silva, Gino Santercole, Anita Strindberg, Guido Alberti, Ray Lovelock

RUDE BOY (Atlantic) Produced and Directed by Jack Hazan, David Mingay; Screenplay, David Mingay, Jack Hazan, Ray Gange; Photography, Jack Hazan; Editors, David Mingay, Peter Goddard; Music, Joe Strummer, Mick Jones; Assistant Director, Peter Goddard; In Dolby Stereo and color; A Michael White presentation; A Buzzy Enterprises production; Rated R; 120 minutes; July release. CAST: Ray Gange (Ray), The Clash (Joe Strummer, Mick Jones, Paul Simonon, Nicky Headon), John Green (Manager), Barry Baker (Roadie), Terry McQuade, Caroline Coon, Elizabeth Young, Sarah Hall, Colin Bucksey, Colin Richards, Lizard Brown, Hicky Etienne, Inch Gordon, Lee Parker, Kenny Joseph, Jimmy Pursey

JUN (New Yorker) Producer, Shigeyoshi Tejima; Direction and Screenplay, Hiroto Yokoyama; Photography, Akira Takada; Music, Toshi Ichiyanagi; Editor, Keiichi Uraoka; In color; In Japanese with English subtitles; Not rated; 90 minutes; August release. CAST: Jun Eto (Jun), Mayumi Asaka (Yoko), Chieko Enomoto, Chiyoko Akaza, Emiko Yamanouchi, Maki Tachibana, Gensen Hanayagi, Kyoko Enami, Hosei Komatsu, Akiyoshi Fukae, Toru Abe, Akiko Mori, Komimasa Tanaka, Goro Hani

ONE WILD MOMENT (Quartet) Producer, Pierre Grunstein; Director, Claude Berri; Photography, Yves Pouffany; Music, Michel Stelio; Editor, Jacques Witta; Not rated; 88 minutes; August release. CAST: Jean-Pierre Marielle (Pierre), Victor Lanoux (Jacques), Agnes Soral (Francoise), Christine Dejoux (Martine), Martine Sarcey (A Woman)

SCANDAL (Entertainment Marketing) Producer, Takashi Koide; Director, Akira Kurosawa; Screenplay, Akira Kurosawa, Ryuzo Kikushima; Photography, Toshio Ubakata; Music, Fumio Hayasaka; In Japanese with subtitles; In black and white; Not rated 105 minutes; August release. CAST: Toshiro Mifune, Yoshiko Yamaguchi, Takashi Shimura

Jun Eto, Mayumi Asaka in "Jun"
© New Yorker Films

MAKE ROOM FOR TOMORROW (Robert A. McNeil) Director, Peter Kassovitz; Screenplay, Peter Kassovitz, E. Pressman; Photography, Etienne Szabo; Music, Georges Moustaki; Not rated; 105 minutes; August release. CAST: Victor Lanoux (Ben/Father), Jane Birkin (Peggy/Wife of Ben), Henri Cremieux (Isaac/Great-Grandfather), Georges Wilson (Elie/Grandfather), Mathieu Kassovitz (Young Boy), Yvonne Clech, Pasquali, Odette Laure, Andre Thorent

BEAR ISLAND (Taft International) Producer, Peter Snell; Director, Don Sharp; 'Screenplay, Don Sharp, David Butler, Murray Smith; Based on novel by Alistair MacLean; Photography, Alan Hume; Editor, Tony Lower; Art Directors, Kenneth Ryan, Peter Childs; Associate Producer, Bill Hill; Assistant Directors, Stuart Freeman, Don Brough, Roy Stevens, Jerry Daly; A Selkirk Films presentation in color; Rated PG; 118 minutes; August release. CAST: Donald Sutherland (Lansing), Vanessa Redgrave (Hedi), Richard Widmark (Otto), Christopher Lee (Lechinski), Barbara Parkins (Judith), Lloyd Bridges (Smithy), Lawrence Dane (Paul), Patricia Collins (Inge), Michael Reynolds, Nicholas Cortland, August Schellenberg, Candace O'Connor, Joseph Golland, Bruce Greenwood, Hagen Beggs, Michael Collins, Terry Kelly, Terry Waterhouse

THE GETTING OF WISDOM (Atlantic) Producer, Philip Adams; Director, Bruce Beresford; Screenplay, Eleanor Witcombe; Based on novel by Henry Handel Richardson; Photography, Don McAlpine; Editor, William Anderson; Design, John Stoddart; Not rated; 100 minutes; August release. CAST: Susannah Fowle (Laura), Hilary Ryan (Evelyn), Alix Longman (Chinky), Sheila Helpmann (Mrs. Gurley), Patricia Kennedy (Miss Chapman), Barry Humphries (Rev. Strachey), John Waters (Rev. Shepherd), Dorothy Bradley, Jan Freidl, Monica Maughan, Candy Raymond (Teachers), Kerry Armstrong, Celia DeBrugh, Kim Deacon, Jo-Anne Moore, Amanda Ring, Janet Shaw, Karen Sutton (Girls)

Toshiro Mifune, Yoshiko Yamaguchi
in "Scandal" © Entertainment

"The Getting of Wisdom"
© Atlantic Films

Mick Ford (L) in "Scum"
© World Northal

"Radio On"
© Unifilm

A PAIN IN THE A— (Corwin Mahler) Producers, Georges Dancigers, Alexandre Mnouchkine; Associated Producer, Robert Amon; Director, Edouard Molinaro; Screenplay, Francis Veber; Adaptation, Edouard Molinaro, Francis Veber; Photography, Raoul Coutard; Editors, Robert Isnardon, Monique Isnardon; Music, Jacques Brel, Francois Gauber; English subtitles; Rated PG; August release. CAST: Lino Ventura (Ralph), Jacques Brel (Pignon), Caroline Cellier (Louise), Nino Castelnuovo (Bellhop), Jeanne Pierre Darras (Fuchs), Andre Vallardy (Cop), Michel Gammino (Future Father), Angela Cardile (Future Mother), Pierre Forget (Felix), Xavier Depraz (Randoni), Lisa Braconnier (Mrs. Randoni)

SCUM (World Northal) Director, Alan Clarke; Screenplay, Roy Minton; Producers, Davina Belling, Clive Parsons; Rated R; 98 minutes; August release. CAST: Ray Winstone (Carlin), Mick Ford (Archer), John Judd (Sands), Phil Daniels (Richards), John Blundell (Banks), Ray Burdis (Eckersley), Julian Firth (Davis), Alrick Riley (Angel)

ANTI-CLOCK (International Film Exchange) Producer, Jack Bond; Executive Producer, Don Boyd; Associate Producer, Louise Temple; Directors, Jane Arden, Jack Bond; Screenplay, Jane Arden; Music, Jane Arden; In black and white; Not rated; 107 minutes; September release. CAST: Sebastian Saville (Prof. Zanof/Joseph Sapha), Suzan Cameron (Sapah's mother), Liz Saville (Sapha's sister), Louise Temple (Madame Aranovitch)

THE TEMPEST (World) Executive Producer, Don Boyd; Producers, Guy Ford, Mordecai Schreiber, Sarah Radclyffe; Direction and Screenplay, Derek Jarman from Shakespeare's play of the same title; Photography, Peter Middleton; Editors, Leslie Walker, Annette D'Alton; Music, Wavemaker, Brian Hodgson, John Lewis; Designer, Yolanda Sonnabend; Choreography, Stuart Hopps; Costumes, Nicolas Ede; In color; Not rated; 96 minutes; September release. CAST: Heathcote Williams (Prospero), Karl Johnson (Ariel), Toyah Willcox (Miranda), Peter Bull (Alonso), Richard Warwick (Antonio), Elizabeth Welch (Goddess), Jack Birkett (Caliban)

RADIO ON (Unifilm) Executive Producers, Peter Sainsbury, Renee Gundelach; Associate Producer, Wim Wenders; Direction and Screenplay, Christopher Petit; Photography, Martin Schafer; Editor, Anthony Sloman; Art Director, Susannan Buxton; In black and white; Not rated; 101 minutes; September release. CAST: David Beames (Robert), Lisa Kreuzer (Ingrid), Sandy Ratcliff (Kathy), Andrew Byatt (Deserter), Sue Jones-Davies (Girl), Sting (Just Like Eddie), Sabina Michael (Aunt), Katja Kersten (German Woman), Paul Hollywood (kid)

THE ALTERNATIVE MISS WORLD (Fred Baker) Producer-Director, Richard Gayer; Executive Producer, Judy McDonald; Associate Producers, Micheal Davis, Simon Mallin, Tony Tye Walker; Editor, Rob Small; In color; Rated R; 93 minutes; September release. CAST: Andrew Logan (Host/Hostess), Luciana Martinez (Secretary), Richard Logan, Peter Logan, Kevin Whitney, Ken Grant, Sophie Parkin, Nigel Adey, Ricardo de Velasco, John Thomas, Rosemary Gibb, Rebecca du Pont de Bie, Jenny Runacre, Stevie Hughes, James Birch, Sarah Parkin, Glinda Von Regensburg, Joanie deVere Hunt, Jill Bruce, John Maybury, Emma Harrison, William Waldron, Janet Slee, John Hopwood, Stephen Holt, Bob Anthony

SECOND CHANCE (United Artists) Direction and Screenplay, Claude Lelouch; Photography, Jacques Lefrancois; Editor, Georges Klotz; Music, Francis Lai; In Eastmancolor; Rated PG; 100 minutes; September release. CAST: Catherine Deneuve (Catherine), Anouk Aimee (Sarah), Charles Denner (Lawyer), Francis Huster (Patrick), Niels Arestrup (Henri), Colette Baudot (Lucienne), Manuella Papatakis (Simon)

HULLABALOO OVER GEORGIE AND BONNIE'S PICTURES (Corinth) Producer, Ismail Merchant; Director, James Ivory; Screenplay, Ruth Prawer Jhabvala; Photography, Walter Lassally; Music, Vic Flick; Editor, Humphrey Dixon; Art Director, Bansi Chandragupta; In color; Not rated; 82 minutes; September release. CAST: Peggy Ashcroft (Lady Gee), Victor Banerjee (Georgie), Jane Booker (Lynn), Larry Pine (Clarke), Aparna Sen (Bonnie), Shamsuddin (Mute), Alladdin Langa (Servant), Jenny Beavan (Governess)

"Anti-Clock"
© International Film Exchange

"Hullabaloo over Georgie and
Bonnie's Pictures" © Corinth

211

**Hazel O'Connor, Jonathan Pryce in
"Breaking Glass" © Paramount**

**Othon Bastos, Isabel Ribeiro in
"Sao Bernardo" © Unifilm**

BREAKING GLASS (Paramount) An Allied Stars presentation; Executive Producer, Dodi Fayed; Producers, Davina Belling, Clive Parsons; Direction and Screenplay, Brian Gibson; Assistant Directors, Roger Simons, Andrew Warren, Nigel Goldsack, Chris Brock; Photography, Stephen Goldblatt; Art Director, Evan Hercules; Choreographer, Eric G. Robarts; Editor, Michael Bradsell; In Panavision, Dolby Stereo and color; Rated PG; September release. CAST: Phil Daniels (Danny), Hazel O'Connor (Kate), Jon Finch (Woods), Jonathan Pryce (Ken), Peter-Hugo Daly (Mick), Mark Wingett (Tony), Gary Tibbs (Dave), Charles Wegner (Campbell), Mark Wing-Davey (Fordyce), Hugh Thomas (Davis), Nigel Humphreys (Brian), Ken Campbell (Publican), Peter Tilbury (Shaw), Gary Holton (Guitarist), Derek Thompson (Andy), Janine Duvitski (Jackie), Lowri Ann Richards (Jane), Gary Olsen (Drunk)

OOPSIE POOPSIE (Joseph Green) Producer, Carolo Ponti; Director, Giorgio Capitani; Screenplay, Ernesto Gastaldi; Editor, Renato Cinquini; Costumes, Art Direction, Enrico Sabbarini; Photography, Alberto Spagnoli; In Eastmancolor; Rated PG; 90 minutes; September release. CAST: Sophia Loren (Poopsie), Marcello Mastroianni (Charlie), Aldo Maccione (Chopin), Pierre Brice (Salvatore)

SAFARI EXPRESS (Joseph Green) Director, Duccio Tessari; Screenplay, Mario Amendola, Bruno Corbucci, Duccio Tessari, Gionfranco Clerici, Antonio Exacoustos; Photography, Claudio Cirillo; Editor, Eugenio Alabisco; Music, Guido Deangelis, Maurizio Deangelis; Costumes, Adriana Spadaro; Art Director, Giovanni Agostinucci; In Eastmancolor; Rated PG; In Techniscope and Eastmancolor; 93 minutes; September release. CAST: Jack Palance, Ursula Andress, Giuliano Gemma, Bibi

GAME FOR VULTURES (New Line Cinema) Executive Producer, Phillip Baird; Producer, Hazel Adair; Director, James Fargo; Screenplay, Phillip Baird from book by Michael Hartmann; A Pyramid Film production; In color; Rated R; 90 minutes; September release. CAST: Richard Harris, Richard Roundtree, Joan Collins, Ray Milland, Sven-Bertil Taube, Denholm Elliott, Ken Gampu, Tony Osoba, Neil Hallett, Alibe Parsons, Elaine Proctor, Mark Singleton, Jana Cilliers, John Parsonson

SAO BERNARDO (Unifilm) Producer, Marcos Farias; Direction and Screenplay, Leon Hirszman; Photography, Lauro Escorel; Editor, Eduardo Escorel; Music, Caetano Veloso; Art Direction, Luis Carlos Ripper; In Portugese with English subtitles; In color; Not rated; 110 minutes; September release. CAST: Othon Bastos (Paulo), Isabel Ribeiro (Madalena), Nildo Parente (Padilha), Vanda Lacerda (Gloria), Mario Lago (Dr. Nogueira), Joseph Guerreiro (Azevedo), Jose Policena (Ribeiro), Andrey Salvador (Marciano), Labanca (Mendonca), Rodolfo Arena (Juiz), Jofre Soares (Padre)

ONCE UPON A TIME IN THE EAST (Public Cinema) Director, Andre Brassard; In black and white and color; 100 Minutes; Not rated; October release. CAST: Denise Filiatrault, Michele Rossignol

MANTHAN (The Churning) Director, Shyam Benegal; October release. CAST: Girish Karnad, Smita Patil, Naseeruddin Shah, Anant Nag, Amrish Puri, Kulbhushan, Mohan Agashe, Sadhu Meher

GOODBYE EMMANUELLE (Miramax) Direction and Screenplay, Francois Leterrier; Based on characters created by Emmanuelle Astier; Photography, Jean Badal; Editor, Marie-Josephe Yoyette; Music, Serge Gainsbourg; In Eastmancolor; Rated R; 95 minutes; October release. CAST: Sylvia Kristel (Emmanuelle), Umberto Orsini (Husband), Alexandra Stewart (Dorothee), Jean-Pierre Bouvier (Lover), Olga Georges Picot (Woman)

THEMROC (Libra) Producer, Jean-Claude Bouriat; Direction and Screenplay, Claude Faraldo; Photography, Jean-Marc Ripert; Editor, Noun Serra; French with English subtitles; In color; Not rated; 100 minutes; October release. CAST: Michel Piccoli (Themroc), Beatrice Romand (His Sister), Marily Tolo (Secretary), Mme. Herviale (His Mother), Francesca R. Coluzzi (Woman across the street), Romain Bouteille (Chief Bureaucrat), and members of the Cafe de la Gare Troupe with Patrick Dewaere, Miou-Miou

**Richard Harris, Richard Roundtree in
"Game for Vultures" © New Line**

**Marcello Mastroianni in "Oopsie
Poopsie" © Joseph Green**

Sylvia Kristel, Jean-Pierre Bouvier
in "Goodbye Emmanuelle" © Miramax

Jamie Lee Curtis, Ben Johnson in "Terror
Train" © 20th Century-Fox

THE DAY AFTER HALLOWEEN (Group 1) formerly "Snap-Shot"; Producer, Anthony I. Ginnane; Executive Producer, William Fayman; Director, Simon Wincer; Screenplay, Chris and Everett DeRoche; Photography, Vincent Monton; Art Directors, Jon Dowding, Jill Eden; Editor, Phil Reid; Music, Brian May; In Eastmancolor; Rated R; 92 minutes; October release. CAST: Chantal Contouri (Madeline), Sigrid Thornton (Angela), Robert Bruning (Elmer), Hugh Keays-Byrne (Linsey),Vincent Gil (Daryl), Denise Drysdale (Lilly), Jacqui Gordon, Peter Stratford, Lulu Pinkus, Stewart Faichney, Julia Blake, Jon Sidney, Christine Amor, Chris Milne, Peter Flemingham, Bob Brown

TERROR TRAIN (20th Century-Fox) Producer, Harold Greenberg; Executive Producer, Lamar Card; Director, Roger Spottiswoode; Music, John Mills-Cockle; Screenplay, T. Y. Drake; Photography, John Alcott; Editor, Anne Henderson; Designer, Glenn Bydwell; Art Director, Guy Comtois; Assistant Director, Ray Sager; In DeLuxe Color; Rated R; 97 minutes; October release. CAST: Ben Johnson (Carne), Jamie Lee Curtis (Alana), Hart Bochner (Doc), David Copperfield (Magician), Derek MacKinnon (Kenny), Sandee Currie (Mitchy), Timothy Webber (Mo), Anthony Sherwood (Jackson), Howard Busgang (Ed), Steve Michaels (Brakeman), Greg Swanson, D. D. Winters, Joy Boushel, Victor Knight

EMANUELLE AROUND THE WORLD (Jerry Gross) Director, Joe D'Amato; Screenplay, Maria Pia Fusco, Gianfranco Clerici; Art Director, Marco Dentici; Costumes, Silvana Scandariato; Music, Nico Fidenco; Editor, Vincenzo Tomassi; Photography, Aristiede Massaccesi; In Metrocolor; Rated R; 92 minutes; October release. CAST: Laura Gemder, Ivan Rassimov, Karin Schubert, Don Powell, George Eastman, Brigitte Petronio, Maria Luigia, Stefania Pecce, Marino Mase, Gia-ni Macchia

THE PERFUMED NIGHTMARE Produced, Directed, Edited and Written by Kidlat Tahimik; Photography, Hartmut Lerch, Mr. Tahimik; Music, Philippine Traditional; In color; Not rated; 93 minutes; November release. CAST: Kidlat Tahimik, Dolores Santamaria, Mang Fely, Georgette Baudry, Katrin Muller, Kidlat Gottlieb, Martmut Lerch, Orlando Nadres

SIR HENRY AT RAWLINSON END (Charisma) Producer, Tony Stratton Smith; Director, Steve Roberts; Screenplay, Vivian Stanshall, Steve Roberts; Editor, Chris Rose; Music, Vivian Stanshall; Not rated; 72 minutes; November release. CAST: Trevor Howard (Sir Henry), Patrick Magee (Rev. Slodden), Denise Coffey (Mrs. E), J. G. Devlin (Old Scrotum), Harry Fowler (Butler), Sheila Reid (Florrie), Vivian Stanshall (Hubert), Suzanna Danielle (Candice), Daniel Gerroll (Rafe), Ben Aris (Lord Tarquin), Liz Smith (Lady Philipa)

ROCKSHOW (Miramax) Producer, MPL Communications; Photography, Jack Priestley; Editor, Robin Clark; In Dolby Stereo and color; Rated G; 105 minutes; November release. With Paul McCartney, Linda McCartney, Jimmy McCulloch, Joe English, Denny Laine

THE MASTER AND MARGARITA (Public Cinema) Director, Aleksandar Petrovic; Based on novel of same title by Mikhail Bulgakov; Music, Aleksandar Petrovic; Photography, Roberto Gerardi; Art Director, Vlastimir Gavrik; Costumes, Divna Jovanovic-Kauzlaric; Editor, Mihailo Ilic; In color, black and white; 120 minutes; Not rated; November release. CAST: Ugo Tognazzi (Master), Mimsy Farmer (Margarita), Alain Cuny (Satan/Prof. Woland), Bata Zivojinovic (Koroviev), Pavle Vujisic (Azazello)

STERNSTEIN MANOR (Public Cinema) Director, Hans Geissendorfer; Photography, Frank Bruhne; Screenplay, Ludwig Anzengruber; Music, Eugen Thomas; In color; Not related; 125 minutes; November release. CAST: Katja Rupe, Tilo Pruckner, Peter Kern, Agnes Fink

GROUP PROTRAIT WITH LADY (Public Cinema) Director, Aleksandar Petrovic; Screenplay, Petrovic, Heinrich Boll; Photography, Pierre William Glenn; Editor, Agape Dorstewitz; Music, Franz Schubert; Art Director, Gunther Nauman; In black and white; Not rated; 107 minutes; November release. CAST: Romy Schneider, Michel Galabru, Brad Dourif, Richard Munch

Kidlat Tahimak
in "The Perfumed Nightmare"

Paul McCartney in "Rockshow"
© Miramax

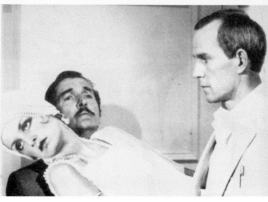

"Shogun Assassin"
© New World Pictures

Twiggy, Graham Stark, Tom Smothers
in "There Goes the Bride" © Vanguard

SHOGUN ASSASSIN (New World) Producers, Shintaro Katsu, Hisaharu Matsubara, David Weisman; Directors, Kenji Misumi, Robert Houston; Story, Kazuo Kioke, Goseki Kojima; Photography, Chriski Makiura; Editor, Toskio Taniguchi; Music, W. Michael Lewis, Mark Lindsay; Screenplay, Robert Houston, David Weisman, Kuzuo Koike; In Dolby Stereo and color; Rated R; 90 minutes; November release. Voices of Lamont Johnson, Marshal Efron, Sandra Bernhard, Vic Davis, Lennie Weinrib, Lainie Cook, Sam Weisman, Mark Lindsay, Robert Houston, David Weisman

CHILDREN OF BABYLON (Rainbow Productions) Produced, Directed, Edited and Written by Lennie Little-White; Photography, Franklyn St. Juste; Music, Harold Butler; Design, Addison; Not rated; 122 minutes; November release. CAST: Tobi (Penny), Don Parchment (Rick), Bob Andy (Luke), Leonie Forbes (Dorcas), Elizabeth de Lisser (Laura), Keith Wheeler (Hitchhiker), Chris Williams, Robin Williams (Boys on beach), Ashton James (Raftsman), Thurston Campbell (Porter), Cordett Duckie (Voice of woman interviewed)

TANYA'S ISLAND (Fred Baker/International Film Exchange) Produced and Written by Pierre Brousseau; Co-Producer, Rainier Energy Resources; Director, Alfred Sole; Executive Producers, Jean-Claude Levesque, Gary Mandell; Photography, Mark Irwin; Art Director, Angelo Stea; Editor, Michael MacLaverty; In color; Rated R; 90 Minutes; December release. CAST: D. D. Winters (Tanya), Richard Sargent (Lobo), Don McCloud (Blue), Mariette Levesque (Commercial Producer)

INVISIBLE ADVERSARIES (Public Cinema) Director, Valie Export; Co-Director, Peter Weibel; Screenplay, Peter Weibel, Valie Export; Photography, Wolfgang Simon, Rudi Palla; Editor, Juno Sylva Englander, Valie Export; In German with subtitles; In color; Not rated; 100 minutes; December release. CAST: Peter Weibel, Josef Plavec, Monika Helfer-Friedrich, Helke Sander, Dominik Dusek, Herbert Schmid, Eduard Neversal

THERE GOES THE BRIDE (Vanguard) Producers, Ray Cooney, Martin Schute; Director, Terence Marcel; Screenplay, Ray Cooney, Terence Marcel, John Chapman; From play by Ray Cooney; Photography, James Devis; Editor, Alan Jones; Music, Harry Robinson; Design, Peter Mullin; Art Director, John Siddall; Choreography, Gilliam Gregory; In color; Rated PG; 88 minutes; December release. CAST: Tom Smothers (Timothy), Twiggy (Polly), Martin Balsam (Babcock), Sylvia Syms (Ursula), Michael Whitney (Shorter), Geoffrey Sumner (Gerald), Graham Stark (Rossi), Hermione Baddeley (Daphne), Toria Fuller (Judy), Margot Moser (Mrs. Babcock), John Terry (Babcock), Jim Backus (Perkins), Phil Silvers (Psychiatrist), Broderick Crawford (Gas Station Attendant), Gonzales Gonzales (Ramirez), Carmen Capata (Mrs. Ramirez), Steve Franken (Organist)

PICTURE SHOW MAN (Limelight) Produced and Written by Joan Long; Director, John Powers; Photography, Geoff Burton; Music, Peter Best; Rated PG; 99 minutes; December release. CAST: Rod Taylor (Palmer), John Meillon (Poo), John Ewart (Freddie), Harold Hopkins (Larry), Patrick Cargill (Fitzwilliam), Yelena Zigon (Mme. Cavalli), Garry McDonald (Lou), Sally Conabere (Lucy), Judy Morris (Miss Lockhart), Jeannie Drynan (Mrs. Duncan)

REGGAE SUNSPLASH (International Harmony) Producer, Kino Arsenal Tubingen; Director, Stefan Paul; Photography, Hans Schalk, Rainer Heinzelmann, Peter Rees; Editor, Hildegard Schroder; In color; Not rated; 107 minutes; December release. CAST: Bob Marley, Peter Tosh, Third World, Burning Spear.

MAGICIANS OF THE SILVER SCREEN In Czechoslovak with English subtitles; Director, Jiri Menzel; Screenplay, Oldrich Vicek, Jiri Menzel; Based on story by Mr. Vicek; Photography, Jaromir Sofr; Music, Jiri Sust; In color; Rated PG; 90 minutes; December release. CAST: Rudolf Krusinsky (Pasparte), Jiri Menzel (Kolenaty), Blazena Holisova (Evzenie), Vlasta Fabianova (Emilie), Vladimir Mensik (Slapeta), Jaromira Milova (Pepicka), Hana Buresova (Aloisie), Oldrich Vicek (Berousek), Josef Kemr (Benjamin)

Bob Andy, Tobi in "Children of Babylon" © Rainbow Productions

D. D. Winters in "Tanya's Island"
© International Film Exchange

| Walter Abel | Brooke Adams | Alan Alda | June Allyson | Alan Arkin |

BIOGRAPHICAL DATA

(Name, real name, place and date of birth, school attended)

ABBOTT, DIAHNNE: NYC, 1945.

ABBOTT, JOHN: London, June 5, 1905.

ABEL, WALTER: St. Paul, MN, June 6, 1898. AADA.

ABRAHAM, F. MURRAY: Pittsburgh, PA, Oct. 24, 1939. UTx.

ADAMS, BROOKE: NYC, 1949. Dalton.

ADAMS, DON: NYC, 1927.

ADAMS, EDIE (Elizabeth Edith Enke): Kingston, PA, Apr. 16, 1929. Juilliard, Columbia.

ADAMS, JULIE (Betty May): Waterloo, Iowa, Oct. 17, 1928. Little Rock Jr. College.

ADAMS, MAUD (Maud Wikstrom): Lulea, Sweden.

ADDAMS, DAWN: Felixstowe, Suffolk, Eng., Sept. 21, 1930. RADA.

ADDY, WESLEY: Omaha, NB, Aug. 4, 1913. UCLA.

ADJANI, ISABELLE: Paris, 1955.

ADLER, LUTHER: NYC, May 4, 1903.

ADRIAN, IRIS (Iris Adrian Hostetter): Los Angeles, May 29, 1913.

AGAR, JOHN: Chicago, Jan. 31, 1921.

AGUTTER, JENNY: London, 1953.

AHERNE, BRIAN: Worcestershire, Eng., May 2, 1902. Malvern College, U. of London.

AIELLO, DANNY: June 20, 1935, NYC.

AIMEE, ANOUK: Paris, Apr. 27, 1934. Bauer-Therond.

AKINS, CLAUDE: Nelson, GA, May 25, 1936. Northwestern U.

ALBERGHETTI, ANNA MARIA: Pesaro, Italy, May 15, 1936.

ALBERT, EDDIE (Eddie Albert Heimberger): Rock Island, IL, Apr. 22, 1908. U. of Minn.

ALBERT, EDWARD: Los Angeles, Feb. 20, 1951. UCLA.

ALBERTSON, JACK: Malden, MA, 1910.

ALBRIGHT, LOLA: Akron, OH, July 20, 1925.

ALDA, ALAN: NYC, Jan. 28, 1936. Fordham.

ALDA, ROBERT (Alphonso D'Abruzzo): NYC, Feb. 26, 1914. NYU.

ALDERSON, BROOKE: Dallas, Tx.

ALEJANDRO, MIGUEL: NYC, 1958.

ALEXANDER, JANE (Quigley): Boston, MA, Oct. 28, 1939. Sarah Lawrence.

ALLEN, NANCY: NYC 1950.

ALLEN, REX: Wilcox, AZ, Dec. 31, 1922.

ALLEN, STEVE: New York City, Dec. 26, 1921.

ALLEN, WOODY (Allen Stewart Konigsberg): Brooklyn, Dec. 1, 1935.

ALLENTUCK, KATHERINE: NYC, Oct. 16, 1954. Calhoun.

ALLYSON, JUNE (Ella Geisman): Westchester, NY, Oct. 7, 1917.

ALVARADO, TRINI: NYC, 1967.

AMECHE, DON (Dominic Amichi): Kenosha, WI, May 31, 1908.

AMES, ED: Boston, July 9, 1929.

AMES, LEON (Leon Wycoff): Portland, IN, Jan. 20, 1903.

AMOS, JOHN: Newark, NJ, Dec. 27, 1940. Colo. U.

ANDERSON, JUDITH: Adelaide, Australia, Feb. 10, 1898.

ANDERSON, MELODY: Canada 1955, Carlton U.

ANDERSON, MICHAEL, JR.: London, Eng., 1943.

ANDERSSON, BIBI: Stockholm, Nov. 11, 1935. Royal Dramatic Sch.

ANDES, KEITH: Ocean City, NJ, July 12, 1920. Temple U., Oxford.

ANDRESS, URSULA: Switz., Mar. 19, 1936.

ANDREWS, DANA: Collins, MS, Jan. 1, 1909. Sam Houston Col.

ANDREWS, EDWARD: Griffin, GA, Oct. 9, 1914. U. VA.

ANDREWS, HARRY: Tonbridge, Kent, Eng., Nov. 10, 1911.

ANDREWS, JULIE (Julia Elizabeth Wells): Surrey, Eng., Oct. 1, 1935.

ANGEL, HEATHER: Oxford, Eng., Feb. 9, 1909. Wycombe Abbey.

ANN-MARGRET (Olsson): Valsjobyn, Sweden, Apr. 28, 1941. Northwestern U.

ANSARA, MICHAEL: Lowell, MA, Apr. 15, 1922. Pasadena Playhouse.

ANTHONY, TONY: Clarksburg, WV, Oct 16, 1937. Carnegie Tech.

ANTON, SUSAN: Yucaipa, CA. 1951. Bernardino Col.

ANTONELLI, LAURA: Pola, Italy.

ARCHER, JOHN (Ralph Bowman): Osceola, NB, May 8, 1915. USC.

ARDEN, EVE (Eunice Quedens): Mill Valley, CA, Apr. 30, 1912.

ARKIN, ALAN: NYC, Mar. 26, 1934. LACC.

ARNAZ, DESI: Santiago, Cuba, Mar. 2, 1915. Colegio de Dolores.

ARNAZ, DESI, JR.: Los Angeles, Jan. 19, 1953.

ARNAZ, LUCIE: Hollywood, July 17, 1951.

ARNESS, JAMES (Aurness): Minneapolis, MN, May 26, 1923. Beloit College.

ARTHUR, BEATRICE: NYC, May 13, 1926. New School.

ARTHUR, JEAN: NYC, Oct. 17, 1905.

ARTHUR, ROBERT (Robert Arthaud): Aberdeen, WA, June 18, 1925. U. Wash.

ASHLEY, ELIZABETH (Elizabeth Ann Cole): Ocala, FL, Aug. 30, 1939.

ASSANTE, ARMAND: NYC, Oct. 4, 1949. AADA.

ASTAIRE, FRED (Fred Austerlitz): Omaha, NB, May 10, 1899.

ASTIN, JOHN: Baltimore, MD, Mar. 30, 1930. U. Minn.

ASTIN, PATTY DUKE (see Patty Duke)

ASTOR, MARY (Lucile V. Langhanke): Quincy, IL, May 3, 1906. Kenwood-Loring School.

ATHERTON, WILLIAM: Orange, CT, July 30, 1947. Carnegie Tech.

ATKINS, CHRISTOPHER: Rye, NY, 1961.

ATTENBOROUGH, RICHARD: Cambridge, Eng., Aug. 29, 1923. RADA.

AUBERJONOIS, RENE: NYC, June 1, 1940. Carnegie Tech.

AUDRAN, STEPHANE: Versailles, Fr., 1933.

AUGER, CLAUDINE: Paris, Apr. 26, 1942. Dramatic Cons.

AULIN, EWA: Stockholm, Sweden, Feb. 14, 1950.

AUMONT, JEAN PIERRE: Paris, Jan. 5, 1909. French Nat'l School of Drama.

AUTRY, GENE: Tioga, TX, Sept. 29, 1907.

AVALON, FRANKIE (Francis Thomas Avallone): Philadelphia, Sept. 18, 1939.

AYRES, LEW: Minneapolis, MN, Dec. 28, 1908.

| Charles Aznavour | Blanche Baker | Warren Beatty | Kathleen Beller | Tom Berenger |

AZNAVOUR, CHARLES (Varenagh Aznourian): Paris, May 22, 1924.

BACALL, LAUREN (Betty Perske): NYC, Sept. 16, 1924. AADA.

BACKUS, JIM: Cleveland, Ohio, Feb. 25, 1913. AADA.

BADDELEY, HERMIONE: Shropshire, Eng., Nov. 13, 1906. Margaret Morris School.

BAILEY, PEARL: Newport News, VA, March 29, 1918.

BAIN, BARBARA: Chicago, Sept. 13, 1934. U. Ill.

BAIO, SCOTT: Brooklyn, 1961.

BAKER, BLANCHE: NYC Dec. 20, 1956.

BAKER, CARROLL: Johnstown, PA, May 28, 1931. St. Petersburg Jr. College.

BAKER, DIANE: Hollywood, CA, Feb. 25, 1938. USC.

BAKER, LENNY: Boston, MA, Jan. 17, 1945. Boston U.

BALABAN, ROBERT: Chicago, Aug. 16, 1945. Colgate.

BALDWIN, ADAM: Chicago, Il. 1962.

BALIN, INA: Brooklyn, Nov. 12, 1937. NYU.

BALL, LUCILLE: Celaron, NY, Aug. 6, 1910. Chatauqua Musical Inst.

BALSAM, MARTIN: NYC, Nov. 4, 1919. Actors Studio.

BANCROFT, ANNE (Anna Maria Italiano): Bronx, NY, Sept. 17, 1931. AADA.

BANNEN, IAN: Airdrie, Scot., June 29, 1928.

BARDOT, BRIGITTE: Paris, Sept. 28, 1934.

BARRAULT, MARIE-CHRISTINE: Paris, 1946.

BARRETT, MAJEL (Hudec): Columbus, OH, Feb. 23. Western Reserve U.

BARRON, KEITH: Mexborough, Eng., Aug. 8, 1936. Sheffield Playhouse.

BARRY, GENE (Eugene Klass): NYC, June 14, 1921.

BARRYMORE, JOHN BLYTH: Beverly Hills, CA, June 4, 1932. St. John's Military Academy.

BARTHOLOMEW, FREDDIE: London, Mar. 28, 1924.

BARYSHNIKOV, MIKHAIL: Riga, Latvia, Jan. 27, 1948.

BASEHART, RICHARD: Zanesville, OH, Aug. 31, 1914.

BATES, ALAN: Allestree, Derbyshire, Eng., Feb. 17, 1934. RADA.

BAXTER, ANNE: Michigan City, IN, May 7, 1923. Ervine School of Drama.

BAXTER, KEITH: South Wales, Apr. 29, 1933. RADA.

BEAL, JOHN (J. Alexander Bliedung): Joplin, MO, Aug. 13, 1909. Pa. U.

BEATTY, ROBERT: Hamilton, Ont., Can., Oct. 19, 1909. U. of Toronto.

BEATTY, WARREN: Richmond, VA, March 30, 1937.

BECK, MICHAEL: Horseshoe Lake, AR, 1948.

BEDELIA, BONNIE: NYC, Mar. 25, 1948. Hunter Col.

BEDI, KABIR: India, 1945.

BEERY, NOAH, JR.: NYC, Aug. 10, 1916. Harvard Military Academy.

BELAFONTE, HARRY: NYC, Mar. 1, 1927.

BELASCO, LEON: Odessa, Russia, Oct. 11, 1902.

BEL GEDDES, BARBARA: NYC, Oct. 31, 1922.

BELL, TOM: Liverpool, Eng., 1932.

BELLAMY, RALPH: Chicago, June 17, 1904.

BELLER, KATHLEEN: NYC, 1957.

BELMONDO, JEAN PAUL: Paris, Apr. 9, 1933.

BENEDICT, DIRK (Niewoehner): White Sulphur Springs, MT. 1945. Whitman Col.

BENJAMIN, RICHARD: NYC, May 22, 1938. Northwestern U.

BENNENT, DAVID: Lausanne, Sept. 9, 1966.

BENNETT, BRUCE (Herman Brix): Tacoma, WA, May 19, 1909. U. Wash.

BENNETT, JILL: Penang, Malay, Dec. 24, 1931.

BENNETT, JOAN: Palisades, NJ, Feb. 27, 1910. St. Margaret's School.

BENSON, ROBBY: Dallas, TX, Jan. 21, 1957.

BERENSON, MARISSA: NYC, Feb. 15, 1947.

BERGEN, CANDICE: Los Angeles, May 9, 1946. U. Pa.

BERGEN, POLLY: Knoxville, TN, July 14, 1930. Compton Jr. College.

BERGER, HELMUT: Salzburg, Aus., 1945.

BERGER, SENTA: Vienna, May 13, 1941. Vienna Sch. of Acting.

BERGER, WILLIAM: Austria, Jan. 20, 1928. Columbia.

BERGERAC, JACQUES: Biarritz, France, May 26, 1927. Paris U.

BERGMAN, INGRID: Stockholm, Sweden, Aug. 29, 1915. Royal Dramatic Theatre School.

BERLE, MILTON (Milton Berlinger): NYC, July 12, 1908. Professional Children's School.

BERLIN, JEANNIE: Los Angeles, Nov. 1, 1949.

BERLINGER, WARREN: Brooklyn, Aug. 31, 1937. Columbia.

BERNARDI, HERSCHEL: NYC, 1923.

BERRI, CLAUDE (Langmann): Paris, July 1, 1934.

BERTO, JULIET: Grenoble, France, Jan. 1947.

BEST, JAMES: Corydon, IN, July 26, 1926.

BETTGER, LYLE: Philadelphia, Feb. 13, 1915. AADA.

BEYMER, RICHARD: Avoca, IA, Feb. 21, 1939.

BIEHN, MICHAEL: Ariz. 1957.

BIKEL, THEODORE: Vienna, May 2, 1924. RADA.

BIRNEY, DAVID: Washington, DC, Apr. 23, 1939. Dartmouth, UCLA.

BISHOP, JOEY (Joseph Abraham Gottlieb): Bronx, NY, Feb. 3, 1918.

BISHOP, JULIE (formerly Jacqueline Wells): Denver, CO, Aug. 30, 1917. Westlake School.

BISSET, JACQUELINE: Waybridge, Eng., Sept. 13, 1944.

BIXBY, BILL: San Francisco, Jan. 22, 1934. U. Cal.

BLACK, KAREN (Ziegler): Park Ridge, IL, July 1, 1942. Northwestern.

BLAINE, VIVIAN (Vivian Stapleton): Newark, NJ, Nov. 21, 1923.

BLAIR, BETSY (Betsy Boger): NYC, Dec. 11, 1923.

BLAIR, JANET (Martha Jane Lafferty): Blair, PA, Apr. 23, 1921.

BLAIR, LINDA: Westport, CT, 1959.

BLAKE, AMANDA (Beverly Louise Neill): Buffalo, NY, Feb. 20, 1921.

BLAKE, ROBERT (Michael Gubitosi): Nutley, NJ, Sept. 18, 1933.

BLAKELY, SUSAN: Frankfurt, Germany 1950. U. Tex.

BLAKLEY, RONEE: Stanley, ID, 1946. Stanford U.

BLOOM, CLAIRE: London, Feb. 15, 1931. Badminton School.

BLYTH, ANN: Mt. Kisco, NY, Aug. 16, 1928. New Wayburn Dramatic School.

BOCHNER, HART: Toronto, 1956. U San Diego.

BOGARDE, DIRK: London, Mar. 28, 1918. Glasgow & Univ. College.

BOLGER, RAY: Dorchester, MA, Jan. 10, 1903.

Florinda Bolkan	Peter Boyle	Jocelyn Brando	Keith Carradine	Leslie Caron

BOLKAN, FLORINDA (Florinda Soares Bulcao): Ceara, Brazil, Feb. 15, 1941.

BOND, DEREK: Glasgow, Scot., Jan. 26, 1920. Askes School.

BOONE, PAT: Jacksonville, FL, June 1, 1934. Columbia U.

BOOTH, SHIRLEY (Thelma Ford): NYC, Aug. 30, 1907.

BORGNINE, ERNEST (Borgnino): Hamden, CT, Jan. 24, 1918. Randall School.

BOTTOMS, JOSEPH: Santa Barbara, CA, 1954.

BOTTOMS, TIMOTHY: Santa Barbara, CA, Aug. 30, 1951.

BOULTING, INGRID: Transvaal, So. Africa, 1947.

BOVEE, LESLIE: Bend, OR, 1952.

BOWKER, JUDI: Shawford, Eng., Apr. 6, 1954.

BOYLE, PETER: Philadelphia, PA, 1937. LaSalle Col.

BRACKEN, EDDIE: NYC, Feb. 7, 1920. Professional Children's School.

BRADY, SCOTT (Jerry Tierney): Brooklyn, Sept. 13, 1924. Bliss-Hayden Dramatic School.

BRAND, NEVILLE: Kewanee, IL, Aug. 13, 1920.

BRANDO, JOCELYN: San Francisco, Nov. 18, 1919. Lake Forest College, AADA.

BRANDO, MARLON: Omaha, NB, Apr. 3, 1924. New School.

BRASSELLE, KEEFE: Elyria, OH, Feb. 7, 1923.

BRAZZI, ROSSANO: Bologna, Italy, Sept. 18, 1916. U. Florence.

BRIAN, DAVID: NYC, Aug. 5, 1914. CCNY.

BRIDGES, BEAU: Los Angeles, Dec. 9, 1941. UCLA.

BRIDGES, JEFF: Los Angeles, Dec. 4, 1949.

BRIDGES, LLOYD: San Leandro, CA, Jan. 15, 1913.

BRISEBOIS, DANIELLE: Brooklyn, June 28, 1969.

BRITT, MAY (Maybritt Wilkins): Sweden, March 22, 1936.

BRODIE, STEVE (Johnny Stevens): Eldorado, KS, Nov. 25, 1919.

BROLIN, JAMES: Los Angeles, July 18, 1940. UCLA.

BROMFIELD, JOHN (Farron Bromfield): South Bend, IN, June 11, 1922. St. Mary's College.

BRONSON, CHARLES (Buchinsky): Ehrenfield, PA, Nov. 3, 1920.

BROWN, BLAIR: Washington, DC, 1948; Pine Manor

BROWN, GEORG STANFORD: Havana, Cuba, June 24, 1943. AMDA.

BROWN, JAMES: Desdemona, TX, Mar. 22, 1920. Baylor U.

BROWN, JIM: St. Simons Island, NY, Feb. 17, 1935. Syracuse U.

BROWN, TOM: NYC, Jan. 6, 1913. Professional Children's School.

BROWNE, CORAL: Melbourne, Aust., July 23, 1913.

BROWNE, LESLIE: NYC, 1958.

BRUCE, VIRGINIA: Minneapolis, Sept. 29, 1910.

BRYNNER, YUL: Sakhalin Island, Japan, July 11, 1915.

BUCHHOLZ, HORST: Berlin, Ger., Dec. 4, 1933. Ludwig Dramatic School.

BUETEL, JACK: Dallas, TX, Sept. 5, 1917.

BUJOLD, GENEVIEVE: Montreal, Can., July 1, 1942.

BUONO, VICTOR: San Diego, CA, 1939. Villanova.

BURKE, PAUL: New Orleans, July 21, 1926. Pasadena Playhouse.

BURNETT, CAROL: San Antonio, TX, Apr. 26, 1933. UCLA.

BURNS, CATHERINE: NYC, Sept. 25, 1945. AADA.

BURNS, GEORGE (Nathan Birnbaum): NYC, Jan. 20, 1896.

BURR, RAYMOND: New Westminster, B.C., Can., May 21, 1917. Stanford, U. Cal., Columbia.

BURSTYN, ELLEN (Edna Rae Gillooly): Detroit, MI, Dec. 7, 1932.

BURTON, RICHARD (Richard Jenkins): Pontrhydyfen, S. Wales, Nov. 10, 1925. Oxford.

BUSEY, GARY: Tulsa, OK, 1944.

BUTTONS, RED (Aaron Chwatt): NYC, Feb. 5, 1919.

BUZZI, RUTH: Wequetequock, RI, July 24, 1936. Pasadena Playhouse.

BYGRAVES, MAX: London, Oct. 16, 1922. St. Joseph's School.

BYRNES, EDD: NYC, July 30, 1933. Haaren High.

CAAN, JAMES: Bronx, NY, Mar. 26, 1939.

CABOT, SUSAN: Boston, July 6, 1927.

CAESAR, SID: Yonkers, NY, Sept. 8, 1922.

CAGNEY, JAMES: NYC, July 17, 1899. Columbia.

CAGNEY, JEANNE: NYC, Mar. 25, 1919. Hunter.

CAINE, MICHAEL (Maurice Michelwhite): London, Mar. 14, 1933.

CAINE, SHAKIRA (Baksh): Guyana, Feb. 23, 1947. Indian Trust Col.

CALHOUN, RORY (Francis Timothy Durgin): Los Angeles, Aug. 8, 1922.

CALLAN, MICHAEL (Martin Calinieff): Philadelphia, Nov. 22, 1935.

CALVERT, PHYLLIS: London, Feb. 18, 1917. Margaret Morris School.

CALVET, CORRINE (Corrine Dibos): Paris, Apr. 30, 1929. U. Paris.

CAMERON, ROD (Rod Cox): Calgary, Alberta, Can., Dec. 7, 1912.

CAMP, COLLEEN: San Francisco, 1953.

CAMPBELL, GLEN: Delight, AR, Apr. 22, 1935.

CANALE, GIANNA MARIA: Reggio Calabria, Italy, Sept. 12.

CANNON, DYAN (Samille Diane Friesen): Tacoma, WA, Jan. 4, 1929.

CANOVA, JUDY: Jacksonville, FL, Nov. 20, 1916.

CAPERS, VIRGINIA: Sumter, SC, 1925. Juilliard.

CAPUCINE (Germaine Lefebvre): Toulon, France, Jan. 6, 1935.

CARA, IRENE: NYC, Mar. 18, 1958.

CARDINALE, CLAUDIA: Tunis, N. Africa, Apr. 15, 1939. College Paul Cambon.

CAREY, HARRY, JR.: Saugus, CA, May 16, 1921. Black Fox Military Academy.

CAREY, MACDONALD: Sioux City, IA, Mar. 15, 1913. U. of Wisc., U. Iowa.

CAREY, PHILIP: Hackensack, NJ, July 15, 1925. U. Miami.

CARMEN, JULIE: Mt. Vernon, NY, Apr. 4, 1954.

CARMICHAEL, HOAGY: Bloomington, IN, Nov. 22, 1899. Ind. U.

CARMICHAEL, IAN: Hull, Eng., June 18, 1920. Scarborough Col.

CARNE, JUDY (Joyce Botterill): Northampton, Eng., 1939. Bush-Davis Theatre School.

CARNEY, ART: Mt. Vernon, NY, Nov. 4, 1918.

CARON, LESLIE: Paris, July 1, 1931. Nat'l Conservatory, Paris.

CARPENTER, CARLETON: Bennington, VT, July 10, 1926. Northwestern.

CARR, VIKKI (Florence Cardona): July 19, 1942. San Fernando Col.

CARRADINE, DAVID: Hollywood, Dec. 8, 1936. San Francisco State.

CARRADINE, JOHN: NYC, Feb. 5, 1906.

CARRADINE, KEITH: San Mateo, CA, Aug. 8, 1951. Colo. State U.

CARRADINE, ROBERT: San Mateo, CA, 1954.

CARREL, DANY: Tourane, Indochina, Sept. 20, 1936. Marseilles Cons.

| Rosalind
Cash | John
Cassavetes | Jill
Clayburgh | Stephen
Collins | Kathleen
Cody |

CARROLL, DIAHANN (Johnson): NYC, July 17, 1935. NYU.

CARROLL, MADELEINE: West Bromwich, Eng., Feb. 26, 1902. Birmingham U.

CARROLL, PAT: Shreveport, LA, May 5, 1927. Catholic U.

CARSON, JOHN DAVID: 1951, Calif. Valley Col.

CARSON, JOHNNY: Corning, IA, Oct. 23, 1925. U. of Neb.

CARSTEN, PETER (Ransenthaler): Weissenberg, Bavaria, Apr. 30, 1929. Munich Akademie.

CASH, ROSALIND: Atlantic City, NJ, Dec. 31, 1938. CCNY.

CASON, BARBARA: Memphis, TN, Nov. 15, 1933. U. Iowa.

CASS, PEGGY (Mary Margaret): Boston, May 21, 1925.

CASSAVETES, JOHN: NYC, Dec. 9, 1929. Colgate College, AADA.

CASSEL, JEAN-PIERRE: Paris, Oct. 27, 1932.

CASSIDY, DAVID: NYC, Apr. 12, 1950.

CASSIDY, JOANNA: Camden, NJ, 1944. Syracuse U.

CASTELLANO, RICHARD: Bronx, NY, Sept. 3, 1934.

CAULFIELD, JOAN: Orange, NJ, June 1, 1922. Columbia U.

CAVANI, LILIANA: Bologna, Italy, Jan. 12, 1937. U. Bologna.

CELI, ADOLFO: Sicily, July 27, 1922, Rome Academy.

CHAKIRIS, GEORGE: Norwood, OH, Sept. 16, 1933.

CHAMBERLAIN, RICHARD: Beverly Hills, CA, March 31, 1935. Pomona.

CHAMPION, MARGE: Los Angeles, Sept. 2, 1925.

CHANNING, CAROL: Seattle, Jan. 31, 1921. Bennington.

CHANNING, STOCKARD (Susan Stockard): NYC, 1944. Radcliffe.

CHAPIN, MILES: NYC, Dec. 6, 1954. HB Studio.

CHAPLIN, GERALDINE: Santa Monica, CA, July 31, 1944. Royal Ballet.

CHAPLIN, SYDNEY: Los Angeles, Mar. 31, 1926. Lawrenceville.

CHARISSE, CYD (Tula Ellice Finklea): Amarillo, TX, Mar. 3, 1922. Hollywood Professional School.

CHASE, CHEVY (Cornelius Crane Chase): NYC, 1943.

CHER (Cherlin Sarkesian): May 20, 1946.

CHIARI, WALTER: Verona, Italy, 1930.

CHRISTIAN, LINDA (Blanca Rosa Welter): Tampico, Mex., Nov. 13, 1923.

CHRISTIAN, ROBERT: Los Angeles, Dec. 27, 1939. UCLA.

CHRISTIE, JULIE: Chukua, Assam, India, Apr. 14, 1941.

CHRISTOPHER, DENNIS (Carrelli): Philadelphia, PA, 1955. Temple U.

CHRISTOPHER, JORDAN: Youngstown, OH, Oct. 23, 1940. Kent State.

CHURCHILL, SARAH: London, Oct. 7, 1916.

CILENTO, DIANE: Queensland, Australia, Oct. 5, 1933. AADA.

CLAPTON, ERIC: London, Mar. 30, 1945.

CLARK, DANE: NYC, Feb. 18, 1915. Cornell, Johns Hopkins U.

CLARK, DICK: Mt. Vernon, NY, Nov. 30, 1929. Syracuse U.

CLARK, MAE: Philadelphia, Aug. 16, 1910.

CLARK, PETULA: Epsom, England, Nov. 15, 1932.

CLARK, SUSAN: Sarnid, Ont., Can., Mar. 8. RADA

CLAYBURGH, JILL: NYC, Apr. 30, 1944. Sarah Lawrence.

CLEMENTS, STANLEY: Long Island, NY, July 16, 1926.

CLERY, CORINNE: Italy, 1950.

CLOONEY, ROSEMARY: Maysville, KY, May 23, 1928.

COBURN, JAMES: Laurel, NB, Aug. 31, 1928. LACC.

COCA, IMOGENE: Philadelphia, Nov. 18, 1908.

COCO, JAMES: NYC, Mar. 21, 1929.

CODY, KATHLEEN: Bronx, NY, Oct. 30, 1953.

COLBERT, CLAUDETTE (Lily Chauchoin): Paris, Sept. 13, 1905. Art Students League.

COLE, GEORGE: London, Apr. 22, 1925.

COLLINS, JOAN: London, May 23, 1933. Francis Holland School.

COLLINS, STEPHEN: Des Moines, IA, Oct. 1, 1947. Amherst.

COMER, ANJANETTE: Dawson, TX, Aug. 7, 1942. Baylor, Tex. U.

CONANT, OLIVER: NYC, Nov. 15, 1955. Dalton.

CONAWAY, JEFF: NYC, Oct. 5, 1950. NYC.

CONNERY, SEAN: Edinburgh, Scot., Aug. 25, 1930.

CONNORS, CHUCK (Kevin Joseph Connors): Brooklyn, Apr. 10, 1921. Seton Hall College.

CONNORS, MIKE (Krekor Ohanian): Fresno, CA, Aug. 15, 1925. UCLA.

CONRAD, WILLIAM: Louisville, KY, Sept. 27, 1920.

CONVERSE, FRANK: St. Louis, MO, May 22, 1938. Carnegie Tech.

CONVY, BERT: St. Louis, MO, July 23, 1935. UCLA.

CONWAY, KEVIN: NYC, May 29, 1942.

CONWAY, TIM (Thomas Daniel): Willoughby, OH, Dec. 15, 1933. Bowling Green State.

COOGAN, JACKIE: Los Angeles, Oct. 25, 1914. Villanova College.

COOK, ELISHA, JR.: San Francisco, Dec. 26, 1907. St. Albans.

COOPER, BEN: Hartford, CT, Sept. 30, 1932. Columbia U.

COOPER, JACKIE: Los Angeles, Sept. 15, 1921.

COOTE, ROBERT: London, Feb. 4, 1909. Hurstpierpont College.

CORBETT, GRETCHEN: Portland, OR, Aug. 13, 1947. Carnegie Tech.

CORBY, ELLEN (Hansen): Racine, WI, June 13, 1913.

CORCORAN, DONNA: Quincy, MA, Sept. 29, 1942.

CORD, ALEX (Viespi): Floral Park, NY, Aug. 3, 1931. NYU, Actors Studio.

CORDAY, MARA (Marilyn Watts): Santa Monica, CA, Jan. 3, 1932.

COREY, JEFF: NYC, Aug. 10, 1914. Fagin School.

CORLAN, ANTHONY: Cork City, Ire., May 9, 1947. Birmingham School of Dramatic Arts.

CORNTHWAITE, ROBERT: Apr. 28, 1917. USC.

CORRI, ADRIENNE: Glasgow, Scot., Nov. 13, 1933. RADA.

CORTESA, VALENTINA: Milan, Italy, Jan. 1, 1925.

COSBY, BILL: Philadelphia, July 12, 1937. Temple U.

COSTER, NICOLAS: London, Dec. 3, 1934. Neighborhood Playhouse.

COTTEN, JOSEPH: Petersburg, VA, May 13, 1905.

COURTENAY, TOM: Hull, Eng., Feb. 25, 1937. RADA.

COURTLAND, JEROME: Knoxville, TN, Dec. 27, 1926.

CRABBE, BUSTER (LARRY) (Clarence Linden): Oakland, CA, Feb. 7, 1908. USC.

CRAIG, JAMES (James H. Meador): Nashville, TN, Feb. 4, 1912. Rice Inst.

CRAIG, MICHAEL: India, Jan. 27, 1929.

CRAIN, JEANNE: Barstow, CA, May 25, 1925.

CRAWFORD, BRODERICK: Philadelphia, Dec. 9, 1911.

Keene Curtis   **Lindsay Crouse**   **Matt Dillon**   **Blythe Danner**   **Alain Delon**

CRENNA, RICHARD: Los Angeles, Nov. 30, 1926. USC.

CRISTAL, LINDA (Victoria Moya): Buenos Aires, Feb. 25, 1934.

CROSBY, HARRY: Los Angeles, CA, 1969.

CROSBY, KATHRYN GRANT: (see Kathryn Grant)

CROSS, MURPHY (Mary Jane): Laurelton, MD, June 22, 1950.

CROUSE, LINDSAY ANN: NYC, May 12, 1948. Radcliffe.

CROWLEY, PAT: Olyphant, PA, Sept. 17, 1932.

CRYSTAL, BILLY: NYC, 1948.

CULLUM, JOHN: Knoxville, TN, Mar. 2, 1930. U. Tenn.

CULP, ROBERT: Oakland, CA., Aug. 16, 1930. U. Wash.

CULVER, CALVIN: Canandaigua, NY, 1943.

CUMMINGS, CONSTANCE: Seattle, WA, May 15, 1910.

CUMMINGS, QUINN: Hollywood, Aug. 13, 1967.

CUMMINGS, ROBERT: Joplin, MO, June 9, 1910. Carnegie Tech.

CUMMINS, PEGGY: Prestatyn, N. Wales, Dec. 18, 1926. Alexandra School.

CURTIS, KEENE: Salt Lake City, UT, Feb. 15, 1925. U. Utah.

CURTIS, TONY (Bernard Schwartz): NYC, June 3, 1924.

CUSACK, CYRIL: Durban, S. Africa, Nov. 26, 1910. Univ. Col.

CUSHING, PETER: Kenley, Surrey, Eng., May 26, 1913.

DAHL, ARLENE: Minneapolis, Aug. 11, 1924. U. Minn.

DALLESANDRO, JOE: Pensacola, FL, Dec. 31, 1948.

DALTON, TIMOTHY: Wales, 1945. RADA.

DALTREY, ROGER: London, Mar. 1, 1945.

DALY, TYNE: NYC, 1947. AMDA.

DAMONE, VIC (Vito Farinola): Brooklyn, June 12, 1928.

DANIELS, WILLIAM: Bklyn, Mar. 31, 1927. Northwestern.

DANNER, BLYTHE: Philadelphia, PA. Bard Col.

DANO, ROYAL: NYC, Nov. 16, 1922. NYU.

DANTE, MICHAEL (Ralph Vitti): Stamford, CT, 1935. U. Miami.

DANTINE, HELMUT: Vienna, Oct. 7, 1918. U. Calif.

DANTON, RAY: NYC, Sept. 19, 1931. Carnegie Tech.

DARBY, KIM: (Deborah Zerby): North Hollywood, CA, July 8, 1948.

DARCEL, DENISE (Denise Billecard): Paris, Sept. 8, 1925. U. Dijon.

DARREN, JAMES: Philadelphia, June 8, 1936. Stella Adler School.

DARRIEUX, DANIELLE: Bordeaux, France, May 1, 1917. Lycee LaTour.

DA SILVA, HOWARD: Cleveland, OH, May 4, 1909. Carnegie Tech.

DAVIDSON, JOHN: Pittsburgh, Dec. 13, 1941. Denison U.

DAVIES, RUPERT: Liverpool, Eng., 1916.

DAVIS, BETTE: Lowell, MA, Apr. 5, 1908. John Murray Anderson Dramatic School.

DAVIS, BRAD: Fla., 1950.

DAVIS, MAC: Lubbock, TX, 1942.

DAVIS, NANCY (Anne Frances Robbins): NYC July 6, 1923, Smith Col.

DAVIS, OSSIE: Cogdell, GA, Dec. 18, 1917. Howard U.

DAVIS, SAMMY, JR.: NYC, Dec. 8, 1925.

DAY, DENNIS (Eugene Dennis McNulty): NYC, May 21, 1917. Manhattan College.

DAY, DORIS (Doris Kappelhoff): Cincinnati, Apr. 3, 1924.

DAY, LARAINE (Johnson): Roosevelt, UT, Oct. 13, 1917.

DAYAN, ASSEF: Israel, 1945. U. Jerusalem.

DEAN, JIMMY: Plainview, TX, Aug. 10, 1928.

DeCARLO, YVONNE (Peggy Yvonne Middleton): Vancouver, B.C., Can., Sept. 1, 1922. Vancouver School of Drama.

DEE, FRANCES: Los Angeles, Nov. 26, 1907. Chicago U.

DEE, JOEY (Joseph Di Nicola): Passaic, NJ, June 11, 1940. Patterson State College.

DEE, RUBY: Cleveland, OH, Oct. 27, 1924. Hunter Col.

DEE, SANDRA (Alexandra Zuck): Bayonne, NJ, Apr. 23, 1942.

DeFORE, DON: Cedar Rapids, IA, Aug. 25, 1917. U. Iowa.

DeHAVEN, GLORIA: Los Angeles, July 23, 1923.

DeHAVILLAND, OLIVIA: Tokyo, Japan, July 1, 1916. Notre Dame Convent School.

DELL, GABRIEL: Barbados, BWI, Oct. 7, 1930.

DELON, ALAIN: Sceaux, Fr., Nov. 8, 1935.

DELORME, DANIELE: Paris, Oct. 9, 1927. Sorbonne.

DEL RIO, DOLORES: (Dolores Ansunsolo): Durango, Mex., Aug. 3, 1905. St. Joseph's Convent.

DeLUISE, DOM: Brooklyn, Aug. 1, 1933. Tufts Col.

DEMAREST, WILLIAM: St. Paul, MN, Feb. 27, 1892.

DEMONGEOT, MYLENE: Nice, France, Sept. 29, 1938.

DENEUVE, CATHERINE: Paris, Oct. 22, 1943.

DeNIRO, ROBERT: NYC, Aug. 17, 1943. Stella Adler.

DENISON, MICHAEL: Doncaster, York, Eng., Nov. 1, 1915. Oxford.

DENNER, CHARLES: Tarnow, Poland, May 29, 1926.

DENNIS, SANDY: Hastings, NB, Apr. 27, 1937. Actors Studio.

DEREK, BO (Mary Cathleen Collins): Long Beach, CA, 1957.

DEREK, JOHN: Hollywood, Aug. 12, 1926.

DERN, BRUCE: Chicago, June 4, 1936. U Pa.

DEWHURST, COLLEEN: Montreal, June 3, 1926. Lawrence U.

DEXTER, ANTHONY (Walter Reinhold Alfred Fleischmann): Talmadge, NB, Jan. 19, 1919. U. Iowa.

DeYOUNG, CLIFF: Los Angeles, CA, Feb. 12, 1945. Cal State.

DHIEGH, KHIGH: New Jersey, 1910.

DICKINSON, ANGIE: Kulm, ND, Sept. 30, 1932. Glendale College.

DIETRICH, MARLENE (Maria Magdalene von Losch): Berlin, Ger., Dec. 27, 1901. Berlin Music Academy.

DILLER, PHYLLIS: Lima, OH, July 17, 1917. Bluffton College.

DILLMAN, BRADFORD: San Francisco, Apr. 14, 1930. Yale.

DILLON, MATT: Larchmont, NY 1964, AADA.

DILLON, MELINDA: Hope, AR, Oct. 13, 1939. Goodman Theatre School.

DOBSON, TAMARA: Baltimore, MD, 1947. Md. Inst. of Art.

DOMERGUE, FAITH: New Orleans, June 16, 1925.

DONAHUE, TROY (Merle Johnson): NYC, Jan. 27, 1937. Columbia U.

DONAT, PETER: Nova Scotia, Jan. 20, 1928. Yale.

DONNELL, JEFF (Jean Donnell): South Windham, ME, July 10, 1921. Yale Drama School.

DONNELLY, RUTH: Trenton, NJ, May 17, 1896.

DOOHAN, JAMES: Vancouver, BC, Mar. 3. Neighborhood Playhouse.

DOOLEY, PAUL: Parkersburg, WV, Feb. 22, 1928. U WV.

DORS, DIANA (Fluck): Swindon, Wilshire, Eng., Oct. 23, 1931. London Academy of Music.

D'ORSAY, FIFI: Montreal, Can., Apr. 16, 1904.

| Robert Duvall | Barbara Eden | Hector Elizondo | Rhonda Fleming | Alan Feinstein |

DOUGLAS, KIRK (Issur Danielovitch): Amsterdam, NY, Dec. 9, 1916. St. Lawrence U.

DOUGLAS, MELVYN (Melvyn Hesselberg): Macon, GA, Apr. 5, 1901.

DOUGLAS, MICHAEL: Hollywood, Sept. 25, 1944. U. Cal.

DOURIF, BRAD: Huntington, WV, Mar. 18, 1950. Marshall U.

DOVE, BILLIE: NYC, May 14, 1904.

DOWN, LESLEY-ANN: London, Mar. 17, 1954.

DRAKE, BETSY: Paris, Sept. 11, 1923.

DRAKE, CHARLES (Charles Ruppert): NYC, Oct. 2, 1914. Nichols College.

DREW, ELLEN (formerly Terry Ray): Kansas City, MO, Nov. 23, 1915.

DREYFUSS, RICHARD: Brooklyn, NY, 1948.

DRIVAS, ROBERT: Chicago, Oct. 7, 1938. U. Chi.

DRU, JOANNE (Joanne LaCock): Logan, WV, Jan. 31, 1923. John Robert Powers School.

DUBBINS, DON: Brooklyn, NY, June 28.

DUFF, HOWARD: Bremerton, WA, Nov. 24, 1917.

DUFFY, PATRICK: Montana, 1949. U Wash.

DUKE, PATTY: NYC, Dec. 14, 1946.

DULLEA, KEIR: Cleveland, NJ, May 30, 1936. Neighborhood Playhouse, SF State Col.

DUNAWAY, FAYE: Bascom, FL, Jan, 14, 1941. Fla. U.

DUNCAN, SANDY: Henderson, TX, Feb. 20, 1946. Len Morris Col.

DUNNE, IRENE: Louisville, KY, Dec. 20, 1898. Chicago College of Music.

DUNNOCK, MILDRED: Baltimore, Jan. 25, 1900. Johns Hopkins and Columbia U.

DUPEREY, ANNY: Paris, 1947.

DURBIN, DEANNA (Edna): Winnipeg, Can., Dec. 4, 1921.

DURNING, CHARLES: Highland Falls, NY, Feb. 28, 1933. NYU.

DUSSOLLIER, ANDRE: Annecy, France, Feb. 17, 1946.

DUVALL, ROBERT: San Diego, CA, 1930. Principia Col.

DUVALL, SHELLEY: Houston, TX, 1950.

EASTON, ROBERT: Milwaukee, Nov. 23, 1930. U. Texas.

EASTWOOD, CLINT: San Francisco, May 31, 1930. LACC.

EATON, SHIRLEY: London, 1937. Aida Foster School.

EBSEN, BUDDY (Christian, Jr.): Belleville, IL, Apr. 2, 1910. U. Fla.

ECKEMYR, AGNETA: Karlsborg, Swed., July 2. Actors Studio.

EDEN, BARBARA (Moorhead): Tucson, AZ, 1934.

EDWARDS, VINCE: NYC, July 9, 1928. AADA.

EGAN, RICHARD: San Francisco, July 29, 1923. Stanford U.

EGGAR, SAMANTHA: London, Mar. 5, 1939.

EICHHORN, LISA: Reading, PA, 1952. Queens Ont. U. RADA.

EKBERG, ANITA: Malmo, Sweden, Sept. 29, 1931.

EKLAND, BRITT: Stockholm, Swed., 1942.

ELIZONDO, HECTOR: NYC, Dec. 22, 1936.

ELLIOTT, DENHOLM: London, May 31, 1922. Malvern College.

ELLIOTT, SAM: Sacramento, CA, 1944. U. Ore.

ELY, RON (Ronald Pierce): Hereford, TX, June 21, 1938.

EMERSON, FAYE: Elizabeth, LA, July 8, 1917. San Diego State Col.

ERDMAN, RICHARD: Enid, OK, June 1, 1925.

ERICKSON, LEIF: Alameda, CA, Oct. 27, 1911. U. Calif.

ERICSON, JOHN: Dusseldorf, Ger., Sept. 25, 1926. AADA.

ESMOND, CARL: Vienna, June 14, 1906. U. Vienna.

EVANS, DALE (Francis Smith): Uvalde, TX, Oct. 31, 1912.

EVANS, GENE: Holbrook, AZ, July 11, 1922.

EVANS, MAURICE: Dorchester, Eng., June 3, 1901.

EVERETT, CHAD (Ray Cramton): South Bend, IN, June 11, 1936.

EWELL, TOM (Yewell Tompkins): Owensboro, KY, Apr. 29, 1909. U. Wisc.

FABARES, SHELLEY: Los Angeles, Jan. 19, 1944.

FABIAN (Fabian Forte): Philadelphia, Feb. 6, 1940.

FABRAY, NANETTE (Ruby Nanette Fabares): San Diego, Oct. 27, 1920.

FAIRBANKS, DOUGLAS JR.: NYC, Dec. 9, 1907. Collegiate School.

FALK, PETER: NYC, Sept. 16, 1927. New School.

FARENTINO, JAMES: Brooklyn, Feb. 24, 1938. AADA.

FARINA, SANDY (Sandra Feldman): Newark, NJ, 1955.

FARR, DEREK: London, Feb. 7, 1912.

FARR, FELICIA: Westchester, NY, Oct. 4, 1932. Penn State Col.

FARRELL, CHARLES: Onset Bay, MA, Aug. 9, 1901. Boston U.

FARROW, MIA: Los Angeles, Feb. 9, 1945.

FAULKNER, GRAHAM: London, Sept. 26, 1947. Webber-Douglas.

FAWCETT, FARRAH: Texas, Feb. 2, 1947.

FAYE, ALICE (Ann Leppert): NYC, May 5, 1912.

FEINSTEIN, ALAN: NYC, Sept. 8, 1941.

FELDON, BARBARA (Hall): Pittsburgh, Mar. 12, 1941. Carnegie Tech.

FELLOWS, EDITH: Boston, May 20, 1923.

FERRELL, CONCHATA: Charleston, WV, Mar. 28, 1943. Marshall U.

FERRER, JOSE: Santurce, P.R., Jan. 8, 1909. Princeton U.

FERRER, MEL: Elberon, NJ, Aug. 25, 1917. Princeton U.

FERRIS, BARBARA: London, 1943.

FERZETTI, GABRIELE: Italy, 1927. Rome Acad. of Drama.

FIELD, SALLY: Pasadena, CA, Nov. 6, 1946.

FIGUEROA, RUBEN: NYC 1958.

FINNEY, ALBERT: Salford, Lancashire, Eng., May 9, 1936. RADA.

FISHER, CARRIE: Los Angeles, CA, 1957. London Central School of Drama.

FISHER, EDDIE: Philadelphia, Aug. 10, 1928.

FITZGERALD, GERALDINE: Dublin, Ire., Nov. 24, 1914. Dublin Art School.

FLANNERY, SUSAN: Jersey City, NJ, July 31, 1943.

FLAVIN, JAMES: Portland, ME, May 14, 1906. West Point.

FLEMING, RHONDA (Marilyn Louis): Los Angeles, Aug. 10, 1922.

FLEMYNG, ROBERT: Liverpool, Eng., Jan. 3, 1912. Haileybury Col.

FLETCHER, LOUISE: Birmingham, AL, July 1934.

FOCH, NINA: Leyden, Holland, Apr. 20, 1924.

FOLDI, ERZSEBET: Queens, NY, 1967.

FONDA, HENRY: Grand Island, NB, May 16, 1905. Minn. U.

FONDA, JANE: NYC, Dec. 21, 1937. Vassar.

FONDA, PETER: NYC, Feb. 23, 1939. U. Omaha.

FONTAINE, JOAN: Tokyo, Japan, Oct. 22, 1917.

| Jodie Foster | Robert Foxworth | Ben Gazzara | Lee Grant | David Marshall Grant |

FORD, GLENN (Gwyllyn Samuel Newton Ford): Quebec, Can., May 1, 1916.

FORD, HARRISON: Chicago, IL, July 13, 1942. Ripon Col.

FOREST, MARK (Lou Degni): Brooklyn, Jan. 1933.

FORREST, STEVE: Huntsville, TX, Sept. 29, 1924. UCLA.

FORSLUND, CONNIE: San Diego, CA, June 19, 1950. NYU.

FORSTER, ROBERT (Foster, Jr.): Rochester, NY, July 13, 1941. Rochester U.

FORSYTHE, JOHN: Penn's Grove, NJ, Jan. 29, 1918.

FOSTER, JODIE: Bronx, NY, 1963.

FOX, EDWARD: London, 1937, RADA.

FOX, JAMES: London, 1939.

FOXWORTH, ROBERT: Houston, TX, Nov. 1, 1941. Carnegie Tech.

FOXX, REDD: St. Louis, MO, Dec. 9, 1922.

FRANCIOSA, ANTHONY (Papaleo): NYC, Oct. 25, 1928.

FRANCIS, ANNE: Ossining, NY, Sept. 16, 1932.

FRANCIS, ARLENE (Arlene Kazanjian): Boston, Oct. 20, 1908. Finch School.

FRANCIS, CONNIE (Constance Franconero): Newark, NJ, Dec. 12, 1938.

FRANCISCUS, JAMES: Clayton, MO, Jan. 31, 1934. Yale.

FRANCKS, DON: Vancouver, Can., Feb. 28, 1932.

FRANK, JEFFREY: Jackson Heights, NY, 1965.

FRANKLIN, PAMELA: Tokyo, Feb. 4, 1950.

FRANZ, ARTHUR: Perth Amboy, NJ, Feb. 29, 1920. Blue Ridge College.

FRANZ, EDUARD: Milwaukee, WI, Oct. 31, 1902.

FRAZIER, SHEILA: NYC, 1949.

FREEMAN, AL, JR.: San Antonio, TX, 1934. CCLA.

FREEMAN, MONA: Baltimore, MD, June 9, 1926.

FREY, LEONARD: Brooklyn, Sept. 4, 1938, Neighborhood Playhouse.

FULLER, PENNY: Durham, NC, 1940. Northwestern U.

FURNEAUX, YVONNE: Lille, France, 1928. Oxford U.

GABEL, MARTIN: Philadelphia, June 19, 1912. AADA.

GABOR, EVA: Budapest, Hungary, Feb. 11, 1920.

GABOR, ZSA ZSA (Sari Gabor): Budapest, Hungary, Feb. 6, 1918.

GALLAGHER, PETER: Armonk, NY, 1956, Tufts U.

GAM, RITA: Pittsburgh, PA, Apr. 2, 1928.

GARBER, VICTOR: Montreal, Can., Mar. 16, 1949.

GARBO, GRETA (Greta Gustafson): Stockholm, Sweden, Sept. 18, 1905.

GARDENIA, VINCENT: Naples, Italy, Jan. 7, 1922.

GARDNER, AVA: Smithfield, NC, Dec. 24, 1922. Atlantic Christian College.

GARFIELD, ALLEN: Newark, NJ, Nov. 22, 1939. Actors Studio.

GARLAND, BEVERLY: Santa Cruz, CA, Oct. 17, 1930. Glendale Col.

GARNER, JAMES (James Baumgarner): Norman, OK, Apr. 7, 1928. Okla. U.

GARNER, PEGGY ANN: Canton, OH, Feb. 3, 1932.

GARR, TERI: Lakewood, OH, 1952.

GARRETT, BETTY: St. Joseph, MO, May 23, 1919. Annie Wright Seminary.

GARRISON, SEAN: NYC, Oct. 19, 1937.

GARSON, GREER: Ireland, Sept. 29, 1906.

GASSMAN, VITTORIO: Genoa, Italy, Sept. 1, 1922. Rome Academy of Dramatic Art.

GAVIN, JOHN: Los Angeles, Apr. 8, 1935. Stanford U.

GAYNOR, JANET: Philadelphia, Oct. 6, 1906.

GAYNOR, MITZI (Francesca Marlene Von Gerber): Chicago, Sept. 4, 1931.

GAZZARA, BEN: NYC, Aug. 28, 1930. Actors Studio.

GEESON, JUDY: Arundel, Eng., Sept. 10, 1948. Corona.

GEORGE, CHIEF DAN (Geswanouth Slaholt): North Vancouver, Can., June 24, 1899.

GERARD, GIL: Little Rock, AR, 1940.

GERE, RICHARD: Philadelphia, PA, Aug. 29, 1949. U. Mass.

GHOLSON, JULIE: Birmingham, AL, June 4, 1958.

GHOSTLEY, ALICE: Eve, MO, Aug. 14, 1926. Okla U.

GIANNINI, GIANCARLO: Spezia, Italy, Aug. 1, 1942. Rome Acad. of Drama.

GIELGUD, JOHN: London, Apr. 14, 1904. RADA.

GILFORD, JACK: NYC, July 25.

GILLIS, ANNE (Alma O'Connor): Little Rock, AR, Feb. 12, 1927.

GILLMORE, MARGALO: London, May 31, 1897. AADA.

GILMORE, VIRGINIA (Sherman Poole): Del Monte, CA, July 26, 1919. U. Calif.

GINGOLD, HERMIONE: London, Dec. 9, 1897.

GISH, LILLIAN: Springfield, OH, Oct. 14, 1896.

GLASER, PAUL MICHAEL: Boston, MA, 1943. Boston U.

GLASS, RON: Evansville, IN, 1946.

GLEASON, JACKIE: Brooklyn, Feb. 26, 1916.

GLENN, SCOTT: Pittsburgh, PA, Jan. 26, 1942; William and Mary Col.

GODDARD, PAULETTE (Levy): Great Neck, NY, June 3, 1911.

GOLDBLUM, JEFF: Pittsburgh, PA, Oct. 22, 1952. Neighborhood Playhouse.

GOLDEN, ANNIE: NYC, 1952.

GONZALES-GONZALEZ, PEDRO: Aguilares, TX, Dec. 21, 1926.

GOODMAN, DODY: Columbus, OH, Oct. 28, 1915.

GORDON, GALE (Aldrich): NYC, Feb. 2, 1906.

GORDON, KEITH: NYC, Feb. 3, 1961.

GORDON, RUTH (Jones): Wollaston, MA, Oct. 30, 1896. AADA.

GORING, MARIUS: Newport, Isle of Wight, 1912. Cambridge, Old Vic.

GORMAN, CLIFF: Jamaica, NY, Oct. 13, 1936. NYU.

GORTNER, MARJOE: Long Beach, CA, 1944.

GOSSETT, LOUIS: Brooklyn, May 27, 1936. NYU.

GOULD, ELLIOTT (Goldstein): Brooklyn, Aug. 29, 1938. Columbia U.

GOULD, HAROLD: Schenectady, NY, Dec. 10, 1923. Cornell.

GOULET, ROBERT: Lawrence, MA, Nov. 26, 1933. Edmonton.

GRAHAME, GLORIA (Gloria Grahame Hallward): Los Angeles, Nov. 28, 1925.

GRANGER, FARLEY: San Jose, CA, July 1, 1925.

GRANGER, STEWART (James Stewart): London, May 6, 1913. Webber-Douglas School of Acting.

GRANT, CARY (Archibald Alexander Leach): Bristol, Eng., Jan. 18, 1904.

GRANT, DAVID MARSHALL: Westport, CT, 1955. Yale.

GRANT, KATHRYN (Olive Grandstaff): Houston, TX, Nov. 25, 1933. UCLA.

GRANT, LEE: NYC, Oct. 31, 1930. Juilliard.

GRANVILLE, BONITA: NYC, Feb. 2, 1923.

**David
Groh** **Julie
Harris** **George
Hamilton** **Audrey
Hepburn** **David
Hedison**

GRAVES, PETER (Aurness): Minneapolis, Mar. 18, 1926. U. Minn.

GRAY, COLEEN (Doris Jensen): Staplehurst, NB, Oct. 23, 1922. Hamline U.

GRAYSON, KATHRYN (Zelma Hedrick): Winston-Salem, NC, Feb. 9, 1922.

GREENE, ELLEN: NYC, Feb. 22. Ryder Col.

GREENE, LORNE: Ottawa, Can., Feb. 12, 1915. Queens U.

GREENE, RICHARD: Plymouth, Eng., Aug. 25, 1914. Cardinal Vaughn School.

GREENWOOD, JOAN: London, Mar. 4, 1919. RADA.

GREER, JANE: Washington, DC, Sept. 9, 1924.

GREER, MICHAEL: Galesburg, IL, Apr. 20, 1943.

GREY, JOEL (Katz): Cleveland, OH, Apr. 11, 1932.

GREY, VIRGINIA: Los Angeles, Mar. 22, 1917.

GRIEM, HELMUT: Hamburg, Ger. U. Hamburg.

GRIFFITH, ANDY: Mt. Airy, NC, June 1, 1926. UNC.

GRIFFITH, MELANIE: NYC, Aug. 9, 1957. Pierce Col.

GRIMES, GARY: San Francisco, June 2, 1955.

GRIMES, TAMMY: Lynn, MA, Jan. 30, 1934. Stephens Col.

GRIZZARD, GEORGE: Roanoke Rapids, NC, Apr. 1, 1928. UNC.

GRODIN, CHARLES: Pittsburgh, PA, Apr. 21, 1935.

GROH, DAVID: NYC, May 21, 1939. Brown U., LAMDA.

GUARDINO, HARRY: Brooklyn, Dec. 23, 1925. Haaren High.

GUINNESS, ALEC: London, Apr. 2, 1914. Pembroke Lodge School.

GUNN, MOSES: St. Louis, MO, Oct. 2, 1929. Tenn. State U.

GUTTENBERG, STEVEN: Brooklyn, NY, 1958. UCLA.

GWILLIM, DAVID: Plymouth, Eng., Dec. 15, 1948. RADA.

HACKETT, BUDDY (Leonard Hacker): Brooklyn, Aug. 31, 1924.

HACKETT, JOAN: NYC, May 1, 1939. Actors Studio.

HACKMAN, GENE: San Bernardino, CA, Jan. 30, 1931.

HADDON, DALE: Montreal, Can., May 26, 1949. Neighborhood Playhouse.

HAGMAN, LARRY (Hageman): Texas, 1939. Bard Col.

HALE, BARBARA: DeKalb, IL, Apr. 18, 1922. Chicago Academy of Fine Arts.

HALL, ALBERT: Boothton, AL, Nov. 10, 1937. Columbia.

HAMILL, MARK: Oakland, CA, Sept. 25, 1952. LACC.

HAMILTON, GEORGE: Memphis, TN, Aug. 12, 1939. Hackley.

HAMILTON, MARGARET: Cleveland, OH, Dec. 9, 1902. Hathaway-Brown School.

HAMILTON, NEIL: Lynn, MA, Sept. 9, 1899.

HAMLIN, HARRY: Pasadena, CA, 1952. Yale

HAMPSHIRE, SUSAN: London, May 12, 1941.

HARDIN, TY (Orison Whipple Hungerford II): NYC, June 1, 1930.

HARDING, ANN (Dorothy Walton Gatley): Fort Sam Houston, TX, Aug. 17, 1901.

HAREWOOD, DORIAN: Dayton, OH, Aug. 6. U Cinn.

HARMON, MARK: Los Angeles, CA, 1951; UCLA.

HARPER, VALERIE: Suffern, NY, Aug. 22, 1940.

HARRINGTON, PAT: NYC, Aug. 13, 1929. Fordham U.

HARRIS, BARBARA (Sandra Markowitz): Evanston, IL, 1937.

HARRIS, JULIE: Grosse Pointe, MI, Dec. 2, 1925. Yale Drama School.

HARRIS, RICHARD: Limerick, Ire., Oct. 1, 1930. London Acad.

HARRIS, ROSEMARY: Ashby, Eng., Sept. 19, 1930. RADA.

HARRISON, GREG: Catalina Island, CA, 1950; Actors Studio.

HARRISON, NOEL: London, Jan. 29, 1936.

HARRISON, REX: Huyton, Cheshire, Eng., Mar. 5, 1908.

HARROLD, KATHRYN: Tazewell, VA. 1950.

HARTMAN, DAVID: Pawtucket, RI, May 19, 1942. Duke U.

HARTMAN, ELIZABETH: Youngstown, OH, Dec. 23, 1941. Carnegie Tech.

HASSETT, MARILYN: Los Angeles, CA, 1949.

HAVER, JUNE: Rock Island, IL, June 10, 1926.

HAVOC, JUNE (June Hovick): Seattle, WA, Nov. 8, 1916.

HAWN, GOLDIE: Washington, DC, Nov. 21, 1945.

HAYDEN, LINDA: Stanmore, Eng. Aida Foster School.

HAYDEN, STERLING (John Hamilton): Montclair, NJ, March 26, 1916.

HAYES, HELEN (Helen Brown): Washington, DC, Oct. 10, 1900. Sacred Heart Convent.

HAYS, ROBERT: San Diego, CA, 1948; SD State Col.

HAYWORTH, RITA (Margarita Cansino): NYC, Oct. 17, 1918.

HEARD, JOHN: Washington, DC, Mar. 7, 1946. Clark U.

HEATHERTON, JOEY: NYC, Sept. 14, 1944.

HECKART, EILEEN: Columbus, OH, Mar. 29, 1919. Ohio State U.

HEDISON, DAVID: Providence, RI, May 20, 1929. Brown U.

HEGYES, ROBERT: NJ, May 7, 1951.

HEMMINGS, DAVID: Guilford, Eng. Nov. 18, 1938.

HENDERSON, MARCIA: Andover, MA, July 22, 1932. AADA.

HENDRY, GLORIA: Jacksonville, FL, 1949.

HENNER, MARILU: NYC, Apr. 4, 1953.

HENREID, PAUL: Trieste, Jan. 10, 1908.

HENRY, BUCK (Zuckerman): NYC, 1931. Dartmouth.

HENRY, JUSTIN: Rye, NY, 1971.

HEPBURN, AUDREY: Brussels, Belgium, May 4, 1929.

HEPBURN, KATHARINE: Hartford, CT, Nov. 8, 1907. Bryn Mawr.

HERRMANN, EDWARD: Washington, DC, July 21, 1943. Bucknell, LAMDA.

HESTON, CHARLTON: Evanston, IL, Oct. 4, 1922. Northwestern U.

HEWITT, MARTIN: San Jose, Ca, 1960; AADA.

HEYWOOD, ANNE (Violet Pretty): Birmingham, Eng., Dec. 11, 1932.

HICKMAN, DARRYL: Hollywood, CA, July 28, 1930. Loyola U.

HICKMAN, DWAYNE: Los Angeles, May 18, 1934. Loyola U.

HILL, ARTHUR: Saskatchewan, Can., Aug. 1, 1922. U. Brit. Col.

HILL, STEVEN: Seattle, WA, Feb. 24, 1922. U. Wash.

HILL, TERENCE (Mario Girotti): Venice, Italy, Mar. 29, 1941. U. Rome.

HILLER, WENDY: Bramhall, Cheshire, Eng., Aug. 15, 1912. Winceby House School.

HILLIARD, HARRIET: (see Harriet Hilliard Nelson)

HINGLE, PAT: Denver, CO, July 19, 1923. Tex. U.

HIRSCH, JUDD: NYC, Mar. 15, 1935. AADA.

HOFFMAN, DUSTIN: Los Angeles, Aug. 8, 1937. Pasadena Playhouse.

HOLBROOK, HAL (Harold): Cleveland, OH, Feb. 17, 1925. Denison.

| Katharine Houghton | Ken Howard | Glenda Jackson | Page Johnson | Diane Keaton |

HOLDEN, WILLIAM: O'Fallon, IL, Apr. 17, 1918. Pasadena Jr. Coll.

HOLLIMAN, EARL: Tenessas Swamp, Delhi, LA, Sept. 11, 1928. UCLA.

HOLLOWAY, STANLEY: London, Oct. 1, 1890.

HOLM, CELESTE: NYC, Apr. 29, 1919.

HOMEIER, SKIP (George Vincent Homeier): Chicago, Oct. 5, 1930. UCLA.

HOOKS, ROBERT: Washington, DC, Apr. 18, 1937. Temple.

HOPE, BOB: London, May 26, 1903.

HOPPER, DENNIS: Dodge City, KS, May 17, 1936.

HORNE, LENA: Brooklyn, June 30, 1917.

HORTON, ROBERT: Los Angeles, July 29, 1924. UCLA.

HOUGHTON, KATHARINE: Hartford, CT, Mar. 10, 1945. Sarah Lawrence.

HOUSEMAN, JOHN: Bucharest, Sept. 22, 1902.

HOUSER, JERRY: Los Angeles, July 14, 1952. Valley Jr. Col.

HOUSTON, DONALD: Tonypandy, Wales, 1924.

HOVEY, TIM: Los Angeles, June 19, 1945.

HOWARD, KEN: El Centro, CA, Mar. 28, 1944. Yale.

HOWARD, RON: Duncan, OK, Mar. 1, 1954. USC.

HOWARD, RONALD: Norwood, Eng., Apr. 7, 1918. Jesus College.

HOWARD, TREVOR: Kent, Eng., Sept. 29, 1916. RADA.

HOWELLS, URSULA: London, Sept. 17, 1922.

HOWES, SALLY ANN: London, July 20, 1930.

HUDSON, ROCK (Roy Scherer Fitzgerald): Winnetka, IL, Nov. 17, 1924.

HUFFMAN, DAVID: Berwin, IL, May 10, 1945.

HUGHES, BARNARD: Bedford Hills, NY, July 16, 1915. Manhattan Col.

HUGHES, KATHLEEN (Betty von Gerkan): Hollywood, CA, Nov. 14, 1928. UCLA.

HULCE, THOMAS: Plymouth, MI, Dec. 6, 1953. N.C.Sch. of Arts.

HUNNICUTT, GAYLE: Ft. Worth, TX, Feb. 6, 1943. UCLA.

HUNT, MARSHA: Chicago, Oct. 17, 1917.

HUNTER, KIM (Janet Cole): Detroit, Nov. 12, 1922.

HUNTER, TAB (Arthur Gelien): NYC, July 11, 1931.

HUPPERT, ISABELLE: Paris, Fr., Mar. 16, 1955.

HURT, WILLIAM: Washington, D.C., Mar. 20, 1950. Tufts, Juilliard.

HUSSEY, RUTH: Providence , RI, Oct. 30, 1917. U. Mich.

HUSTON, JOHN: Nevada, MO, Aug. 5, 1906.

HUTTON, BETTY (Betty Thornberg): Battle Creek, MI, Feb. 26, 1921.

HUTTON, LAUREN (Mary): Charleston, SC, Nov. 17, 1943. Newcomb Col.

HUTTON, ROBERT (Winne): Kingston, NY, June 11, 1920. Blair Academy.

HUTTON, TIMOTHY: Malibu, CA, 1960.

HYDE-WHITE, WILFRID: Gloucestershire, Eng., May 13, 1903. RADA.

HYER, MARTHA: Fort Worth, TX, Aug. 10, 1924. Northwestern U.

INGELS, MARTY: Brooklyn, NY, Mar. 9, 1936.

IRELAND, JOHN: Vancouver, B.C., Can., Jan. 30, 1914.

IVES, BURL: Hunt Township, IL, June 14, 1909. Charleston Ill. Teachers College.

JACKSON, ANNE: Alleghany, PA, Sept. 3, 1926. Neighborhood Playhouse.

JACKSON, GLENDA: Hoylake, Cheshire, Eng., May 9, 1936. RADA.

JACOBI, LOU: Toronto, Can., Dec. 28, 1913.

JACOBS, LAWRENCE-HILTON: Virgin Islands, 1954.

JACOBY, SCOTT: Chicago, Nov. 19, 1956.

JAECKEL, RICHARD: Long Beach, NY, Oct. 10, 1926.

JAFFE, SAM: NYC, Mar. 8, 1892.

JAGGER, DEAN: Lima, OH, Nov. 7, 1903. Wabash College.

JAMES, CLIFTON: NYC, May 29, 1921. Ore. U.

JARMAN, CLAUDE, JR.: Nashville, TN, Sept. 27, 1934.

JASON, RICK: NYC, May 21, 1926. AADA.

JEAN, GLORIA (Gloria Jean Schoonover): Buffalo, NY, Apr. 14, 1927.

JEFFREYS, ANNE (Carmichael): Goldsboro, NC, Jan. 26, 1923. Anderson College.

JEFFRIES, LIONEL: London, 1927, RADA.

JERGENS, ADELE: Brooklyn, Nov. 26, 1922.

JESSEL, GEORGE: NYC, Apr. 3, 1898.

JOHNS, GLYNIS: Durban, S. Africa, Oct. 5, 1923.

JOHNSON, CELIA: Richmond, Surrey, Eng., Dec. 18, 1908. RADA.

JOHNSON, PAGE: Welch, WV, Aug. 25, 1930. Ithaca.

JOHNSON, RAFER: Hillsboro, TX, Aug. 18, 1935. UCLA.

JOHNSON, RICHARD: Essex, Eng., 1927. RADA.

JOHNSON, ROBIN: Brooklyn, NY; May 29, 1964.

JOHNSON, VAN: Newport, RI, Aug. 28, 1916.

JONES, CAROLYN: Amarillo, TX, Apr. 28, 1933.

JONES, CHRISTOPHER: Jackson, TN, Aug. 18, 1941. Actors Studio.

JONES, DEAN: Morgan County, AL, Jan. 25, 1936. Ashburn College.

JONES, JACK: Bel-Air, CA, Jan. 14, 1938.

JONES, JAMES EARL: Arkabutla, MS, Jan 17, 1931. U. Mich.

JONES, JENNIFER (Phyllis Isley): Tulsa, OK, Mar. 2, 1919. AADA.

JONES, SAM J.: Chicago, IL, 1954.

JONES, SHIRLEY: Smithton, PA, March 31, 1934.

JONES, TOM (Thomas Jones Woodward): Pontypridd, Wales, June 7, 1940.

JONES, TOMMY LEE: San Saba, TX, Sept. 15, 1946. Harvard.

JORDAN, RICHARD: NYC, July J9, 1938. Harvard.

JORY, VICTOR: Dawson City, Can., Nov. 28, 1901. Cal. U.

JOURDAN, LOUIS: Marseilles, France, June 18, 1920.

JULIA, RAUL: San Juan, PR, Mar. 9, 1940. U PR.

JURADO, KATY (Maria Christina Jurado Garcia): Guadalajara, Mex., 1927.

KAHN, MADELINE: Boston, MA, Sept. 29, 1942. Hofstra U.

KANE, CAROL: Cleveland, OH, 1952.

KAPLAN, JONATHAN: Paris, Nov. 25, 1947. NYU.

KATT, WILLIAM: Los Angeles, CA, 1955.

KAUFMANN, CHRISTINE: Lansdorf, Graz, Austria, Jan. 11, 1945.

KAYE, DANNY (David Daniel Kominski): Brooklyn, Jan. 18, 1913.

KAYE, STUBBY: NYC, Nov. 11, 1918.

KEACH, STACY: Savannah, GA, June 2, 1941. U. Cal., Yale.

KEATON, DIANE (Hall): Los Angeles, CA, Jan. 5, 1946. Neighborhood Playhouse.

Marthe Keller	Aron Kincaid	Nancy Kelly	Leigh Lawson	Jessica Lange

KEATS, STEVEN: Bronx, NY, 1945.

KEDROVA, LILA: Greece, 1918.

KEEL, HOWARD (Harold Keel): Gillespie, IL, Apr. 13, 1919.

KEELER, RUBY (Ethel): Halifax, N.S., Aug. 25, 1909.

KEITH, BRIAN: Bayonne, NJ, Nov. 14, 1921.

KELLER, MARTHE: Basel, Switz., 1945. Munich Stanislavsky Sch.

KELLERMAN, SALLY: Long Beach, CA, June 2, 1938. Actors Studio West.

KELLEY, DeFOREST: Atlanta, GA, Jan. 20, 1920.

KELLY, GENE: Pittsburgh, Aug. 23, 1912. U. Pittsburgh.

KELLY, GRACE: Philadelphia, Nov. 12, 1929. AADA.

KELLY, JACK: Astoria, NY, Sept. 16, 1927. UCLA.

KELLY, NANCY: Lowell, MA, Mar. 25, 1921. Bentley School.

KELLY, PATSY: Brooklyn, Jan. 12, 1910.

KEMP, JEREMY: Chesterfield, Eng., 1935, Central Sch.

KENNEDY, ARTHUR: Worcester, MA, Feb. 17, 1914. Carnegie Tech.

KENNEDY, GEORGE: NYC, Feb. 18, 1925.

KERR, DEBORAH: Helensburg, Scot., Sept. 30, 1921. Smale Ballet School.

KERR, JOHN: NYC, Nov. 15, 1931. Harvard, Columbia.

KHAMBATTA, PERSIS: Bombay, Oct. 2, 1950.

KIDDER, MARGOT: Yellow Knife, Can., Oct. 17, 1948. UBC.

KIER, UDO: Germany, Oct. 14, 1944.

KILEY, RICHARD: Chicago, Mar. 31, 1922. Loyola.

KINCAID, ARON (Norman Neale Williams III): Los Angeles, June 15, 1943. UCLA.

KING, ALAN: (Irwin Kniberg): Brooklyn, Dec. 26, 1927.

KING, PERRY: Alliance, OH, Apr. 30. Yale.

KINSKI, NASTASSIA: Germany, 1960.

KITT, EARTHA: North, SC, Jan. 26, 1928.

KLEMPERER, WERNER: Cologne, Mar. 22, 1920.

KLUGMAN, JACK: Philadelphia, PA, Apr. 27, 1925. Carnegie Tech.

KNIGHT, ESMOND: East Sheen, Eng., May 4, 1906.

KNIGHT, SHIRLEY: Goessel, KS, July 5, 1937. Wichita U.

KNOWLES, PATRIC (Reginald Lawrence Knowles): Horsforth, Eng., Nov. 11, 1911.

KNOX, ALEXANDER: Strathroy, Ont., Can., Jan. 16, 1907.

KNOX, ELYSE: Hartford, CT, Dec. 14, 1917. Traphagen School.

KOENIG, WALTER: Chicago, IL, Sept. 14. UCLA.

KOHNER, SUSAN: Los Angeles, Nov. 11, 1936. U. Calif.

KORMAN, HARVEY: Chicago, IL, Feb. 15, 1927. Goodman.

KORVIN, CHARLES (Geza Korvin Karpathi): Czechoslovakia, Nov. 21. Sorbonne.

KOSLECK, MARTIN: Barkotzen, Ger., Mar. 24, 1907. Max Reinhardt School.

KOTTO, YAPHET: NYC, Nov. 15, 1937.

KREUGER, KURT: St. Moritz, Switz., July 23, 1917. U. London.

KRISTOFFERSON, KRIS: Brownsville, TX, 1936, Pomona Col.

KRUGER, HARDY: Berlin, Ger., April. 12, 1928.

KULP, NANCY: Harrisburg, PA, 1921.

KUNTSMANN, DORIS: Hamburg, 1944.

KWAN, NANCY: Hong Kong, May 19, 1939. Royal Ballet.

LACY, JERRY: Sioux City, IA, Mar. 27, 1936. LACC.

LADD, CHERYL (Stoppelmoor): Huron, SD, 1951.

LADD, DIANE (Ladnier): Meridian, MS, Nov. 29, 1932. Tulane U.

LAHTI, CHRISTINE: Detroit, MI, Apr. 4, 1950; U Mich.

LAMARR, HEDY (Hedwig Kiesler): Vienna, Sept. 11, 1913.

LAMAS, FERNANDO: Buenos Aires, Jan. 9, 1920.

LAMAS, LORENZO: Los Angeles, Jan. 1958.

LAMB, GIL: Minneapolis, June 14, 1906. U. Minn.

LAMOUR, DOROTHY: Dec. 10, 1914. Spence School.

LANCASTER, BURT: NYC, Nov. 2, 1913. NYU.

LANCHESTER, ELSA (Elsa Sullivan): London, Oct. 28, 1902.

LANDAU, MARTIN: Brooklyn, NY, 1931. Actors Studio.

LANDON, MICHAEL (Eugene Orowitz): Collingswood, NJ, Oct. 31, 1936. USC.

LANE, ABBE: Brooklyn, Dec. 14, 1935.

LANE, DIANE: NYC, Jan. 1965.

LANGAN, GLENN: Denver, CO, July 8, 1917.

LANGE, HOPE: Redding Ridge, CT, Nov. 28, 1933. Reed Col.

LANGE, JESSICA: Minnesota, 1950. U. Minn.

LANGTON, PAUL: Salt Lake City, Apr. 17, 1913. Travers School of Theatre.

LANSBURY, ANGELA: London, Oct. 16, 1925. London Academy of Music.

LANSING, ROBERT (Brown): San Diego, CA, June 5, 1929.

LAURE, CAROLE: Montreal, Can., 1951.

LAURIE, PIPER (Rosetta Jacobs): Detroit, Jan. 22, 1932.

LAW, JOHN PHILLIP: Hollywood, Sept. 7, 1937. Neighborhood Playhouse, U. Hawaii.

LAWFORD, PETER: London, Sept. 7, 1923.

LAWRENCE, BARBARA: Carnegie, OK, Feb. 24, 1930. UCLA.

LAWRENCE, CAROL (Laraia): Melrose Park, IL, Sept. 5, 1935.

LAWRENCE, VICKI: Inglewood, CA, 1949.

LAWSON, LEIGH: Atherston, Eng., July 21, 1945. RADA.

LEACHMAN, CLORIS: Des Moines, IA, Apr. 30, 1930. Northwestern U.

LEAUD, JEAN-PIERRE: Paris, 1944.

LEDERER, FRANCIS: Karlin, Prague, Czech., Nov. 6, 1906.

LEE, CHRISTOPHER: London, May 27, 1922. Wellington College.

LEE, MICHELE (Dusiak): Los Angeles, June 24, 1942. LACC.

LEIBMAN, RON: NYC, Oct. 11, 1937. Ohio Wesleyan.

LEIGH, JANET (Jeanette Helen Morrison): Merced, CA, July 6, 1926. College of Pacific.

LEMBECK, HARVEY: Brooklyn, Apr. 15, 1923. U. Ala.

LEMMON, JACK: Boston, Feb. 8, 1925. Harvard.

LENZ, RICK: Springfield, IL, Nov. 21, 1939. U. Mich.

LEONARD, SHELDON (Bershad): NYC, Feb. 22, 1907. Syracuse U.

LEROY, PHILIPPE: Paris, Oct. 15, 1930. U. Paris.

LESLIE, BETHEL: NYC, Aug. 3, 1929. Brearley School.

LESLIE, JOAN (Joan Brodell): Detroit, Jan. 26, 1925. St. Benedict's.

LESTER, MARK: Oxford, Eng., July 11, 1958.

LEWIS, JERRY: Newark, NJ, Mar. 16, 1926.

LIGON, TOM: New Orleans, LA, Sept. 10, 1945.

LILLIE, BEATRICE: Toronto, Can., May 29, 1898.

LINCOLN, ABBEY (Anna Marie Woolridge): Chicago, Aug. 6, 1930.

Cleavon Little	Sophia Loren	Lee Majors	Janet Margolin	Roddy McDowall

LINDFORS, VIVECA: Uppsala, Sweden, Dec. 29, 1920. Stockholm Royal Dramatic School.

LISI, VIRNA: Rome, 1938.

LITHGOW, JOHN: Rochester, NY, Oct. 19, 1945. Harvard.

LITTLE, CLEAVON: Chickasha, OK, June 1, 1939. San Diego State.

LOCKE, SONDRA: Shelbyville, TN, 1947.

LOCKHART, JUNE: NYC, June 25, 1925. Westlake School.

LOCKWOOD, GARY: Van Nuys, CA, Feb. 21, 1937.

LOCKWOOD, MARGARET: Karachi, Pakistan, Sept. 15, 1916. RADA.

LOLLOBRIGIDA, GINA: Subiaco, Italy, July 4, 1927. Rome Academy of Fine Arts.

LOM, HERBERT: Prague, Czechoslovakia, 1917. Prague U.

LOMEZ, CELINE: Montreal, Can., 1953.

LONDON, JULIE (Julie Peck): Santa Rosa, CA, Sept. 26, 1926.

LONOW, MARK: Brooklyn, N.Y.

LOPEZ, PERRY: NYC, July 22, 1931. NYU.

LORD, JACK (John Joseph Ryan): NYC, Dec. 30, 1928. NYU.

LOREN, SOPHIA (Sofia Scicolone): Rome, Italy, Sept. 20, 1934.

LOUISE, TINA (Blacker): NYC, Feb. 11, 1934. Miami U.

LOVELACE, LINDA: Bryan, TX, 1952.

LOWITSCH, KLAUS: Berlin, Apr. 8, 1936. Vienna Academy.

LOY, MYRNA (Myrna Williams): Helena, MT, Aug. 2, 1905. Westlake School.

LUCAS, LISA: Arizona, 1961.

LULU: Glasglow, Scot., 1948.

LUND, JOHN: Rochester, NY, Feb. 6, 1913.

LUPINO, IDA: London, Feb. 4, 1916. RADA.

LYDON, JAMES: Harrington Park, NJ, May 30, 1923.

LYNDE, PAUL: Mt. Vernon, OH, June 13, 1926. Northwestern U.

LYNLEY, CAROL (Jones): NYC, Feb. 13, 1942.

LYNN, JEFFREY: Auburn, MA, 1909. Bates College.

LYON, SUE: Davenport, IA, July 10, 1946.

LYONS, ROBERT F.: Albany, NY. AADA.

MacARTHUR, JAMES: Los Angeles, Dec. 8, 1937. Harvard.

MacGINNIS, NIALL: Dublin, Ire., Mar. 29, 1913. Dublin U.

MacGRAW, ALI: NYC, Apr. 1, 1938. Wellesley.

MacLAINE, SHIRLEY (Beatty): Richmond, VA, Apr. 24, 1934.

MacMAHON, ALINE: McKeesport, PA, May 3, 1899. Barnard College.

MacMURRAY, FRED: Kankakee, IL, Aug. 30, 1908. Carroll Col.

MACNEE, PATRICK: London, Feb. 1922.

MacRAE, GORDON: East Orange, NJ, Mar. 12, 1921.

MADISON, GUY (Robert Moseley): Bakersfield, CA, Jan. 19, 1922. Bakersfield Jr. College.

MAHARIS, GEORGE: Astoria, NY, Sept. 1, 1928. Actors Studio.

MAHONEY, JOCK (Jacques O'-Mahoney): Chicago, Feb. 7, 1919. U. of Iowa.

MAJORS, LEE: Wyandotte, MI, Apr. 23, 1940. E. Ky. State Col.

MAKEPEACE, CHRIS: Toronto, Can., 1964.

MALDEN, KARL (Mladen Sekulovich): Gary, IN, Mar. 22, 1914.

MALONE, DOROTHY: Chicago, Jan. 30, 1925. S. Methodist U.

MANN, KURT: Roslyn, NY, July 18, 1947.

MANZ, LINDA: NYC, 1961.

MARAIS, JEAN: Cherbourg, France, Dec. 11, 1913. St. Germain.

MARGO (Maria Marguerita Guadalupe Boldoay Castilla): Mexico City, May 10, 1917.

MARGOLIN, JANET: NYC, July 25, 1943. Walden School.

MARIN, JACQUES: Paris, Sept. 9, 1919. Conservatoire National.

MARLOWE, HUGH (Hugh Hipple): Philadelphia, Jan. 30, 1914.

MARSHALL, BRENDA (Ardis Anderson Gaines): Isle of Negros, P.I., Sept. 29, 1915. Texas State College.

MARSHALL, E. G.: Owatonna, MN, June 18, 1910. U. Minn.

MARSHALL, PENNY: Bronx, NY, Oct. 15, 1942. U. N. Mex.

MARSHALL, WILLIAM: Gary, IN, Aug. 19, 1924. NYU.

MARTIN, DEAN (Dino Crocetti): Steubenville, OH, June 17, 1917.

MARTIN, DEAN PAUL: Los Angeles, CA, 1952. UCLA.

MARTIN, MARY: Weatherford, TX, Dec. 1, 1914. Ward-Belmont School.

MARTIN, STEVE: Waco, TX; 1946; UCLA.

MARTIN, TONY (Alfred Norris): Oakland, CA, Dec. 25, 1913. St. Mary's College.

MARVIN, LEE: NYC, Feb. 19, 1924.

MASON, JAMES: Huddersfield, Yorkshire, Eng., May 15, 1909. Cambridge.

MASON, MARSHA: St. Louis, MO, Apr. 3, 1942. Webster Col.

MASON, PAMELA (Pamela Kellino): Westgate, Eng., Mar. 10, 1918.

MASSEN, OSA: Copenhagen, Den., Jan. 13, 1916.

MASSEY, DANIEL: London, Oct. 10, 1933. Eton and King's Col.

MASSEY, RAYMOND: Toronto, Can., Aug. 30, 1896. Oxford.

MASTERSON, PETER: Angleton, TX, June 1, 1934. Rice U.

MASTROIANNI, MARCELLO: Fontana Liri, Italy, Sept. 28, 1924.

MATTHAU, WALTER (Matuschanskayasky): NYC, Oct. 1, 1920.

MATTHEWS, BRIAN: Philadelphia, PA. 1953. St. Olaf.

MATURE, VICTOR: Louisville, KY, Jan. 29, 1915.

MAY, ELAINE (Berlin): Philadelphia, Apr. 21, 1932.

MAYEHOFF, EDDIE: Baltimore, July 7. Yale.

MAYO, VIRGINIA: (Virginia Clara Jones): St. Louis, Mo; Nov. 30, 1920.

McCALLUM, DAVID: Scotland, Sept. 19, 1933. Chapman Coll.

McCAMBRIDGE, MERCEDES: Jolliet, IL, March 17, 1918. Mundelein College.

McCARTHY, KEVIN: Seattle, WA, Feb. 15, 1914. Minn. U.

McCLORY, SEAN: Dublin, Ire., March 8, 1924. U. Galway.

McCLURE, DOUG: Glendale, CA, May 11, 1935. UCLA.

McCOWEN, ALEC: Tunbridge Wells, Eng., May 26, 1925. RADA.

McCREA, JOEL: Los Angeles, Nov. 5, 1905. Pomona College.

McDERMOTT, HUGH: Edinburgh, Scot., Mar. 20, 1908.

McDOWALL, RODDY: London, Sept. 17, 1928. St. Joseph's.

McDOWELL, MALCOLM (Taylor): Leeds, Eng., June 15, 1943. LAMDA.

McENERY, PETER: Walsall, Eng., Feb. 21, 1940.

McFARLAND, SPANKY: Dallas, TX, 1936.

McGAVIN, DARREN: Spokane, WA, May 7, 1922. College of Pacific.

McGUIRE, BIFF: New Haven, CT, Oct. 25, 1926. Mass. State Col.

McGUIRE, DOROTHY: Omaha, NB, June 14, 1918.

| Jayne Meadows | Barry Miller | Mary Tyler Moore | Roger Moore | Patricia Neal |

McKAY, GARDNER: NYC, June 10, 1932. Cornell.

McKEE, LONETTE: Detroit, MI, 1954.

McKENNA, VIRGINIA: London, June 7, 1931.

McKUEN, ROD: Oakland, CA, Apr. 29, 1933.

McLERIE, ALLYN ANN: Grand Mere, Can., Dec. 1, 1926.

McNAIR, BARBARA: Chicago, March 4, 1939. UCLA.

McNALLY, STEPHEN (Horace McNally): NYC, July 29, 1913. Fordham U.

McNICHOL, KRISTY: Los Angeles, CA, Sept. 11, 1962.

McQUEEN, BUTTERFLY: Tampa, FL, Jan. 8. 1911. UCLA.

MEADOWS, AUDREY Wuchang, China, 1919. St. Margaret's.

MEADOWS, JAYNE (formerly, Jayne Cotter): Wuchang, China, Sept. 27, 1920. St. Margaret's.

MEDWIN, MICHAEL: London, 1925. Instut Fischer.

MEEKER, RALPH (Ralph Rathgeber): Minneapolis, Nov. 21, 1920. Northwestern U.

MEKKA, EDDIE: Worcester, MA, 1932. Boston Cons.

MELATO, MARIANGELA: Milan, Italy, 1941. Milan Theatre Acad.

MELL, MARISA: Vienna, Austria, Feb. 25, 1939.

MERCADO, HECTOR JAIME: NYC, 1949. HB Studio.

MERCOURI, MELINA: Athens, Greece, Oct. 18, 1915.

MEREDITH, BURGESS: Cleveland, OH, Nov. 16, 1908. Amherst.

MEREDITH, LEE (Judi Lee Sauls): Oct., 1947. AADA.

MERKEL, UNA: Covington, KY, Dec. 10, 1903.

MERMAN, ETHEL (Ethel Zimmerman): Astoria, NY, Jan. 16, 1908.

MERRILL, DINA (Nedinia Hutton): NYC, Dec. 9, 1925. AADA.

MERRILL, GARY: Hartford, CT, Aug. 2, 1915. Bowdoin, Trinity.

MICHELL, KEITH: Adelaide, Aus., Dec. 1, 1926.

MIFUNE, TOSHIRO: Tsingtao, China, Apr. 1, 1920.

MILES, SARAH: Ingatestone, Eng., Dec. 31, 1941. RADA.

MILES, SYLVIA: NYC, Sept. 9, 1932.

MILES, VERA (Ralston): Boise City, OK, Aug. 23, 1929. UCLA.

226

MILFORD, PENELOPE: Winnetka, IL.

MILLAND, RAY (Reginald Trustcott-Jones): Neath, Wales, Jan. 3, 1908. King's College.

MILLER, ANN (Lucille Ann Collier): Chireno, TX, Apr. 12, 1919. Lawler Professional School.

MILLER, BARRY: NYC 1958.

MILLER, JASON: Long Island City, NY, Apr. 22, 1939. Catholic U.

MILLER, LINDA: NYC, Sept. 16, 1942. Catholic U.

MILLER, MARVIN: St. Louis, July 18, 1913. Washington U.

MILLS, HAYLEY: London, Apr. 18, 1946. Elmhurst School.

MILLS, JOHN: Suffolk, Eng., Feb. 22, 1908.

MILNER, MARTIN: Detroit, MI, Dec. 28, 1931.

MIMIEUX, YVETTE: Los Angeles, Jan. 8, 1941. Hollywood High.

MINNELLI, LIZA: Los Angeles, Mar. 12, 1946.

MIRANDA, ISA (Isabella Sampietro): Milan, Italy, July 5, 1909.

MITCHELL, CAMERON: Dallastown, PA, Nov. 4, 1918. N.Y. Theatre School.

MITCHELL, JAMES: Sacramento, CA, Feb. 29, 1920. LACC.

MITCHUM, JAMES: Los Angeles, CA, May 8, 1941.

MITCHUM, ROBERT: Bridgeport, CT, Aug. 6, 1917.

MONTALBAN, RICARDO: Mexico City, Nov. 25, 1920.

MONTAND, YVES (Yves Montand Livi): Mansummano, Tuscany, Oct. 13, 1921.

MONTGOMERY, BELINDA: Winnipeg, Can., July 23, 1950.

MONTGOMERY, ELIZABETH: Los Angeles, Apr. 15, 1933. AADA.

MONTGOMERY, GEORGE (George Letz): Brady, MT, Aug. 29, 1916. U. Mont.

MONTGOMERY, ROBERT (Henry, Jr.): Beacon, NY, May 21, 1904.

MOOR, BILL: Toledo, OH, July 13, 1931. Northwestern.

MOORE, CONSTANCE: Sioux City, IA, Jan. 18, 1919.

MOORE, DICK: Los Angeles, Sept. 12, 1925.

MOORE, FRANK: Bay-de-Verde, Newfoundland, 1946.

MOORE, KIERON: County Cork, Ire., 1925. St. Mary's College.

MOORE, MARY TYLER: Brooklyn, Dec. 29, 1936.

MOORE, ROGER: London, Oct. 14, 1927. RADA.

MOORE, TERRY (Helen Koford): Los Angeles, Jan. 7, 1929.

MORE, KENNETH: Gerrards Cross, Eng., Sept. 20, 1914.

MOREAU, JEANNE: Paris, Jan. 3, 1928.

MORENO, RITA (Rosita Alverio): Humacao, P.R., Dec. 11, 1931.

MORGAN, DENNIS (Stanley Morner): Prentice, WI, Dec. 10, 1910. Carroll College.

MORGAN, HARRY (HENRY) (Harry Bratsburg): Detroit, Apr. 10, 1915. U. Chicago.

MORGAN, MICHELE (Simone Roussel): Paris, Feb. 29, 1920. Paris Dramatic School.

MORIARTY, CATHY: Bronx, NY, 1961.

MORIARTY, MICHAEL: Detroit, MI, Apr. 5, 1941. Dartmouth.

MORISON, PATRICIA: NYC, 1915.

MORLEY, ROBERT: Wiltshire, Eng., May 26, 1908. RADA.

MORRIS, GREG: Cleveland, OH, 1934. Ohio State.

MORRIS, HOWARD: NYC, Sept. 4, 1919. NYU.

MORROW, VIC: Bronx, NY, Feb. 14, 1932. Fla. Southern College.

MORSE, DAVID: Hamilton, MA, 1953.

MORSE, ROBERT: Newton, MA, May 18, 1931.

MOSS, ARNOLD: NYC, Jan. 28, 1910. CCNY.

MULLIGAN, RICHARD: NYC, Nov. 13, 1932.

MURPHY, GEORGE: New Haven, CT, July 4, 1902. Yale.

MURPHY, MICHAEL: Los Angeles, CA, 1949.

MURRAY, BILL: Evanston, IL, Sept. 21, 1950; Regis Col.

MURRAY, DON: Hollywood, July 31, 1929. AADA.

MURRAY, KEN (Don Court): NYC, July 14, 1903.

MUSANTE, TONY: Bridgeport, CT, June 30, 1936. Oberlin Col.

NADER, GEORGE: Pasadena, CA, Oct. 19, 1921. Occidental College.

NAPIER, ALAN: Birmingham, Eng., Jan. 7, 1903. Birmingham University.

NATWICK, MILDRED: Baltimore, June 19, 1908. Bryn Mawr.

NAUGHTON, JAMES: Middletown, CT, Dec. 6, 1945. Yale.

NEAL, PATRICIA: Packard, KY, Jan. 20, 1926. Northwestern U.

NEFF, HILDEGARDE (Hildegard Knef): Ulm, Ger., Dec. 28, 1925. Berlin Art Academy.

NELL, NATHALIE: Paris, Oct. 1950.

Don Nute	Jennifer O'Neill	Ron O'Neal	Estelle Parsons	Jameson Parker

NELSON, BARRY (Robert Nielsen): Oakland, CA, 1920.

NELSON, DAVID: NYC, Oct. 24, 1936. USC.

NELSON, GENE (Gene Berg): Seattle, WA, Mar. 24, 1920.

NELSON, HARRIET HILLIARD (Peggy Lou Snyder): Des Moines, IA, July 18.

NELSON, LORI (Dixie Kay Nelson): Santa Fe, NM, Aug. 15, 1933.

NELSON, RICK (Eric Hilliard Nelson): Teaneck, NJ, May 8, 1940.

NESBITT, CATHLEEN: Cheshire, Eng., Nov. 24, 1889. Victoria College.

NEWHART, BOB: Chicago, IL, Sept. 5, 1929. Loyola U.

NEWLEY, ANTHONY: Hackney, London, Sept. 21, 1931.

NEWMAN, BARRY: Boston, MA, Mar. 26, 1938. Brandeis U.

NEWMAN, PAUL: Cleveland, OH, Jan. 26, 1925. Yale.

NEWMAR, JULIE (Newmeyer): Los Angeles, Aug. 16, 1935.

NEWTON-JOHN, OLIVIA: Cambridge, Eng., 1949.

NICHOLAS, PAUL: London, 1945.

NICHOLS, MIKE (Michael Igor Peschkowsky): Berlin, Nov. 6, 1931. U. Chicago.

NICHOLSON, JACK: Neptune, NJ, Apr. 22, 1937.

NICKERSON, DENISE: NYC, 1959.

NICOL, ALEX: Ossining, NY, Jan. 20, 1919. Actors Studio.

NIELSEN, LESLIE: Regina, Saskatchewan, Can., Feb. 11, 1926. Neighborhood Playhouse.

NIMOY, LEONARD: Boston, MA, Mar. 26, 1931. Boston Col., Antioch Col.

NIVEN, DAVID: Kirriemuir, Scot., Mar. 1, 1909. Sandhurst College.

NOLAN, LLOYD: San Francisco, Aug. 11, 1902. Stanford U.

NOLTE, NICK: Omaha, NB, 1941.

NORRIS, CHRISTOPHER: NYC, Oct. 7, 1943. Lincoln Square Acad.

NORTH, HEATHER: Pasadena, CA, Dec. 13, 1950. Actors Workshop.

NORTH, SHEREE (Dawn Bethel): Los Angeles, Jan. 17, 1933. Hollywood High.

NORTON, KEN: Aug. 9, 1945.

NOVAK, KIM (Marilyn Novak): Chicago, Feb. 18, 1933. LACC.

NUREYEV, RUDOLF: Russia, Mar. 17, 1938.

NUTE, DON: Connellsville, PA, Mar. 13. Denver U.

NUYEN, FRANCE (Vannga): Marseilles, France, July 31, 1939. Beaux Arts School.

OATES, WARREN: Depoy, KY, July 5, 1928.

O'BRIAN, HUGH (Hugh J. Krampe): Rochester, NY, Apr. 19, 1928. Cincinnati U.

O'BRIEN, CLAY: Ray, AZ, May 6, 1961.

O'BRIEN, EDMOND: NYC, Sept. 10, 1915. Fordham, Neighborhood Playhouse.

O'BRIEN, MARGARET (Angela Maxine O'Brien): Los Angeles, Jan. 15, 1937.

O'BRIEN, PAT: Milwaukee, Nov. 11, 1899. Marquette U.

O'CONNELL, ARTHUR: NYC, Mar. 29, 1908. St. John's.

O'CONNOR, CARROLL: Bronx, NY, Aug. 2, 1925. Dublin National Univ.

O'CONNOR, DONALD: Chicago, Aug. 28, 1925.

O'CONNOR, GLYNNIS: NYC, Nov. 19, 1956. NYSU.

O'CONNOR, KEVIN: Honolulu, HI, May 7. U. Hi.

O'HANLON, GEORGE: Brooklyn, NY, Nov. 23, 1917.

O'HARA, MAUREEN (Maureen FitzSimons): Dublin, Ire., Aug. 17, 1920. Abbey School.

O'HERLIHY, DAN: Wexford, Ire., May 1, 1919. National U.

O'KEEFE, MICHAEL: Paulland, NJ, 1955, NYU.

OLIVIER, LAURENCE: Dorking, Eng., May 22, 1907. Oxford.

O'LOUGHLIN, GERALD S.: NYC, Dec. 23, 1921. U. Rochester.

OLSON, NANCY: Milwaukee, WI, July 14. UCLA.

O'NEAL, PATRICK: Ocala, FL, Sept. 26, 1927. U. Fla.

O'NEAL, RON: Utica, NY, Sept. 1, 1937. Ohio State.

O'NEAL, RYAN: Los Angeles, Apr. 20, 1941.

O'NEAL, TATUM: Los Angeles, Nov. 5, 1963.

O'NEIL, TRICIA: Shreveport, LA, Mar. 11, 1945. Baylor U.

O'NEILL, JENNIFER: Rio de Janeiro, Feb. 20, 1949. Neighborhood Playhouse.

O'SULLIVAN, MAUREEN: Byle, Ire., May 17, 1911. Sacred Heart Convent.

O'TOOLE, ANNETTE: Houston, TX, 1953. UCLA

O'TOOLE, PETER: Connemara, Ireland, Aug. 2, 1932. RADA.

PACINO, AL: NYC, Apr. 25, 1940.

PAGE, GERALDINE: Kirksville, MO, Nov. 22, 1924. Goodman School.

PAGET, DEBRA (Debralee Griffin): Denver, Aug. 19, 1933.

PAIGE, JANIS (Donna Mae Jaden): Tacoma, WA, Sept. 16, 1922.

PALANCE, JACK (Walter Palanuik): Lattimer, PA, Feb. 18, 1920. UNC.

PALMER, BETSY: East Chicago, IN, Nov. 1, 1929. DePaul U.

PALMER, GREGG (Palmer Lee): San Francisco, Jan. 25, 1927. U. Utah.

PALMER, LILLI: Posen, Austria, May 24, 1914. Ilka Gruning School.

PALMER, MARIA: Vienna, Sept. 5, 1924. College de Bouffement.

PAMPANINI, SILVANA: Rome, Sept. 25, 1925.

PAPAS, IRENE: Chiliomodion, Greece, Mar. 9, 1929.

PARKER, ELEANOR: Cedarville, OH, June 26, 1922. Pasadena Playhouse.

PARKER, FESS: Fort Worth, TX, Aug. 16, 1927. USC.

PARKER, JAMESON: 1947, Beloit Col.

PARKER, JEAN (Mae Green): Deer Lodge, MT, Aug. 11, 1912.

PARKER, SUZY (Cecelia Parker): San Antonio, TX, Oct. 28, 1933.

PARKER, WILLARD (Worster Van Eps): NYC, Feb. 5, 1912.

PARKINS, BARBARA: Vancouver, Can., May 22, 1943.

PARSONS, ESTELLE: Lynn, MA, Nov. 20, 1927. Boston U.

PARTON, DOLLY: Sevierville, TN, 1946.

PATRICK, DENNIS: Philadelphia, Mar. 14, 1918.

PATRICK, NIGEL: London, May 2, 1913.

PATTERSON, LEE: Vancouver, Can., Mar. 31, 1929. Ontario Col.

PAVAN, MARISA (Marisa Pierangeli): Cagliari, Sardinia, June 19, 1932. Torquado Tasso College.

PEACH, MARY: Durban, S. Africa, 1934.

PEARSON, BEATRICE: Denison, TX, July 27, 1920.

PECK, GREGORY: La Jolla, CA, Apr. 5, 1916. U. Calif.

PEPPARD, GEORGE: Detroit, Oct. 1, 1928. Carnegie Tech.

PERKINS, ANTHONY: NYC, Apr. 14, 1932. Rollins College.

PERREAU, GIGI (Ghislaine): Los Angeles, Feb. 6, 1941.

PERRINE, VALERIE: Galveston, TX, Sept. 3, 1944. U. Ariz.

PESCOW, DONNA: Brooklyn, NY, 1954.

PETERS, BERNADETTE: Jamaica, NY, Feb. 28, 1948.

PETERS, BROCK: NYC, July 2, 1927. CCNY.

| Suzanne Pleshette | Barry Primus | Kathleen Quinlan | Thalmus Rasulala | Debbie Reynolds |

PETERS, JEAN (Elizabeth): Canton, OH, Oct. 15, 1926. Ohio State U.

PETTET, JOANNA: London, Nov. 16, 1944. Neighborhood Playhouse.

PHILLIPS, MacKENZIE: Hollywood, CA, 1960.

PHILLIPS, MICHELLE (Holly Gilliam): NJ, June 4, 1944.

PICERNI, PAUL: NYC, Dec. 1, 1922. Loyola U.

PICKENS, SLIM (Louis Bert Lindley, Jr.): Kingsberg, CA, June 29, 1919.

PIDGEON, WALTER: East St. John, N.B., Can., Sept. 23, 1897.

PINE, PHILLIP: Hanford, CA, July 16, 1925. Actors' Lab.

PISIER, MARIE-FRANCE: Vietnam, May 10, 1944. U. Paris.

PLACE, MARY KAY: Port Arthur, TX, Sept., 1947. U. Tulsa.

PLAYTEN, ALICE: NYC, Aug. 28, 1947. NYU.

PLEASENCE, DONALD: Workshop, Eng, Oct. 5, 1919. Sheffield School.

PLESHETTE, SUZANNE: NYC, Jan. 31, 1937. Syracuse U.

PLUMMER, CHRISTOPHER: Toronto, Can., Dec. 13, 1927.

PODESTA, ROSSANA: Tripoli, June 20, 1934.

POITIER, SIDNEY: Miami, FL, Feb. 27, 1924.

POLITO, LINA: Naples, Italy, Aug. 11, 1954.

POLLARD, MICHAEL J. Pacific, NJ, May 30, 1939.

PORTER, ERIC: London, Apr. 8, 1928, Wimbledon Col.

POWELL, ELEANOR: Springfield, MA, Nov. 21, 1912.

POWELL, JANE (Suzanne Burce): Portland, OR, Apr. 1, 1928.

POWELL, ROBERT: London, June 1, 1944.

POWELL, WILLIAM: Pittsburgh, July 29, 1892. AADA.

POWER, TARYN: Los Angeles, CA, 1954.

POWERS, MALA (Mary Ellen): San Francisco, Dec. 29, 1921. UCLA.

PRENTISS, PAULA (Paula Ragusa): San Antonio, TX, Mar. 4, 1939. Northwestern U.

PRESLE, MICHELINE (Micheline Chassagne): Paris, Aug. 22, 1922. Rouleau Drama School.

PRESNELL, HARVE: Modesto, CA, Sept. 14, 1933. USC.

PRESTON, ROBERT (Robert Preston Meservey): Newton Highlands, MA, June 8, 1913. Pasadena Playhouse.

PRICE, VINCENT: St. Louis, May 27, 1911. Yale.

PRIMUS, BARRY: NYC, Feb. 16, 1938. CCNY.

PRINCE, WILLIAM: Nicholas, NY, Jan. 26, 1913. Cornell U.

PRINCIPAL, VICTORIA: Tokyo, Jan. 3, 1945. Dade Jr. Col.

PROVAL, DAVID: Brooklyn, NY, 1943.

PROVINE, DOROTHY: Deadwood, SD, Jan. 20, 1937. U. Wash.

PROWSE, JULIET: Bombay, India, Sept. 25, 1936.

PRYOR, RICHARD: Peoria, IL, Dec. 1, 1940.

PURCELL, LEE: Cherry Point, NC, June 15, 1947. Stephens.

PURCELL, NOEL: Dublin, Ire., Dec. 23, 1900. Irish Christian Brothers.

PURDOM, EDMUND: Welwyn Garden City, Eng., Dec. 19, 1924. St. Ignatius College.

PYLE, DENVER: Bethune, CO, 1920.

QUAYLE, ANTHONY: Lancashire, Eng., Sept. 7, 1913. Old Vic School.

QUINE, RICHARD: Detroit, MI, Nov. 12, 1920.

QUINLAN, KATHLEEN: Mill Valley, CA, Nov. 19, 1954.

QUINN, ANTHONY: Chihuahua, Mex., Apr. 21, 1915.

RAFFERTY, FRANCES: Sioux City, IA, June 16, 1922. UCLA.

RAFFIN, DEBORAH: Los Angeles, Mar. 13, 1953. Valley Col.

RAINES, ELLA (Ella Wallace): Snoqualmie Falls, WA, Aug. 6, 1921. U. Wash.

RAMPLING, CHARLOTTE: Surmer, Eng., Feb. 5, 1946. U. Madrid.

RAMSEY, LOGAN: Long Beach, CA, Mar. 21, 1921. St. Joseph.

RANDALL, TONY: Tulsa, OK, Feb. 26, 1920. Northwestern U.

RANDELL, RON: Sydney, Australia, Oct. 8, 1920. St. Mary's Col.

RASULALA, THALMUS (Jack Crowder): Miami, FL, Nov. 15, 1939. U. Redlands.

RAY, ALDO (Aldo DeRe): Pen Argyl, PA, Sept. 25, 1926. UCLA.

RAYE, MARTHA (Margie Yvonne Reed): Butte, MT, Aug. 27, 1916.

RAYMOND, GENE (Raymond Guion): NYC, Aug. 13, 1908.

REAGAN, RONALD: Tampico, IL, Feb. 6, 1911. Eureka College.

REASON, REX: Berlin, Ger., Nov. 30, 1928. Pasadena Playhouse.

REDDY, HELEN: Australia, Oct. 25, 1942.

REDFORD, ROBERT: Santa Monica, CA, Aug. 18, 1937. AADA.

REDGRAVE, CORIN: London, July 16, 1939.

REDGRAVE, LYNN: London, Mar. 8, 1943.

REDGRAVE, MICHAEL: Bristol, Eng., Mar. 20, 1908. Cambridge.

REDGRAVE, VANESSA: London, Jan. 30, 1937.

REDMAN, JOYCE: County Mayo, Ire., 1919. RADA.

REED, DONNA (Donna Mullenger): Denison, IA, Jan. 27, 1921. LACC.

REED, OLIVER: Wimbledon, Eng., Feb. 13, 1938.

REED, REX: Ft. Worth, TX, Oct. 2, 1939. LSU.

REEMS, HARRY (Herbert Streicher): Bronx, NY, 1947. U. Pittsburgh.

REEVE, CHRISTOPHER: NJ, Sept. 25, 1952. Cornell, Juilliard.

REEVES, STEVE: Glasgow, MT, Jan. 21, 1926.

REID, ELLIOTT: NYC, Jan. 16, 1920.

REINER, CARL: NYC, Mar. 20, 1922. Georgetown.

REINER, ROBERT: NYC, 1945. UCLA.

REMICK, LEE: Quincy, MA, Dec. 14, 1935. Barnard College.

RETTIG, TOMMY: Jackson Heights, NY, Dec. 10, 1941.

REVILL, CLIVE: Wellington, NZ, Apr. 18, 1930.

REY, FERNANDO: La Coruna, Spain, 1917.

REYNOLDS, BURT: West Palm Beach, FL, Feb. 11, 1935. Fla. State U.

REYNOLDS, DEBBIE (Mary Frances Reynolds): El Paso, TX, Apr. 1, 1932.

REYNOLDS, MARJORIE: Buhl, ID, Aug. 12, 1921.

RHOADES, BARBARA: Poughkeepsie, NY, 1947.

RICH, IRENE: Buffalo, NY, Oct. 13, 1891. St. Margaret's School.

RICHARDS, JEFF (Richard Mansfield Taylor): Portland, OR, Nov. 1. USC.

RICHARDSON, RALPH: Cheltenham, Eng., Dec. 19, 1902.

RICKLES, DON: NYC, May 8, 1926. AADA.

RIEGERT, PETER: NYC Apr. 11, 1947; U Buffalo.

RIGG, DIANA: Doncaster, Eng., July 20, 1938. RADA.

RITTER, JOHN: Burbank, CA, 1949. U. S. Cal.

ROBARDS, JASON: Chicago, July 26, 1922. AADA.

| **Cliff Robertson** | **Ann Ruymen** | **Raymond St. Jacques** | **Susan St. James** | **William Shatner** |

ROBERTS, ERIC: Biloxi, MS, 1956. RADA.

ROBERTS, RALPH: Salisbury, NC, Aug. 17, 1922. UNC.

ROBERTS, TANYA: (Leigh) NYC 1965.

ROBERTS, TONY: NYC, Oct. 22, 1939. Northwestern U.

ROBERTSON, CLIFF: La Jolla, CA, Sept. 9, 1925. Antioch Col.

ROBERTSON, DALE: Oklahoma City, July 14, 1923.

ROBINSON, CHRIS: Nov. 5, 1938, West Palm Beach, FL. LACC.

ROBINSON, JAY: NYC, Apr. 14, 1930.

ROBINSON, ROGER: Seattle, WA, May 2, 1941. USC.

ROBSON, FLORA: South Shields, Eng., Mar. 28, 1902. RADA.

ROCHEFORT, JEAN: Paris, 1930.

ROGERS, CHARLES "BUDDY": Olathe, KS, Aug. 13, 1904. U. Kan.

ROGERS, GINGER (Virginia Katherine McMath): Independence, MO, July 16, 1911.

ROGERS, ROY (Leonard Slye): Cincinnati, Nov. 5, 1912.

ROGERS, WAYNE: Birmingham, AL, Apr. 7, 1933. Princeton.

ROLAND, GILBERT (Luis Antonio Damaso De Alonso): Juarez, Mex., Dec. 11, 1905.

ROMAN, RUTH: Boston, Dec. 23, 1922. Bishop Lee Dramatic School.

ROMERO, CESAR: NYC, Feb. 15, 1907. Collegiate School.

ROONEY, MICKEY (Joe Yule, Jr.): Brooklyn, Sept. 23, 1920.

ROSS, DIANA: Detroit, MI, Mar. 26, 1945.

ROSS, KATHARINE: Hollywood, Jan. 29, 1943. Santa Rosa Col.

ROSSITER, LEONARD: Liverpool, Eng., Oct. 21, 1926.

ROUNDS, DAVID: Bronxville, NY, Oct. 9, 1938. Denison U.

ROUNDTREE, RICHARD: New Rochelle, NY, Sept. 7, 1942. Southern Ill.

ROWLANDS, GENA: Cambria, WI, June 19, 1936.

RUBIN, ANDREW: New Bedford, MA, June 22, 1946. AADA.

RUDD, PAUL: Boston, MA, May 15, 1940.

RULE, JANICE: Cincinnati, OH, Aug. 15, 1931.

RUPERT, MICHAEL: Denver, CO, Oct. 23, 1951. Pasadena Playhouse.

RUSH, BARBARA: Denver, CO, Jan. 4. 1929. U. Calif.

RUSSELL, JANE: Bemidji, MI, June 21, 1921. Max Reinhardt School.

RUSSELL, JOHN: Los Angeles, Jan. 3, 1921. U. Calif.

RUSSELL, KURT: Springfield, MA, March 17, 1951.

RUTHERFORD, ANN: Toronto, Can., Nov. 2, 1917.

RUYMEN, AYN: Brooklyn, July 18, 1947. HB Studio.

SACCHI, ROBERT: Bronx, NY, 1941; NYU.

SAINT, EVA MARIE: Newark, NJ, July 4, 1924. Bowling Green State U.

ST. JACQUES, RAYMOND (James Arthur Johnson): CT.

ST. JAMES, SUSAN: Los Angeles, Aug. 14. Conn. Col.

ST. JOHN, BETTA: Hawthorne, CA, Nov. 26, 1929.

ST. JOHN, JILL (Jill Oppenheim): Los Angeles, Aug. 19, 1940.

SALMI, ALBERT: Coney Island, NY, 1925. Actors Studio.

SALT, JENNIFER: Los Angeles, Sept. 4, 1944. Sarah Lawrence Col.

SANDS, TOMMY: Chicago, Aug. 27, 1937.

SAN JUAN, OLGA: NYC, Mar. 16, 1927.

SARANDON, CHRIS: Beckley, WV, July 24, 1942. U. WVa., Catholic U.

SARANDON, SUSAN (Tomaling): NYC, Oct. 4, 1946. Catholic U.

SARGENT, RICHARD (Richard Cox): Carmel, CA, 1933. Stanford.

SARRAZIN, MICHAEL: Quebec City, Can., May 22, 1940.

SAVAGE, JOHN (Youngs): Long Island, NY, Aug. 25, 1949. AADA.

SAVALAS, TELLY (Aristotle): Garden City, NY, Jan. 21, 1925. Columbia.

SAVOY, TERESA ANN: London, July 18, 1955.

SAXON, JOHN (Carmen Orrico): Brooklyn, Aug. 5, 1935.

SCARWID, DIANA: Savannah, GA; AADA, Pace U.

SCHEIDER, ROY: Orange, NJ, Nov. 10, 1935. Franklin-Marshall.

SCHELL, MARIA: Vienna, Jan. 15, 1926.

SCHELL, MAXIMILIAN: Vienna, Dec. 8, 1930.

SCHNEIDER, MARIA: Paris, Mar. 27, 1952.

SCHNEIDER, ROMY: Vienna, Sept. 23, 1938.

SCHRODER, RICKY: Staten Island, NY, Apr. 13, 1970.

SCHWARZENEGGER, ARNOLD: Austria, 1947.

SCOFIELD, PAUL: Hurstpierpoint, Eng., Jan. 21, 1922. London Mask Theatre School.

SCOTT, DEBRALEE: Elizabeth, NJ, Apr. 2.

SCOTT, GEORGE C.: Wise, VA, Oct. 18, 1927. U. Mo.

SCOTT, GORDON (Gordon M. Werschkul): Portland, OR, Aug. 3, 1927. Oregon U.

SCOTT, MARTHA: Jamesport, MO, Sept. 22, 1914. U. Mich.

SCOTT, RANDOLPH: Orange County, VA, Jan. 23, 1903. UNC.

SCOTT-TAYLOR, JONATHAN: Brazil, 1962.

SEAGULL, BARBARA HERSHEY (Herzstein): Hollywood, Feb. 5, 1948.

SEARS, HEATHER: London, 1935.

SECOMBE, HARRY: Swansea, Wales, Sept. 8, 1921.

SEGAL, GEORGE: NYC, Feb. 13, 1934. Columbia.

SELLARS, ELIZABETH: Glasgow, Scot., May 6, 1923.

SELWART, TONIO: Watenberg, Ger., June 9, 1906. Munich U.

SERNAS, JACQUES: Lithuania, July 30, 1925.

SEYLER, ATHENE (Athene Hannen): London, May 31, 1889.

SEYMOUR, ANNE: NYC, Sept. 11, 1909. American Laboratory Theatre.

SEYMOUR, JANE (Joyce Frankenberg): Hillingdon, Eng., Feb. 15, 1951.

SHARIF, OMAR (Michel Shalboub): Alexandria, Egypt, Apr. 10, 1932. Victoria Col.

SHARKEY, RAY: Brooklyn, NY, 1952; HB Studio.

SHATNER, WILLIAM: Montreal, Can., Mar. 22, 1931. McGill U.

SHAW, SEBASTIAN: Holt, Eng., May 29, 1905. Gresham School.

SHAW, STAN: Chicago, IL, 1952.

SHAWLEE, JOAN: Forest Hills, NY, Mar. 5, 1929.

SHAWN, DICK (Richard Shulefand): Buffalo, NY, Dec. 1, 1929. U. Miami.

SHEARER, MOIRA: Dunfermline, Scot., Jan. 17, 1926. London Theatre School.

SHEARER, NORMA: Montreal, Can., Aug. 10, 1900.

SHEEN, MARTIN (Ramon Estevez): Dayton, OH, Aug. 3, 1940.

SHEFFIELD, JOHN: Pasadena, CA, Apr. 11, 1931. UCLA.

SHEPARD, SAM (Rogers): Ft. Sheridan, IL, Nov. 5, 1943.

SHEPHERD, CYBIL: Memphis, TN, Feb. 18, 1950. Hunter, NYU.

SHIELDS, BROOKE: NYC, May 31, 1965.

SHIRE, TALIA: Lake Success, NY. Yale.

229

William Smithers	Elke Sommer	Gary Springer	Connie Stevens	Woody Strode

SHORE, DINAH (Frances Rose Shore): Winchester, TN, Mar. 1, 1917. Vanderbilt U.

SHOWALTER, MAX (formerly Casey Adams): Caldwell, KS, June 2, 1917. Pasadena Playhouse.

SIDNEY, SYLVIA: NYC, Aug. 8, 1910. Theatre Guild School.

SIGNORET, SIMONE (Simone Kaminker): Wiesbaden, Ger., Mar. 25, 1921. Solange Sicard School.

SILVERS, PHIL (Philip Silversmith): Brooklyn, May 11, 1911.

SIMMONS, JEAN: London, Jan. 31, 1929. Aida Foster School.

SIMON, SIMONE: Marseilles, France, Apr. 23, 1910.

SIMPSON, O. J. (Orenthal James): San Francisco, CA, July 9, 1947. UCLA.

SINATRA, FRANK: Hoboken, NJ, Dec. 12, 1915.

SINDEN, DONALD: Plymouth, Eng., Oct. 9, 1923. Webber-Douglas.

SKALA, LILIA: Vienna; U. Dresden.

SKELTON, RED (Richard): Vincennes, IN, July 18, 1910.

SKERRITT, TOM: Detroit, MI, 1935. Wayne State U.

SLEZAK, WALTER: Vienna, Austria, May 3, 1902.

SMITH, ALEXIS: Penticton, Can., June 8, 1921. LACC.

SMITH, CHARLES MARTIN: Los Angeles, CA, 1954. CalState U.

SMITH, JOHN (Robert E. Van Orden): Los Angeles, Mar. 6, 1931. UCLA.

SMITH, KATE (Kathryn Elizabeth): Greenville, VA, May 1, 1909.

SMITH, KENT: NYC, Mar. 19, 1907. Harvard U.

SMITH, LOIS: Topeka, KS, Nov. 3, 1930. U. Wash.

SMITH, MAGGIE: Ilford, Eng., Dec. 28, 1934.

SMITH, ROGER: South Gate, CA, Dec. 18, 1932. U. Ariz.

SMITHERS, WILLIAM: Richmond, VA, July 10, 1927. Catholic U.

SNODGRESS, CARRIE: Chicago, Oct. 27, 1946. UNI.

SNOWDEN, LEIGH: Memphis, TN, June 28, 1932. Lambeth Col.

SOLOMON, BRUCE: NYC, 1944. U. Miami, Wayne State U.

SOMERS, SUZANNE (Mahoney): San Bruno, CA, Oct. 16, 1946. Lone Mt. Col.

SOMMER, ELKE (Schletz): Berlin, Nov. 5, 1940.

SONNY (Salvatore Bono): 1935.

SORDI, ALBERTO: Rome, Italy, 1919.

SORVINO, PAUL: NYC, 1939. AMDA.

SOTHERN, ANN (Harriet Lake): Valley City, ND, Jan. 22, 1907. Washington U.

SPACEK, SISSY: Quitman, TX, Dec. 25, 1949. Actors Studio.

SPENSER, JEREMY: Ceylon, 1937.

SPRINGER, GARY: NYC, July 29, 1954. Hunter Col.

STACK, ROBERT: Los Angeles, Jan. 13, 1919. USC.

STADLEN, LEWIS J.: Brooklyn, Mar. 7, 1947. Neighborhood Playhouse.

STALLONE, SYLVESTER: NYC, 1946. U. Miami.

STAMP, TERENCE: London, 1940.

STANDER, LIONEL: NYC, Jan. 11, 1908. UNC.

STANG, ARNOLD: Chelsea, MA, Sept. 28, 1925.

STANLEY, KIM (Patricia Reid): Tularosa, NM, Feb. 11, 1925. U. Tex.

STANWYCK, BARBARA (Ruby Stevens): Brooklyn, July 16, 1907.

STAPLETON, JEAN: NYC, Jan. 19, 1923.

STAPLETON, MAUREEN: Troy, NY, June 21, 1925.

STEEL, ANTHONY: London, May 21, 1920. Cambridge.

STEELE, TOMMY: London, Dec. 17, 1936.

STEENBURGEN, MARY: Newport, AR, 1953. Neighborhood Playhouse.

STEIGER, ROD: Westhampton, NY, Apr. 14, 1925.

STERLING, JAN (Jane Sterling Adriance): NYC, Apr. 3, 1923. Fay Compton School.

STERLING, ROBERT (William Sterling Hart): Newcastle, PA, Nov. 13, 1917. U. Pittsburgh.

STERN, DANIEL: Bethesda, MD, 1957.

STEVENS, ANDREW: Memphis, TN, June, 1955.

STEVENS, CONNIE (Concetta Ann Ingolia): Brooklyn, Aug. 8, 1938. Hollywood Professional School.

STEVENS, KAYE (Catherine): Pittsburgh, July 21, 1933.

STEVENS, MARK (Richard): Cleveland, OH, Dec. 13, 1920.

STEVENS, STELLA (Estelle Eggleston): Hot Coffee, MS, Oct. 1, 1936.

STEVENSON, PARKER: CT, 1953.

STEWART, ALEXANDRA: Montreal, Can., June 10, 1939. Louvre.

STEWART, ELAINE: Montclair, NJ, May 31, 1929.

STEWART, JAMES: Indiana, PA, May 20, 1908. Princeton.

STEWART, MARTHA (Martha Haworth): Bardwell, KY, Oct. 7, 1922.

STIMSON, SARA: Helotes, TX, 1973.

STOCKWELL, DEAN: Hollywood, March 5, 1936.

STORM, GALE (Josephine Cottle): Bloomington, TX, Apr. 5, 1922.

STRAIGHT, BEATRICE: Old Westbury, NY, Aug. 2, 1916. Dartington Hall.

STRASBERG, SUSAN: NYC, May 22, 1938.

STRAUD, DON: Hawaii, 1943.

STRAUSS, PETER: NY, 1947.

STREEP, MERYL (Mary Louise): Basking Ridge, NJ, Sept. 22, 1950. Vassar, Yale.

STREISAND, BARBRA: Brooklyn, Apr. 24, 1942.

STRITCH, ELAINE: Detroit, MI, Feb. 2, 1925. Drama Workshop.

STRODE, WOODY: Los Angeles, 1914.

STRUDWICK, SHEPPERD: Hillsboro, NC, Sept. 22, 1907. UNC.

STRUTHERS, SALLY: Portland, OR, July 28, 1948. Pasadena Playhouse.

SULLIVAN, BARRY (Patrick Barry): NYC, Aug. 29, 1912. NYU.

SUTHERLAND, DONALD: St. John, New Brunswick, Can., July 17, 1934. U. Toronto.

SVENSON, BO: Goteborg, Swed., Feb. 13, 1941. UCLA.

SWANSON, GLORIA (Josephine May Swenson): Chicago, Mar. 27, 1897. Chicago Art Inst.

SWEET, BLANCHE: Chicago, 1896.

SWINBURNE, NORA: Bath, Eng., July 24, 1902. RADA.

SWIT, LORETTA: Passaic, NJ, Nov. 4, AADA.

SYLVESTER, WILLIAM: Oakland, CA, Jan. 31, 1922. RADA.

SYMS, SYLVIA: London, June 1, 1934. Convent School.

TABORI, KRISTOFFER (Siegel): Los Angeles, Aug. 4, 1952.

TAKEI, GEORGE: Los Angeles, CA, Apr. 20. UCLA.

TALBOT, LYLE (Lysle Hollywood): Pittsburgh, Feb. 8, 1904.

TALBOT, NITA: NYC, Aug. 8, 1930. Irvine Studio School.

TAMBLYN, RUSS: Los Angeles, Dec. 30, 1934.

| Marlo Thomas | Rip Torn | Brenda Vaccaro | Ben Vereen | Genevieve Waite |

TANDY, JESSICA: London, June 7, 1909. Dame Owens' School.

TAYLOR, DON: Freeport, PA, Dec. 13, 1920. Penn State U.

TAYLOR, ELIZABETH: London, Feb. 27, 1932. Byron House School.

TAYLOR, KENT (Louis Weiss): Nashua, IA, May 11, 1906.

TAYLOR, ROD (Robert): Sydney, Aust., Jan. 11, 1929.

TAYLOR-YOUNG, LEIGH: Wash., DC, Jan. 25, 1945. Northwestern.

TEAGUE, ANTHONY SKOOTER: Jacksboro, TX, Jan. 4, 1940.

TEEFY, MAUREEN: Minneapolis, MN, 1954; Juilliard.

TEMPLE, SHIRLEY: Santa Monica, CA, Apr. 23, 1927.

TERRY-THOMAS (Thomas Terry Hoar Stevens): Finchley, London, July 14, 1911. Ardingly College.

TERZIEFF, LAURENT: Paris, June 25, 1935.

THACKER, RUSS: Washington, DC, June 23, 1946. Montgomery Col.

THAXTER, PHYLLIS: Portland, ME, Nov. 20, 1921. St. Genevieve.

THOMAS, DANNY (Amos Jacobs): Deerfield, MI, Jan. 6, 1914.

THOMAS, MARLO (Margaret): Detroit, Nov. 21, 1938. USC.

THOMAS, PHILIP: Columbus, OH, May 26, 1949. Oakwood Col.

THOMAS, RICHARD: NYC, June 13, 1951. Columbia.

THOMPSON, JACK (John Payne): Sydney, Aus., 1940. U. Brisbane.

THOMPSON, MARSHALL: Peoria, IL, Nov. 27, 1925. Occidental.

THOMPSON, REX: NYC, Dec. 14, 1942.

THOMPSON, SADA: Des Moines, IA, Sept. 27, 1929. Carnegie Tech.

THULIN, INGRID: Solleftea, Sweden, Jan. 27, 1929. Royal Drama Theatre.

TICOTIN, RACHEL: Bronx, NY, 1958.

TIERNEY, GENE: Brooklyn, Nov. 20, 1920. Miss Farmer's School.

TIERNEY, LAWRENCE: Brooklyn, Mar. 15, 1919. Manhattan College.

TIFFIN, PAMELA (Wonso): Oklahoma City, Oct. 13, 1942.

TODD, RICHARD: Dublin, Ire., June 11, 1919. Shrewsbury School.

TOLO, MARILU: Rome, Italy, 1944.

TOMLIN, LILY: Detroit, MI, Sept. 1, 1939. Wayne State U.

TOPOL (Chaim Topol): Tel-Aviv, Israel, Sept. 9, 1935.

TORN, RIP: Temple, TX, Feb. 6, 1931. U. Tex.

TORRES, LIZ: NYC, 1947. NYU.

TOTTER, AUDREY: Joliet, IL, Dec. 20, 1918.

TRAVERS, BILL: Newcastle-on-Tyne, Eng., Jan. 3, 1922.

TRAVIS, RICHARD (William Justice): Carlsbad, NM, Apr. 17, 1913.

TRAVOLTA, JOEY: Englewood, NJ, 1952.

TRAVOLTA, JOHN: Englewood, NJ, Feb. 18, 1954.

TREMAYNE, LES: London, Apr. 16, 1913. Northwestern, Columbia, UCLA.

TREVOR, CLAIRE (Wemlinger): NYC, March 8, 1909.

TRINTIGNANT, JEAN-LOUIS: Pont-St. Esprit, France, Dec. 11, 1930. Dullin-Balachova Drama School.

TRYON, TOM: Hartford, CT, Jan. 14, 1926. Yale.

TSOPEI, CORINNA: Athens, Greece, June 21, 1944.

TUCKER, FORREST: Plainfield, IN, Feb. 12, 1919. George Washington U.

TURNER, LANA (Julia Jean Mildred Frances Turner): Wallace, ID, Feb. 8, 1921.

TUSHINGHAM, RITA: Liverpool, Eng., 1940.

TUTIN, DOROTHY: London, Apr. 8, 1930.

TUTTLE, LURENE: Pleasant Lake, IN, Aug. 20, 1906. USC.

TWIGGY (Lesley Hornby): London, Sept. 19, 1949.

TYLER, BEVERLY (Beverly Jean Saul): Scranton, PA, July 5, 1928.

TYRRELL, SUSAN: San Francisco, 1946.

TYSON, CICELY: NYC, Dec. 19.

UGGAMS, LESLIE: NYC, May 25, 1943.

ULLMANN, LIV: Tokyo, Dec. 10, 1938. Webber-Douglas Acad.

USTINOV, PETER: London, Apr. 16, 1921. Westminster School.

VACCARO, BRENDA: Brooklyn, Nov. 18, 1939. Neighborhood Playhouse.

VALLEE, RUDY (Hubert): Island Pond, VT, July 28, 1901. Yale.

VALLI, ALIDA: Pola, Italy, May 31, 1921. Rome Academy of Drama.

VALLONE, RAF: Riogio, Italy, Feb. 17, 1916. Turin U.

VAN CLEEF, LEE: Somerville, NJ, Jan. 9, 1925.

VAN DE VEN, MONIQUE: Holland, 1957.

VAN DEVERE, TRISH (Patricia Dressel): Englewood Cliffs, NJ, Mar. 9, 1945. Ohio Wesleyan.

VAN DOREN, MAMIE (Joan Lucile Olander): Rowena, SD, Feb. 6, 1933.

VAN DYKE, DICK: West Plains, MO, Dec. 13, 1925.

VAN FLEET, JO: Oakland, CA, 1922.

VAN PATTEN, DICK: NYC, Dec. 9, 1928.

VAN PATTEN, JOYCE: NYC, Mar. 9, 1934.

VAUGHN, ROBERT: NYC, Nov. 22, 1932. USC.

VEGA, ISELA: Mexico, 1940.

VENNERA, CHICK: Herkimer, NY, Mar. 27, 1952. Pasadena Playhouse.

VENTURA, LINO: Parma, Italy, July 14, 1919.

VENUTA, BENAY: San Francisco, Jan. 27, 1911.

VERA-ELLEN (Rohe): Cincinnati, Feb. 16, 1926.

VERDON, GWEN: Culver City, CA, Jan. 13, 1925.

VEREEN, BEN: Miami, FL, Oct. 10, 1946.

VILLECHAIZE, HERVE: Paris, Apr. 23, 1943.

VINCENT, JAN-MICHAEL: Denver, CO, July 15, 1944. Ventura.

VIOLET, ULTRA (Isabelle Collin-Dufresne): Grenoble, France.

VITALE, MILLY: Rome, Italy, July 16, 1938. Lycee Chateaubriand.

VOHS, JOAN: St. Albans, NY, July 30, 1931.

VOIGHT, JON: Yonkers, NY, Dec. 29, 1938. Catholic U.

VOLONTE, GIAN MARIA: Milan, Italy, Apr. 9, 1933.

VON SYDOW, MAX: Lund, Swed., July 10, 1929. Royal Drama Theatre.

WAGNER, LINDSAY: Los Angeles, 1949.

WAGNER, ROBERT: Detroit, Feb. 10, 1930.

WAHL, KEN: Chicago, IL, 1957.

WAITE, GENEVIEVE: South Africa, 1949.

WALKEN, CHRISTOPHER: Astoria, NY, Mar. 31, 1943. Hofstra.

WALKER, CLINT: Hartfold, IL, May 30, 1927. USC.

WALKER, NANCY (Ann Myrtle Swoyer): Philadelphia, May 10, 1921.

WALLACH, ELI: Brooklyn, Dec. 7, 1915. CCNY, U. Tex.

WALLACH, ROBERTA: NYC, Aug. 2, 1955.

WALLIS, SHANI: London, Apr. 5, 1941.

WALSTON, RAY: New Orleans, Nov. 22, 1917. Cleveland Playhouse.

Jessica Walter	Orson Welles	Cindy Williams	Michael York	Susannah York

WALTER, JESSICA: Brooklyn, NY, Jan. 31, 1940. Neighborhood Playhouse.

WANAMAKER, SAM: Chicago, June 14, 1919. Drake.

WARD, BURT (Gervis): Los Angeles, July 6, 1945.

WARD, SIMON: London, 1941.

WARDEN, JACK: Newark, NJ, Sept. 18, 1920.

WARNER, DAVID: Manchester, Eng., 1941. RADA.

WARREN, JENNIFER: NYC, Aug. 12, 1941. U. Wisc.

WARREN, LESLEY ANN: NYC, Aug. 16, 1946.

WARRICK, RUTH: St. Joseph, MO, June 29, 1915. U. Mo.

WASHBOURNE, MONA: Birmingham, Eng., Nov. 27, 1903.

WATERSTON, SAM: Cambridge, MA, Nov. 15, 1940. Yale.

WATLING, JACK: London, Jan. 13, 1923. Italia Conti School.

WATSON, DOUGLASS: Jackson, GA, Feb. 24, 1921. UNC.

WAYNE, DAVID (Wayne McKeehan): Travers City, MI, Jan. 30, 1914. Western Michigan State U.

WAYNE, PATRICK: Los Angeles, July 15, 1939. Loyola.

WEAVER, DENNIS: Joplin, MO, June 4, 1924. U. Okla.

WEAVER, MARJORIE: Crossville, TN, Mar. 2, 1913. Indiana U.

WEAVER, SIGOURNEY: NYC, 1949. Stanford, Yale.

WEBB, ALAN: York, Eng., July 2, 1906. Dartmouth.

WEBB, JACK: Santa Monica, CA, Apr. 2, 1920.

WEBBER, ROBERT: Santa Ana, CA, Sept. 14, 1925. Compton Jr. Col.

WEDGEWORTH, ANN: Abilene, TX, Jan. 21. U. Tex.

WEISSMULLER, JOHNNY: Chicago, June 2, 1904. Chicago U.

WELCH, RAQUEL (Tejada): Chicago, Sept. 5, 1940.

WELD, TUESDAY (Susan): NYC, Aug. 27, 1943. Hollywood Professional School.

WELDON, JOAN: San Francisco, Aug. 5, 1933. San Francisco Conservatory.

WELLES, GWEN: NYC, Mar. 4.

WELLES, ORSON: Kenosha, WI, May 6, 1915. Todd School.

WERNER, OSKAR: Vienna, Nov. 13, 1922.

WESTON, JACK (Morris Weinstein): Cleveland, OH, Aug. 21, 1915.

WHITAKER, JOHNNY: Van Nuys, CA, Dec. 13, 1959.

WHITE, CAROL: London, Apr. 1, 1944.

WHITE, CHARLES: Perth Amboy, NJ, Aug. 29, 1920. Rutgers U.

WHITE, JESSE: Buffalo, NY, Jan. 3, 1919.

WHITMAN, STUART: San Francisco, Feb. 1, 1929. CCLA.

WHITMORE, JAMES: White Plains, NY, Oct. 1, 1921. Yale.

WHITNEY, GRACE LEE: Detroit, MI, Apr. 1, 1930.

WIDDOES, KATHLEEN: Wilmington, DE, Mar. 21, 1939.

WIDMARK, RICHARD: Sunrise, MN, Dec. 26, 1914. Lake Forest.

WILCOX-HORNE, COLIN: Highlands NC, Feb. 4, 1937. U. Tenn.

WILCOXON, HENRY: British West Indies, Sept. 8, 1905.

WILDE, CORNEL: NYC, Oct. 13, 1915. CCNY, Columbia.

WILDER, GENE (Jerome Silberman): Milwaukee, WI, June 11, 1935. U. Iowa.

WILLIAMS, BILLY DEE: NYC, Apr. 6, 1937.

WILLIAMS, CINDY: Van Nuys, CA, Aug. 22, 1947. LACC.

WILLIAMS, DICK A.: Chicago, IL, Aug. 9, 1938.

WILLIAMS, EMLYN: Mostyn, Wales, Nov. 26, 1905. Oxford.

WILLIAMS, ESTHER: Los Angeles, Aug. 8, 1921.

WILLIAMS, GRANT: NYC, Aug. 18, 1930. Queens College.

WILLIAMS, JOHN: Chalfont, Eng., Apr. 15, 1903. Lancing College.

WILLIAMS, TREAT (Richard): Rowayton, CT. 1952.

WILLIAMSON, FRED: Gary, IN, Mar. 5, 1938. Northwestern.

WILSON, DEMOND: NYC, Oct. 13, 1946. Hunter Col.

WILSON, FLIP (Clerow Wilson): Jersey City, NJ, Dec. 8, 1933.

WILSON, NANCY: Chillicothe, OH, Feb. 20, 1937.

WILSON, SCOTT: Atlanta, GA, 1942.

WINDE, BEATRICE: Chicago, Jan. 6.

WINDOM, WILLIAM: NYC, Sept. 28, 1923. Williams Col.

WINDSOR, MARIE (Emily Marie Bertelson): Marysvale, UT, Dec. 11, 1924. Brigham Young U.

WINFIELD, PAUL: Los Angeles, 1940. UCLA.

WINKLER, HENRY: NYC, Oct. 30, 1945. Yale.

WINN, KITTY: Wash., D.C., 1944. Boston U.

WINTERS, JONATHAN: Dayton, OH, Nov. 11, 1925. Kenyon Col.

WINTERS, ROLAND: Boston, Nov. 22, 1904.

WINTERS, SHELLEY (Shirley Schrift): St. Louis, Aug. 18, 1922. Wayne U.

WINWOOD, ESTELLE: Kent, Eng., Jan. 24, 1883. Lyric Stage Academy.

WITHERS, GOOGIE: Karachi, India, Mar. 12, 1917. Italia Conti.

WITHERS, JANE: Atlanta, GA, 1926.

WOOD, NATALIE (Natasha Gurdin): San Francisco, July 20, 1938.

WOODLAWN, HOLLY (Harold Ajzenberg): Juana Diaz, PR, 1947.

WOODS, JAMES: Vernal, UT, Apr. 18, 1947. MIT.

WOODWARD, JOANNE: Thomasville, GA, Feb. 27, 1930. Neighborhood Playhouse.

WOOLAND, NORMAN: Dusseldorf, Ger., Mar. 16, 1910. Edward VI School.

WOPAT, TOM: Lodi, WI, 1950.

WORONOV, MARY: Brooklyn, Dec. 8, 1946. Cornell.

WRAY, FAY: Alberta, Can., Sept. 15, 1907.

WRIGHT, TERESA: NYC, Oct. 27, 1918.

WYATT, JANE: Campgaw, NJ, Aug. 10, 1911. Barnard College.

WYMAN, JANE (Sarah Jane Fulks): St. Joseph, MO, Jan. 4, 1914.

WYMORE, PATRICE: Miltonvale, KS, Dec. 17, 1926.

WYNN, KEENAN: NYC, July 27, 1916. St. John's.

WYNN, MAY (Donna Lee Hickey): NYC, Jan. 8, 1930.

WYNTER, DANA (Dagmar): London, June 8, 1927. Rhodes U.

YORK, DICK: Fort Wayne, IN, Sept. 4, 1928. De Paul U.

YORK, MICHAEL: Fulmer, Eng., Mar. 27, 1942. Oxford.

YORK, SUSANNAH: London, Jan. 9, 1941. RADA.

YOUNG, ALAN (Angus): North Shield, Eng., Nov. 19, 1919.

YOUNG, LORETTA (Gretchen): Salt Lake City, Jan. 6, 1912. Immaculate Heart College.

YOUNG, ROBERT: Chicago, Feb. 22, 1907.

ZACHARIAS, ANN: Stockholm, Sw., 1956.

ZETTERLING, MAI: Sweden, May 27, 1925. Ordtuery Theatre School.

ZIMBALIST, EFREM, JR.: NYC, Nov. 30, 1918. Yale.

OBITUARIES

FLOYD TALIAFERRO ALDERSON, 84, Montana-born retired actor, died of pneumonia, Feb. 12, 1980 in Sheridan, WY. Began his career in 1915 as an extra and became a featured player in 1921 in "Western Hearts." In 1925 he changed his name to Wally Wales and starred in "Tearin' Loose," subsequently appearing in over 60 films. In 1940 he again changed his name to Hal Taliaferro and became a supporting actor until his retirement in 1952. His other credits include "The Man with Nine Lives," "Cherokee Strip," "Sons of the Pioneers," "Yellow Rose of Texas," "Tombstone," "American Empire," "Utah," "Fallen Angel," "Red River," "Brimstone," "Junction City," "Savage Horde," "Sea Hornet," "Saddle Mates," "Duel in the Sun," "Ramrod," "San Antonio," and "Blood on the Moon." No reported survivors.

RAYMOND BAILEY, 75, San Francisco-born actor, died Apr. 15, 1980 in His home in Irvine, CA. He was best known as banker Milburn Drysdale in the tv series "Beverly Hillbillies." His film credits include "Hell's Kitchen," "Tidal Wave," "Girl in the Red Velvet Swing," "Picnic," "The Girl He Left Behind," "Incredible Shrinking Man," "Band of Angels," "No Time for Sergeants," "Vertigo," "I Want to Live!," "Al Capone," "From the Terrace" and "Five Weeks in a Balloon." No reported survivors.

LEONARD BARR, nee Barri, 77, comedian, died Nov. 22, 1980 after a stroke in West Hollywood, CA. After a career in vaudeville, he appeared in such films as "The Sting," "Diamonds Are Forever," "Skatetown U.S.A.," and his last "Under the Rainbow." He was co-starred in the tv series "Syznyck," and appeared in night clubs. Surviving are his nephew, actor Dean Martin, and a niece.

DONALD (RED) BARRY, nee Donald Barry de Acosta in Texas, 69, actor, shot and killed himself July 17, 1980 in his home in North Hollywood, CA. He was best known for his "Red Ryder" series in the 1940's. Other films include "Night Waitress," "Duke of "West Point," "The Crowd Roars," "Calling Dr. Kildare," "Only Angels Have Wings," "Days of Jesse James," "Tulsa Kid," "Stagecoach Express," "Remember Pearl Harbor," "The Purple Heart," "My Buddy," "The Chicago Kid," "The Last Crooked mile," "The Dalton Gang," "Red Desert," "The plainsman and the Lady," "Ringside," "I'll Cry Tomorrow," "Twilight of Honor," "Alvarez Kelly," "Fort Utah," "The Last Mile," "Walk on the Wild Side," "King Gun."

CECIL BEATON, 76, British designer and photographer, died in his sleep in his home in Broad Chalke, Eng., Jan. 18, 1980. He received Academy Awards for his designs on "Gigi" in 1959 and "My Fair Lady" in 1965. There were no immediate survivors.

TONY BECKLEY, 52, English-born stage and screen actor, died of cancer Apr. 19, 1980 in Los Angeles, CA. His screen credits include "Falstaff" also titled "Chimes at Midnight," "A Kind of Loving," "The Penthouse," "A Long Day's Dying," "The Italian Job," "Gold," "When a Stranger Calls" and "Revenge of the Pink Panther." No immediate survivors.

RICHARD BONNELLI, 91, NY-born operatic baritone, died June 7, 1980 in his Los Angeles home. After his 12 years with the Metropolitan Opera, he became a teacher, and appeared in the films "There's Magic in Music" and "Enter Madame." His second wife survives.

BARBARA BRITTON, 59, California-born screen, tv and stage actress, died of cancer Jan. 17, 1980 in her NYC home. Her film career began in 1940 in "Secrets of the Wasteland" and "Louisiana Purchase," and subsequently she appeared in over 30 movies, including "Wake Island," "The Fleet's In," "Mrs. Wiggs of the Cabbage Patch," "Reap the Wild Wind," "So Proudly We Hail," "The Story of Dr. Wassell," "Till We Meet Again," "Captain Kidd," "The Virginian," "The Return of Monte Cristo," "Gunfighters," "Albuquerque," "I Shot Jesse James," "Champagne for Caesar," "The Raiders," "Bwana Devil," "The Great John L.," "Ain't Misbehavin'," "The Spoilers" and "Night Freight." On tv she was the distaff side of the detective couple "Mr. and Mrs. North," and appeared in the series "One Life to Live." Surviving is her husband, Dr. E. J. Czukor, a son and a daughter.

KATHLEEN BURKE, 66, Indiana-born actress, died Apr. 9, 1980 in Chicago, IL. Her career began as the "Panther Woman" in the 1932 film "Island of Lost Souls," and she subsequently appeared in over 30 pictures, including "Murders in the Zoo," "Mad Game," "Good Dame," "Bulldog Drummond Strikes Back," "Lives of a Bengal Lancer," "Last Outpost," "Craig's Wife," "Boy of the Streets" and "Rascals." Surviving are her husband, Forrest Smith, and her mother.

DEE CARROLL, 54, nee Betty Jean Marsh, screen and tv actress, died Apr. 28, 1980 in Burbank, CA., after corrective surgery following a stroke. She had appeared in over 100 films and tv programs, and was a regular on the tv serial "Days of Our Lives." Her pictures credits include "Airport," "Sweet Charity," "Uptown Saturday Night," "Busting," "Terminal Man" and "Prisoner of Second Avenue." She is survived by her son.

GOWER CHAMPION, 61, Illinois-born director, choreographer and former dancer, died in NYC Aug. 25, 1980 of a rare cancer of the blood, a few hours before his last project, "42nd Street," opened on Broadway. With his former wife Marge, he had appeared in the pictures "'Til the Clouds Roll By," "Mr. Music," "Show Boat," "Lovely to Look at," "Everything I Have Is Yours," "Give a Girl a Break," "Jupiter's Darling" and "Three for the Show." Surviving are his second wife, and two sons by his first wife.

OLGA CHEKHOVA, 83, Russian-born actress, died Mar. 9, 1980 in her home in Munich, Ger. She fled Russia in 1921 for Germany, and subsequently appeared in more than 200 films, including "Moulin Rouge," "Pawns of Passion," "His Late Excellency," and "City of Temptation." No reported survivors.

CICELY COURTNEIDGE, 87, Australian-born comedienne and actress, died Apr. 26, 1980 in London. She first appeared on the British stage in 1901, subsequently becoming one of its most popular stars. In 1972 she was made a Dame of the British Empire. Her film credits include "Ghost Train," "Night and Day," "Woman in Command," "Along Came Sally," "The Perfect Gentleman," "The L-Shaped Room," "Wrong Box," "Not Now, Darling," "Aunt Sally" "Those Magnificent Men in Their Flying Machines." She was the widow of musical star Jack Hulbert. A daughter survives.

LIL DAGOVER, 82, nee Marta Maria Liletts in Java, actress died Jan. 23, 1980 in West Germany. She first appeared in "The Cabinet of Dr. Caligari," and subsequently in "Between Worlds," "Beyond the Wall," "Tartuffe," "Discord," "Two brothers," "Congress Dances," "Hungarian Rhapsody," "The White Devil," "The Spiders," "Woman from Monte Carlo," "Kreuzer Sonata" and "Fredericus." No reported survivors.

ADOLPH DEUTSCH, 82, London-born composer-conductor-arranger, died Jan. 1, 1980 in his home in Palm Desert, CA. He received Academy Awards for his film scores of "Annie Get Your Gun," "Seven Brides for Seven Brothers" and "Oklahoma!" He was founder and president of the Screen Composers Association, and a member of the American Society of Composers, Authors and Publishers. His widow and son survive.

JIMMY DURANTE, 86, one of America's most beloved comedians, died Jan. 29, 1980 of pneumonitis in Santa Monica, CA. From New York's lower East Side, he parlayed a raspy voice, a large nose and a great talent into one of the world's most honored entertainers for 60 years on stage, radio, film, tv and in night clubs. After playing the piano in saloons, and appearing in vaudeville, he established himself on Broadway before he was lured to Hollywood and films. His popularity reached new heights with his weekly radio and tv shows. Among his film credits are "Roadhouse Nights," "The Cuban Love Song," "Speak Easily," "Blondie of the Follies," "Palooka," "Strictly Dynamite," "George White's Scandals," "Sally, Irene and Mary," "Little Miss Broadway," "Melody Ranch," "The Man Who Came to Dinner," "Two Girls and a Sailor," "Music for Millions," "The Great Rupert," "The Milkman," "Jumbo" and "It's a Mad, Mad, Mad, Mad World." He is survived by his second wife and adopted daughter.

| Barbara Britton | Gower Champion | Lil Dagover | Jimmy Durante | Reginald Gardiner | Hugh Griffith |

KATHERINE EMERY, 73, Alabama-born screen and stage actress, died of a pulmonary illness Feb. 7, 1980 in Portland, ME. After several Broadway successes, and her marriage to Paul Eaton in 1944, she moved to Hollywood where she appeared in films until her retirement in 1954. She was featured in such pictures as "Eyes in the Night," "Isle of the Dead," "The Walls Came Tumbling Down," "The Locket," "Chicken Every Sunday," "The Intruder" and "Kid Galahad." A son and a daughter survive.

TOM FADDEN, 85, film, stage and tv actor, died Apr. 14, 1980 in his home in Vero Beach, FL. After appearing in vaudeville and on Broadway, his film credits include "I Stole a Million," "Destry Rides Again," "Zanzibar," "Shepherd of the Hills," "Wings for the Eagle," "Edge of Darkness," "The Hairy Ape," "Tomorrow the World," "That Hagen Girl," "State of the Union," "Singing Guns," "Prince of Players," "Invasion of the Body Snatchers," "Toby Tyler," "Pocketful of Miracles," "They Shoot Horses, Don't They?" and "Empire of the Ants." He is survived by his wife.

VIRGINIA BROWN FAIRE, 75, retired actress, died June 30, 1980 in Laguna Beach, CA. She had appeared in over 50 films before her retirement in the late 1930's. She was John Gilbert's leading lady in "Monte Cristo," and Tinker Bell in the 1924 "Peter Pan." Other credits include "Welcome Stranger," "Friendly Enemies," "Proud Heart," "The Temptress" and "The Donovan Affair." She also appeared in several westerns. No reported survivors.

HERBIE FAYE, 81, stage, tv and film comedian and character actor, died June 28, 1980 in his home in Las Vegas, Nv. He had appeared in such pictures as "Top Banana," "The Shrike," "The Harder They Fall," "Requiem for a Heavyweight," "Thoroughly Modern Millie," "The Night They Raided Minsky's," "Come Blow Your Horn," "Family Jewels," "Fortune Cookie," "Melvin and Howard." Surviving are his widow and a son.

REGINALD GARDINER, 77, English-born comedian and character actor, died of pneumonia July 7, 1980 in his home in Westwood, CA. He came to the U.S. in 1935, and after appearing successfully on Broadway, he had roles in approximately 100 films. He also appeared on tv in "Mr. Belvedere" and "The Pruitts of Southhampton." His film credits include "Born to Dance," "A Damsel in Distress," "Marie Antoinette," "Sweethearts," "The Great Dictator," "Dulcy," "A Yank in the R.A.F.," "The Man Who Came to Dinner," "Immortal Sergeant," "Claudia," "Molly and Me," "The Dolly Sisters," "Cluny Brown," "Fury at Furnace Creek," "Halls of Montezuma," "Androcles and the Lion," "The Story of Mankind," "Back Street," "Mr. Hobbs Takes a Vacation," "What a Way to Go," and his last in 1964 "Do Not Disturb." Surviving are his widow and a son.

HUGH GRIFFITH, 67, Welsh character actor on stage, screen and tv, died May 14, 1980 after a long illness in his London home. In 1959 he received an Academy Award for his supporting role in "Ben-Hur" and was nominated for his performance in the 1963 film "Tom Jones." Other screen credits include "The First Gentleman," "So Evil My Love," "Kind Hearts and Coronets," "The Beggar's Opera," "Sleeping Tiger," "Lucky Jim," "Exodus," "The Inspector," "Mutiny on the Bounty," "Hide and Seek," "How to Steal a Million," "Oh, Dad, Poor Dad," "Oliver!" "The Last Remake of Beau Geste," "The Hound of the Baskervilles," and his last "A Nightingale Sang in Berkeley Square." He is survived by his widow.

KAY HAMMOND, 71, English stage and film actress, died May 4, 1980 in Brighton, Eng. Among her screen credits are "The Trespasser," "Her Private Affair," "Abraham Lincoln," "Racetrack," "Double Harness," "Eight Girls in a Boat," "Jeannie," "Blithe Spirit," "Five Golden Hours," and "The Girl in the Red Velvet Swing." She was the wife of actor and director Sir John Clements.

DICK HAYMES, 63, Argentina-born singing star, died of lung cancer Mar. 28, 1980 in Los Angeles, CA. After a successful career as a popular singer in the Big Band era of WWII, he appeared in 35 films, including "Four Jills in a Jeep," "Irish Eyes Are Smiling," "Billy Rose's Diamond Horseshoe," "State Fair," "Do You Love Me," "The Shocking Miss Pilgrim," "Carnival in Costa Rica," "Up in Central Park," "One Touch of Venus," "All Ashore" and "Cruisin' Down the River." At one time he had his own national radio show, and also had nine gold records, including "It Had to Be You," "Little White Lies" and "It Might As Well Be Spring." He was married and divorced six times, including actresses Joanne Dru and Rita Hayworth.

CHARLOTTE HENRY, 65, Brooklyn-born stage and screen actress, died Apr. 11, 1980 in San Diego, CA. After her Broadway success at 13, she went to Hollywood in 1930 to recreate on film her stage role in "Courage," and subsequently appeared in "Huckleberry Finn," "Arrowsmith," "Lena Rivers," "Forbidden," "Rebecca of Sunnybrook Farm," "Forbidden," "Alice in Wonderland," "The Human Side," "The Last Gentleman," "Babes in Toyland," "Laddie," "Three Kids and a Queen," "Charlie Chan at the Opera," "Bowery Blitzkreig," "Stand and Deliver" "She's in the Army." She retired in 1942. Surviving is her husband, Dr. James Dempsey.

ALFRED HITCHCOCK, 80, London-born director and master of suspense, died of a heart attack Apr. 29, 1980 in his Bel Air, CA., home. He had been in failing health for the past two years. After working briefly as a technical calculator, advertising layout draftsman, writer of title cards for silent films, script writer, art director and assistant director, he became the world-celebrated director of 54 films. The list includes his Academy Award "Rebecca" (Best Film), "The Lodger," "Easy Virtue," "The Farmer's Wife," "Blackmail," "Juno and the Paycock," "Murder," "The Man Who Knew Too Much," "The 39 Steps," "Secret Agent," "Sabotage," "The Lady Vanishes," "Jamaica Inn," "Foreign Correspondent," "Mr. and Mrs. Smith," "Suspicion," "Shadow of a Doubt," "Notorious," "The Paradine Case," "Rope," "Under Capricorn," "Stage Fright," "Strangers on a Train," "Dial 'M' for Murder," "To Catch a Thief," "The Wrong Man," "Vertigo," "North by Northwest," "The Birds," "Torn Curtain," "Topaz," "Frenzy" and "Family Plot" his last in 1976. He was nominated for a director's "Oscar" five times but never won for "Rebecca," "Lifeboat," "Spellbound," "Rear Window" and "Psycho." He moved to Hollywood in 1939 and became a citizen in 1955. He was knighted by Queen Elizabeth II in 1979. Surviving are his widow and actress daughter Patricia Hitchcock O'Connell.

ALLEN HOSKINS, 59, retired actor, died of cancer July 26, 1980 in Oakland, CA. As a child he was the wide-eyed, pig-tailed "Farina" in the "Our Gang" and "Little Rascals" series. He retired at 19 and after army service worked with the handicapped. He is survived by his widow, four sons and two daughters.

JOSE ITURBI, 84, Spanish-born pianist, conductor and actor, died from a heart ailment June 28, 1980 in Hollywood, CA. After success as a pianist and conductor, he became a film actor in 1942 and appeared in "Thousands Cheer," "Two Girls and a Sailor," "Music for Millions," "Anchors Aweigh," "Holiday in Mexico," "Three Daring Daughters" and "That Midnight Kiss." Surviving are two grandchildren.

| Dick Haymes | Alfred Hitchcock | Jose Iturbi | Leon Janney | David Janssen | Dick Kallman |

HATTIE JACQUES, 56, one of England's leading comedy actresses, died of a heart attack Sept. 6, 1980 in her London home. She appeared in over 20 films including the "Carry On" series, and "Chance of a Lifetime," "The Gay Lady," "The Adventures of Sadie," "School for Scoundrels," "Make Mine Mink," "Follow a Star," "The Pickwick Papers," "Oliver Twist," "Watch Your Stern" and "The Bobo." No reported survivors.

LEON JANNEY, 63, one of the few actors to enjoy a lifelong career in radio, theatre, films and tv, despite fame as a child actor, died of cancer Oct. 28, 1980 in Guadalajara, Mexico. Born in Ogden, Utah, he began his career at age 2 in vaudeville and at 10 was a star in movies. In addition to "Our Gang Comedies" he appeared in such pictures as "Courage," "Hand Full of Clouds," "Father's Son," "Doorway to Hell," "Old English," "Penrod and Sam," "Fame Street," "Should Ladies Behave?," "Stolen Paradise" and "The Last Mile." On radio he was Richard Parker of "The Parker Family" for 5 years, a role he recreated on tv. He also appeared on the tv series "The Edge of Night" and "Another World." He is survived by his fourth wife and a son, Donald.

DAVID JANSSEN, 49, nee David Harold Meyer in Naponee, NE., film and tv actor, died of a heart attack Feb. 13, 1980 in his home in Malibu, CA. Although he had appeared in 34 films, he was probably best known for his tv series "Richard Diamond, Private Detective" and "The Fugitive," the latter an Emmy-Award winning series. His film credits include "Chief Crazy Horse," "To Hell and Back," "Francis in the Navy," "The Girl He Left Behind," "Never Say Goodbye," "Hell to Eternity," "Ring of Fire," "Man Trap," "Belle Sommers," "The Green Berets" and "The Shoes of the Fisherman." His second wife survives.

RICHARD (DICK) KALLMAN, 46, antiques dealer, former stage, film tv actor, and clothing designer, was found shot to death in his NYC home on Feb. 22, 1980. His film credits include "Hell Canyon Outlaws," "Born to Be Loved," "Verboten," "Back Street," "It's All Happening," "Doctor, You've Got to Be Kidding!" He starred in the 1965 tv series "Hank." No reported survivors.

IDA KAMINSKA, 80, Russian-born actress-director-producer, died of a heart ailment May 21, 1980 in NYC. For 21 years she headed the Jewish State Theater of Poland, but left in 1968, and made her home in NYC. Her film credits include "Without a Home," "A Vilna Legend," "The Angel Levine," and "The Shop on Main Street." A son and daughter survive.

PEGGY KNUDSEN, 57, Minnesota-born stage, film, radio and tv actress, died of cancer July 11, 1980 in her home in Encino, CA. After Broadway success, she went to Hollywood and appeared in "The Big Sleep," "Never Say Goodbye," "A Stolen Life," "Humoresque," "Stallion Road," "Roses Are Red," "Half Past Midnight," "Perilous Waters," "Copper Canyon," "Unchained," "Good Morning, Miss Dove," "Bottom of the Bottle," "Hilda Crane" and "Istanbul." She retired in 1960. Surviving are three daughters.

MILIZA KORJUS, 72, Warsaw-born coloratura soprano died of a heart attack Aug. 26, 1980 in Culver City, CA. Cast as Johann Strauss' mistress in the 1938 "The Great Waltz," her performance won her an Academy Award nomination for best supporting actress. A serious automobile accident in 1940 prevented her appearing immediately in other films. Her only other picture was the Mexican produced "Imperial Cavalry." She subsequently made many concert appearances. She is survived by three children.

FLORENCE LAKE, 75, retired actress, died Apr. 11, 1980 in Woodland Hills, CA. She had appeared in such films as "Thru Different Eyes," "The Rogue Song," "Romance," "Ladies of the Jury," "Night World," "Sweetheart of Sigma Chi," "Midshipman

Jack," "Two Fisted," "To Mary with Love," "Quality Street," "I Met My Love Again," "Condemned Woman," "Stage Coach," "Crash Dive" and "San Diego I Love You." She was the sister of actor Arthur Lake. No reported survivors.

PAUL LANGTON, 65, radio, film and tv actor, died of a heart attack Apr. 15, 1980 in Burbank, CA. Among his over 50 screen credits are "Destination Tokyo," "30 Seconds over Tokyo," "Gentle Annie," "The Thin Man," "They Were Expendable," "Till the Clouds Roll By," "My Brother Talks to Horses," "What Next, Cpl. Hargrove?," "A Song Is Born," "Jack Slade," "Return from the Sea," "Murder Is My Beat," "To Hell and Back," "The Big Knife," "The Incredible Shrinking Man," "Chicago Confidential," "Juke Box Jamboree," "The Cosmic Man," "The Big Night," "Dime with a Halo" and "Shock Treatment." A son survives.

CHESTER H. LAUCK, 79, Arkansas-born character actor, died Feb. 21, 1980 after a brief illness in Hot Springs, AR. With his friend Norris Goff who died in 1978, they were Lum and Abner on one of radio's most popular programs, five nights per week from 1931 to 1955. They also made six feature films. He opened a public relations firm in Little Rock, and retired in 1966. He leaves his widow, a son and a daughter.

JOHN LAURIE, 83, Scottish-born actor whose career spanned 60 years, died June 23, 1980 in a hospital near London. His more than 100 film credits include "Juno and the Paycock," "39 Steps," "East Meets West," "As You Like It," "Edge of the World," "Four Feathers," "Convoy," "The Life and Death of Col. Blimp," "Henry V," "Hamlet," "Mine Own Executioner," "Treasure Island," "Laughter in Paradise," "Pandora and the Flying Dutchman," "Bonnie Prince Charlie," "Hobson's Choice," "Richard III" and "Kidnapped." Surviving are his widow and a daughter.

SOL LESSER, 90, one of the film industry giants, died of a heart condition Sept. 19, 1980 in his Hollywood apartment. At an early age his family moved from Spokane, WA., to San Francisco where his father opened one of the first nickelodeons, and young Lesser began his career. He subsequently produced 117 films, including 10 of the Tarzan series starring Johnny Weissmuller, and "When a Man's a Man," "Thunder Mountain," "Let's Sing Again," "Border Patrolman," "Rainbow on the River," "Peck's Bad Boy," "My Boy," "Trouble," "Boy of Flanders," "Daddy," "Oliver Twist," "Rawhide," "Fisherman's Wharf," "Way Down South," "Tuttles of Tahiti," "Stage Door Canteen," "3 Is a Family," "The Red House," and his Oscar-Award winning documentary "Kon-Tiki." In his later years he taught cinematography at Univ. of S. Calif. He is survived by his son and a daughter.

JOHN LENNON, 40, one of the original four Beatles, was shot to death Dec. 8, 1980 in the entrance way of his apartment building in NYC. In addition to writing, playing and recording many songs, he appeared in "A Hard Day's Night," "Help!" and "How I Won the War." He also contributed to the score for "Yellow Submarine." Surviving is his second wife, Yoko Ono, and two sons.

SAM LEVENE, 75, Russian-Born character actor on stage and screen, died of a heart attack Dec. 26, 1980 in his NYC apartment. In his career of over 50 years, his film credits include "Three Men on a Horse," "After the Thin Man," "Yellow Jack," "Shopworn Angel," "Golden Boy," "Shadow of the Thin Man," "The Big Street," "Action in the North Atlantic," "Gung Ho!," "Purple Heart," "The Killers," "Brute Force," "Crossfire," "Dial 1119," "Three Sailors and a Girl," "Sweet Smell of Success," "Slaughter on Tenth Avenue," "A Farewell to Arms," "Act One," "A Dream of Kings," ". . . And Justice for All," "The Last Embrace" and "The Champ." A son survives.

| Ida Kaminska | Paul Langton | John Lennon | Sam Levene | Strother Martin | Mary McCarty |

BARBARA LODEN, 48, North Carolina-born stage, tv and film actress, died of cancer Sept. 5, 1980 in NYC. She appeared in the films "Wild River," "Splendor in the Grass" and "Wanda" that she also produced and directed, and that won the International Critics Award at the Venice Film Festival in 1970. She is survived by her second husband, director Elia Kazan, and two sons.

STROTHER MARTIN, 61, screen, stage and tv actor, died of a heart attack Aug. 1, 1980 in Thousand Oaks, CA. In his 30-year career his film credits include "Storm over Tibet," "Strategic Air Command," "The Big Knife," "Target Zero," "Attack!," "Copper Sky," "The Shaggy Dog," "Sanctuary," "The Man Who Shot Liberty Valance," "McLintock," "Invitation to a Gunfighter," "Shenandoah," "The Sons of Katie Elder," "Harper," "Cool Hand Luke," "Flim-Flam Man," "Butch Cassidy and the Sundance Kid," "The Champ," "Nightwing," "The Villain" and "Love and Bullets." His widow survives.

MARY McCARTY, 56, Kansas-born singer-actress on stage, screen and tv, died of a heart attack Apr. 30, 1980 in her home in Westwood, CA. She was appearing as Nurse Starch on the tv series "Trapper John." Her film credits include "Rebecca of Sunnybrook Farm," "Keep Smiling," "The Sullivans," "The French Line," "Babes in Toyland" and "My Six Loves." She had no reported survivors.

CHARLES McGRAW, 66, nee Charles Butters in the Orient, character actor on stage, film and tv died July 30, 1980 from injuries suffered when he fell through the glass shower in his home in Studio City, CA. His screen credits include "The Killers," "The Big Fix," "The Imposter," "The Long Night," "Roses Are Red," "Blood on the Moon," "Once More, My Darling," "The Threat," "His Kind of Woman," "One Minute to Zero," "The Bridges at Toko-Ri," "Slaughter on Tenth Avenue," "The Defiant Ones," "Spartacus," "Cimarron," "It's a Mad, Mad, Mad World," "In Cold Blood" and "Twilight's Last Gleaming." He starred in the tv series "The Falcon" and "Casablanca." No reported survivors.

STEVE McQUEEN, 50, Indianapolis-born stage and screen actor, died Nov. 7, 1980 of a heart attack following surgery for cancer in Juarez, Mex. By the end of the '60's he was one of the most popular and highest paid actors in films. His credits include "The Blob," "Never Love a Stranger," "The Magnificent Seven," "Hell Is for Heroes," "The War Lover," "The Great Escape," "Love with the Proper Stranger," "Baby, the Rain Must Fall," "The Cincinnati Kid," "Nevada Smith," "The Sand Pebbles," "The Thomas Crown Affair," "Bullitt," "The Reivers," "On Any Sunday," "Le Mans," "Junior Bonner," "Papillon," "The Towering Inferno," "Tom Horn," "An Enemy of the People" and "The Hunter." He is survived by his third wife, and a son and daughter by his first wife, actress Neile Adams.

KAY MEDFORD, 59, nee Maggie O'Regin, film, stage and tv actress, died of cancer Apr. 10, 1980 in her native NYC. She made her screen debut in 1942 in "The War against Mrs. Hadley," followed by "Swing Shift Maisie," "Adventure," "Guilty Bystander," "A Face in the Crowd," "Jamboree," "The Rat Race," "Girl of the Night," "Butterfield 8," "Two Tickets to Paris," "Ensign Pulver," "A Fine Madness," "Funny Girl," "Angel in My Pocket," "Twinky," "Fire Sale," and "Windows." She is survived by a sister.

IRIS MEREDITH, 64, character actress, died Jan. 22, 1980 in Los Angeles, CA. She began her career as a Goldwyn Girl, but worked primarily in serial adventures and westerns. Surviving is a daughter.

LEWIS MILESTONE, 84, Oscar-winning director, nee Lewis Milstein in Russia, died Sept. 25, i980 in Los Angeles, CA. He emigrated to the U.S. in 1914 and became a citizen. He directed his first film "Bobbed Hair" in 1925, followed by such credits as "The Garden of Eden," "Betrayal," "The Front Page," "Rain," "Anything Goes," "The General Died at Dawn," "Of Mice and Men," "Lucky Partners," "Edge of Darkness," "The North Star," "The Purple Heart," "A Walk in the Sun," "Arch of Triumph," "The Red Pony," "Halls of Montezuma," "Les Miserables," "Pork Chop Hill," "Ocean's Eleven," "Mutiny on the Bounty" and his Academy Award winners "Two Arabian Nights" and "All quiet on the Western Front." Two sisters survive.

CARMEL MYERS, 80, San Francisco-born silent film star, died of a heart attack Nov. 9, 1980 in Los Angeles, CA. She appeared in over 50 pictures, frequently as a vamp or femme fatale. Among her credits are "Slave of Desire," "Beau Brummell," 'Broadway after Dark," "Babbitt," "Tell It to the Marines," "Sorrell and Son," "Dream of Love," "The Ghost Walks," "Broadway Scandals," "Show of Shows," "Svengali," "Ben Hur" (1925 & 1931), "Nice Women," "Countess of Monte Cristo," "Lady for a Night," and "Whistle Stop." She had also appeared in vaudeville, the theatre, on radio and tv. She was married three times, and is survived by a son and two daughters.

DAVID NEWELL, 75, makeup artist and retired stage and screen actor, died Jan. 25, 1980 in Los Angeles, CA. His film credits include "Dangerous Curves," "Marriage Playground," "The Kibitzer," "Runaway Bride," "Let's Go Native," "Woman Hungry," "The Flood," "New Morals for Old," "Hell Below," "Made on Broadway," "White Heat," "Educating Father" and "Polo Joe." After a disfiguring auto accident, he became a makeup artist for screen and tv until his retirement in 1967. No reported survivors.

ELLIOTT NUGENT, 83, Ohio-born writer-actor-director on stage, screen and tv, died in his sleep Aug. 9, 1980 in his NYC home. He began his professional career with his parents in vaudeville at 4. He went to Hollywood in 1929 and ultimately worked on more than 20 pictures, appearing in "So This Is College," "Not So Dumb," "Unholy Three," "Sins of the Children," "Romance," "Virtuous Husband," "The Last Flight," "Stage Door Canteen" and "My Outlaw Brother." His directing credits include "Whistling in the Dark," "Three-Cornered Moon," "Strictly Dynamite," "She Loves Me Not," "Professor Beware," "The Cat and the Canary," "Nothing but the Truth," "The Male Animal," "Up in Arms," "My Favorite Brunette," "Welcome Stranger," "Mr. Belvedere Goes to College," "The Great Gatsby" and "Just for You." Surviving are his widow, former actress Norma Lee, and two daughters.

BARBARA O'NEIL, 70, stage and film actress, died Sept. 3, 1980 in her home in Cos Cob, CT. After her Broadway success, she went to Hollywood in 1937 and subsequently appeared in "Stella Dallas," "Love, Honor and Behave," "The Sun Never Sets," "When Tomorrow Comes," "Tower of London," "Gone with the Wind" (Scarlett's mother), "All This and Heaven Too," "Shining Victory," "I Remember Mama," "Whirlpool," "Angel Face" and "The Nun's Story." Two brothers survive. She was divorced from director Joshua Logan.

GEORGE PAL, 72, Hungarian-born producer-director, died of a heart attack May 2, 1980 in his home in Beverly Hills, CA. In 1939 he came to the U.S. and was signed by Paramount. He and his crews won 8 Academy Awards, beginning with "Destination Moon" in 1958, followed by "When Worlds Collide," "War of the Worlds" and "The Time Machine." He was also the creator of Puppetoons. Other film credits include "Tom Thumb," "The Wonderful World of the Brothers Grimm," "Atlantis, the Lost Continent," "Conquest of Space," "The Seven Faces of Dr. Lao," "Houdini," and "The Power." He is survived by his widow and two sons.

Charles McGraw	Steve McQueen	Kay Medford	Carmel Myers	David Newell	Barbara O'Neil

GAIL PATRICK, 69, actress-producer, nee Margaret Fitzpatrick in Birmingham, AL., died of leukemia July 6, 1980 in her Hollywood home. After more than 50 films, she gave up her career to enter tv production with Erle Stanley Gardner, creator for the Perry Mason series. Among her screen credits are "Murders in the Zoo," "Cradle Song," "Death Takes a Holiday," "Murder at the Vanities," "Wagon Wheels," "Artists and Models," "Stage Door," "Disbarred," "Reno," "My Favorite Wife," "The Doctor Takes a Wife," "Tales of Manhattan," "Hit Parade of 1943," "Up in Mabel's Room," "Brewster's Millions," "Claudia and David," "The Plainsman and the Lady," "Calendar Girl" and "Inside Story." She is survived by her fourth husband, John E. Velde, Jr., and a son and daughter by her third husband, Thomas C. Jackson.

GEORGE RAFT, 85, nee George Ranft in NYC, died of leukemia Nov. 24, 1980 in Los Angeles, CA. He had suffered from emphysema for several years. After some success as a dancer and actor, he went to Hollywood and appeared in over 60 movies. His credits include, "Quick Millions," "Scarface," "Dancers in the Dark," "Madame Racketeer," "Night after Night," "The Bowery," "All of Me," "Bolero," "Limehouse Blues," "Rumba," "Yours for the Asking," "Souls at Sea," "Spawn of the North," "Each Dawn I Die," "The House across the Bay," "They Drive by Night," "Broadway," "Hollywood Canteen," "Follow the Boys," "Nob Hill," "Johnny Angel," "Manpower," "Nocturne," "Whistle Stop," "Intrigue," "Johnny Allegro," "A Bullet for Joey," "Around the World in 80 Days," "Some Like It Hot," "Intrigue," "The Patsy," "Casino Royale," "Skidoo!," "Sextette," "Sam Marlow, Private Eye." His life was the subject of a 1961 film "The George Raft Story." His wife, Grace Mulrooney, from whom he was separated, died in 1970. A son survives. He was interred at Forest Lawn Memorial Park.

LILLIAN RANDOLPH, 65, screen, radio and tv actress for 40 years, died of cancer Sept. 12, 1980 in Arcadia, CA. Her film credits include "Little Men," "West Point Widow," "Mexican Spitfire Sees a Ghost," "Gentleman from Dixie," "All American Coed," "The Great Gildersleeve," "Adventures of Mark Twain," "Three Little Sisters," "Child of Divorce," "The Bachelor and Bobby-Soxer," "Sleep My Love," "Once More, My Darling," "Hush, Hush, Sweet Charlotte," "The Onion Field" and "Magic." She was probably best known for her roles as Madame Queen in "Amos 'n' Andy" series, housekeeper Birdie in the radio and tv "Great Gildersleeve," and the title role in the radio comedy "Beulah" in which she replaced Hattie McDaniel. A son survives.

MARSHALL REED, 62, Colorado-born actor-director-producer-writer, died of a massive hemorrhage on Apr. 15, 1980 in Los Angeles, CA. His first featured part was in 1943 in the title role of "The Texas Kid," subsequently he acted in "Haunted Harbor," "Law of the Valley," "Chicago Kid," "Drifting Along," "Gentleman Joe Palooka," "Stampede," "The Cowboy and the Prizefighter," "O, Susanna," "Abilene Trail," "Hurricane Island," "Purple Heart Diary," "Sound Off!," "Texas City," "The Night the World Exploded," "Angel and the Badman," "Ghost of Zorro" and "A Time for Killing." He also appeared in many tv series. Survivors include his fifth wife, and a daughter by a previous marriage.

DUNCAN RENALDO, 76, film and tv character actor, nee Renault Renaldo Duncan in Spain, died of heart failure Sept. 3, 1980 in Goleta, CA. He appeared in "Trader Horn," "Moonlight Murder," "Rose of the Rio Grande," "Spawn of the North," "For Whom the Bell Tolls," "The Fighting Seabees," "Sword of the Avenger," "Gay Amigo," "The Lady and the Bandit," "The Capture" and "Zorro Rides Again." It was his role as the Cisco Kid in the tv series that made him the idol of millions, especially of children. He served a year in the penitentiary for illegally entering the U.S. but was later pardoned by Pres. Roosevelt. His widow survives.

GALE ROBBINS, 58, Chicago-born singer-actress and WWII pin-up girl, died of lung cancer Feb. 18, 1980 in Los Angeles, CA. She performed as a band singer before making her film debut in 1944 in "In the Meantime, Darling," followed by "My Girl Tisa," "My Dear Secretary," "Oh, You Beautiful Doll," "Three Little Words," "The Fuller Brush Girl," "Between Midnight and Dawn," "Strictly Dishonorable," "Belle of New York," "Calamity Jane," "Double Jeopardy," "Girl in the Red Velvet Swing" and "Gunsmoke in Tucson." Two daughters survive.

RACHEL ROBERTS, 53, Welsh-born stage, tv and screen actress, was found dead Nov. 26, 1980 in her home in Bel Air, CA. A medical report said she died of acute barbiturate intoxication and her death was a suicide. Her film credits include "Valley of Song," "The Weak and the Wicked," "The Good Companions," "Alpha Beta," "Our Man in Havana," "Saturday Night and Sunday Morning," "Girl on Approval," "This Sporting Life," "A Flea in Her Ear," "Murder on the Orient Express," "Picnic at Hanging Rock," "Foul Play," "Yanks," and "Charlie Chan and The Curse of The Dragon Queen." She was married and divorced from actors Alan Dobie and Rex Harrison. A sister survives.

LILLIAN ROTH, 69, Boston-born singer and actress, died May 12, 1980 after a massive stroke and a long illness in NYC. She entered show business at 6 and appeared in vaudeville, the theatre, on tv and film. Her screen credits include "Illusion," "The Love Parade," "The Vagabond King," "Animal Crackers," "Sea Legs," "Paramount on Parade," "Madame Satan," "Honey," "Take a Chance," "Ladies They Talk About," "The Sound of Laughter," and "Boardwalk." Her autobiography, "I'll Cry Tomorrow" was filmed with Susan Hayward in an Oscar-nomination performance. She had been married six times, but left no immediate survivors.

DORE SCHARY, 74, producer, director, screenwriter and playwright, died in his sleep July 7, 1980 in his NYC home after a long illness. After small parts on Broadway, he went to Hollywood where he was hired as a writer, subsequently penning over 40 screenplays, and became MGM's executive producer. In 1938 his "Boys Town" was awarded an "Oscar." Other films with which he was involved are "I'll Be Seeing You," "The Spiral Staircase," "The Farmer's Daughter," "Broadway Melody of 1940," "Edison the Man," "Sunrise at Campobello," "Plymouth Adventure," "Bad Day at Black Rock," "The Swan," "Executive Suite," "Blackboard Jungle," and "Lust for Life." Surviving are his widow and two daughters.

SARAH SELBY, 74, character actress for 50 years, died Jan. 7, 1980 in Los Angeles, CA. Among her many film credits are "The Beautiful Cheat," "Stork Bites Man," "Trapped by Boston Blackie," "Beyond the Forest," "Battle Cry," "An Affair to Remember," "Moon Pilot," "Tower of London," "Taggart" and "Don't Make Waves." On tv she appeared as Ma Smalley in the "Gunsmoke" series. Two daughters survive.

PETER SELLERS, 54, British comedian, died after a massive heart attack, July 24, 1980 in London. Considered by many as a comic genius, he began his film career in 1956 with "Ladykillers," subsequently appearing in such films as "Up the Creek," "Tom Thumb," "The Mouse That Roared," "Battle of the Sexes," "I'm All Right, Jack," "The Millionairess," "Only Two Can Play," "Lolita," "The Road to Hong Kong," "Waltz of the Toreadors," "Trial and Error," "Dr. Strangelove," "The World of Henry Orient," "The Pink Panther," "Return of the Pink Panther," "The Pink Panther Strikes Again," "Undercover Hero," "A Shot in the Dark," "What's New Pussycat?," "The Wrong Box," "Casina Royale," "Murder by Death," "The Party," "Being There" and "The Fiendish Plot of Dr. Fu Man Chu." He is survived by his fourth wife, actress Lynne Frederick, and a son and two daughters by previous marriages. He was cremated.

Gail Patrick	George Raft	Rachel Roberts	Peter Sellers	Bobby Van	Mae West

JAY SILVERHEELS, 62, Ontario-born Mohawk Indian, died Mar. 5, 1980 of complications from pneumonia in Woodland Hills, CA. He appeared as Tonto in all 221 episodes of "The Lone Ranger" on tv from 1949 to 1957 and is still being re-run. His other credits include "Captain from Castile," "Fury at Furnace Creek," "Key Largo," "Sand," "Broken Arrow," "The Will Rogers Story," "Walk the Proud Land," "Alias Jesse James," "Smith," "The Man Who Loved Cat Dancing," "True Grit" and "The Phynx." Surviving are his widow, a son and three daughters.

MILBURN STONE, 75, Kansas-born character actor, died of a heart failure June 12, 1980 in La Jolla, CA. He appeared in over 250 films but made his fame and fortune for 20 years as Doc Adams in the tv series "Gunsmoke." Among his film credits are "China Clipper," "Crime School," "Blind Alley," "Young Mr. Lincoln," "Sherlock Holmes Faces Death," "Gung Ho!," "The Impostor," "Jungle Woman," "Branded," "Atomic City," "Arrowhead," "Pickup on South Street," "Black Tuesday," "The Long Gray Line" and "Drango." He retired in 1975 when the tv series ended its record run. Surviving are his widow, and a daughter.

BILLY THOMAS, 49, "Buckwheat" in the "Our Gang" series, was found dead of natural causes Oct. 10, 1980 in his home in Los Angeles, CA. He joined the "gang" at the age of 3 and appeared in 89 films. He is survived by a son.

GEORGE TOBIAS, 78, NYC-born character actor, died of cancer Feb. 27, 1980 in Hollywood, CA. His acting career began at 15. In 1938 he abandoned Broadway for Hollywood and subsequently appeared in "Maisie," "Ninotchka," "Hunchback of Notre Dame," "Balalaika," "Music in My Heart," "Saturday's Children," "Torrid Zone," "They Drive by Night," "The Bride Came C.O.D.," "You're in the Army Now," "Sgt. York," "My Sister Eileen," "Yankee Doodle Dandy," "This Is the Army," "Mission to Moscow," "Mildred Pierce," "Sinbad the Sailor," "Adventures of Casanova," "Glenn Miller Story," "The 7 Little Foys," "Silk Stockings," "Marjorie Morningstar," "The Glass Bottom Boat" and "The Phynx." He was Abner Kravitz on the tv series "Bewitched." A brother survives.

IVAN TRIESAULT, 80, Russian-born former ballet dancer and character actor, died of a heart failure Jan. 3, 1980 in Los Angeles, CA. After appearing in many Broadway productions, he moved to Hollywood in 1942. His film credits include "Uncertain Glory," "The Hitler Gang," "Days of Glory," "Cry of the Werewolf," "Counter-Attack," "Notorious," "The Return of Monte Cristo," "Golden Earrings," "Johnny Allegro," "Kim," "Five Fingers," "The Bad and the Beautiful," "Jet Pilot," and "The Young Lions." Surviving are his widow, and a son Jon who is an assistant director.

ROMOLO VALLI, 55, one of Italy's most respected stage and film actors, died Feb. 1, 1980 in an auto accident in Rome. For six years he was artistic director of the Festival of Two Worlds in Spoleto. His film credits include "Girl with a Suitcase," "La Viaccia," "The Leopard," "Mandragola," "Boom!," "Death in Venice," "The Great War" and "Garden of the Finzi-Continis." No reported survivors.

BOBBY VAN, 49, actor, comedian, dancer and singer, nee Robert King in the Bronx, died of cancer July 31, 1980 in Los Angeles, CA. He had appeared in night clubs, on stage, screen and tv. His films include "Because You're Mine," "Small Town Girl," "Affairs of Dobie Gillis," "Kiss Me, Kate," "The Navy vs. the Night," "Skirts Ahoy," "That's Entertainment," "Lost Flight" and the re-make of "Lost Horizons." He is survived by his widow, actress Elaine Joyce, and a daughter.

ODILE VERSOIS, 50, French stage and screen actress, born Militza de Poliakoff-Baidarov, died of cancer June 23, 1980 in Paris. She had appeared in more than 30 films including "Man in the Dinghy," "Paolo and Francesca," "To Paris with Love," "Change Meeting," "Checkpoint," "Room 43," "Nude in a White Car," "Cartouche," "Benjamin." She is survived by four children and her three sisters, actresses Olga Poliakoff, Helene Vallier and Marina Vlady.

MAE WEST, 88, the legendary forever-blond stage and screen actress and writer, died Nov. 22, 1980 apparently of natural causes following a stroke in her apartment in Los Angeles, CA. The Brooklyn-born sex symbol began her career as a child in vaudeville at 5 and made her last film in 1977. Vanity Fair Magazine had called her "the greatest female impersonator of all time." After her first film "Night after Night" in 1932, her name and inimitable act became known world-wide, and made her a millionairess by wise investments from record salaries. During WWII her name was applied to various military equipment and was added to the dictionary. Other film credits include "She Done Him Wrong," "I'm, No Angel," "Bell of the Nineties," "Goin' to Town," "Klondike Annie," "Go West, Young Man," "Every Day's a Holiday," "My Little Chickadee," "The Heat's On," "Myra Breckenridge" and her last "Sextette." In 1911 she was secretly married to her vaudeville partner Frank Wallace but soon realized it was a mistake, and continued her career without him. She divorced him in 1941. A sister survives. She was interred with her parents in Brooklyn's Cypress Hills Cemetery.

RAOUL WALSH, 93, one of the industry's most versatile and important directors for almost 50 years, died of a heart attack Dec. 31, 1980 in Simi Valley, CA. Born in NYC, he moved west, finally ending up in California and being hired in 1913 by D. W. Griffith. He directed over 100 pictures including "Thief of Bagdad," "East of Suez," "What Price Glory," "Loves of Carmen," "Sadie Thompson," "The Honor System," "In Old Arizona," "The Bowery," "Going Hollywood," "Artists and Models," "Strawberry Blonde," "The Roaring Twenties," "They Drive by Night," "High Sierra," "Manpower," "They Died with Their Boots On," "Gentleman Jim," "White Heat," "Lion in the Streets," "The Big Trail," "Objective Burma," "The Horn Blows at Midnight," "Capt. Horatio Hornblower," "The Naked and the Dead" and "A Distant Trumpet." He retired in 1964. In addition to his widow, he leaves a brother, former film actor, George Walsh.

RAY WALKER, 76, retired stage, film, radio and tv actor died of heart failure Oct. 6, 1980 in Los Angeles, CA. His many screen credits include "Devil's Mate," "Baby, Take a Bow," "Million Dollar Baby," "The Girl Friend," "Princess O'Rourke," "Crazy House," "Tars and Spars," "April Showers," "Blue Gardenia," "Rebel City," "Pride of the Blue Grass" and "Kiss Them for Me." He retired in 1970. His widow survives.

VICTOR SEN YUNG, 65, film and tv actor, was found dead under mysterious circumstances in his North Hollywood home on Nov. 9, 1980. He had appeared as No. 2 son in 34 of the Charlie Chan film series, and was a regular on the "Bonanza" and "Bachelor Father" tv series, playing the family cook in the former. Other film credits include "The Letter," "A Yank on the Burma Road," "Manila," "China," "The Breaking Point," "Woman on the Run," "Blood Alley," "Flower Drum Song" and "Sam Marlow, Private Eye." There were no reported survivors.

240

244

245

246

247

249

255

256